# Corpora, Corpses and Corps

Federico Pio Gentile

# Corpora, Corpses and Corps

A Multimodal Study of Contemporary Canadian TV Crime Series

palgrave
macmillan

Federico Pio Gentile
Scholar in Multimodality
Modena, Italy

ISBN 978-3-030-78275-7        ISBN 978-3-030-78276-4    (eBook)
https://doi.org/10.1007/978-3-030-78276-4

© The Editor(s) (if applicable) and The Author(s), under exclusive licence to Springer Nature
Switzerland AG 2021
This work is subject to copyright. All rights are solely and exclusively licensed by the Publisher, whether
the whole or part of the material is concerned, specifically the rights of translation, reprinting, reuse of
illustrations, recitation, broadcasting, reproduction on microfilms or in any other physical way, and transmission or information storage and retrieval, electronic adaptation, computer software, or by similar or
dissimilar methodology now known or hereafter developed.
The use of general descriptive names, registered names, trademarks, service marks, etc. in this publication
does not imply, even in the absence of a specific statement, that such names are exempt from the relevant
protective laws and regulations and therefore free for general use.
The publisher, the authors and the editors are safe to assume that the advice and information in this book
are believed to be true and accurate at the date of publication. Neither the publisher nor the authors or
the editors give a warranty, expressed or implied, with respect to the material contained herein or for any
errors or omissions that may have been made. The publisher remains neutral with regard to jurisdictional
claims in published maps and institutional affiliations.

Cover illustration: © Alex Linch / shutterstock.com

This Palgrave Macmillan imprint is published by the registered company Springer Nature Switzerland AG.
The registered company address is: Gewerbestrasse 11, 6330 Cham, Switzerland

# Acknowledgements

Federico would like to thank Cathy Scott and Steven Fassioms from Palgrave Macmillan for their editorial support. The author would also like to thank Anne Marie La Traverse and Bill Mustos from Flashpoint All Seasons Inc., for their exceptional kindness and warmth in granting permission to use several visual materials included in the book.

# Conventions

## (a) POS tagging conventions

| Tag | Description | Tag | Description |
|---|---|---|---|
| CC | Coordinating conjunction | PRP$ | Possessive pronoun |
| CD | Cardinal number | RB | Adverb |
| DT | Determiner | RBR | Adverb, comparative |
| EX | Existential *there* | RBS | Adverb, superlative |
| FW | Foreign word | RP | Particle |
| IN | Preposition or subordinating conj. | SYM | Symbol |
| JJ | Adjective | TO | *to* |
| JJR | Adjective, comparative | UH | Interjection |
| JJS | Adjective, superlative | VB | Verb, base form |
| LS | List item marker | VBD | Verb, past tense |
| MD | Modal | VBG | Verb, gerund or present part. |
| NN | Noun, singular or mass | VBN | Verb, past participle |
| NNP | Proper noun, singular | VBP | Verb, non-3rd person singular present |
| NNS | Noun, plural | VBZ | Verb, 3rd person singular present |
| NNPS | Proper noun, plural | WDT | Wh-determiner |
| PDT | Predeterminer | WP | Wh-pronoun |
| POS | Possessive ending | WP$ | Wh-pronoun, possessive |
| PRP | Personal pronoun | WBB | Wh-adverb |

viii    Conventions

**(b) Multimodal annotation conventions (Heydon 2005: xi)**

| Symbol | Description | Symbol | Description |
|---|---|---|---|
| // | Overlapping speech commences | (word) | Uncertain transcription |
| * | Overlapping speech ends | ( ) | Incomprehensible utterance |
| = | Latching | (( )) | Transcriber's remarks or comments |
| (0.6) | Silence measured in seconds | ^ | Low rise intonation |
| (.) | Micro-pause of less than 0.2 sec. | ↓ | Falling intonation |
| (..) | Pause, > 0.2 sec; < 3 sec. | ⇒ | Level intonation |
| °word° | Softer than surrounding speech | - | Truncated word |
| WORD | Louder than surrounding speech | :: | Syllab. sound lengthened for each : |
| <u>word</u> | Syllables having greater stress | h | Audible outbreath |
| ↑ | High rise intonation | .h | Audible inbreath |
| (h) | Explosive aspiration (e.g. laughter) | | |

**(c) Cinematic annotation conventions (adapted from Baldry in O'Halloran 2004: 86)**

| | |
|---|---|
| Time: | Min. = hh:mm:ss (h = hour; m = minute; s = second). |
| PHASES: | Ph = Phase; SP = Subphase; |
| | MovA = In-motion actions; NMovA = Stationary actions. |
| METAFUNCTIONS: | EXP = Experiential; INT = Interpersonal; TEX = Textual. |
| VISUAL IMAGE: | CP = Camera Position; VS = Visual salience; |
| | SH = Shot; CLS = Close shot; D = Distance; MCS = Medium close shot; CLU = Close up; ECLU = Extreme close up; |
| | CU-in = Cut in; CU-a = Cutaway; MS = Medium shot; |
| | WS = Wide shot; EWS = Extreme wide shot; |
| | SV = Side view; FV = Front view; BV = Back view; |
| | OSS = Over the Shoulder Shot; Det. = Detail; |
| | I = Inside; O = Outside; I/O = Inside looking outside; |
| | O/I = Outside looking inside. |
| PARTICIPANTS: | P = Participant; M = Male; F = Female; NB = Non-binary. |
| SOUNDTRACK: | ST = Soundtrack; |
| | AS = Ambient sound; M/S = Music and singing (*with transcription of spoken or sung words in italics*). |
| TRANSITIONS: | T = Transition; <> = Transition lasting a subphase; </> = Transition crossing a phasal boundary. |

*(continued)*

(continued)

| | |
|---|---|
| RESOURCE COMBINATIONS (RC): | H = High integration of resources;<br>K = Medium integration of resources;<br>L = Low integration of resources (e.g. body movement + music). |
| OTHER SYMBOLS: | Movt = Movement description;<br>≈ = The same semiotic selections hold true as compared with the previous frame (e.g. same phase or subphase but some changes have occurred); ≈+E = The configuration is as before but a new element has been added to those previously present (e.g. a new participant, being it either clearly recognisable or just recognised by its body parts entering the scene—like a protruded arm—or its voice is heard). |

*Other symbols pertaining to the multimodal annotation are listed in (b)*

# References

Heydon, G. (2005). *The Language of Police Interviewing: A Critical Analisys*. Palgrave Macmillan.

O'Halloran, K. L. (Ed.). (2004). *Multimodal Discourse Analisys. Systemic Functional Perspectives*. London and New York: Continuum.

# Contents

**1 Introduction** — 1
Communication as a Quibbling Concept — 1
References — 11

**2 The Research Methodology** — 15
Corpus Linguistics as a Methodological Tool — 15
Transcript Process and Tagging Tools — 17
Multimodality and the Extra-Linguistic Gap — 21
    Annotation Procedure — 33
Beyond the Screen: Film Studies, Language and
Communication — 36
Naturalness vs. Forgery: Cinematic Language Comprehension — 43
Specialised Discourse Conveyance and Popularised Knowledge
Appraisal — 48
References — 58

**3 The Linguistic and Cultural Environment of Canadian
Television** — 71
Television as a Medium — 71
The Power of Media over the Masses — 73
Media Ecology and Regulation Policies — 76
The Canadian Television Background — 81

xii    Contents

| | | |
|---|---|---|
| | The 'Cancon' Contemporary Context | 89 |
| | Crime Genre and Television Seriality | 93 |
| | References | 102 |

**4  *Flashpoint* as in-Group Psychological and Action Narrative**   109

| | |
|---|---|
| The Broadcast | 110 |
| The *Flashpoint* Visual Narrative | 112 |
| The *Flashpoint Corpus* Structure | 117 |
| Communication in the *Flashpoint* TV Series | 124 |
| Narrativity and Popularisation | 128 |
| The Vocative Function | 130 |
| Tactics | 136 |
| Weaponry Occurrence | 140 |
| Localisation Operations | 145 |
| The Psychological Communication Slant | 148 |
| Psychology and Profiling | 155 |
| The *Flashpoint Corpus* Results | 167 |
| References | 172 |

**5  The *Motive* 'Whydunit' Television Hybrid**   177

| | |
|---|---|
| The Broadcast | 178 |
| The *Motive* Narrative Core | 179 |
| The *Motive Corpus* Structure | 182 |
| The *Motive* TV Series Language(s) | 189 |
| The Characters' Portrayal | 192 |
| Procedural Language: The *Whydunnit* Reconstructive Approach to Homicides | 194 |
| Interrogation Room Talks | 203 |
| The Crime Scene Dialogues | 207 |
| Who's Killing the Killstreak? | 214 |
| The *Motive* Forensics: Language, Discourse and Terminology | 218 |
| The Medical Communication Supports | 221 |
| IT and Finances | 228 |
| The Legal Context Crystallised Praxis | 230 |

Contents xiii

| | | |
|---|---|---|
| | Observation | 233 |
| | The *Motive Corpus* Results | 234 |
| | References | 238 |
| **6** | **The *19-2* Anglified Police Procedural *Noir*** | 241 |
| | The *19-2 Corpus* Structure | 244 |
| | The Broadcast | 252 |
| | The *19-2* Expressive Spectum | 253 |
| | Procedural Language: Authority | 255 |
| | Misdemeanours Citywide | 262 |
| | Specialised Knowledge, Subcodes and Popularisation | 275 |
| | The Linguistic Characterisation | 280 |
| | Lingo, Slang and Jargon | 286 |
| | The *19-2 Corpus* Results | 292 |
| | References | 300 |
| **7** | **Contrastive Analysis and Results** | 305 |
| | Normalisation and Speech Performance Metrics | 310 |
| | The Languages of the *Corpora* | 313 |
| | Popularised Knowledge, Natural Language and Characterisation Blend | 321 |
| | Narrating the *Corpora* Visual and Acoustic Dimensions | 324 |
| | The Canadian Contemporary TV Crime Drama | 332 |
| | References | 340 |
| **8** | **Concluding Remarks** | 345 |
| | References | 356 |
| **Appendix** | | 359 |
| **Further Reading** | | 367 |
| **Index** | | 371 |

# List of Figures

| | | |
|---|---|---|
| Fig. 1.1 | Shares of total volume of film and television production in Canada, by province and territory, 2017/2018 | 7 |
| Fig. 2.1 | Information transmission model | 24 |
| Fig. 2.2 | Language system stratification: the socio-semiotic functional perspective | 25 |
| Fig. 2.3 | Non-verbal behaviour (NVB) vs. Non-verbal communication (NVC) scheme | 32 |
| Fig. 2.4 | Metz's overview of visual iconic codes relevant for the filmic image track revised with respect to multiplicity and movement | 41 |
| Fig. 2.5 | Trimble's schematisation of the rhetorical inferences model in SD communication | 51 |
| Fig. 2.6 | Appraisal framework model | 55 |
| Fig. 3.1 | Representational 'user-medium-purpose' relationship | 73 |
| Fig. 3.2 | Representation of Thomson's model of 'sit' and 'situation' confronting each other | 78 |
| Fig. 3.3 | Chinese boxes reboot of Thomson's 'sit' and 'situation' model | 79 |
| Fig. 3.4 | Detection TV transposition periodisation scheme | 93 |
| Fig. 4.1 | *Flashpoint*, seasons 1 and 2 theme still captures | 114 |
| Fig. 4.2 | *Flashpoint*, season 3 episodes' opening frames | 116 |
| Fig. 4.3 | *Flashpoint*, s01e01. Flashback narration | 127 |
| Fig. 4.4 | *Flashpoint Corpus* weaponry display | 144 |
| Fig. 4.5 | *Flashpoint Corpus* topnym map | 146 |

**xvi**     **List of Figures**

Fig. 4.6  *Flashpoint*, s02e13, min. 00:02:17–18/00:30:18–21. Pursuit
multimodal observation                                                                                      147
Fig. 6.1  *19-2 Corpus* City of Montreal topnym map                                      271
Fig. 6.2  *19-2 Corpus* law violations chart                                                       294
Fig. 7.1  *Total Corpus* noun topicalisation                                                     336

# List of Tables

| | | |
|---|---|---|
| Table 4.1 | *Flashpoint*, s02e02. Multimodal annotation aligned with frames | 122 |
| Table 4.2 | *Flashpoint Corpus* noun frequency list | 130 |
| Table 4.3 | *Flashpoint*, s03e07. Investigator's assessment multimodal annotation | 132 |
| Table 4.4 | *Flashpoint*, s01e02. Professional discourse and sarcasm multimodal annotation | 137 |
| Table 4.5 | The *Flashpoint Corpus* weaponry lexicon | 141 |
| Table 4.6 | *Flashpoint Corpus* topnym list | 146 |
| Table 4.7 | *Flashpoint Corpus*, 'subject', 'hostage', 'bomb' word sketches | 150 |
| Table 4.8 | *Flashpoint*, s02e10. Bomb explosion multimodal annotation | 152 |
| Table 4.9 | *Flashpoint*, s01e01. Culprit identification multimodal annotation | 161 |
| Table 4.10 | The *Flashpoint Corpus* results | 167 |
| Table 5.1 | *Motive*, s03e01. Multimodal annotation aligned with minutes | 187 |
| Table 5.2 | *Motive Corpus* word frequency list | 196 |
| Table 5.3 | *Motive Corpus* "what" word sketch | 196 |
| Table 5.4 | *Motive Corpus* verb frequency list | 197 |
| Table 5.5 | *Motive*, s03e07. Medical examination multimodal observation | 199 |

xviii  **List of Tables**

| | | |
|---|---|---|
| Table 5.6 | *Motive*, s02e11. Interrogatory flashback narration and multimodal observation | 204 |
| Table 5.7 | *Motive* TV series, season 1, killers and victims report | 215 |
| Table 5.8 | *Motive* TV series, season 2, killers and victims report | 215 |
| Table 5.9 | *Motive* TV series, season 3, killers and victims report | 216 |
| Table 5.10 | *Motive Corpus*, noun frequency list | 221 |
| Table 5.11 | *Motive Corpus*, "victim" word sketch | 222 |
| Table 5.12 | *Motive*, s01e02. Medical report multimodal observation | 224 |
| Table 5.13 | *Motive*, s01e04. Detectives' vs. lawyers' authority multimodal | 231 |
| Table 5.14 | The *Motive Corpus* results | 235 |
| Table 6.1 | *19-2* TV series intro frames description | 245 |
| Table 6.2 | *19-2*, s02e07. Evidence tampering footage multimodal annotation aligned with frames | 249 |
| Table 6.3 | *19-2 Corpus* verb word list | 255 |
| Table 6.4 | *19-2*, s01e05. Police briefing multimodal observation | 258 |
| Table 6.5 | *19-2 Corpus* adjective word list | 263 |
| Table 6.6 | *19-2*, s01e01. Culprit description multimodal observation | 264 |
| Table 6.7 | *19-2 Corpus* crimes classification | 268 |
| Table 6.8 | *19-2 Corpus* toponym list | 270 |
| Table 6.9 | *19-2 Corpus*, "assault" word sketch | 272 |
| Table 6.10 | *19-2*, s01e05. RMP chitchat multimodal observation | 274 |
| Table 6.11 | *19-2*, s01e01. 'Nick performing CPR' multimodal observation | 277 |
| Table 6.12 | *19-2 Corpus*, "atta-" prefixation word sketch | 282 |
| Table 6.13 | *19-2*, s01e01. Gunfight multimodal observation | 288 |
| Table 6.14 | The *19-2 Corpus* results | 293 |
| Table 7.1 | *Flashpoint*, *Motive* and *19–2 Corpora* total statistics | 307 |
| Table 7.2 | *Flashpoint*, *Motive* and *19-2 Corpora* seasonal statistics | 308 |
| Table 7.3 | *Total Corpus* noun frequency list | 334 |
| Table A.1 | List of the *Flashpoint* episodes, season 1 | 359 |
| Table A.2 | List of the *Flashpoint* episodes, season 2 | 360 |
| Table A.3 | List of the *Flashpoint* episodes, season 3 | 360 |
| Table A.4 | List of the *Motive* episodes, season 1 | 362 |
| Table A.5 | List of the *Motive* episodes, season 2 | 362 |
| Table A.6 | List of the *Motive* episodes, season 3 | 363 |
| Table A.7 | List of the *19-2* episodes, season 1 | 364 |
| Table A.8 | List of the *19-2* episodes, season 2 | 364 |

# 1

# Introduction

## Communication as a Quibbling Concept

Communication might link up to a social sharing process (Halliday, 1978). Its performance summons a mutual exchange where the speaker's *oral* linguistic skills (Like proficiency and effectiveness) largely facilitate its success as well. The cooperative (or non-cooperative) receiver's attitude would work for the essential information apprehension to exploit the interaction fully (Scott-Phillips, 2015). Nonetheless, fundamental studies on language systems strongly underpin the human codes' more complex structure (ibid.).

During the nineteenth century, the American mathematician and philosopher Charles S. Peirce was already considering languages' semiotic charge (Hardwick, 1977, pp. 85–86). He established a three-level hierarchy of signs (*visually* detectable) determined by a *signifier*—the form of the code transmitting the meaning—and a *signified*—the concept or the object described (Houser et al., 1998, p. 478). He labelled those signs as *icons*, *indexes* and *symbols*, all having different deictic peculiarities (ibid.). Generally speaking, graphics (and graphemes) represent the *conventional* relationship between what is told (signified) and the way it is described

© The Author(s), under exclusive license to Springer Nature Switzerland AG 2021
F. P. Gentile, *Corpora, Corpses and Corps*,
https://doi.org/10.1007/978-3-030-78276-4_1

(signifier). Observing those categories more deeply, one could notice some relevant mental schemata defining this co-dependency. Peirce identified *icons* as reproducing the original through physical resemblance (like portraits and photographs). *Indexes* correspond to the direct manifestation of a phenomenon (i.e., smoke denoting fire). Eventually, *symbols* funnel a cultural or metaphoric association. These latter are arbitrary but shared by all community members (i.e., smoke not simplistically representing fire but meaning 'war', 'disasters', 'tragedy').

The said expressive characteristics unify language communicativeness on the visual dimension. When synchronised with sound, they also mark out a clear polysemiotic objective. Different content-enriched elements express themselves in diverse modes. Their denotative/connotative *strata* transmit as many encoded bits of information that constitute the final meaningful linguistic evidence.

Therefore, those studies continued in time via diverse disciplinary approaches. A few decades later, during the 1960s, another scholar, the Armenian-American psychologist Albert Mehrabian, focused on meaningful language features, which appeared to occur on expressive modes that diverged from the verbal one (Mehrabian 1972, 1981). Through his famous '7-38-55' rule, Mehrabian formulated an equation stating that only 7 per cent of natural communication is verbal (oral). By contrast, 38 per cent is non-verbal (gestures and mimics), and 55 per cent is para-verbal (tone, rhythm, prosody). This approach statistically screened the relevance of extra-linguistic traits over the linguistic ones to shape the transparent multilayered stratification of communication codes.

The psychologist's theory misinterpretations wanted it as per se extendable to every context, although Mehrabian only investigated emotionally connoted interactions (ibid.). Yet, despite its limited applicability, the equation affects the myriads of informative possibilities transferring knowledge from person to person and from community to community.

The twentieth-century initial polysemiotic approach to languages launched the improved label of *multimodality* (Baldry & Thibault, 2001, 2006; Bateman, 2008; Bateman & Schmidt, 2012; Kress, 2010; Kress & van Leeuwen, 1996, 2011). From this renewed perspective, the "semiotic modes, similarily, are shaped by both the intrinsic characteristics and potentialities of the medium and by the requirements, histories and values of societies and their cultures" (Kress & van Leeuwen, 1996, p. 35).

# 1 Introduction    3

The theoretical basis validating the polyvalent methodological approach to communication could not exclude associated thoughts about the channels used to convey some discourses and the ideological and cultural premises casting them.

In the late 1920s, linguistic relativity formulations presupposed language as conditioning the speakers' worldview and cognition; this speculation became famous as the 'Sapir–Whorf hypothesis' (after its most eminent advocates). Following this mutual influence between the language system and thought, an ecolinguistic vista is necessary. Although focusing mostly on language, scholars (see Fill & Mühlhäusler, 2001; Halliday, 1990) started scouting communication according to the social environment hosting it. They associated language to compartmental communicative areas like 'language and gnosis', 'language and science', 'language and politics'. There, they recognised that communication is not static but that it mutates following the given patterns exploited in diverse situations. The study of semiotics first, and then multimodality contributed to shaping the polyhedral linguistic and extralinguistic expressive possibilities of those many contexts. This said vista helped the utter evaluation of the situational backgrounds guiding the iterative events. Likewise, the ecology of media (Granata, 2015; Postman, 1970, 1979) field of application is responsible for developing an improved assessment of mass-oriented messages (Lamberti, 2012; McLuhan, 1964, 1967) and their ways of functioning.

Hence, multimodality has become fundamental as the primary method to observe and interpret any communicative situation. It forbids every *sēma* to be read as the product of a mere sign combination. The approach prefers its definition under an interrelated compound of graphic, linguistic, corporeal, proxemic, metaphoric, modal, sociocultural, historical and performative implementations. Those many aspects enhance the sēmas significance within the media transmitting them.

In light of that, the present survey benefits from the essential multimodal support for carrying out the examination. Other pivotal methodologies assist the process. Alongside this primary disciplinary study, corpus linguistic tools help construct some solid corpora for the analysis. Appraisal framework evaluations and specialised communication perspectives would apply to sift through the monitored and artificial television contexts explained by Media Studies theorisations. The second chapter of the work presents these fundamental disciplines and their practical contribution to the investigation.

Having once defined the multidisciplinary and multimodal methodological ground, the study delves into the mediatic and cultural dimensions.

Suppose that a list of recurring patterns and stereotypical contexts of use can decode language systems. In that case, the diverse communication channels participate in the characterisation process. An ample array of expressive modes serves information transmission. The entire study concentrates on the analysis of television as an informative tool and as a powerful medium that forges and casts linguistic and communicative social knowledge through its content. Still, one should bear in mind the planned and monitored iterative, interactive and discoursal structure of onscreen situations. Despite the non-spontaneous, and thus non-natural, quality of television languages, they tend to employ some expressive features that emulate actual communicative contexts. In like manner, televised scenarios parade before the public of end-users through a plausibly and trustworthy attitude, and with themes galore (ranging from news to documentaries and from historically reconstructive movies to sci-fi series).

Supported also by Film Studies (Metz, 1966, 1974; Messaris, 1994; Monaco, 2009; Sikov, 2000; Miller & Stam, 2004; Piazza et al., 2011; Bateman & Schmidt, 2012; Wildfeuer, 2016), the survey includes the perusal of the main strategies adopted for the making of the television products. They synchronise with linguistic and extra-linguistic data to achieve a proper comprehension of the medium recounting patterns. Together with the modal contextualisation, the cultural background is necessary.

Canada's TV productions generally contrast the overwhelmingly dominant US cinematic industry in the crime drama genre.[1] In Chap. 3, television falls under the Canadian and cultural studies' lens to understand domestic television history and evolution, in conjunction with the rise of national consciousness.

The subsequent analysis involves reading Canadian television crime narratives via several series surveys (*Flashpoint*, Canada: *CTV*, 2008–2012;

*Motive*, Canada: *CTV*, 2013–2016; *19–2*, Canada: *Bravo!*, 2014–2016, *CTV*, 2017). The examination of three emblematic contemporary dramas aims to retrieve the genre's main expressive and communicative features. Here different 'languages' (verbal, non-verbal, para-verbal) combine to convey pre-arranged meanings simultaneously.

Television fitted the goal more than the cinema (and other media) from the thematic contextualisation perspective, as the former offers spectators—as individuals—the chance to switch from one channel to the other, and consequently from one narrative typology to another in a very short space of time. In contrast, cinema forces its ticket holders—as the collective multitude crammed into the theatre—to sit through the movie without any zapping arbitrariness. Indeed, this medium is most popular and of effortless accessibility. TVs lay siege to almost every house worldwide, and they represent an aggregative social instrument.

The choice of series instead of films had similar reasons. The former (meant as multiple-instalment shows) grant more continuity to the analytical work. Movies, in fact, would provide insufficient conversational contexts and a limited vocabulary compared to the series collectable data.

A further TV inner differentiation distinguishes series from serials. Onscreen fictions of a varying number of episodes have two labels depending on their narrative slant. On the one hand, TV series work through a centrifugal complexity. They target their affiliation goal through capturing and fascinating plot structures that recount many unitary and compartmented episodes. On the other hand, serials tend to a more centripetal perspective. These latter propose one mainly exciting event, and they carry it along throughout the show's season. Only a few collateral situations embellish the storyline during the instalments succession.

Given such final differentiation, the study has not excluded one narrative structure or the other since its overall goal is to describe genre-related peculiarities. This difference does not characterise crime narratives only, as the separation between serial and series belongs to every televised possibility (either fiction or non-fiction). Yet, crime has always been a fascinating topic on- and offscreen, thus representing the study's ideal environment. Heterogeneous colliding audiences seem to agree in appreciating its main patterns, capable of catching one's attention via specifically designed arrangements:

> Tzvetan Todorov's *The Typology of Detective Fiction*, which remains one of the most significant contribution to the field, sought to uphold the distinction between 'genre fiction' and 'literature'. However, his identification of the two orders of the story, inquest and crime, as equivalents to the Russian formalist distinction between *sjužet* and *fabula* (often translated as '*discourse*' and '*story*' respectively), makes the detective story, as Peter Brooks writes, 'the narrative of narratives', its classical structure a laying bare of the structure of all narrative in that it dramatizes the role of *sjužet* and *fabula* and the nature of their relation. (Kracauer, 1974, p. 119)

Crime drama enjoys a commonly shared favour. Its major strategies polarised the examination for their right-on-point aim to meet the receiver's taste and combine linguistic and extra-linguistic traits fit for the medium of broadcasting. Such registers happen to blend multiple set of elements belonging to different interactive and descriptive dimensions. These workings offer the public a kaleidoscopic experience that spectators seem to embrace (more than like) fully. Onscreen, non- and paralingual audiovisual multimodality features integrate with everyday conversations and scant terminology. Even specialised discourses would easily co-occur in their popularised form with natural language. In those cases, no incomprehension threats would rise, where countless culturally related implementations support communication to make the TV product more palatable to its end-users.

Of course, despite the broad-*spectrum* cover, this study could not proceed to the actual and complete observation of *every* TV series on crime ever produced in Canada. Here, the focus concentrates on three exemplary case studies.

According to the 2018 *Economic Report on the Screen-Based Media Production Industry in Canada* (*ERSMP*; Fig. 1.1), 92 per cent of the entire cinematic productions intended for television broadcasting belongs to the three main film industry poles comprising: Quebec 20 per cent; Ontario 32 per cent; and British Columbia 40 per cen, that, together with the remaining 8 per cent of the other provinces, has led to an income of $8.9 billion of production volume increasing Canada's 2017/2018 GDP to +6 per cent ($12.8 bn and +19 per cent of foreign investments ($5.6 bn) in Canadian productions more than the previous biennium

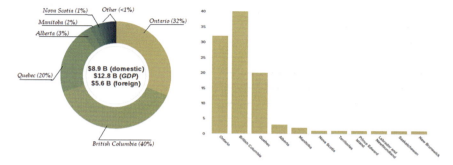

**Fig. 1.1** Shares of total volume of film and television production in Canada, by province and territory, 2017/2018. (The figure is mine, based on *Profile 2018*, n.d.; 'Estimates based on data collected from CAVCO, CRTC, CBC/Radio-Canada and the Association of Provincial Funding Agencies. *[Territories are] Yukon, Nunavut and Northwest Territories. Note: some totals may not sum the due rounding'. *Profile 2018—Economic Report on the Screen-Based Media Production Industry in Canada* (n.d.). Canadian Media Producers Association, Department of Canadian Heritage, Telefilm Canada, Association québécoise de la production médiatique, Nordcity. [22nd edition]. p. 10. https://cmpa.ca/wp-content/uploads/2019/03/Profile-2018.pdf (accessed June, 6, 2019))

(ibid.: 4). The trend did not stop in the two-year period 2018/2019, reaching $9.3 bn of production volume (*Profile 2019*).[2]

Fiction genre investments decreased by 18.1 per cent to $1.53 bn between 2016/2017 and 2017/2018, but their projects remained decidedly relevant. Other genres like documentaries and shows on lifestyle and customs outnumbered fiction, annihilating other narrative forms like movies and variety shows via the serial typology employment (*Profile 2018*, n.d., pp. 27–29). Seventy-four per cent of productions were Anglophone, only contrasted by 26 per cent of French-language content and the remaining 1 per cent of bilingual products (or adopting other minor codes, *ivi*). Compared to the previous two-year period, 2017/2018 TV formats experienced a commodification overturn of −8.8 per cent of Canadian content ($3.04 bn), affected by non-local productions and investments.

Nevertheless, the multidisciplinary methodological approach also affects Canadian television's sociocultural background. It offers a relevant analytical description of the said expressive modes occurring in contemporary crime drama.

Some of the statistical data has reported the programming investments of current Canadian broadcasting policies. Coherently with that, the survey's core dissects three main TV products ascribable to as many leading provinces on the mediatic panorama. The involved British Columbia, Ontario and Quebec productions achieved resounding success in their respective broadcasting periods. Also, the series underwent a periodisation process to discuss their content structures and communicative peculiarities through a dynamic and evolving path. The evaluation included a ten-year gap between the first episode premiere and the last broadcast airing analysed.

These involved shows represent three exciting narrative shades of the whole genre. The *Flashpoint* TV series—set in Toronto—recounts tactical corps' perilous actions defeating terrorist threats and other major crimes (Chap. 4). The *Motive* TV hybrid is midway between series and serial: it narrates the murders occurring in a gloomy Vancouver supervised by a skilled homicide department (Chap. 5). Eventually, the *19–2* TV serial relates a quibbling Anglophone rendition of the francophone original *Dix Neuf-Deux* police procedural in a *noir* Montreal (Chap. 6).

The corpus linguistic approach was fundamental for the collecting and building procedures of the *corpora*. However, it consisted of a tool deployed to accomplish the transcription and tagging steps. It limited its pragmatical support to attaining relevant frequency lists and extrapolating several illustrative examples. Also, corpus linguistics usefulness granted the study some generalisable statistical observations to highlight the genre communication trends. Interactive modes, however, present a primary performative power that implements their linguistic banks.

Consequently, the observation and description of multimodally and cinematically annotated passages had a leading role in this work. Those aspects allowed the (de)codification of countless non- and para-verbal features. That kind of information tells users about prosodic and rhythmic additions boosting verbality. The televised products performative nature necessitates a more profound reading that summons all the fundamental expressive peculiarities. This way, the onscreen act translates into a *unicum*, out of many communication layers, for the utmost understanding of the Canadian contemporary crime drama.

The seventh chapter outlines its main communication patterns. Here, the entire study contemplates the 'reading' of three representative bodies, elicited from the title itself.

The linguistic—verbal—body corresponds to *corpora*. It consists of the textual dimension given by transcription procedures.

*Corpses* stand for the visual body, determined by the corporeal dissection of multimodal elements. For example, non- and para-verbality include cinematic language (for frame and sequence descriptions), use of colours, sociological metadata (i.e., details on age, gender, social class, dress code).

The third and final body refers to *corps*. It is ideological since it reflects on the extra-linguistic and cinematic implicatures harnessing the narrative schemata.

A similar contribution could, once more, raise the bar of Multimodal Studies. It would implement the comprehension of the expressive schemata in media—television especially. In turn, these monitored contexts could operate as educational and formative modes contributing to moulding social, linguistic and cultural proficiency and awareness of large communities. Indeed, the state of the art is still under-investigated. It mostly concentrates on reading the visual, cultural or linguistic dimensions on their own and concerning limited case studies. Many works on the Film Studies sphere face the television environment as their ideal and challenging habitat for the utmost study of its expressive qualities. In truth, they remain anchored to interesting cases, mostly exclusively belonging to the mesmerising US cinematographic area. For example, amid the many instances, several cognate surveys work on *Cagney & Lacey* (USA: CBS, 1982–1988) or *X-Files* (USA: Fox, 1993–2002). This latter's extensive production filmed many of its seasons in Vancouver instead of Los Angeles, still portraying it as an entirely US trade-off. Along with said series, *The Shield* (USA: FX, 2002–2008) is another over-investigated series, especially for the *thematic* or *sociologic* structures of the products. Merely assessing either of the two aspects, dated works generally forget to consider other content-enriched layers (see Jenner, 2016;

Longworth, 2000; Moorti & Cuklaz, 2017; Nelson, 2007; Richardson, 2010).

Other scholars ventured into the meanders of multimodality to offer competent readers or *theoretical* manuals on the visual implicatures affecting communication. This time, they spent no words for the topics behind the products and exiling the linguistic dimension in the scrapheap of salient features (i.e., De Saint-Georges, 2004; Jewitt, 2013; Kress & van Leeuwen, 1996; O'Halloran, 2004; O'Toole, 1994) but for a few cases (Bednarek, 2010, 2011, 2018). The compartmental approach falls outside the aura of the discipline. To that extent, this literature represents an immense patrimony of incomparable knowledge yet fails in the primary condition of assembling all communication dimensions at once.

The methodology bases its quintessential interpretative task on the combined and simultaneous *covalent* occurrence of the diverse communicative *strata* involved in whatsoever type of communication. In like manner, discipline-related analyses could in no eventuality relinquish any expressive aspect to prefer another.

Opposite to similar contradicting conduct, the main objective of the examination presented in the following chapters is to investigate all-inclusive modes of television information transmissibility. On this occasion, the study falls on the crime drama genre emblematic context, rallying vast plateaux of receivers for its appealing qualities. Here, the foregrounding requirements of multimodality finally unify the cultural, sociological, political, thematic, narrative and cinematic reflections to the linguistic and extra-linguistic content associated with them. The linguistic layer is not anymore the sole result of verbal features (as traditionally reckoned). It *indissolubly* melts with its non- and para-verbal expressive stages. This *continuum* simultaneously (and unprecedentedly) intervenes onto both the natural language dimension and the specialised discourse usage.

Moreover, this multimodal (spoken and performative) language always comes together with its connected backgrounds. Themes and storylines convey agglomerates of culture, social and political statements. Topics rendition through cinematic features to not leave behind any relevant data.

On this silver thread, the work is an advisable option for diverse users aiming to bolster up new and creative understandings and successfully expanding the actual knowledge frontiers.

## Notes

1. Listing a huge quantity of famous genre-related TV series and serials like *Criminal Minds* (USA: *CBS*, 2005–), *CSI* (USA and Canada: *CBS*, 2000–2015, and its related U.S. on-going spin-offs), *NCIS* (USA: *CBS*, 2003–), *Dexter* (USA: *Showtime*, 2006–2013), *Castle* (USA: *ABC*, 2009–2016), *BlueBlood* (USA: *CBS*, 2010–), *TheMentalist* (USA: *CBS*, 2008–2015), *ColdCase* (USA: *CBS*, 2003–2010), *Numb3rs* (USA: *CBS*, 2005–2010), and others.
2. *Profile 2019—Economic Report on the Screen-Based Media Production Industry in Canada* (n.d.). Canadian Media Producers Association, Department of Canadian Heritage, Telefilm Canada, Association québécoise de la production médiatique, Nordcity. p. 4. https://cmpa.ca/wp-content/uploads/2020/04/CMPA_2019_E_FINAL.pdf (accessed March 4, 2021).

## References

Baldry, A., & Thibault, P. J. (2001). Towards Multimodal Corpora. In G. Aston & L. Burnard (Eds.), *Corpora in the Description and Teaching of English-Papers from the 5th ESSE Conference* (pp. 87–102). Cooperativa Libraria Universitaria Editrice Bologna.

Baldry, A., & Thibault, P. J. (2006). *Multimodal Transcription and Text Analysis: A Multimedia Toolkit and Course Book*. Equinox.

Bateman, J. A. (2008). *Multimodality and Genre*. Palgrave Macmillan.

Bateman, J. A., & Schmidt, K. H. (2012). *Multimodal Film Analysis. How Films Mean*. Routledge.

Bednarek, M. (2010). Corpus Linguistics and Systemic Functional Linguistics: Interpersonal Meaning, Identity and Bonding In Popular Culture. In M. Bednarek & J. R. Martin (Eds.), *New Disourse on Language: Functional Perspectives on Multimodality, Identity and Affiliation* (pp. 237–266). Continuum.

Bednarek, M. (2011). Expressivity and Television Characterisation. *Language and Literature, 20*(1), 3–21.

Bednarek, M. (2018). *Language and Television Series. A Linguistic Approach to Television Dialogue.* Cambridge University Press.

De Saint-Georges, I. (2004). Materiality in Discourse: The Influence of Space and Layout in Making Meaning. In P. LeVine & R. Scollon (Eds.), *Discourse and Technology. Multimodal Discourse Analysis* (pp. 71–87). Georgetown University Press.

Fill, A., & Mühlhäusler, P. (Eds.). (2001). *The Ecolinguistics Reader: Language, Ecology and Environment.* Continuum.

Granata, P. (2015). *Ecologia dei media. Protagonisti, scuole, concetti chiave.* Franco Angeli Editore.

Halliday, M. A. K. (1978). *Language as Social Semiotic: The Social Interpretation of Language and Meaning.* Edward Arnold.

Halliday, M. A. K. (1990 [2001]). New Ways of Meaning: The Challenge to Applied Linguistics. In A. Fill & P. Mühlhäusler (Eds.), *The Ecolinguistics Reader: Language, Ecology and Environment* (pp. 175–202). Continuum.

Hardwick, C. (Ed.). (1977). *Semiotics and Significs.* Indiana University Press.

Houser, N., et al. (Eds.). (1998). *The Essential Peirce. Selected Philosophical Writings* (Vol. 2). Indiana University Press.

Jenner, M. (2016). *American TV Detective Dramas: Serial Investigation.* Palgrave Macmillan.

Jewitt, C. (Ed.). (2013). *The Routledge Handbook of Multimodal Analysis.* Routledge.

Kracauer, S. (1974). *Saggi di Sociologia Critica. Sociologia Come Scienza. Sociologia del Romanzo Poliziesco.* Bari: De Donato Editore. [Original Title: *Der DeEtektiv-Roman. Ein philosophischer Traktat,* 1971].

Kress, G. (2010). *Multimodality. A Social Semantic Approach to Contemporary Communication.* Routledge.

Kress, G., & van Leeuwen, T. (1996). *Reading Images: The Grammar of Visual Design.* Routledge.

Kress, G., & van Leeuwen, T. (2011). *Multimodal Discourse. The Modes and Media of Contemporary Communication.* Bloomsbury Academic.

Lamberti, E. (2012). *Marshall McLuhan's Mosaic: Probing the Literary Origins of Media Studies.* University of Toronto Press.

Longworth, J. L. (2000). *TV Creations: Conversations with America's Top Producers of Television Drama.* Syracuse University Press.

McLuhan, M. (1964). *Understanding Media. The Extensions of Man*. McGraw-Hill. Retrieved October 4, 2018, from http://robynbacken.com/text/nw_research.pdf

McLuhan, M. (1967 [2001]). *Medium Is the Massage: An Inventory on Effects*. Gingko Press Inc.

Mehrabian, A. (1972). *Nonverbal Communication*. Aldeine-Atherton.

Mehrabian, A. (1981). *Silent Messages: Implicit Communication of Emotions and Attitude*. Wardsworth Pub Co.

Messaris, P. (1994). *Visual Literacy*. Westview Press.

Metz, C. (1966). La grande syntagmatique du film narratif. *Communications. Recherches Sémiologique: L'Analyse Stucturale du Récit, 8*, 120–124.

Metz, C. (1974). *Film Language: A Semiotics of the Cinema* (M. Taylor, Trans.). Oxford and Chicago: Oxford University Press and Chicago University Press. [Original Title: *Essays sur la Signification au Cinéma*, 1968].

Miller, T., & Stam, R. (2004). *A Companion to Film Theory*. Blackwell.

Monaco, J. (2009). *How to Read a Film: Movies, Media and Beyond*. Oxford University Press.

Moorti, S., & Cuklaz, J. (2017). *All-American TV Crime Drama: Feminism and Identity Policy in Law&Order—Special Victims Unit*. I.B. Tauris.

Nelson, R. (2007). *State of Play: Contemporary 'High-End' TV Drama'*. Manchester University Press.

O'Halloran, K. L. (Ed.). (2004). *Multimodal Discourse Analysis. Systemic Functional Perspectives*. Continuum.

O'Toole, M. (1994). *The Language of Displayed Art*. Leicester University Press.

Piazza, R., Bednarek, M., & Rossi, F. (Eds.). (2011). *Telecinematic Discourse. Approaches to the Language of Films and Television Series*. John Benjamins Publishing Company.

Postman, N. (1970). The Reformed English Curriculum. In A. C. Eurich (Ed.), *High-School 1980: The Shape of the Future in American Secondary Education* (pp. 160–168). Pitman.

Postman, N. (1979). *Teaching as a Conversing Activity*. Delacorte Press.

*Profile 2018—Economic Report on the Screen-Based Media Production Industry in Canada*. (n.d.). Canadian Media Producers Association, Department of Canadian Heritage, Telefilm Canada, Association québécoise de la production médiatique, Nordcity. [22nd ed.]. Retrieved June, 6, 2019, from https://cmpa.ca/wp-content/uploads/2019/03/Profile-2018.pdf

*Profile 2019—Economic Report on the Screen-Based Media Production Industry in Canada*. (n.d.). Canadian Media Producers Association, Department of

Canadian Heritage, Telefilm Canada, Association québécoise de la production médiatique, Nordcity. p. 4. Retrieved March 4, 2021, from https://cmpa.ca/wp-content/uploads/2020/04/CMPA_2019_E_FINAL.pdf

Richardson, K. (2010). *Television Dramatic Dialogue. A Sociolinguistic Study*. Oxford University Press.

Scott-Phillips, T. (2015). *Speaking Our Minds: Why Human Communication is Different, and How Language Evolved to Make It Special*. Palgrave Macmillan.

Sikov, E. (2000). *Film Studies. An Introduction*. Columbia University Press.

Wildfeuer, J. (2016 [2014]). *Film Discourse Interpretation. Towards a New Paradigm for Multimodal Film Analysis*. Routledge.

# 2

# The Research Methodology

## Corpus Linguistics as a Methodological Tool

The Corpus Linguistics approach (Stubbs, 1983, 1996a: 41) is an invaluable resource bestowing users a tool for scanning language in search of "actual patterns of use" (Biber et al., 1998: 4). Such methodology funnels the researchers' interests in retrieving and investigating syntax peculiarities and linguistic schemata (see Swales 1988, 1990). It tracks back main language apparatuses frequency and occurrences, and their prosodic, semantic and cultural associations of a lexical thesaurus in natural discourse. Therefore, Corpus Analysis (Conrad, 2002) involves enormous amounts of data to conduct a satisfying and well-accomplished survey on language use. Large-scale multimillion-word corpora represent the main models of a similar process. To that extent, scholars cannot manually perform similar studies, as their analytical development demands the application of software processing countless linguistic data in no time and provide users with precise results:

> There might be a large number of potentially meaningful patterns that escape the attention of the traditional linguist; these will not be recorded in

© The Author(s), under exclusive license to Springer Nature Switzerland AG 2021
F. P. Gentile, *Corpora, Corpses and Corps*,
https://doi.org/10.1007/978-3-030-78276-4_2

traditional reference works and may not even be recognised until they are forced upon the corpus analyst by the sheer visual presence of the emerging patterns in a concordance page. (Tognini-Bonelli, 2001: 86)

Corpus Analysis (intended as corpus-based analysis in the manuscript) is largely used to evaluate foreseen patterns expected to be retrieved within extensive linguistic data collections. Nonetheless, the present investigation circumvents the deductive approach based on sheer results (Calabrese, 2004, 2008) and observes "the integrity of the data as a whole" (Tognini-Bonelli, 2001: 84–85).Then, it proceeds to describe them "with respect to corpus evidence" from a corpus-driven perspective, since it is the corpus *itself* (and not its *linguistics*) to embody "a theory of language" (ibid.: 84–85, 86; see also Biber, 2012). This inductive approach generalises the linguistic rule through the corpus interpretation and study, and it does not confirm or rejects pre-existing constructs.

The data collection procedures and researchers' expertise contribute detecting register shifts. Nonetheless, the mode (generally written or spoken) represents an outstanding limit for the approach. When processing data from corpora based on series of written texts, the work seems to be exploitable in a relatively linear manner (as they are already in the written form) (Ochs, 1979). Spoken words consist of language data in the form of transcriptions here (but they may also include other document formats like audio-files, etc.); however, written documents, including visual, graphic, audio format, etc., represent something else:

> Languages contain not only words, phrases and sentences but languages also have imagery; they have a global, instantaneous non-compositional component that is as defining as the existence of a language as are the familiar linguistic components. (McNeill et al., 1994: 223)

Indeed, "we speak with our vocal organs [...], we converse with our whole body" (Abercrombie, 1963: 55). Hence, according to speculations formulated by Albert Mehrabian, Professor of Psychology at UCLA, spoken contexts (although mostly associated with emotionality) are summarisable in the '7-38-55 equation' (Mehrabian, 1972). The sequence demonstrates that actual utterances (or simply, words) only represent 7 per cent of communication in dialogic situations, where the best of information is given by non-verbal patterns (55 per cent) and paralanguage (38 per cent), displaying meaningful elements such as tone of voice and rhythm, or gestuality and mimics. These features add extra meanings to mere oral dimension, signifying beyond word's linguistics (the speculation was already pioneered by Searle's speech act theory; Searle, 1969). Nonetheless, advanced researches on the matter allowed programmers to elaborate complete software managing to process complex data involving the vast range of information conveyed by these 'new generation' corpora (see Saferstein, 2004; Crane et al., 2007; Crosthwaite, 2020). There, further multimodal supportive analysis can flank language case studies with respective audio-video frames. Such tools operate on audio-video and textual-registration (or transcription) inclusive corpora to carry out a complete analysis involving different computational levels where metadata are extracted separately and then re-aligned into a single stream of information (Burnard, 2005). Thus every *mode* of the corpus—whether it be visual, rather than acoustic or transcript—could be easily analysed singularly or in pairs with and assimilated to another, projecting every colour shading the spectrum of the language examined.

At this point of the survey, it has to be acknowledged that the literature does not entirely support such idea of *multimodality* involving computational analysis (see Hoslanova, 2012; O'Halloran, 2011, 2012); nevertheless, the label of 'multimodal corpus' as described so far is present throughout the study for ease of reference.

## Transcript Process and Tagging Tools

As a methodological tool, Corpus Linguistics' early empirical applications focused on retrieving the existing patterns stabilized in language-in-use and inclusive of the lexicon, grammar, language acquisition devices, etc. However, before computers, corpora used to be moderately small and qualitative-based, since speculations on language deriving from the quantitative-based study of similar textual collections appeared insufficient or even deceptive (Wonner, 2005; Engwall et al., 2014). Consequently, methodological contentions jeopardizing the approach led to an era of "discontinuity", receptive to new perspectives jettisoning empiricism and embracing rationalism (McEnery & Wilson, 1996: 4; see also Carroll, 1956; McEnery & Hardie, 2012). According to that perspective, electronically parsed data could be somewhat misleading compared to well-collected large-scale corpora consisting of 'trustworthy'data that derived from unmonitored sources. The arrival of computers eventually revolutionized investigation methods and allowed scholars and users to gather useful data through digital records, and subsequently accelerated the analysis process. The technological enhancement described so far took researchers to create databases such as the Brown Corpus, built in 1963. Further knowledge implementations improved the capacity of processors, which then could handlehuge amounts of data (Kennedy, 1998: 5) such as those included in the British National Corpus (BNC) (1991–1994), or the Bank of English (BoE) (began in 1991 as well).

Over time, the computer science revolution underwent substantial growth responsible for further enhancements permitting users to map their surveys' language contexts, analysing frequency information, lexical and grammatical associations, occurrence patterns, and peculiar language functions with higher levels of precision. Nonetheless, as discussed in the previous paragraph, 'recent' theories used those implementations to get the discipline up to a new pace that involved different contexts and communicative situations to be examined simultaneously. Transcription-based corpora had a new bone of contention on maintaining consistency and coherence in research concerned with two main issues.

On the one hand, canons used to investigate just *one* communicative aspect.

On the other, by praxis, corpora analysis founded the observation merely on written sentences out of linguistic situations that had occurred in a spoken mode and inclusive of other undeniable conversational elements (like gestures, head-nods, gaze; see Wilcox, 2004; Saferstein, 2004). That contingency led to the need for creating multimodal corpora mapping the language and scanning every level—or mode—of communication. They had to detect the meaningful features and structures that belong to surveyed conversational situations. Aside from verbal elements, the new focus was on non-verbal behaviours and paralanguage that a transcript would not express adequately (Saferstein, 2004: 213):

## 2 The Research Methodology 19

> [Multimodal corpus is] an annotated collection of coordinated content and communication channels including speech, gaze, hand gesture and body language, and is generally based on recorded human behavio[u]r. (Foster & Oberlander, 2007: 307–308)

Hence, the use of computers to build a corpus involves a huge range of tools required to provide users with the proper facilities for textualising the pieces of information to be analysed. Software including essential ease for transcription, annotation and coding devices offer examiners the fundamental features for studying corpora. Other programs display the possibility of integrating data and metadata belonging to different modes. Moreover, some online freely available software such as MuTra and MultiTool (Cerrato & Skhiri, 2003: 255) is programmed to "simultaneously display the video and orthographic transcription of dialogues so that the operator can easily observe when gestures are produced together with speech" (ibid.). ANVIL (Kipp et al., 2014) is another freely available online software for multimodal corpus analysis.[1] It permits researchers to align audio/video features with their related transcripts and gestural annotation blueprints describing its visual iconicity. However, metadata needs manual codification.

It is worth noting that corpus-driven filing of electronically stored data and metadata[2] (Firth, 1957; Sinclair, 1996) also involves different stages for designing such collection of materials. The most salient of them are discussed in the present paragraph to illustrate the strategies and procedures adopted in the research. The study's aim involves a language screening of situational, conversational and communicative contexts, here displayed by three major Canadian contemporary television crime dramas being studied here.

For the carrying out of the survey, three different multimodal corpora were built and analysed to retrieve the peculiarities of each. Secondly, a conjoined examination portrays the crucial linguistic tendencies and schemata associated with the crime genre onscreen communication, language use, verbal patterns, non-verbal and para-verbal features. All these aspects influence conversation (adding meaning rather than undermining the scenario's semantics) and occur in everyday exchanges as much as in specialised discourse, changing the terminological ratio and its blendability with *natural language* in such contexts (Halliday, 1978, 1990, 2003; Halliday & Matthiessen, 2004).[3] Moreover, specific examination levels also operate through Textual Linguistics. They search the main negotiation strategies that plot patrols against perpetrators and pin staged situational control marks and turn-taking dynamics (De Beaugrande & Dressler, 1994) to harness the psycho-linguistic clash and achieve the goal of prosecuting criminals.

There are efficient and valid tools aplenty on the web, all useful for tagging corpora in compliance with different criteria. They range from semantic to grammatical tagsets. CLAWS4 (Constituent Likelihood Automatic Word-tagging System)—C5 or C7 tagsets employed—for example, is one available, freely accessible, online software and is often used for attributing Part-of-Speech (POS) tagging for grammatical evidence of words constituting the corpora (Garside, 1987; Leech et al., 1994; Garside & Smith, 1997; Garside et al., 1997: 102–121). The tagging tool is considered reliable, with an accuracy ratio reaching 97–98 per cent. Nevertheless, it could fail to parse some rare iteration uses correctly.Developed in the early 1980s, this software "[…] was used to POS tag c. 100 million words of the British National Corpus (BNC)".[4]

The total amount of data collected consists of 113 episodes ranging from 39 to 45 minutes in length—around 4741 minutes—and ~523,853 words transcribed (become ~505,127 once corpora have been deprived of empty words).[5] Concerning the array of free/paid online parsers, Sketch Engine (Kilgarriff et al., 2004, 2014) has been another key resource. After the collection, the three corpora underwent a POS-tagging process, and their observation through said software allowed the qualitative and quantitative corpus-based analysis.[6] The corpus-driven focus, using a corpus-based parser such as the one mentioned above would integrate the inductive approach with deductive theoretical linguistic expectations. It would generate what some analysts would call a 'hybrid' corpus linguistic approach.

**Example#1**

(a) *Motive Corpus, Motive*, **min. 00: 21: 47–00: 21: 49 [Transcript]**

London: Those five men are not the only ones to die because of my father's greed.

(b) *Motive Corpus, Motive*, **min. 00: 21: 47–00: 21: 49 [POS tagged]**

London: [EX]Those [CD]five [NN]men [VB]are [RB]not [DT]the [RB]only [NNS]ones [TO]to [VB]die [IN]because [IN]of [PRP$]my [NN]father [POS]'s [NN]greed [.].

The choice of POS-tagging (through the use of the Penn Treebank model (Taylor et al. 2003)), implying the proceeding with a strictly grammatical focus that excludes other layers of interest, is dictated by the need for preliminarily assessing language construction modalities and praxis at first glance. However, thanks to the multimodal aim, such a purely linguistic approach, only considering the written text by itself, benefits from a lens alternating focus supportive system. The grammar-schemata linguistic value helps the comprehension via tagging verbal aspects of the language (example 1(b)). Yet, the understanding of some extra-linguistic data is reached through annotation procedures for describing prosody, tone and pitch disparities (*para*-verbal) and for reporting events happening in the film scene. Indeed, these latter features would not be perceivable through the simple action of reading the plain text (*non*-verbal) and the superimposition of the visual and sound dimensions in addition to transcripts.

## Multimodality and the Extra-Linguistic Gap

To proceed with a satisfying comprehension level in conversational situations, one should first acknowledge the main "criteria that show how different resources contextualise each other" (Baldry & Thibault, 2001: 88) in communication. Hence, such contingencies naturally tend to employ a range of (non- and para-verbal) elements co-occurring with (verbal) iterations: "information in both communication channels complement each other to convey the full meaning of a single cognitive representation" (Holler & Bettie, 2003: 81). As a crucial disciplinary approach, multimodality has already been introduced and associated with Corpus Linguistics, aiming at supporting the computational analysis involved in the examination that focuses on language patterns and peculiarities, and that consider different features beyond the linguistic ones. The following chapters of the research adopt a combined slant of

## 22 F. P. Gentile

Multimodal Studies applied to Corpus Linguistics,[7] although the field of investigation covered by such theoretical perspective is much broader (Holler & Bettie, 2002, 2004; Clark & Krych, 2004; De Saint-Georges, 2004).

In their volume entitled *Multimodal Discourse: The Modes and Media of Contemporary Communication*, on the one hand, Gunther Kress and Theo van Leeuwen (2011) describe multimodality as the contemporary tendency that, nowadays, is relentlessly facing the past Western culture of monomodal communication formerly dominating even the academic context. There, scholars used to adopt separately "one language to speak about language (linguists), another to speak about art (art history), yet another to speak about music (musicology), and so on" (Kress & van Leeuwen, 2011: 11; see also van Leeuwen, 2004).

On the other hand, the twentieth-century studies on semiotics have seemingly long annihilated such ideology, mostly facilitating inter-disciplinarity and multifocal approaches, especially in the film context since images convey actions. Moreover, it is the sync with sound and music to fetch emotional connotation and realism, then transposed by the integration code of editing (van Leeuwen, 1985). In many cases, the TV product format and the highly schematised genre narrative allow viewers to fully understand situational communicativeness via the simple fruition of the iconic visual dimension even in absentia of any linguistic knowledge on the film (because those spectators do not speak the language conveyed or even experience the situation by selecting mute mode on their devices), since "all discourse [...] are grounded in local knowledge, but due to the universality of the semiotic model being used, they are applicable to similar texts in any culture" (O'Halloran, 2004: 2). Such an idea also takes roots in a sociological context where "discourses are socially constructed knowledge of (some aspect of) reality" (Kress & van Leeuwen, 2011: 4; 24–44). They have to be communicatively and situationally transposed via the combination of ad hoc semiotic resources. Moreover, their "design" (ibid.: 45–65) would be responsible for the correct interpretation of messages by the receiver, while the sender is carefully balancing the related "production" active processes as the "organisation of materials" (ibid.: 6; 66–85) and "distribution" (ibid.: 86–110). Indeed:

In a Social Semiotic theory, signs are *made*—not *used*—by a sign-*maker* who brings meaning into an *apt* conjunction with a form, a selection/choice shaped by the sign-maker's *interest*. In the process of *representation* sign-makers remake concepts and 'knowledge' in a constant new shaping of the cultural resources for dealing with the social world. (Kress, 2010: 62)

As a consequence, the final accessibility *of* and *to* the message eventually involves two more categories: "provenance" and "experiential meaning potential" (ibid.: 10). The first one is related to the message articulatory essence since individuals tend to reproduce semiotic modes lent by different codes and part of both personal and social backgrounds. While that aspect might be in tighter connection with productive actions, the second one is instead ascribable to understanding the message, its related mental patterns, and actual previous knowledge and experiences creating memories. According to Kristine Lund, an expert in cognitive sciences:

The term multimodality encompasses a wide variety of phenomena in literature, including emotions and attitudes conveyed through prosody, applause, laugher or silence in answer to a question, body movements, object manipulations and proxemics, layout and posture [...] [I]n a different vein, the term multimodal is also often used to signify the medium in which a particular message can be expressed, for example text and graphics. (Lund, 2007: 289–290)

Such linguistic and extra-linguistic information involving prosodic features, gaze and gesture, and haptic perception (Anolli, 2006: 155–156) are structured in a dynamic pattern involving a linguistic exchange to be organized by a source and then sent to a receiver participating in the iteration and being aware of the situational context that they are in (Fig. 2.1). In multimodal contexts, encoding processes enrich messages with the sender's emotional information carried by tone and rhythm (see Lund, 2007) that provide the receiver with all the facilities for proper decoding. Further signals intercepted by receivers could involve gaze and gestures, implying a multilayered channel comparing language with mimicry and conveying a more comprehensive array of codes that participants may embrace and share throughout the decoding step as well.

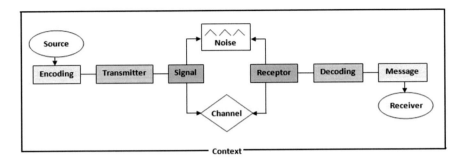

**Fig. 2.1** Information transmission model. (The figure is mine, adapted from Shannon and Weaver's model of 1949 [Shannon & Weaver, 1963])

Yet, the over-use of non-verbal and para-verbal features (and codes) could increase the *noise*, disturbing communication and potentially impeding the receiver to access the message (Shannon & Weaver, 1963).

Considering the verbal context, "language is by no mean a unitary, atomistic concept—its description involves many essential semiotic dimensions" (Bateman & Schmidt, 2012: 31) enhanced by time. According to such an idea (Fig. 2.2), the "local time-scale of individual texts and interactions (logo genesis)" evolves to a "medium time-scale of an individual child's acquisition of the system (ontogenesis)". Then, it turns onto "long-term scales of historical change (phylogenesis)", since language and communication systems are "in constant flux" (Bateman & Schmidt, 2012: 37). As reported by Ingrid de Saint-Georges, Professor of Sociolinguistics at Georgetown University, "there is no discourse, knowledge, or social practice that stands outside of a social, historical, and physical space" (LeVine & Scollon, 2004: 71). Nonetheless, as for linguistics, the multimodal system proceeds the same way, and different semiotic modes always cooperate by combining for the retrieval of a *quintessential* meaning.

Multimodality, per se, refuses the notion of diverse semiotic channels acting independently to convey any textual meaning. Conversely, it affirms the co-dependence of those channels oriented towards delivering a composite semantically processed message by integrating all the available communicative resources involved (Thibault, 2000: 321). Moreover, according to Professor Jerrold Levinson, proceedings might produce

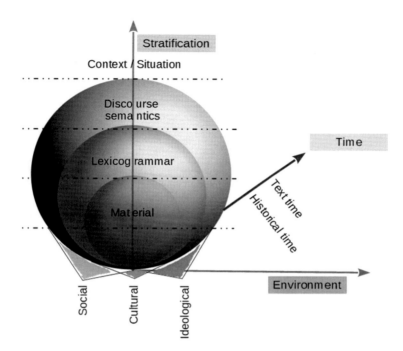

**Fig. 2.2** Language system stratification: the socio-semiotic functional perspective. (The figure is mine, adapted from Bateman & Schmidt [2012: 36]; Bateman and Schmidt's model proposed concentric circles pertaining to the linguistic and multimodal stratification of discourses. The adaptation of the figure opted for a tridimensional reconsideration of the original model, where Time and Environment are the main actors of a Cartesian plane, where the Stratification process happens both depending on them and along with them, also projecting its Social, Cultural and Ideological halos, onto those two more interrelated trajectories, consequentially moulding them)

three different hybrids: juxtaposition, transformation—or alteration—and synthesis. Anyhow, "multi- or mixed-media phenomena would [rather] be […] juxtapositional hybrids" (Levinson, 1990: 31) since semiotic modes tend not to blend and lose their individuality. They also maintain their own set of features and peculiarities to be mixed harmoniously (and yet singularly), lending themselves at the disposal of the semantic aim of communication. To that extent, "one medium appears inside another as its content […] when one sensory channel of semiotic function is woven together with another more or less seamlessly" (Mitchell, 2007: 401).

Also, quoting Professor Sigrid Norris, the conversational environment is full of "disembodied modes [...] giving off messages". Those modes entail "some frozen actions, where the term *frozen action* does not imply one static form but rather a higher level of permanency of a communicative mode" (LeVine & Scollon, 2004: 103). Subsequently, as for many fields of study, the context is the communicative aspect that makes the difference and allows modes to be distinguishable and analysable from single or multiple perspectives:

> [...] [Multimodal] Discourse Analysis was intended to highlight the recognition [...] that all discourse is multimodal. That is, language in use, whether this is in the form of spoken language or text, is actually inevitably constructed across multiple modes of communication, including speech and gesture not just in spoken language but through such 'contextual' phenomena as the use of physical spaces in which we carry out our discourse actions or the design, papers, and typography of the documents within which our texts are presented. (Ibid.: 1–2)

The present survey shares Theo van Leeuwen's social semiotic approach. The scholar's position on the matter proceeds through a ten-point thesis listing the main reasons apt to justify multimodal slants to be applied to communicative situations:

I. The expressiveness of voiced iterations or unvoiced meanings conveyed through illocutionary and perlocutionary signification patterns carry the same linguistic power of the locutionary ones, even if the vocal element is the minor part of the message itself. Thus, "speech acts should be renamed communicative acts and understood as [multimodal] microevents in which all the signs present combine to determine its communicative intent" (ibid.: 8).

II. Since the heterogeneous nature of speech acts, involving different mode combinations to be exploited—such as the use of language and actions in conversations, or the use of language and graphics in written texts—"speech genres should therefore be renamed 'performed' genres and written genres 'inscribed' genres" (10).

III. "The communicative acts that define the stages of 'performed' genres may or may not include speech, just as communicative acts that define the stages of genres of 'inscribed' communication may or may not include writing" (ibid.).

IV. "The boundaries between the elements or stages of both performed and inscribed genres are often signal[l]ed visually" (11).

V. "Even at the level of a single 'proposition', the visual and the verbal can be integrated into a single syntagmatic unit" (14).

VI. In the contemporary era, where media proliferation proffers plenty of possibilities of expressing messages via as many modalities, writing techniques (and oral) are no longer confined to one limited formulaic (or articulatory) way of expression. To that extent, even the choice of a certain mode despite another contributes to the connoting procedure affecting language. "Typography and handwriting are no longer just vehicles for linguistic meaning, but semiotic modes in their own right" (ibid.), which, however, also participate in the semantic transmission of their content.

VII. "Critical discourse analysis needs to take account of non-verbal as well as verbally realized" (15) aspects of discourse, where the deployment of image visual iconicity instead of—as well as along with—textual products could alter or contrast the actual meaning to be rendered via ambiguous realisations, intricate denotative schemata, and so forth.

VIII. "Many of the concepts developed in the study of grammar and text are not specific to language" (16).

IX. "The concepts that have been used for describing the structure of language as a resource and the 'footing' of talk can also be applied multimodally" (18).

X. "Students of visual communication should also pay attention to linguists, as many linguistic concepts and methods are directly applicable to and highly productive for the study of visual communication" (19).

More concisely, the study of multimodal communicative situations should fundamentally lean on Halliday's conceptualisation of ideational, interpersonal and textual metafunctions. The first deals with the unconscious *representation* of the world (along with the grammatical choices and the logical inferences that enable the speakers to formulate and send messages efficiently; point VI to IX); the second represents the actual *exchange* established by interaction participants (the social relevance of this communication layer—systemic functional linguistics—underlines the establishment of a phatic channel/bond; points I to IV); the latter is the ultimate *message* produced (via the unconstrained organisation and combination of the experiential and interpersonal metafunctions; mainly points V and X, but it synthesises all of them). In those three metafunctions, one should also include both the experiential and logical meaning (see Halliday, 1994), and "Gregory's notion of phase and transition" (O'Halloran, 2004: 98; see also Gregory, 2002), where different communicative events, narrations or contexts (phases) alternate during the conversation by means of certain expressive patterns or situations (transitions) that consistently escort the discourse from one phase to the other. This last theorisation proposes that discourses are social practices constituted by many parts signalling different contexts, plus the ability to move from one type of discourse or medium of conveyance to another intermittently and without creating coherence inconsistencies.

The boundaries between the modes in communication are as evident as their links. Focusing on them, one could individuate the different levels of stratification giving off messages. Such relationships would easily be ascribable to the "anchorage" concept (the text directs the reader through the meaning) described by Roland Barthes (Barthes, 1977: 38; see also Barthes, 1972). For instance, in newspapers, photograph meanings and purposes are fixed and captured by descriptive tag-lines just for readers' ease. A further process involves "relay" (ibid.: 41) relations, such as comics or film dubbing (text and image are complementary), where written and visual channels are interdependent for the conveyance of the stripe— or scene—meaning: in the absence of either one of these elements, the whole comics—or film—would be unreadable.

Despite the large spectrum of the discipline, the present survey mainly focuses on multimodal strategies and structures applicable to the cinematic context, discussed by Film Studies, and limited by the Corpus Linguistics examination of multimodal corpora built in the interest of the research. The intersemiotic approach of multimodality also highlights some pragmatic points of (dis-)continuity along with the theoretical discourse on the discipline. Multimodal communication indeed entails different channels that aim to inform the number of participants in the conversation. This process includes details on what social actors are speaking about, who is (and who is not) involved, what emotions are displayed by speakers and recalled by the facts recounted, what phatic elements signal one's attention or interest, etc. Nonetheless, communication is not just a 'medium' or 'tool'. It represents the psychological dimension of an iterating subject who deliberately decides its level of communicativeness and the channels to be used to funnel the intended pieces of information.

Communication is a participatory and eminently cognitive phenomenon, tightly connected to the field of 'actions' (Anolli, 2006: 13–14). According to Anolli (ibid.), users cannot deliberately decide whether being completely communicative or not, because of a solid unconsciuous set of expressions (gestures and mimicry) that our body naturally activates whenever we interact. Yet, it represents a disagreeable question in the opinion of the present study, also following fundamental works in the field of linguistics, such as Paul Grice's "cooperative principle" and its non-cooperative implicatures (Grice, 1981, 1989; Potts, 2005). However, in both cases, the prominent role of performativity is unmistakable (Austin, 1962; Searle, 1979; Butler, 1993; Sindroni et al., 2017). It represents an important aspect in terms of visual communication on the television. Indeed, this context of communication envisions as preordered, highly schematised and staged to convey precise messages (often stereotyping linguistic and gestural aspects of interaction). Multimodality mainly investigates the features and devices supporting verbal statements to understand the communication equation managing social exchanges. Community members inevitably interact under certain rules, comprehend and interpret each other's meaningful (written, spoken or performed) acts through a shared code, create (back)channels, and potentially respond by choosing the most adequate (or merely most convenient) mode. Situational conversations do not demand that communicative *stimuli* and respective reactions happen on the same level at any time. According to Professor John R. Bateman:

# 30    F. P. Gentile

> Meaning construction thus operates as a process of finding discourse relations to 'glue' contributions together. This is in stark contrast both to the compositionality found in syntax (the stratum below) and in the realm of common-sense reasoning, beliefs, mental states and problem solving (the stratum above) [...]. The division of logic and strata allows the process of discourse interpretation to be restricted to just what is necessary to fill in certain 'gaps' created by linguistic forms and their sequential presentation in discourse. (Bateman & Schmidt, 2012: 42)

On a psycho-linguistic level, mimics and gestures are one primary alternative to verbal-language systems allowing humans (and animals) to access communication. Strictly interconnected with social behaviours, "the system of gestures is very different in its underlying principles from the system of language" (Chomsky, 1983: 40), and many experts have been observing gesture-in-talk (Rimé & Schiaratura, 1991; Beattie & Shovelton, 1999) through the years. Scholars have mostly focused on gaze (Griffin & Bock, 2000; Cerrato & Skhiri, 2003), head nods and facial expressions (Ekman, 1982; Black, 1984; Black & Yacoob, 1998), head, arm and body movements (Thompson & Massaro, 1986; Rimé & Schiaratura, 1991) and their related connections with speech.

Nonetheless, despite the divergent and thus *discontinuous* relationship with language, some points of *continuity* emerge to emphasize interaction-facilitating codependencies between participants in communicative situations, due to their different structural systems. Relationships between language and gesture seem to be tighter than a simple combination of modes (Birdwhistell, 1952).Those two channels simultaneously take place and vary synchronically with words (Brown, 1986; Kendon, 1972). In light of this, gesture-in-talk appears to be "truly part of speech in that they contribute to meaning just as words and phrases do" (Bavelas, 1994: 205), actively participating in the creation of communicative events interacting or even "counteracting" with the discourse (Maynard, 1987: 590). Despite their physical rather than vocal displayability, gesture and mimics reflect psychological actions of speech (McNeill, 1992: 30). They convey the speakers'—or better performers'—indisputable mental schemata and communicative behaviours to be exploited unanimously with verbal iterations. Considering the label of 'performers' attributed to conversation participants, the concept of performativity extends to communication by its nature. Thus, it is worth noting that the corporeal expressiveness and the message psychological reception are also influenced by other extra-linguistic aspects that transcend non-verbal aspects and include the para-verbal visual and sociological layer (e.g., data about ethnicity, gender, age, social class, dress code). Hence, linguistic events cannot deny—nor happen beyond—psychologically-set non-verbal patterns befalling the discourse: according to Paul Waltzlawick, psychologist, philosopher and communication theorist, "one cannot *not* behave" (Walzlawick et al., 1967: 48). Gesture-in-talk points of both continuity and discontinuity with speech became a crucial aspect being integrated and analysed within the linguistic discourse of multimodal corpora in the present study. The nonverbal human behaviours potentiality of "forming communicative messages" (Richmond et al., 1991: 7) is a crucial perspective discussed by Kinesic Studies (Birdwhistell, 1952). Any subject participating in communication might mean something, just showing/moving their bodies because of the gestural signifying value implied. To that extent, one could easily distinguish nonverbal *behaviours*—depending on neuronal links connecting a brain to the body and creating psychological inferences stimulating movement during one's speech—from nonverbal *communication,* as the actual making of such interactive wish through common gestural patterns and so on (Richmond et al., 1991; Norris, 2004). Despite the importance of the former type of gestural meaning, the latter does not *behave* for pure nonverbal instinct, for it intentionally performs communication in the attempt of forwarding only deictic messages (Fig. 2.3). In dialogic situations, individuals participating in the exchange will inevitably recur to gestural behaviours. Nonetheless, when non-verbal communication is intended, such context supposes receivers to recognize body movement behaviours performed by related sources and classify them as messages de facto, regardless of whether or not intentionally displayed or denoting anything. However, as reported in the scheme (Fig. 2.3), it is always the receiver who defines nonverbal situation types according to his/her perception of the source's ways of interact.

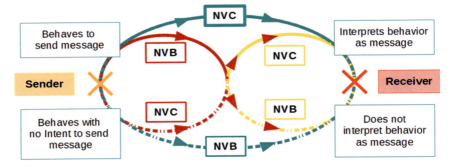

**Fig. 2.3** Non-verbal behaviour (NVB) vs. Non-verbal communication (NVC) scheme. (The figure is mine, adapted from Knight [2011: 61])

It is possible to narrow down five main categories of gesticulation and descriptive of different gestural modes of interaction or meaning addition to verbal communication:

1. Iconic, involving spontaneous hand movement series, etc. (Schegloff, 1984; Kendon, 1987; McNeill, 1992);
2. Metaphoric, conveying more significant meanings than those strictly enacted by lexis (McNeill et al., 1994);
3. Beats, which comprise (generally two) repetitive movements (Efron, 1941; Ekman & Friesen, 1969). They usually coordinate with speech prosody and intonation (Bolinger, 1986; Haiman, 1998; Wilcox, 2004) slightly related to talk-semantics;
4. Cohesive (Halliday & Hasan, 1976; McNeill, 1992) properties dealing with hand gestures that "tie together thematically related by temporally separated parts of discourse" (McNeill, 1992: 16);
5. Deictics consists of conscious gestures being ascribable to the so-called "kinetograph" forms of speech (Richmond et al., 1991: 58) for indicating, pointing and denoting objects within the physical conversational space.

Consequently, thinking of multimodality and multimodal corpora, it is worth noting that such precise classification of gestures and gesture-in-talk would be useful to understand the analysed contexts. Nonverbal behaviours

(NVB) could indeed represent unmotivated actions, spasms or pure instinct. Nevertheless, gestures are *body language* (Ekman, 1971; Ekman & Friesen, 2003; Ekman et al., 2013; Kilma & Bellugi, 1979; Burgoon et al., 1996; Moore, 2010). Thus, as a *language*, nonverbal communication (NVC) has by its right the actual capability of conveying meaningful messages through a huge range of semiotic structures (such as the language of signs for deaf people) that could substitute verbal-linguistic events to exploit (almost) any communicative situation and achieve higher understandability.

In adherence to the given theorisations, TV broadcasts can be perceived and observed as texts about a multilayered communicative stratification of diverse modes and codes. The perusal of those features is enacted by the deployment of an integrative multisemiotic model that can "bring together and incorporate the systemic-functional matrices and frameworks currently available in the field of multimodality" (O'Halloran, 2004: 220) and responsible for the utter reading and evaluation of said products from their related communicative slants.

## Annotation Procedure

The present survey analyses specific corpora involving multimodal aspects of communication. Corpus Linguistics examination tools are numerous and quite different from each other. Moreover, they undergo multiple constraints imposed by time, traditions and so on (Strassel & Cole, 2006: 2). Nonetheless, the current description of the corpora built and discussed throughout this study—and in terms of multimodality—is delivered according to the "investigator's goal" (Cameron, 2001: 29). The final aim is to retrieve relevant data along with peculiar linguistic features and patterns. The procedure mostly sifts through fragmentsof specialised discourse, terminology and knowledge in association with linguistic evaluative approaches of the codes and the messages summoned. For the sake of the objectivity of the research, the filing practice is construed through definite concern, rigour and consistency (Wynne, 2005).

A corpus, irrespective of how large it is, "is not guaranteed to exemplify *all* the language patterns in roughly their normal proportions" (Sinclair, 2008: 30). The present investigation aims not at the study of *any* linguistic phenomena involved in the English language. It delves into the observation of multimodal expedients and linguistic features mostly co-occurring or associated with communication in given contexts. The research only considers chosen cinematic situations reproducing monitored communicative events. In those specific cases, language happens to be cast and moulded to emulate its natural conversational aspects, placing the role of multimodality under the spotlight to provide different audiences with all the information required for a proper understanding of the plot. By said premises, corpora are designed with and supported by fully documented schemes offering information about the characters taking part in the TV series, contents, and transcription strategies to facilitate the reading and the interpretation of given heterogeneous situational contexts.

Furthermore, the analysis required a preliminary stratified process for its proper exploitation. The *making of corpora*—and multimodal corpora—demands three main steps:

(a) Frame the focus of examination;
(b) Collection of data and transcription process;
(c) Mark-up (Bird & Liberman, 2001).

After that, corpora are finally in the condition of being analysed through combined multimodal–corpus linguistics approaches. Hence, data (enriched by metadata) could be presented and discussed. Yet, for what concerns the framing of the focus and the collection step, it is worth noting that the scenario depicted by the materials involved in the analysis is uncommon. Film contexts *simplify* speakers' iteration renditions (see Eco, 1984, 2016c; also described in the following paragraph), where every communicative situation is already recorded and *eternalized* onscreen. Moreover, language and behaviours observable might result even more *natural* than audio-video recordings of ordinary people, as actors are used to performing naturally in front of a public or a troupe. Thus, the presence of cameras should not deflect the conversational path or intimidate speakers, according to the range of misleading effects that people could bump into. Those features were reunited by William Labov within the *observer's paradox* (see Labov, 1972) concept. Copyright

## 2 The Research Methodology

represents one further issue. When recording people's speech in the interest of any study, subjects have to grant permission of being filmed, where frame fragments of their voices may occur, or their faces appear on the screen. At any moment, they could restrain scholars or researchers from divulging such audio-video contents, subsequently pinching possible sensible data crucial for the survey. The case study presented throughout these chapters jumped the hurdle by choosing to construct three corpora built on TV series episodes. Here, not only professional actors would easily avoid goosebumps in front of the camera's intimidating *eye*—as already said, producing natural communicative results—moreover the investigation falls on FTA television series. Subsequently, audio-video records are already publicly available because of the medium of broadcast and consultable even on-demand whenever needed.[8]

The previous section has already given a partial description of mark-up procedures by clarifying tagging criteria (POS tagging via Penn Treebank). Nonetheless, such a step also implies qualitative annotations to be added to the multimodal corpora—and beyond grammatical structures— including information about backchannels, tone, rhythm, prosody, facial expressions, turn-taking, gesture-in-talk and other metadata. There are several tools a researcher could use to prepare corpora for the analysis and annotate those bits of information, such as Transcriber and iTranscriber, or the well-known Transana (Silver & Lewins, 2009).

On the one hand, Transcriber (freely available online) and iTranscriber software are basically "tools for assisting manual annotation of speech signals".[9] Their Snack Sound Extension provides users with functional, user-friendly ease for transcribing multimodal corpora segmenting long-duration speeches and offering the possibility of annotating and labelling data with turn-taking, topics and potential noise surrounding the scene. Nonetheless, according to Transcriber releasers, the software is "specifically designed for the annotation of broadcast news recordings, for creating corpora used in the development of automatic broadcast news transcription systems", which would represent a limit in multimodal analysis applied to films.[10]

On the other hand, Transana software supports multiple simultaneous transcriptions and offers users a huge array of facilities. It could "integrate text, still image, audio and video in a single analysis; categorize and code

## 36 F. P. Gentile

segments of [...] data analytically; code still images using coding shapes, including screenshots from video data; [...]".[11] Analysts could also benefit from the possibility of sharing their work (or just data) with other users and colleagues in the distance through multiple access platforms.

Considering the numerous valid alternatives, the present study takes advantage of the qualitative annotation criteria by Georgina Heydon (Heydon, 2005: xi), here reckoned as effectively informative. Anthony P. Baldry's detailed model (O'Halloran, 2004: 85–86, and chaps. 3–6 for contextualised examples) integrates Heydon's schematisation.

As a consequence, multimodal annotation operates on the tagged corpora. It aligns data with *secondary* information (like prosody, rhythm, tone, and transcriber's annotations about the visual relevance of the scene), completing and enhancing written textual details with others conveying conversational meanings given by conventionalised symbols (see Conventions).Those image-descriptive features operate with visual supporting devices, facial expressions and gestural reports.All these aspects are substitutive of sounds and music (to be annotated in double-round brackets or reported in the schemes).

## Beyond the Screen: Film Studies, Language and Communication

As for multimodality, Film Studies (Bordwell, 1985; Branigan, 1992; Bordwell & Thompson, 2008; Richardson, 2010; Bednarek, 2010, 2018, 2019; Piazza et al., 2011; Davis, 2021) cover a wide array of potential fields of investigation. However, the present paragraph considers them as a discipline for the examination of the main strategies involved with onscreen communication: quoting Alan Parker, chair of the British Film Institute, "[the] film needs theory like it needs a scratch on the negative" (Lapsley & Westlake, 1988: vi). From such a point of view, an exact comparison between the TV and the literary product could emerge, leading to mediatic content observation. Here, diverse communicative modes (e.g., camera effects, images, soundtracks, gesture-in-talk) synchronically interact with the textual, linguistic dimension to establish a connection with the spectator. Just like literary texts, they would vary their message target via the deployment of multiple editing and typing strategies (e.g., font, size, special characters, textual elements implemented by illustrations), whose "*intersemiosis* accounts for the diverse meanings which have to be identified by a recipient when watching a movie" (Wildfeuer, 2016: 3), thus unconsciously investigating—or more neutrally witnessing—the film textuality. In particular, throughout the filmic product survey, its description, shooting techniques, narration methodologies, plots, and other peculiar features are discussed under the significant perspective of facilitating and expediting communication, regardless of their actual technicality of procedures. According to this point of view:

> Films appear to more or less directly inform viewers which pieces of information have to be brought together, which not, and when. It is only this 'pre-structuring', we suggest, that keeps common sense from running wild—after all, many things might be compatible with what is shown, but films do not often leave their viewers guessing about which lines of interpretation to follow and which not. (Bateman & Schmidt, 2012: 1)

Like any textual genre, films represent an *opera aperta* (Eco, 2016c [1962]), where meaningful structures and semantics are dynamic and tend to undergo multiple reshaping processes following the spectator's interpretative eye. Such communicative events, it seems, do not belong at all to the list of closed texts where messages parade hierarchically and with unilateral, absolute, pedagogical claims. Films appear more similar to the Baroque liveliness of an open text replacing tactile preponderance with visual taste. The reality of facts makes room for the readability of them: yet empiricism becomes perception (Eco, 2016c: 50–51).

Nonetheless, onscreen representations do have narrative structures that need substantial respect for the correct-sequence-sake of the events. Despite filmic sign interpretability, their semiotic system communicates through some paradigms, funnelling storyline bits of information and setting the succession planning rhythm. On that silver thread, the grammar of films has lately tended to give huge preponderance to forms—the representations of objects and actions—over contents—as narrative story components. Other psycho-sensorial strategies have supplanted the linear recount efficiency, implementing the iconic and indexical power of cinema—e.g., via the use and exploit of special effects, CGI editing, stunt doubles, soundtrack expressivity (see Chatman, 1980; Durovicova & Newman, 2010; Bednarek, 2010; Davis, 2021). Subsequently, in this phase, any film study survey would be conducted in adherence to interpretative studies investigating the building plan to construct narrative schemata that authors should consider when creating their (film) texture. Of course, film narrative (Bordwell, 2007) slightly differs from literary narrations as much as the latter *only* involves authors writing their texts provided with a narrator and narrative structures (and strategies) intended for a narratee (to be distinguished between intended or real).

However, screen productions may have more than one single author. On the one hand, script-making schemata and procedures may supplant the authorial process (Bartlett, 1932), including scriptwriters with producers, directors, and all the different professionals responsible for what has to be displayed. On the other hand, narrative structures transform as well. Film narration does not just include the actual detailed textual recount of what is arranged to happen during a particular scene. Onscreen narrators and narrations involve film crew and troupes, technologies and media for shooting and broadcasting, shooting strategies and characters (e.g., POV shots, where single actors are not only characters but their sight becomes the narrator's and the viewers' ones) as the path within the environment influencing the staged situation. Eventually, as for literary texts, films have to deal with implied and real spectators as well. The difference is that onscreen productions have wider audiences (including occasional spectators) and that *real* spectators are likely quite different from the *implied* ones meant for the view. Thus, broadcasters require commodification processes to render content attractive to any end-user (see Chap. 3).

Moreover, unless the creators intend narrations as ambiguous and obscure, comprehension and interpretation are two further disjunctive points between filmic contexts and others. In literature, for instance, text narrations want precise semantic balance. Developing plots through the pages demands *dynamic object* conveyance, qua the relationship that connects and determines a sign to its representation. It leads readers to figure implied *immediate objects* (Eco, 2016b: 23–32)—or their mental pictures. In similar situations, an evocative register is crucial for the achievement of the semantic goal. Conversely, the use of multimodal "complex 'signs'" in films implies visual representations with acoustic and spatial ones, plus a massive array of other features such as proxemics, social conventions, etc. (Bateman & Schmidt, 2012: 28).

A similar practice facilitates comprehension through the direct display of the scene and circumvents the issue of evoking fatiguing mental models:

> Films and novels are alike in that they require us to make inferences to the intentions of a maker; they are unlike in that, while literature requires also a linguistic competence on the reader's part, film requires only a naturally given competence with visual depiction (Currie, 1997: 54)

It seems that films do not need to depict any *dynamic object* since they can present the public with *immediate objects* that already correspond to *facts*. Through film perception, every potential issue carried out or introduced by the arbitrariness of linguistic connections between the word and the 'object' revolves around the image display. However:

> It is possible for a sequence of moving images to signal meanings that are *not limited* to redescription of what the images show, that are describable *independently* of any putative authorial intent, and which enter into *active negotiations* of more abstract interpretations with recipients as more than equal partners (i.e. 'pre-arrange' and 'pre-figure'). This means that we will argue that there is information that is beyond the 'referential' story events but which must nevertheless be seen as 'non-negotiable' with respect to the film. The film consequently 'commits to' more than is directly portrayed. (Bateman & Schmidt, 2012: 4)

Besides the audience's perception, it is possible to distinguish two possibilities from a broader point of view. Film comprehension, that "is intended to pick out meanings that are in some sense 'explicitly' recoverable from the work analy[s]ed," and film interpretation, which includes "further interferences made by the analyst to reveal more abstract, 'implicitly' made meanings" (Bordwell, 1989: 8–9). Speculations discussed so far have been reporting examinations that focused on comprehension, perception and interpretation of films.

Nonetheless, in the interest of the research, it would be worth studying how films mean—that is, what are the features constituting film language. This perspective would lead the observer's eye to a semiotic analysis that should consider the 1960s studies on the matter. In those years, Christian Metz developed the *Grande Syntagmatique* (Metz, 1966, 1972a, 1972b, 1973, 1974): a system for the classification of film scenes—or *syntagmas* (Metz, 1966)—based on montage techniques (see Pudovkin, 1926; Eisenstein, 1963; Wees, 1973). The forerunning model gained criticism at the time because of its lack of "detailed semiotic framework capable of addressing issues of multimodality and discourse", and any further enhancement of the work was blocked (Bateman & Schmidt, 2012: 99):

> One of Metz's goals in the work within which the development of the *Grande Syntagmatique* took place was considered very critically the question of whether film could be considered in any sense to be a 'language'. To the extent that similarities could be found, this would naturally offer explanations for how film could work as a carrier of meaning. (Ibid.: 100)

However, such a starting point would set a premise according to which no image is ever entirely alike another one. Hence Metz came up with the idea that films are made of sets or combinations of single small episodes or scenes. In turn, those units can be part of more extensive sequences related to narrative schemata defining different kinds of segments. The bottom-up point of view, rather than the similar up-to-bottom perspective, was meant to illustrate the infinite variety of possible shots—and semantics—a cinematic fragment could convey (Metz, 1972a, 1972b, 1974; Monaco, 2009). Indeed:

> Although each image is a free creation, the arrangement of these images into an intelligible sequence—cutting and montage—brings us to the heart of the semiological dimension of film. It is a rather paradoxical situation: those proliferating (and not very discrete!) units—the *images*—when it is a matter of composing a film, suddenly accept with reasonably good grace the constraint of a few large syntagmatic structures. (Metz, 1974: 101)

Despite the hierarchical specificity of semiotic modes, many of those are not particularly of film contexts. Films produce meaning in terms of *transmediality* and *intermediality* (Wolf, 2005). The first term represents the possibility of narrating a story through multiple formats, also via the support of as many devices, platforms and digital technologies, whose approach dates back to the early 1960s (Jenkins, 2008: 110). The second term refers to the "interconnectedness of modern media of communication" (Jensen, 2016: 1), as they are all distinct but codependent and their mapping creates a precious opportunity to also understand their meaning-making mechanisms. Those two concepts are mainly responsible for the unique visual iconicity of TV (and films in general), resulting out of a balanced combination of mechanical duplication devices, channel diversity and shooting techniques allowing motion (Fig. 2.4). What distinguishes figurative arts from films is the specificity of the latter of recurring at the same time to such different features and devices to construct a product that would be efficient in terms of multimodal 'communicativeness', according to both semiotic and pragmatic levels.

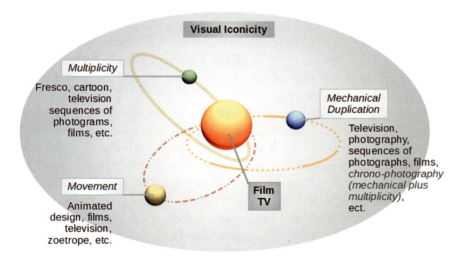

**Fig. 2.4** Metz's overview of visual iconic codes relevant for the filmic image track revised with respect to multiplicity and movement. (The figure is mine, adapted from Bateman & Schmidt [2012: 136])

Such an idea, it seems, is tightly connected to the concept of film perception described previously. Audiences peruse combinations of visual, acoustic, verbal suggestions, social conversational habits involving tone, rhythm and prosody (in speech), proxemics and other *stimuli*. All those aspects are useful to create or evoke meaningful images communicating something in the spectator's mind (Hochberg & Brooks, 1978; Smith et al., 1985; Hobbs et al., 1988). The perspective urges researchers to also concentrate their attention on the specific field of *cognitive* film theory (Bordwell, 2007). Audiences' concern in terms of knowledge and beliefs have implications with "psychological, sociological, educational, consumer, criminological, and political promises and anxieties" (Miller & Stam, 2004: 2) that condition interpreting.

Cognitive and interpretative investigations on Film Studies and Television Studies need to consider a tripartite line of reasoning: filmmakers, filmgoers, film theorists (ibid.: 3).

The filmmaker group is composed of those professionals using imagination and practical knowledge to create plots and make decisions about how to shoot a scene, what are the fittest locations for setting the film, etc. They *produce* meaning according to their creative notions and ideas (design, production and distribution of multimodal messages).

On the other hand, filmgoers represent the public enjoying the experience through the screen. Those consumers *receive* semiotic messages to be interpreted, working with common sense and experience (provenance and experiential meaning potential).

Eventually, theorists unravel the magic and tear apart the cinema to examine every formal aspect and get to the bottom, *analysing* meanings.

Besides all the possibilities of building, interpreting and discussing implications, cognitivism in Film Studies also covers a crucial object of analysis in terms of actual language(s) employed throughout onscreen productions. Mostly depending on the genre a language is related to, is worth noting that films aim to reproduce and emulate real-life contexts as much as natural languages. Simultaneously, further speculations also involve film viewers being aware of those conditions and the subsequent 'natural' perception of such monitored, motivated and 'artificial' communicative codes.

## Naturalness vs. Forgery: Cinematic Language Comprehension

Film language mostly depends on scriptwriters' and directors' dexterity to emulate real-life linguistic situations applied to a scenic related multimodal context being read as plausible by its spectators. Moreover, those *teams* of professionals have to make the TV products concretely. Hence the poietic acts of conceiving, projecting and writing down narrations involve multiple individuals working on the same final mediatic merchandise to output stories to be transposed onscreen. There, different people turnover when building the episode *skeleta* and change from one instalment to the other throughout the seasons (especially when dealing with TV series/serials). As a unit, the entire team eventually participates in releasing a heterogeneous product in terms of language, themes, and creative writing strategies. Those same episodes and seasons structured by said ample number of scriptwriters correspond to a handful of directors assigned to various instalments to managing the interpretative slant and the filming procedures. To that extent, many instalments can be attributed to the same group of scriptwriters and likewise have different directors (§ Appendix). That may produce plenty of slightly different narrative focuses or adopt various cinematic techniques for televising similar scenarios, thus contributing to shading the kaleidoscopic variety of film language expressive and communicative *spectra*.

Every linguistic situation has its elements and *stimuli* arranged and displayed in a precise order and (possibly) with crystallised structures identifying the field of knowledge recalled by said monitored codes. According to Umberto Eco, one could affirm that languages are fundamental means that *constitute* interaction (2016c). Yet, their nature is artificial. Languages represent the Shakespearean 'quintessence' of communication, compared to which any other symbolic system appears as just accessory or derivational (ibid.: 71). In Eco's theory, language *naturalness* is not the same as the glare emitted by a beam of stimulated photons. That emphasises the complexity and the *specificity* of language. A beam produces a dynamic, vanishing glare, yet it is a phenomenon that requires photonic *stimulations* to be observed. Likewise, language is a

**44**     **F. P. Gentile**

constantly evolving system, which we can study only under certain contextual circumstances (e.g., 'diaphasic', 'diastratic', 'diamesic', 'diatopic', 'diachronic' variations). Those events allow performative communication and facilitate its examination: the shortage of similar preconditions (ranging from the 'mere' social need to change certain language usages to the researcher's interest in the investigation itself) entails the absence of communication, just like the lack of proper stimulation would leave photons unseen.

From the information-exchange point of view, languages appear as intricate. First structuralist methodologies assumed that texts were thoroughly and objectively analysable as linguistic objects (Eco, 2016a: 29–32). To those scholars, they were rigorously structured and wholly empirically describable (ibid.). Reactions to similar speculations arose throughout the 1960s when focusing on the matter became less stiff and ranged through a wider perspective. Some other formulations proposed some unprecedented concepts (and roles) to be involved in the examination. Reception Theory reader-oriented criticism (Hulob, 1984) introduced 'authors' and 'implied authors' (Booth, 1983). These speculations recovered formalist concepts of artificiality, estrangement and dominant textual types from the Constance School (Iser, 1989, 2000; De Bruyn, 2012). Along with the former two, further thoughts included receivers' interpretatory activity frames (Ingarden, 1973; McCormick, 1985) and the ideal reader's role.

Eco thoroughly thought out whether it would be better to analyse linguistic works according to the *intentio auctoris* rather than the *intentio operis* or *lectoris* (Eco, 2016a: 36 and ff.). Besides the possible solutions and methodologies offered by similar studies it is in the opinion of the present study that texts are basically all ascribable to a general *Communication-Instructions-Textual* (CIT) linguistic model (Weinrich & Segre, 1988: 15–16).According to the model, the establishment of a common code sets *Communication*; then, the exchange becomes dynamic when the speaker starts giving *Instructions* (or information) to the receiver; eventually, once all the instructions have been provided and structured (including turn-taking and interruptions) a communicative *Textual model* emerges and results become available. Such a model could be a useful tool not only for the comprehension of facts. It could fit the portraying of those individuals participating in the conversation as well, according to the entire series of communicative choices they make:

> Language is not simply a means of communicating information [...]. It is also a very important means of establishing and maintaining relationships with other people.

> [...] Two aspects of language behavio[u]r are very important from a social point of view: first, the function of language in establishing social relationships; and, second, the role played by language in conveying information about the speaker. (Trudgill, 2000: 1–2)

When listening to somebody's speech, one of the first things we notice is their gender—and it happens quite unconsciously—then their race (ibid.: 61), and their linguistic and prosodic peculiarities varying language in terms of tenor, domain, elocution pace and more.

Any fictional communicative situation is built on conversations and speeches exploited during a plot progression and adapted to its pace. The related proceedings move through the narration and representation of facts along two parallel paths: "*story*—the event or sequence of events— and *discourse*—how the story is conveyed" (Puckett, 2016: 4). Genres play a fundamental role in identifying languages and discourses conveyed in such narrative schemata. Moreover:

> Current debates on the status of film genres arise, in part, because of the different reasons for invoking them: film scholars, tend to define genres for purposes of interpretation and critical analysis, while producers, publicists, and audiences may use them as descriptive tools. (Berry-Flint, 2004: 25)

Regardless of their expert/non-expert nature, both scholars' and audiences' points of view seem worthy. Despite the analytical purpose, it is possible to identify and describe films through their genres in particular contexts. Genre films are "commercial feature films [that], through repetition and variation, tell familiar stories with familiar characters and familiar situations" (Grant, 2007: 1) in a given genre. They relate to their genres differently, and a broader approach not confining them within single-genre boundaries would allow researchers to picture inter-generic connections (Altman, 1995) as well as retrieving complete information about the type of language(s) involved in similar contexts: "discourses, in other words, are culturally specific frameworks of knowledge that determine what can be considered fiction, news, entertainment, obscenity, history, etc." (Berry-Flint, 2004: 38). Consequently, we consider genres according to their interpretative and critical-analytical aspects and identifying set of peculiarities. That offers a more complete theoretical and practical examination of genres related to corpora throughout the survey. The genre discussed and involved in the examination is the TV crime drama, whose narrative context per se allows sporadic *intrusions* of other genres typically co-occurring with it, such as medical, legal, scientific, etc., and with their linguistic peculiarities.

Notwithstanding the importance of language naturalness, linguistic communicative situations happening onscreen are always monitored and prearranged to perfectly fit into the filmic contexts they are designed for. To that extent, crime drama needs officers to speak their language and jargon. Medical drama necessitates terminology and medical procedures. Fictions on law recall justice systems in force in one country rather than others, and lawyers haranguing their summations. Scientific TV series involves formulas and maths. Secondarily, any onscreen production requires specific narrative schemata to be receivable and identifiable by its audiences. Thus, films use the language both to perform conversational fragments of a scene (or a sequence of scenes) and as a proper generic peculiarity immediately recognizable and creating affiliation:

> Contemporary linguistic theory is by and large committed to the view that such languages need to be described in terms of rules which determine the meaning of a combination of signs as a function of the meaning of the components. While a few kinds of short-combination in cinema have acquired the status of recurrent and familiar patterns, these in no sense constitute or even approach the status of meaning-determining rules.
>
> […] Of course most films employ language in the ordinary sense, as when the characters speak or the interlines announce, but the 'language of film' thesis was supposed to be something more exciting than the platitude

that you have to be competent with English to understand the utterances of English characters. It was the claim that there is a specifically cinematic language or 'sign system', and this is a claim unsupported by the psychology of language and of perception. (Currie, 2004: 109)

The core of the argument lays, once more, on cognitivism. The language of film thesis—introducing film specificity as residing in its unconventional sign system altering standard inferential processes—destabilised the psychology of language theorists discussing the power of visual images on the spectators' minds. On an anthropological level, many hypotheses support the cinematic vision of language as culture-conditioning content-enriched preconditions such as opinions and beliefs that can be changed or reshaped through perspective representations offered by some film contexts (Pylyshyn, 1981; Messaris, 1994). Other speculations in the field of philosophy, quite similar to the perception theories approach, emphasize the natural interpretability of visual images. They mostly focus on the idea that inferential mechanisms triggered by spectators' sight work separately from their content states (Marr, 1982; Schier, 1986). Indeed, just like Joseph Greenberg's 'linguistic universals' (multimodal) communication may deploy some "general principles [...] and means and processes of meaning in any culture and in any mode [...] shared by all human cultures, as well as by many other species" (Kress, 2010: 10). That contributes to the final internalisation of messages irrespective of source/target culture disparities, etc.

However, "if understanding cinematic images is not assimilable to understanding language, how is it done?" (Currie, 2004: 109). Films function within the field of multimodality. The best part of their meaning corresponds to *immediate objects* (Eco, 2016b: 23–32), that are images shown without any linguistic mediation and, thus, corresponding to what they stand for. They skip the inferential process linking signs (or words) to the reality that they shall denote. Crime fiction novels must describe the minutiae of the revolver used to kill someone to transmit the exact idea that reconstructs the weapon inside the reader's mind. Conversely, crime drama TV episodes would simplistically show the gun for an immediate and more precise result. To that extent, vision workings cooperate with sound. Hence language comprehension in filmic

48 F. P. Gentile

multimodal contexts is hardly ever integrated by the direct display of images of objects or actions referring to conversational segments or solely described by interlines. As a consequence, spectators' content-enriched states remain divided from sight inferential mechanisms, although they operate simultaneously in firing up mind implicatures that tend to combine these two aspects on a cognitive level that would facilitate the propelling of actual comprehension.

## Specialised Discourse Conveyance and Popularised Knowledge Appraisal

At this point, it would be clear that film language is intended here as a blending of several, diverse communicative contexts and situations. It is not merely the language that parades before the public through the screen product, which, however, does not necessarily correspond to the ordinary set of usages, depending on the genre.[12] Along with what is uttered beyond the screen, film language also included behind-the-scene interactions (like scriptwriting, shooting terminology, etc.) and cinematic language (i.e., visual communication, sound and music narrations). As discussed so far, is it now clear that film language is always artificially built to achieve the communicative goals fore-ordained by scripts. Nevertheless, such a premise does not automatically imply a kind of language that would sound phony or openly fictional to the receivers. Unless receivers find themselves catapulted to the dreamlike worlds of Lewis Carroll's *Alice in Wonderland* (1865) or Tim Burton's adaptation of *Big Fish* by Daniel Wallace (1998), where the surreal atmosphere hovering around drenches language as well to burst fantastic (visual and linguistic) images inside one's mind, it is also a fact that films demand language naturalness. Moreover:

> Some critics would require the novel to do justice to reality, to be true to life, to be natural, or real, or intensely alive. Others would cleanse it of impurities, of the inartistic, of the all-too-human. On the one hand, the request is for 'dramatic vividness', 'conviction', 'sincerity', 'genuineness', an 'air of reality', 'a full realization of the subject', 'intensity of illusion'; on the other hand, for 'dispassionateness', 'impersonality', 'poetic purity', 'pure form'. (Booth, 1983: 37–38)

## 2 The Research Methodology    49

Indeed, focusing on the linguistic level, films and novels seem to work the same way.[13] Like literature, cinematic language requires verisimilitude in its peculiar narrative and conversational schemata that should render respective real-life narration and conversational situations. Filmic scenarios apart from fantasy—and other similar genres—should portray characters as representative of men and women behaving in actual social contexts by commonly-shared hierarchical conversation patterns (Ekman & Friesen, 1969; Ekman, 1982; Anolli, 2006). Any spectator would recognise those recounts as plausible.

According to the data retrieved, specific traits and structures of communication—such as 'discommunication', negotiation strategies, etc. (Anolli, 2006)—are discussed in the examination. In the interest of the present paragraph, however, the uses of specialised communication onscreen are treated coherently with the genre(s), to which the analysed corpora pertain.

Thinking of ancient societies such as Greece with its well-known philosophers, the natural language was ordinarily counterpoised to some more prestigious usages orators adopted to spread their thoughts. The notion of 'terminology' is here comparable to the Aristotelian idea of 'literary language', where everyday expressive formulae and words (*kurion*) get supplanted by some others, the terms (*glotta*), which are less common and understandable by laypeople and finalised to fulfil some specific goals (Coletti, 1978: 1). The said *glotta* often convey particular meanings related to proper professional fields. They enhance the level of complexity of the registers used (Gunnarsson, 1997; Faini, 2014), along with specific contexts whenever individuals "employ English in a restricted range of social and thematic areas" (Gramley & Pätzold, 1992: 246; Fairclough, 1992). Focusing on the English for Specific Purposes (ESP hereafter), it is possible to track back its origins in the 1960s, when John Swales retrieved one of the leading early articles on the matter by Charles L. Barber (1962). The writing depicted the significant characteristics of modern scientific prose. ESP was "influenced by developments and changes in Applied Linguistics" (Dudley-Evans & St. John, 2012: 19; see also Swales 1985, 1988, 1990, 1992). In its origin, "the growth of science and technology, the increased use of English as the international language of science, technology and business, the increased power of certain oil-rich countries and the increased number of students studying in the UK, USA and Australia" (Dudley-Evans & St. John, 2012: 19; see also Hutchinson & Waters, 1987) fostered the development of a specialised knowledge to be transmitted by a specialised code (Howatt, 1984). However, languages are not all concerning the same dimension as ESP does not consist of one *single* English language. It represents a *system* of languages (yet its purposes are plural), which are the appanage of different communities. Many experts (and sometimes laypeople when divulgation occurs) speak multiple codes that vary according to their areas of interest and applicability. The wor(l)d of "specialised discourse is by no means homogeneous as it may at first appear. There is a clear distinction between different specialised languages, though any distinction based mainly on lexis is far too simplistic" (Gotti, 2003: 25; see also Gotti and Giannoni, 2006). Moreover, the upstream canons characterising ESP limit the verbal channel trustworthiness because of its polysemous attitude (a feature instead often ignored by natural languages).[14] Instead, this language recurrently prefers and performs a type of communication that would result out of a combination of "a wealth of formulae, symbols, flow-charts, diagrams and other non-verbal conventional codes" (ibid.: 27), supporting the need for a multimodal analytical approach to such languages and fields.

Languages have their patterns. Yet, knowledge (and specific knowledge) cannot be constrained within static linguistic cages crystallising how one could express and divulge it. Consequently, it is better to describe specialised discourse (and ESP) as a field of knowledge that studies specific occupational contexts, articulatory processes, and language uses, rather than a stiffly-structured linguistic product (Hutchinson & Waters, 1987: 19). Hence, such written and spoken communication modes also involve rhetoric strategies, intended as "the process a writer uses to produce a desired piece of text" (Trimble, 1985: 10), aiming to present facts and hypothesize and convey information. Following such preconditions, in 1985, Louis Trimble introduced a four-levels up-to-bottom scheme (Fig. 2.5), setting rhetorical inferences in specialised communicative contexts. According to Trimble, an A level gives the general objectives of the total discourse. Then, further B, C and D sub-levels observe and explain the related rhetorical functions connecting each to the previous one (Hutchinson & Waters, 1987: 11; see also Selinker et al., 1978; Wood, 1982; Trimble, 1985).

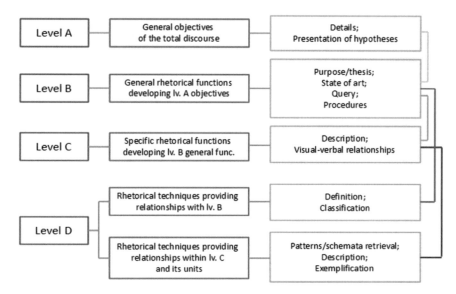

**Fig. 2.5** Trimble's schematisation of the rhetorical inferences model in SD communication. (The figure is mine, based on Hutchinson & Waters, 1987)

A similar point of view would recall the relationship connecting language form and language use theorized between the 1960s and 1970s (Ewer & Latorre, 1969) and leading to acknowledging the supremacy of *usage* over form (Widdowson, 1978, 1979, 1989). Whatsoever would be the form adopted to describe any linguistic object in specialised contexts, the use of the language involved should portray and transmit some given characteristics typically identifying Discourse, as pointed out by Lothar Hoffman's main features list (Gotti, 2005):

| | | |
|---|---|---|
| 1. Exactitude, simplicity, clarity | 2. Objectivity | 3. Abstractness |
| 4. Generalization | 5. Density of information | 6. Brevity of laconism |
| 7. Emotional neutrality | 8. Unambiguousness | 9. Impersonality |
| 10. Logical consistency | 11. Use of technical terms and figures | |

Therefore, ESP and Communication for Specific Purposes do not only involve terminology. It also summons different levels of technicality and technicity. Those aspects are responsible for the density of information varying degrees of texts that convey specific knowledge and put natural-language words and terminology in a relationship. This combination also highlights the lexical complexity of such communicative situations compared with ordinary iterations (Cabrè, 1993, 2003). According to the theories reported by Riccardo Gualdo and Stefano Telve (Gualdo & Telve, 2011) in their work on the Italian LSPs, extensible to ESP as well, here, a general stratification of specialised lexicon is observable.

It separates into four different *strata*, to the Italian theorists. Like a terrestrial model, where a chamber of magmatic fluids wobbles between the nucleus and the crust, exploding through and pouring into each other's place, the linguistic domains are not rigorously stiff. The boundaries—or layers—tend to be permeable and allow their elements be flexible as belonging to one level rather than another according to specific situations. Moreover, the stratification also offers users a multiple-range spectrum for composing and formulating their texts, allowing them to vary their discourses regarding register and lexical density of information when communicating with different individuals. Hence, the existence of three primary levels of interaction (Gotti, 2003: 25–27): (1) expert-to-expert (E2E)—basically happening in the written mode and benefiting from the use of loanwords, highly specialised lexicon, etc.; (2) expert/professional-to-professional (P2P)—very fast and effective, also including communication at pedagogical levels and jargon; (3) expert/professional-to-lay audience (P2L)—usually happening in the spoken mode and involving regionalisms and dialects—which is the most detechnified one (Gualdo & Telve, 2011: 26–30).

To be understood by the totality of their public, film contexts involving LSPs tend to organise their iterative features according to an 'intermediate level', halfway between divulging and expert-to-layman communication. Language should be transmitted (and so, recognised) in a simple, straightforward way to let its audience assimilate the pieces of information conveyed. Nonetheless, such discourses cannot wholly relinquish their peculiar language use characterised by elements of complexity, technicity and technicality, even if those who listen to, participate in, or witness such conversational situations are not experts at all.

## 2 The Research Methodology    53

Cinematic contexts tend to deal with specialised knowledge more than language, overusing explanatory glosses and multimodal devices integratedwith LSPs, terminology or generic linguistic usages rather than vice versa. Indeed, the cinematic strength resides in the consistent power of its visual iconicity. Any context is already communicative because of the image flow shown onscreen, which is just supported and not specified or preceded by verbal occurrences. Any utterance or text could transmit its meaning despite specialised discourse (and language) occurrence, or terms that would otherwise have an obscure meaning to the general audience thanks to collateral data compresence that boosts the communication. To that extent, it is clear that linguistic events do not initiate the understanding process, and images are not at all a mere expedient introduced to facilitate film comprehension.

On the contrary, the visual dimension represents the actual trigger that ignites the mental connections. It resolves the understanding of filmic scenes, establishing a communicative channel. Iterative linguistic events only come to confirm what has a few moments earlier been assimilated by the receivers. Corpus Linguistics observes the prominence of linguistic data over extra-linguistic factors. Instead, the multimodal point of view demonstrates the irrevocable communicative power of the visual salience. Hence, the non-/para-verbal integrated reading vastly applies to some relevant linguistic passages conveyed within the surveyed TV products. However, the increasing importance of the multimodal analytical needs also affects other (as pivotal as crystallised) disciplines.

Besides the iconic layer, and by communicative expressiveness heterogeneity, language is indeed a social fact. It responds to several cultural, political, historical and environmental real-time evolving contingencies, giving off messages within hierarchically structured situations.

Corpus-based and corpus-driven orientations could lead to stiff observations of language needs, cognitive and evaluative approaches. In some cases, even their hybrid blend might funnel possible biases because of the connoted nature of the extra-linguistic qualities (linguistic behaviours parading along with the communicative and emotive ones). The perusal of "disembodied modes" (LeVine & Scollon, 2004: 108) transmitting contents via semantic (and potentially non-linguistic) implications could only originate from disciplinary hypotheses like the anthropological or

**54     F. P. Gentile**

the philosophical ones such as the already mentioned Perception Theory. From the linguistic perspective, though, similar studies would be mirrored by the Appraisal framework theorisation (Martin & White, 2005; Martin, 1992) capable of evaluating the actual properties and qualities of data related to language conveyance and concerning with the role played by conversation participants, when:

> [...] The speaker/writer negotiates relationships of alignment/disalignment vis-à-vis the various value positions referenced by the text and hence vis-à-vis the socially-constituted communities of shared attitude and belief associated with those positions [...] with respect to [...] assumptions about the nature of the world, its past history, and the way it ought to be. (Ibid.: 95)

The approach appears to concentrate on the understanding of the identities built by the texts that authors formulate. Their ideal predisposition regards the potential responder role to impersonate once forwarded the message. The final goal, then, is creating a phatic channel between speakers/writers and receivers.

A similar bond arises through the actual linguistic metafunctional attitude. It shapes the intended audience, in adherence with the assumption of languages "conveying information about the speaker" (Trudgill, 2000: 2). Nonetheless, this attitude influences listeners expecting to be addressed several foreseen contents as well. The pivotal "stance" concept (Martin & White, 2005: 92; see Stubbs, 1996b; Hyland, 2005) originates a ramified scheme, where three main branches survey appraisal objectives. In turn, those ramifications separate into even more classifying labels (Fig. 2.6).

In terms of the Appraisal Framework, scholars could preliminarily evaluate diverse linguistic situations via a dialogic organisation. This first difference presupposes 'monoglossia' if the utterer's point of view is the only one expressed, or 'heteroglossia' if elements of the speaker's discourse recall different perspectives (according to...; quoting...; as explained by...; etc.), both reunited under the 'engagement' label. Secondarily, many factors can influence language. One could think of cultural associations with the contextual exchange and feelings towards the people involved in the discussion, to name two. Those aspects frame communication into an emotive dimension. Here, the participants' 'attitude' fissures into 'affect' for emotional states (happy; sad; positive; confident;

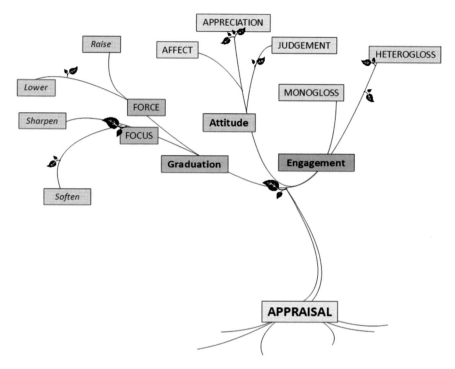

**Fig. 2.6** Appraisal framework model. (The figure is mine)

etc.), 'judgement' implying normative or ethic appraisals (right; wrong; reprehensible; etc.), and 'appreciation' (beautiful; horrific; eerie; etc.) related to aesthetic (dis-)likes.

Eventually, a third path allows concentrating on 'graduation'. It concerns the 'raising' or 'lowering force' of phenomena manifestation (big; enormous; minimal; etc.), and its related 'sharpening' or 'softening focus' (by itself; sort of…; somewhat like…; etc.) whenever contexts happen to deal with non-gradable situations.

Taking into account Ken Hayland's specifications, when dealing with academic or professional discourses, as interactive situations involving 'positioning':

> Writers seek to create a recognizable social world through rhetorical choices which allow them to conduct interpersonal negotiations and balance claims

for the significance, originality and plausibility of their work against the convictions and expectations of their readers. (Hyland, 2005: 175–176)

The appraisal method can provide a considerable contribution in terms of communication comprehension. Nonetheless, grammatical levels seem to control the evident perspectival inclination to analyse speakers/ writers characterised speeches. This influence also limits the framework applicability to contexts that move further than the sole syntactic layer. Multimodal situations are the exact contexts where such analysis could be detrimental. Instead of mere grammatical classifications, they include other elements typical of the para-verbal and non-verbal expressiveness, prosodic features, soundtrack and noises.

Moreover, what Hyland wrote apropos professional speeches is without a doubt valid for academic writing or E2E interactions, as well. These latter exchanges presuppose a scholar or specialist who would vigorously defend their thesis and corroborate it with effective rhetorical tinsels. Yet, the discipline would forfeit its validity if extended to specialised communication broader iterative contexts. There, the emotional neutrality and the authorial identity concealment are mostly mandatory and would instead contribute to foil the observation slant:

> […] Many texts are mediated by the 'mass media', which are defined as 'institutions' that connect different social events and move meaning from one social practice to another […]. In this manner, a media genre 'recontextualises' and transforms other social practices (political, governmental, etc.) and is 'recontextualised' in the texts and interactions of different practices, including, everyday life, where it contributes to the shaping of everyday conversations. (Russo, 2018: 40)

To that extent, television as a medium (see Chap. 3) could influence *even*—perhaps *especially*—those (extra-)linguistic products belonging to the sphere of specialised communication. It would alter their essence and possibly apply connoted discoursal aspects to originally denotative formulations. Those iterations—if not detechnified and emotionally loaded—could be misinterpreted by their receivers. Consequently, the present examination studies neutral E2E or P2P levels of interaction, generalisable specialised discourse patterns and knowledge conveyance modes mediated and *popularised* by the crime drama genre. The analysis that follows flanks the hybrid-corpus approach to the multimodal lens. This combination of practical-analytical tool and methodological criteria also benefits from the synchronisation with the appraisal framework to cover any detectable shade of the expressive and communicative qualities. Such a procedure aims to understand the television processes influencing discourse salience and attitudes. Simultaneously, it parses the discoursal schemata, as they may deflect media and ordinary linguistic structures to cast new communicative models.

# Notes

1. The present research has partially used it, although the best part has urged a qualitative observation.
2. While data commonly consists of the actual words that constitute the *thesaurus* of the corpus, metadata involves information like age, gender, ethnicity, etc., of the individual participating in the conversation.
3. Here, 'natural language' is not used in its proper meaning since filmic situations involve monitored iterations prearranged for the *medium* of broadcasting conveying the language. Thus, the phrase throughout the study will signify the attempt to emulate actual natural language in fictional contexts reproducing real-life situations.
4. CLAWS part-of-speech tagger for English. http://ucrel.lancs.ac.uk/claws/ on (accessed 07/21/2017).
5. "Empty words are principally uninflected forms, they are not members of the formal structure, they cannot be independent sentence members" (Shengelaia, 2001: 149). The opposite of an 'empty' word is a 'full' word.
6. Sketch Engine software. http://www.sketchengine.eu/ (accessed 10/13/2018). Moreover, the Sketch Engine software can provide results employing different tag and annotation models set on phrase structures as the Penn Treebank (Marcus et al., 1993) rather than schemes focusing on dependency structures such as the Prague Dependency Treebank (Hajič et al., 2001) and others mainly analysing prosodic or pragmatic elements.
7. As anticipated, the Corpus Linguistic approach here mostly represents a 'medium' for retrieving statistically valid instances to be multimodally analysed. Thus, the tool only serves the relevant word frequency lists and projective percentages relating to words and terms.

8. Nevertheless, the Broadcaster has to grant permission to use TV series frames in case of works to be published.
9. Transcriber. A tool for segmenting, labelling and transcribing speech. http://trans.sourceforge.net/en/presentation.php (accessed 07/27/2017).
10. Ibid.
11. Transana-Qualitative analysis software for text, still image, audio and video data. http://transana.com/ (accessed 07/27(2017).
12. TV narrates all of its linguistic formulations as plausible. However, it has vast arrays of contexts and expresisons at its disposal. Action movie language is inevitably different from sci-fi dialogues; historical drama old fashion talks nothing like comedies; etc.
13. The main focus of the research is TV dramas. Nonetheless, given the amplitude and the complexity of film language, the term is often used to describe the language of the TV series—as a subcategory of TV language—in lieu of their similar expressive structures.
14. Films are not ESP per se but they represent texts simultaneously conveying multiple 'natural' and 'specialised' discourses during the same plot articulations (Stewart, 2015; Bonsignori, 2018).

# References

Abercrombie, D. (1963). *Studies in Phonetics and Linguistics*. Oxford University Press.

Altman, R. (1995). A Semantic/Syntactic Approach to Film Genre. In B. K. Grant (Ed.), *Film Genre Reader II* (pp. 26–40). University of Texas.

Anolli, L. (2006). *Fondamenti di Psicologia della Comunicazione*. Il Mulino.

Austin, J. L. (1962). *How to Do Things with Words*. Oxford University Press.

Baldry, A., & Thibault, P. J. (2001). Towards Multimodal Corpora. In G. Aston & L. Burnard (Eds.), *Corpora in the Description and Teaching of English-Papers from the 5th ESSE Conference* (pp. 87–102). Cooperativa Libraria Universitaria Editrice Bologna.

Barber, C. L. (1962 [1985]). Some Measurable Characteristics of Modern Scientific Prose. In J. Swales (Ed.), *Episodes in ESP*. Pergamon.

Barthes, R. (1972). *Mythologies* (A. Lavers, Trans.). The Noonday Press. [Original Title: *Mythlogies*, 1972]. Retrieved June 13, 2018, from http://faculty.georgetown.edu/irvinem/theory/Barthes-MythToday-excerpt.pdf

Barthes, R. (1977). *Image, Music, Text*. Fontana.

Bartlett, F. (1932). *Remembering*. Cambridge University Press.

Bateman, J. A., & Schmidt, K. H. (2012). *Multimodal Film Analysis. How Films Mean*. Routledge.

Bavelas, J. B. (1994). Gestures as Part of Speech: Methodological Implications. *Research on Language and Social Interaction, 27*(3), 201–221.

Beattie, G., & Shovelton, H. (1999). Mapping the Range of Information Contained in the Iconic Hand Gestures that Accompany Speech. *Journal of Language and Social Psychology, 18*, 438–463.

Bednarek, M. (2010). *The Language of Fictional Television: Drama and Identity*. Continuum.

Bednarek, M. (2018). *Language and Television Series. A Linguistic Approach to TV Dialogue*. Cambridge University Press.

Bednarek, M. (2019). *Creating Dialogue for TV: Screenwriters Talk Television*. Routledge.

Berry-Flint, S. (2004). Genre. In T. Miller & R. Stam (Eds.), *A Companion to Film Theory* (pp. 25–44). Blackwell.

Biber, D. (2012). Corpus-based and Corpus-Driven Analyses of Language Variation and Use. In B. Heine & H. Narrog (Eds.), *The Oxford Handbook of Linguistic Analysis* (pp. 160–191). Oxford University Press.

Biber, D., Conrad, S., & Reppen, R. (1998). *Corpus Linguistics: Investigating Language Structure and Use*. Cambridge University Press.

Bird, S., & Liberman, M. (2001). A Formal Framework for Linguistic Annotation. *Speech Communication, 33*(1–2), 23–60.

Birdwhistell, R. L. (1952). *Introduction to Kinesics: An Annotated System for the Analysis of Body Motion and Gesture*. University of Louisville Press.

Black, D. W. (1984). Laughter. *Journal of American Medical Association, 252*, 2995–2998.

Black, D. W., & Yacoob, Y. (1998). Recognizing Facial Expression in Image Sequences Using Local Parameterised Modes of Image Motion. *International Journal on Computer Vision, 25*(1), 23–48.

Bolinger, D. (1986). *Intonation and Its Parts*. Stanford University Press.

Bonsignori, V. (2018). Using Films and TV Series for ESP Teaching: A Multimodal Perspective. *System, 77*, 58–69.

Booth, W. C. (1983). *The Rhetoric of Fiction*. Chicago University Press.

Bordwell, D. (1985). *Narration in the Fiction Film*. University of Wisconsin Press.

Bordwell, D. (1989). *Making Meaning. Inference and Rhetoric in the Interpretation of Cinema*. Harvard University Press.

Bordwell, D. (2007). *Poetics of Cinema*. Routledge.

Bordwell, D., & Thompson, K. (2008). *Film Art: An Introduction* (8th ed.). McGraw-Hill.

Branigan, E. (1992). *Narrative Comprehension and Film*. Routledge.

Brown, R. (1986). *Social Psychology*. Free Press.

Burgoon, J. K., Buller, D. B., & Woodall, W. G. (1996). *Nonverbal Communication: The Unspoken Dialogue*. McGraw-Hill.

Burnard, L. (2005). Developing Linguistic Corpora: Metadata for Corpus Work. In M. Wynne (ed.), *Developing Linguistic Corpora: A Guide to Good Practice* (pp. 30–46). Oxbow Books. Retrieved July 21, 2017, from http://ota.ox.ac.uk/documents/creating/dlc/

Butler, J. (1993). *Bodies that Matter: On the Discursive Limits of 'Sex*. Routledge.

Cabrè, M. T. (1993). *La Terminologia. Teoria, Metodologia, Aplicaciones*. Editorial Antártide.

Cabrè, M. T. (2003). Theories of Terminology: Their Description, Prescription and Explanation. *Terminology, 9*(2), 163–200.

Calabrese, R. (2004). *La linguistica dei corpora e l'inglese come lingua straniera*. Massa Editore.

Calabrese, R. (2008). *Insights into the Lexicon-Syntax Interface in Italian Learners' English. A Generative Framework for a Corpus-based Analysis*. Aracne.

Cameron, D. (2001). *Working with Spoken Discourse*. Sage.

Carroll, J. B. (Ed.). (1956). *Language, Thought and Reality: Selected Writings of Benjamin Lee Whorf*. MIT Press.

Cerrato, L., & Skhiri, M. (2003). Analysis and Measurement of Head Movements Signaling Feedback in Face-to-Face Human Dialogues. *Proceedings of AVSP* (pp. 251–256). [Online]. Retrieved July 21, 2017, from http://citeseerx.ist.psu.edu/viewdoc/download?doi=10.1.1.3.2626&rep=rep1&type=pdf

Chatman, S. (1980). *Story and Discourse. Narrative Structure in Fiction and Film*. Cornell University Press.

Chomsky, N. (1983). Noam Chomsky's Views on the Psychology of Language and Thought. In R. Rieber (Ed.), *Dialogues on the Psychology of Language and Thought* (pp. 33–46). Plenum.

Clark, H. H., & Krych, M. A. (2004). Speaking While Monitoring Addresses for Understanding. *Journal of Memory and Language, 50*(1), 62–81.

Coletti, V. (1978). *Il Linguaggio Letterario*. Zanichelli.

Conrad, S. (2002). Corpus Linguistic Approaches for Discourse Analysis. *Annual Review of Applied Linguistics, 22*, 75–95.

Crane, G., Stewart, G., & Babeu, A. (Eds.). (2007). *A New Generation of Textual Corpora: Mining Corpora from Very Large Collections*. Joint Conference on Digital Libraries (JCDL). Proceedings. Vancouver.

Crosthwaite, P. (Ed.). (2020). *Data-Driven Learing for the Next Generation.* Routledge.

Currie, G. (1997). The Film Theory That Never Was: A Nervous Manifesto. In R. Allen & L. Smith (Eds.), *Film Theory and Philosophy* (pp. 42–59). Oxford University Press.

Currie, G. (2004). Cognitivism. In T. Miller & R. Stam (Eds.), *A Companion to Film Theory* (pp. 105–122). Blackwell.

Davis, M. (2021). The TV and Movies Corpora. *International Journal of Corpus Linguistics, 26*(1), 10–37.

De Beaugrande, R.-A., & Dressler, W. U.. (1994). *Introduzione alla Linguistica Testuale.* Il Mulino. [Original Title: *Einführunh in die Textlinguistik,* 1981].

De Bruyn, B. (2012). *Wolfgang Iser: A Companion.* De Gruyter.

De Saint-Georges, I. (2004). Materiality in Discourse: The Influence of Space and Layout In Making Meaning. In P. LeVine & R. Scollon (Eds.), *Discourse and Technology: Multimodal Discourse Analysis* (pp. 71–87). Georgetown University Press.

Dudley-Evans, T., & St. John, M. J. (2012). *Developments in English for Specific Purposes: A Multi-Disciplinary Approach.* Cambridge University Press.

Durovicova, N., & Newman, K. (Eds.). (2010). *World Cinemas, Transnational Perspectives.* Routledge.

Eco, U. (1984). *The Role of the Reader: Explorations in the Semiotics of Texts.* Indiana University Press.

Eco, U. (2016a, 1st ed. 1990). *I Limiti* dell'Interpretazione. La Nave di Teseo.

Eco, U. (2016b). *Lector in Fabula.* Bompiani.

Eco, U. (2016c, 1st ed. 1962). *Opera Aperta. Forma e Indeterminazione nelle Poetiche Contemporanee.* Bompiani.

Efron, D. (1941). *Gesture, Race and Culture.* Mouton & Co.

Eisenstein, S. (1963). *Film Form: Essays in the Film Theory.* Dennis Dobson.

Ekman, P. (1971). Universal and Cultural Differences in Facial Expression of Emotion. *Nebraska Symposium of Motivation,* 19, 207–283. Retrieved July 29, 2017, from http: //www.ekman international.com/ResearchFiles/ Universals-And-Cultural-Differences-In-Facial-Expressions-Of.pdf

Ekman, P. (1982). *Emotion in the Human Face.* Cambridge University Press.

Ekman, P., & Friesen, W. V. (1969). The Repertoire of Non-Verbal Behavior: Categories, Origins, Usage and Coding. *Semiotica, 1*(1), 49–98.

Ekman, P., & Friesen, W. V. (2003). *Unmasking the Face: A Guide to Recognising Emotion from Facial Clues.* Malor Books.

Ekman, P., Friesen, W. V., & Ellsworth, P. (2013). *Emotion in the Human Face: Guidelines for Research and an Integration of Findings.* Pergamont Press Inc.

Engwall, L., et al. (Eds.). (2014). Computer Corpus Linguistics. An Innovation in the Humanities'. *Organisational Transformation and Scientific Change: The Impact of Institutional Restructuring on Universities and Intellectual Innovation (Research in the Sociology of Organisations),* Vol. 42. Pp. 331–365.

Ewer, J., & Latorre, G. (1969). *A Course in Basic Scientific English.* Longman.

Faini, P. (2014). *Terminology Management and the Translator. From Project Planning to Database Creation.* Tangram Edizioni Scientifiche.

Fairclough, N. (1992). *Discourse and Social Change.* Polity.

Firth, J. (1957). *Papers in Linguistics.* Oxford University Press.

Foster, M. E., & Oberlander, J. (2007). Corpus-based Generation of Head and Eyebrow Motion for an Embodies Conversational Agent. *Language Resources and Evaluation, 41*(3/4), 305–323.

Garside, R. (1987). The CLAWS word-tagging system. In R. Garside, G. Leech & G. Sampson (Eds.). *The Computational Analysis of English: A Corpus-Based Approach.* Longman (accessed July, 21, 2017).

Garside, R., & Smith, N. (1997). A Hybrid Grammatical Tagger: CLAWS4. In R. Garside, G. Leech, & A. McEnery (Eds.), *Corpus Annotation: Linguistic Information from Computer Text Corpora* (pp. 102–121). Longman. Retrieved July 21, 2017, from http://ucrel.lancs.ac.uk/papers/HybridTaggerGS97.pdf

Garside, R., Leech, G., & McEnery, A. (Eds.). (1997). *Corpus Annotation. Linguistic Information from Computer Text Corpora.* Longman.

Gotti, M. (2003). *Specialized Discourse. Linguistic Features and Changing Conventions.* Peter Lang.

Gotti, M. (2005). *Investigating Specialized Discourse.* Peter Lang.

Gotti, M., & Giannoni, D. S. (Eds.). (2006). *New Trends in Specialized Discourse Analysis.* Peter Lang.

Gramley, S., & Pätzold, K.-M. (1992). *A Survey of Modern English.* Routledge.

Grant, B. K. (2007). *Film Genre: From Iconography to Ideology.* Wallflower Press.

Gregory, M. (2002). Phasal Analysis Within Communication Linguistics: Two Contrastive Discourses. In P. Fries, M. Cummings, D. Lockwood, & W. Sprueill (Eds.), *Relations and Functions within and Around Language* (pp. 316–345). Continuum.

Grice, P. H. (1981). Presupposition and Conversational Implicature. In P. Cole (Ed.), *Radical Pragmatics* (pp. 183–198). Academic Press.

Grice, P. H. (1989). *Studies in the Way of Words.* Harvard University Press.

Griffin, Z. M., & Bock, K. (2000). 'What the Eye Say about Speaking. *Psychological Science, 11*(4), 274–279.

Gualdo, R., & Telve, S. (2011). *I Linguaggi Specialistici dell'Italiano.* Carocci.

## 2 The Research Methodology　63

Gunnarsson, B.-L. (1997). Language for Special Purposes. In G. R. Tucker & D. Corson (Eds.), *Encyclopedia of Language and Education.Second Language Education* (vol. 4, pp. 105–117). [Online]. Springer. Retrieved August 31, 2017, from https: //link.springer.com/chapter/10.1007/978-94-011-4419-3_11

Haiman, J. (1998). The Metalinguistics of Ordinary Language. *Evolultion of Communication, 2*(1), 117–135.

Hajič, J., Vidová Hladká, B., Panevová, J., Hajičová, E., Sgall, P., & Pajas, P. (2001). Prague Dependency Treebank 1.0. CDROM. CAT: LDC2001T10. ISBN: 1-58563-212-0. Linguistic Data Consortium. University of Pennsylvania, Philadelphia, USA. Retrieved July 21, 2017, from http://ufal.mff.cuni.cz/pdt/

Halliday, M. A. K. (1978). *Language as Social Semiotic: The Social Interpretation of Language and Meaning.* Edward Arnold.

Halliday, M. A. K. (1990 [2001]). New Ways of Meaning: The Challenge to Applied Linguistics. In A. Fill & P. Mühlhäusler (Eds.), *The Ecolinguistics Reader: Language, Ecology and Environment* (pp. 175–202). Continuum.

Halliday, M. A. K. (1994). *An Introduction to Functional Grammar.* Edward Arnold.

Halliday, M. A. K. (2003). *On Language and Linguistics. Collected Works* (Vol. 3). Equinox.

Halliday, M. A. K., & Hasan, R. (1976). *Cohesion in English.* Longman.

Halliday, M. A. K., & Matthiessen, C. M. I. M. (2004). *An Introduction to Functional Grammar.* Edward Arnold.

Heydon, G. (2005). *The Language of Police Interviewing: A Critical Analysis.* Palgrave Macmillan.

Hobbs, R., Frost, R., Davis, A., & Stauffer, J. (1988). How First Time Viewers Comprehend Editing Conversations. *Journal of Communication, 38*(4), 50–60.

Hochberg, J., & Brooks, V. (1978). The Perception of Motion Pictures. In M. Friedman & E. Carterette (Eds.), *Handbook of Perception* (Vol. X). Academic Press.

Holler, J., & Bettie, G. W. (2002). A Micro-Analytic Investigation on How Iconic Gestures and Speech Represent Core Semantic Features in Talk. *Semiotica, 142*(1–4), 31–69.

Holler, J., & Bettie, G. W. (2003). How Iconic Gesture and Speech Interact In the Representation of Meaning: Are Both Aspects Really Integral to the Process? *Semiotica, 146*(1–4), 81–116.

Holler, J., & Bettie, G. W. (2004). The Interpretation of Iconic Gestures and Speech. *5th International Gesture Workshop*. Genova (Italy). Springer Verlag, pp. 15–17.

Hoslanova, J. (2012). New Methods for Studying Visual Communication and Multimodal Integration. *Journal of Visual Communication, 11*(3), 251–257.

Howatt, A. P. R. (1984). *A History of English Language Teaching*. Oxford University Press.

Hulob, R. C. (1984). *Reception Theory: A Critical Introduction*. Methuen.

Hutchinson, T., & Waters, A. (1987). *English for Specific Purposes: A Learning-Centred Approach*. Cambridge University Press.

Hyland, K. (2005). *Metadiscourse. Exploring Interaction in Writing*. Continuum.

Ingarden, R. (1973). *The Literary Work of Art* (G. G. Grabowicz, Trans.). Northwestern University Press. [Original Title: *O Dziele Literackim*, 1960].

Iser, W. (1989). *Prospecting: From Reader Response to Literal Anthropology*. Johns Hopkins University Press.

Iser, W. (2000). *The Range of Interpretation*. Columbia University Press.

Jenkins, H. (2008). *Convergence Culture: Where Old and New Media Collide*. New York University Press.

Jensen, K. B. (2016). *Intermediality. The International Encyclopedia of Communication Theory and Philosophy* (pp. 1–12). Retrieved April 26, 2021, from https://onlinelibrary.wiley.com/doi/full/10.1002/9781118766804.wbiect170

Kendon, A. (1972). Some Relationships between Body Motion and Speech. In A. Seigman & B. Pope (Eds.), *Studies in Dyadic Communication* (pp. 177–216). Pergamon Press.

Kendon, A. (1987). On Gesture: Its Complementary Relationship with Speech. In A. W. Siegman & S. Feldstein (Eds.), *Nonverbal Behavior and Communication* (pp. 65–97). Lawrence Erlbaum Associates.

Kennedy, G. D. (1998). *An Introduction to Corpus Linguistics*. Longman.

Kilgarriff, A., et al. (2004). The Sketch Engine. *Information Technology*. Retrieved October 13, 2018, from https://www.sketchengine.eu/wp-content/uploads/The_Sketch_Engine_2004.pdf

Kilgarriff, A., et al. (2014). The Sketch Engine. Ten Years On. *Lexicography, 1*, 7–36. Retrieved October 13, 2018, from https://www.sketchengine.eu/wp-content/uploads/The_Sketch_Engine_2014.pdf

Kilma, E., & Bellugi, U. (1979). *The Signs of Language*. Harvard University Press.

Kipp, M., von Hollen, L., Hrstka, M.C., & Zamponi, F. (2014). Single-Person and Multi-party 3D Visualizations for Nonverbal Communication Analysis. In *Proceedings of the Ninth International Conference on Language Resources and Evaluation (LREC)*, ELDA, Paris.

Kress, G. (2010). *Multimodality. A Social Semantic Approach to Contemporary Communication*. Routledge.

Kress, G., & van Leeuwen, T. (2011). *Multimodal Discourse: The Modes and Media of Contemporary Communication*. Bloomsbury Academic.

Labov, W. (1972). *Sociolinguistic Patterns*. University of Pennsylvania Press.

Lapsley, R., & Westlake, M. (1988). *Film Theory: An Introduction*. Manchester University Press.

Leech, G., Garside, R., & Bryant, M. (1994). CLAWS4: The Tagging of the British National Corpus. *Proceedings of the 15th International Conference of Computational Linguistics (COLING94)* (pp. 622–628). Kyoto, Japan. Retrieved July 21, 2017, from http://ucrel.lancs.ac.uk/papers/coling1994 paper.pdf

LeVine, P., & Scollon, R. (Eds.). (2004). *Discourse and Technology. Multimodal Discourse Analysis* (pp. 71–87). Georgetown University Press.

Levinson, J. (1990). *Music and Metaphysics. Essay in Philosophical Aesthetics*. Cornwell University Press.

Lund, K. (2007). The Importance of Gaze and Gesture in Interactive Multimodal Explanation. *Language Resources and Evaluation, 41*(3), 289–303.

Marcus, M., Santorini, B., & Marcinkiewicz, M. (1993). Building a Large Annotated Corpus of English: The Penn Treebank. *Computational Linguistics, 19*, 313–330.

Marr, D. (1982). *Vision*. W.H. Freeman.

Martin, J. R. (1992). *English Text: Systems and Structures*. John Benjamins Publishing Company.

Martin, J. R., & White, P. R. R. (2005). *The Language of Evaluation: Appraisal in English*. Palgrave Macmillan.

Maynard, S. K. (1987). Interaction Functions of a Nonverbal Sign. Head Movement in Japanese Dyadic Casual Conversation. *Journal of Pragmatics, 11*, 589–606.

McCormick, P. J. (Ed.). (1985). *Selected Papers in Aesthetics*. Philosophie Verlag. [Original Work: Ingarden, R., *Studia z Estetyki*, 1957–1958].

McEnery, T., & Hardie, A. (2012). *Corpus Linguistics: Method, Theory and Practice*. Cambridge University Press.

McEnery, T., & Wilson, A. (1996). *Corpus Linguistics*. Edinburgh University Press.

McNeill, D. (1992). *Head and Mind: What Gesture Reveal about Thought*. University of Chicago Press.

McNeill, D., Cassell, J., & McCullough, K.-E. (1994). Communicative Effects of Speech-Mismatches Gestures. *Research on Language and Social Interacton, 27*(3), 223–237.

Mehrabian, A. (1972). *Nonverbal Communication*. Aldeine-Atherton.

Messaris, P. (1994). *Visual Literacy*. Westview Press.

Metz, C. (1966). La grande syntagmatique du film narratif. *Communications. Recherches Sémiologique: L'Analyse Stucturale du Récit, 8*, 120–124.

Metz, C. (1972a). *Essays sur la Signification au Cinéma, Volume 2*. Klincksieck.

Metz, C. (1972b). Ponctuation et démarcations dans le film de diégèse. *Cahiers du Cinéma* (pp. 73–78). [Reprinted in Metz 1972a: 111–137].

Metz, C. (1973). Methodological Propositions for the Analysis of Films. *Screen, 14*(1–2), 89–101 (D. Matias, Trans.). [Original French Article of 1968 Reprinted in Metz 1972a: 97–110].

Metz, C. (1974). *Film Language: A Semiotics of the Cinema*. Oxford University Press and Chicago University Press. (M. Taylor, Trans.). [Original Title: *Essays sur la Signification au Cinéma*, 1968].

Miller, T., & Stam, R. (2004). *A Companion to Film Theory*. Blackwell.

Mitchell, W. (2007). There Are No Visual Media. In O. Grau (Ed.), *Media Art Histories* (pp. 395–406). MIT Press.

Monaco, J. (2009). *How to Read a Film: Movies, Media and Beyond*. Oxford University Press.

Moore, N. (2010). *Nonverbal Communication: Studies and Applications*. Oxford University Press.

Norris, S. (2004). Multimodal Discourse Analysis: A Conceptual Framework. In P. LeVine & R. Scollon (Eds.), *Discourse and Technology: Multimodal Discourse Analysis* (pp. 1–6). Georgetown University Press.

O'Halloran, K. L. (Ed.). (2004). *Multimodal Discourse Analysis. Systemic Functional Perspectives*. Continuum.

O'Halloran, K. (2011). Multimodal Analisys within an Interactive Software Environment: Critical Discourse Perspectives. *Critical Discourse Studies, 8*(2), 109–125.

O'Halloran, K. (2012). Interactive Software for Multimodal Analysis. *Journal of Visual Communication, 11*(3), 363–381.

Ochs, E. (1979). Transcription as Theory. In E. Ochs & B. B. Schieffelin (Eds.), *Developmental Pragmatics* (pp. 43–72). Academic Press.

Piazza, R., Bednarek, M., & Rossi, F. (Eds.). (2011). *Telecinematic Discourse. Approaches to the Language of Films and Television Series*. John Benjamins Publishing Company.

Potts, C. (2005). *The Logic of Conversational Implicature*. Oxford University Press.

Puckett, K. (2016). *Narrative Theory. A Critical Introduction.* Cambridge University Press.

Pudovkin, V. I. (1926). *Film Technique and Film Acting: The Cinema Writings of V.I. Pudovkin* (I. Montagu, Trans.). Bonanza Books. [Republished by Sims Press (2007)].

Pylyshyn, Z. (1981). The Image Debate: Along Media vs Tacit Knowledge. In N. Block (Ed.), *Imagery.* MIT Press.

Richardson, K. (2010). *Television Dramatic Dialogue. A Sociolinguistic Study.* Oxford University Press.

Richmond, V. P., McCroskey, J. C., & Payne, S. K. (1991). *Nonverbal Behavior in Interpersonal Relations.* Prentice Hall.

Rimé, B., & Schiaratura, L. (1991). Gesture and Speech. In R. S. Feldman & B. Rimé (Eds.), *Foundamentals of Nonverbal Behavior* (pp. 239–284). Cambridge University Press.

Russo, K. E. (2018). *The Evaluationof Risk in Institutional and Newspaper Discourse. The Case of Climate Change and Migration.* Editoriale Scientifica.

Saferstein, B. (2004). Digital Technology-Methodological Adoption: Text and Video as a Resource for Analytical Reflectivity. *Journal of Applied Linguistics, 1*(2), 197–223.

Schegloff, E. A. (1984). On Some Gestures' Relation to Talk. In J. M. Atkinson & E. J. Heritage (Eds.), *Structures of Social Action: Studies in Conversation Analysis* (pp. 266–296). Cambridge University Press.

Schier, F. (1986). *Deeper into Pictures.* Cambridge University Press.

Searle, J. (1969). *Speech Acts. An Essay in the Philosophy of Language.* Cambridge University Press.

Searle, J. (1979). *Expression and Meaning. Studies in the Theory of Speech Acts.* Cambridge University Press.

Selinker, L., Trimble, M. T., & Trimble, L. (1978). Rhetorical Function-Shifts in EST Discourse. *TESOL Quaterly, 12*(3), 311–320.

Shannon, C. E., & Weaver, W. (1963). *The Mathematical Theory of Communication.* University of Illinois Press.

Shengelaia, N. (2001). On the General Semantics of Empty Words. *The 1999 Batumi Conference Proceedings* (pp. 149–52). Retrieved April 26, 2021, from https://archive.illc.uva.nl/Tbilisi/Borjomi2001/Proceedings/borj-proc.pdf

Silver, C., & Lewins, A. (2009). *Transana 2.40: Distinguishing Features and Functions.* QUIC Working Papers: University of Guildford.

Sinclair, J. (1996). The Search for Units of Meaning. *Textus, 9*(1), 71–106.

Sinclair, J. (2008). Borrowed Ideas. In A. Gerbig & O. Mason (Eds.), *Language, People, Numbers—Corpus Linguistics and Society* (pp. 21–42). Rodopi BV.

Sindroni, M. G., Wildfeuer, J., & O'Halloran, K. L. (Eds.). (2017). *Mapping Multimodal Performance Studies*. Routledge.

Smith, R., Anderson, D. R., & Fischer, C. (1985). Young Children's Comprehension of Montage. *Child Development, 56*, 962–971.

Stewart, C. (2015). *VCE Media: New Ways and Meanings. Units 3&4*. John Wiley and Sons Australia, Ltd..

Strassel, L., & Cole, A. W.. (2006). Corpus Development and Publication. *Proceedings of the 5th International Conference on Language Resources and Evaluation (LREC) 2006* [Online]. Retrieved July 26, 2017, from http://papers.ldc.upenn.edu/LREC

Stubbs, M. (1983). *Discourse Analysis. The Sociolinguistic Analysis of Natural Language*. University of Chicago Press.

Stubbs, M. (1996a). *Text and Corpus Analysis: Computer-Assisted Studies of Language and Culture*. Blackwell.

Stubbs, M. (1996b). Towards a Modal Grammar of English: A Matter of Prolonged Fieldwork. In M. Stubbs (Ed.), *Text and Corpus Analysis*. Blackwell.

Swales, J. M. (Ed.). (1985). *Episodes in ESP*. Pergamon.

Swales, J. M. (1988). Discourse Communities, Genres and English as International Language. *World Englishes, 7*(2), 211–220.

Swales, J. M. (1990). *Genre Analysis: English in Academic and Research Settings*. Cambridge University Press.

Swales, J. M. (1992). Language for Specific Purposes. In W. Bright (Ed.), *International Encyclopedia of Linguistics* (Vol. 2, pp. 300–302). Oxford University Press.

Taylor, A., Marcus, M., & Santorini, B. (2003). The Penn Treebank: An Overview. In A. Abeillé (Ed.), *Treebanks: Text, Speech and Language Technology* (Vol. 20). Springer.

Thibault, J. P. (2000). The Multimodal Transcription of a Television Advertisement: Theory and Practice. In A. Baldry (Ed.), *Multimodality and Multimediality in the Distance Learning Age* (pp. 311–385). Palladino Editore.

Thompson, L. A., & Massaro, D. W. (1986). Evaluation of Integration of Speech and Pointing Gestures during Referential Understanding. *Journal of Experimental Child Psychology, 42*(1), 144–168.

Tognini-Bonelli, E. (2001). *Corpus Linguistics at Work*. John Benjamins Publishing.

Trimble, L. (1985). *English for Science and Technology. A Discourse Approach*. Cambridge University Press.

Trudgill, P. (2000). *Sociolinguistics. An Introduction to Language and Society*. Penguins Book.

van Leeuwen, T. (1985). Rhythmic Structure of the Film Text. In T. Van Dijk (Ed.), *Discourse and Communication: New Approaches to the Analysis of Mass Media Discourse and Communication* (pp. 69–93). De Gruyter.

van Leeuwen, T. (2004). Ten Reasons Why Linguists Should Pay Attention to Visual Communication. In P. LeVine & R. Scollon (Eds.), *Discourse and Technology: Multimodal Discourse Analysis* (pp. 7–19). Georgetown University Press.

Walzlawick, P., Beavin, J., & Jackson, D. (1967). *Pragmatics of Human Communication*. W.W. Norton.

Wees, W. C. (1973). Dickens, Griffith and Eisenstein: Form and Image in Literature and Film. *The Humanities Association Review/La Revue de l'Association des Humanités, 24*, 266–276.

Weinrich, H., & Segre, C. (Eds). (1988). *Lingua e Linguaggi nei Testi* (E. Bolla, Trans.). Feltrinelli. [Original Title: *Sprache in Texten*, 1976].

Widdowson, H. G. (1978). *Teaching Language as Communication*. Oxford University Press.

Widdowson, H. G. (1979). The Description of Scientific Language. In H. G. Widdowson (Ed.), *Explorations in Applied Linguistics* (pp. 51–61). Oxford University Press.

Widdowson, H. G. (1989). Language Ability for Use. *Applied Linguistics, 10*(2), 128–137.

Wilcox, S. (2004). Language from Gesture. *Behavioral and Brain Sciences, 27*(4), 524–525.

Wildfeuer, J. (2016 [2014]). *Film Discourse Interpretation. Towards a New Paradigm for Multimodal Film Analysis*. Routledge.

Wolf, W. (2005). Metalepsis as a Transgeneric and Transmedial Phenomenon: A Case Study of the Possibilities of 'Exploring' Narratological Concepts. In J. C. Meister, T. Kindt, W. Schermus, & M. Stein (Eds.), *Narrative Beyond Literary Criticism* (pp. 83–107). De Gruyter.

Wonner, B. (2005). *The Deveopment of Corpus Linguistics to Its Present-Day Concept*. GRIN Verlag.

Wood, A. S. (1982). An examination of the rhetorical structures of authentic chemistry texts. *Applied Linguistics, 3*(2), 121–143 (accessed September, 1, 2017).

Wynne, M. (2005). Archiving, Distribution and Preservation. In M. Wynne (Ed.), *Developping Linguistic Corpora: A Guide to Good Practice* (pp. 30–46). Oxbow Books. Retrieved July 21, 2017, from http://ota.ox.ac.uk/documents/creating/dlc/

# 3

# The Linguistic and Cultural Environment of Canadian Television

## Television as a Medium

A tree could only thrive because the florid ground is nurturing its roots. Similarly, any communicative situation has languages to convey it. They represent the utter branches of the tree. It sucks its sap from the cultural environments and contexts bolstering its flourishing expressiveness. Therefore, iterations represent the actual *skeleta* produced out of a tricky balance between the languages involved in the exchange and media. In this precise relationship, the latter is to be considered not as mere 'couriers' but as a gathering of multiple factors *including* the 'traditional' idea of medium—as "a method or way of expressing something"—[1] along with all contingent, collateral linguistic, cultural and semantic elements. The context itself could be a channel. Nonetheless, that does not describe the totality of its functions.

During the 1980s, the British sociologist Denis McQuail insisted on the etymological value of communication as strictly related to the Latin word 'communis', which represented the concept of sharing. In the sense of 'mass communication', it involved creating a channel for transmitting informative content with vast amounts of people at any distance in no

© The Author(s), under exclusive license to Springer Nature Switzerland AG 2021
F. P. Gentile, *Corpora, Corpses and Corps,*
https://doi.org/10.1007/978-3-030-78276-4_3

time (McQuail, 2010 [1983]). This initial idea evolved over the years, along with the increase of Media Studies interests and preciseness in investigating and understanding the concept's actual realisation. Twelve years after McQuail's observations, John Thompson, another sociologist, set the bar to a higher level when he defined a five-point list of main features characterising mass media (Thompson, 1995, pp. 20–28; see also Thompson, 2000). They were to let information circulate everywhere and be always available—as formerly stated by McQuail (point four). That required building an information distribution system (point five) in tight connection with the technical and institutional methods to be adopted for disseminating news across the world (point one). A similar organisation demanded a neat separation between the very moment in which pieces of information were *produced* and the one in which media reached their audience to be finally *consumed* (point three), within a process of commodification of the contents (point two). These points represented the necessary and sufficient conditions for achieving the mediatic goal.

These very foundations contribute to position television onto the mass mediatic panorama in a paramount role. Indeed, it impairs the authority of other means of communication thanks to its charming audio-visual transmission mode mostly preferred to mono-modal media (e.g., newspapers, radio), and its peculiar domestic connotation.[2] Moreover, the incredible power of television resides in the transitory nature of this medium. Just like the radio (and unlike the press), one significant aspect to be considered when dealing with TV is the fidelisation goal pursued by broadcasters. A more attentive overlook into the communication field reveals the weak point of printed media as their democratic aptitude to being purchased and consulted at any time of the day without the risk of missing any interesting facts, where printed news is static. The transience of television appears as one of the most undemocratic information systems to be conveyed. And yet, it still earns appraisal by those users who just cannot avoid staying tuned because missing a single content could knock their up-to-date statuses over within a consumerist society indiscriminately devouring news together with culture, entertainment and publicity. Consequently, television also fantastically fits the commodification requirements longing for and counting on the commercialisation of onscreen products fostering the mass media economy.

## 3 The Linguistic and Cultural Environment of Canadian Television

# The Power of Media over the Masses

Some persons could reckon a medium is an empty tool. It should be strictly functional to its purpose, used up to drain its usefulness to the last bit, and then stashed back onto the shelf until the next time one might need it. Nevertheless, if one reconsiders the relationship between the tool and its task, it could somehow evolve and resolve itself into something new that is nobler and more vivid as if its nature were relieved. There, rather than assisting to the decay of the medium, users become part of it. Like a mirror trick, people reflect themselves into and simultaneously get reflected by both the communication task they pursue and the channel employed for fulfilling it (Fig. 3.1). In like manner, the separate elements in the three-way correlation originate a final image embodying the synthesis of a process that unifies them into a mental and theoretical action conveying (or, more properly, *mediating* the transmission of) the meaning.

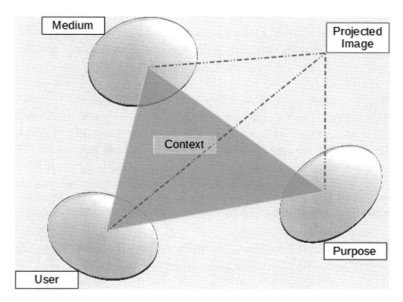

**Fig. 3.1** Representational 'user-medium-purpose' relationship (the figure is mine)

In the 1920s, Charles K. Ogden and Ivor A. Richards theorised a triangulation connecting the 'sign', the 'though of reference' and the 'referent' via as many relationships (Ogden & Richards, 2013 [1923]). Here, the sign determines the though of reference thanks to a causal motivation by symbolisation.

The correctness of this former binomial is responsible for communication adequacy, where the referent must have a clear reference idea to denote its linguistically descriptive aspects. Consequently, the third bond in the triangulation sets the true and arbitrary relationship between the referent (as the sign maker) and the sign itself (as the referent denotative artifact). The given speculation well fits a tangible realisation of the triangle applied to media. The person becomes the task completion through the medium; the sender becomes the messages through the words s/he used *and* the channel transmitting them.

Such an outlook also reveals the change that occurred in time. By the late 1990s, "the world was experiencing a technological revolution [...]: the planet had shrunk into a global village; the internet medium was the new message; individuals were living outside their bodies, on-air or through the Web", said Elena Lamberti (2012, p. 5), an expert on English literature and mass media, in a reflection of the foreseeing criticism anticipated years before by Marshall McLuhan:

> Why is the title of the book *Medium is the Massage* and not *Medium is the Message*? Actually, the title was a mistake. When the book came back from the typesetter's, it had on the cover 'Massage' and it still does. The title was supposed to have read *Medium is the Message* but the typesetter had made an error. When McLuhan saw the title he exclaimed, 'Leave it alone! It's great, and right on target!' Thus, there are now four possible readings for the last word of the title, all of them accurate: *Message* and *Mess Age*, *Massage* and *Mass Age*.[3]

To the scholar, the *medium* is neither a mere and void carrier of contents meant to be unfolded afterward by some hideous receiver, nor is it a negligible part of them. To the Canadian expert, the channel already coincides with the message transmitted. Indeed, it also consists of encryption and decryption codes, comprised along with the pieces of information to be communicated and represent their key to interpretation.

## 3 The Linguistic and Cultural Environment of Canadian Television 75

Moreover, McLuhan's theory (see McLuhan, 1967) also matches the mediatic power included in the excellent conceptualisation of sharing content with—potentially—any audience. Media spread mass-oriented messages (m-e/a-ssages) that aim to reach any person in the world by their nature: via such attempt to meet understandability criteria and wide-spectrum transmission also incorporate the conventional inner substance of language. Communication already *is* a medium per se, born to facilitate exchanges through a set of common shared and acknowledged schemata.

At the turn of the nineteenth and twentieth centuries, Ferdinand De Saussure expressed the relationship between *langue* and *parole* (De Saussure, 1959 [1916]).[4] The former consisted of the symbol system constituting the codes of a language (aka, French *langue* + *langage*). These structural features establish the social convention and the norms. Oppositely, the latter corresponds to the concrete linguistic act, that is univocal and unique (aka, speech; Carroll, 1956). One could retrieve the perfect correspondence between media and meanings in this specular relationship since it is their mutual, final goal. The cooperative (as much as potentially non-cooperative) formulaic attitude of individuals who want to either express or receive some content-enriched, informative codes also establishes a further connection between language and its users. Like the Saussurian dichotomy *langue/parole*, orators get involved in a synthetic relationship with their speeches.

Nonetheless, television has aspects which characterise it as a medium and make it different from the other ones. However, one significant feature of the channel remains its audio-visual transmissibility, responsible for its attention-seeking connotation. Such a quality seems to be quite different from the aseptic news-conveyance provided by newspapers and journals—to name a few. It circumvents the impasse of forcing people to sit and focus on reading the medium, giving up any different activities. Television and the radio are otherwise audio-communicative means which allow individuals to interact with them—(sometimes) violently or even subliminally—by sneaking into their minds, urging the audiences to witness their presence and eventually pay attention to what they have to *say*. Moreover, besides the aural intake, screens play an emblematic role

# 76 F. P. Gentile

as well. The implements of running images outstand the radio's auditive power, as the former are finalised to hypnotically capture spectators' interests through the broadcast of some audience's taste-designed contents to be ad hoc soci(-o-logic-)ally produced.

## Media Ecology and Regulation Policies

The conjoining late 1960s and early 1970s signed a turning point for the Media Studies approach to understand of mass communication when the US scholar Neil Postman ventured himself into the hazardous parallelism between *media* and *ecology*, establishing a brand new perspective on the matter (Postman, 1970). Such speculation was based on the future possibility that 1980s High Schools would have substituted the English subject with media ecology. Such a perspective would have observed these informative tools via an environmental magnifying glass to be focusing on them as a *milieu* that surrounded the globalised population of the entire world (ibid., p. 161). Quoting the Media Studies scholar Paolo Granata, the position taken by the North American sociologist became even clearer about ten years later:

> All'interno dell'etichetta proposta dallo studioso americano il termine ecologia è infatti utilizzato secondo l'etimo—dal greco *oikos*, 'casa', 'abitazione', 'dimora', combinato col suffisso *logos*, 'discorso'—, ovvero è attribuita all'ecologia un'accezione sociale, politica, culturale, come d'altronde è facile intuire se si considera l'apparentamento con il termine 'economia', del quale condivide la stessa radice di senso. (Granata, 2015, p. 12)

Postman emphasises the concept once more, this time mostly gravitating around the etymological value of 'ecology' as the harmonic combination of the Greek stem *oikos*, meaning 'home', and the suffixation *logos*, standing for 'discourse'. The expert insists on the deep connection between 'humans' and 'media', the latter to be considered and analysed as an integral part of everybody's life, in a sort of vestigial relationship breeding humanity throughout their whole existence. There, McLuhan's idea of media as "extensions of man" (McLuhan, 1964) is not only acceptable: it

## 3 The Linguistic and Cultural Environment of Canadian Television

also clarifies the contemporary age where the correlation between these informative tools and their users has gone much further than Ong's personalistic approach (Ong, 1962, 1986; Dance & Larson, 1976, Levinson, 1988, 1997; see also the concept of 'hermeneutics' in Ricoeur, 1997 [1969]). Media have provocatively become quite symbiotic, as technologies' prosthetic value has turned into a sort of self-representation of the hosting organism. On a theoretical level, the situation is remarked by David Thomson as well, when describing the high level of acquaintance spectators nowadays have with television (or generally screens), somehow *assaulting* everybody's public and private life almost automatically:

> It was said for decades that television was a service: it covered live events, news reportage, and the commodity all too easily encoded as entertainment or fun. It also encouraged us to buy certain goods [...]. Those functions still operate, despite enormous shifts in technology. But the medium had another role [...]: it prompted the principle that it was sufficient for the world to be witnessed, or have it pass by. It did not require the effort of understanding or criticism. (Thomson, 2016, p. 34)

From such a perspective, the original *noble* aim of mass-media transmitting to, and communicating with, global communities for the sake of sharing unlimited amounts of information with unlimited audiences, however, eventually got corrupted by the eagerness of entertaining and reporting facts at any costs.

In light of such speculation, people witnessing TV shows have lately become unconscious sponge-like beings ready to assimilate contents without preliminary assessments responsible for the correct understanding—and thus criticism—of what they assist to. Accordingly, the media experience is like a static condition where people watch television and television watches people attempt to create some (im)possible interaction or exchange. Although a similar dichotomic description of "dream" and "domesticity" as "two cubes confront[ing] each other" (Thomson, 2016, p. 80), the parallelism could rather be depicted as a game of Chinese boxes, one shaping the other. Thomson sketches two separated crates that he names 'sit' (as for sitcom)—consisting in the mediated representation of the world—and 'situation'—the world itself—which he counterposes one opposite to the other in a reciprocal contemplation (Fig. 3.2).

Nonetheless, similar speculation disregards the fundamental premise that the piece of furniture television once was meant to be, today, has utterly become an integral part of anybody's daily routine. Such awareness would subsequently refuse to consider the world and the media as two separate and independent (even if correlated) entities preserving their initial natural status from 'contamination', and would instead prefer to reckon them as an agglomerate of boxes infinitely containing each other (Fig. 3.3). In extending the Sapir–Whorf hypothesis (Chap. 1) on language and thought influencing each other to Media Studies, one could conclude that they have changed the world that originated (and contained) mass media. The world is now itself, time after time, transforming media into different channels adapted to its new representations (and thus capable of simultaneously being contained by, and containing, the outside world and its reshapings). The contamination between situation and sit is not just theoretical. Each medium always proposesits version of reality. The subsequent bulk of alternatives does not entirely correspond to the world itself, but the imagery is identifiable mostly through

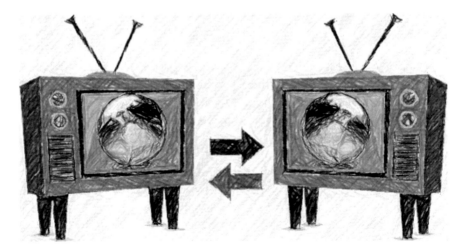

**Fig. 3.2** Representation of Thomson's model of 'sit' and 'situation' confronting each other (the figure is mine, based on Thomson [2016, p. 80])

## 3 The Linguistic and Cultural Environment of Canadian Television

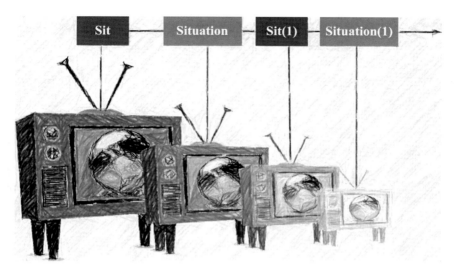

**Fig. 3.3** Chinese boxes reboot of Thomson's 'sit' and 'situation' model (the figure is mine)

narrational, descriptional, audio-visual supportive patterns and schemata. Those aspects, therefore, maintain an outstanding presence that biases people's beliefs and overwhelms their general iterative habits.

Thus, the pivotal role of cinematic language appears like a mixture of communicative linguistic and extra-linguistic features enhanced by "modern technologies visual style and effective use of sound[track]" (Nelson, 2007, p. 11; see also Newcomb, 2007; Tulloch, 2000; Jacobs & Peacock, 2013). It allows spectators to assimilate some expressive peculiarities from television to be reproduced in ordinary contexts.

On the linguistic level, "interactions [...] are deliberately scripted and designed or constructed and prefabricated" (Beers-Fägersten, 2016, p. 3) to emulate ordinary communicative situations. However, any misspeaking, mishearing, pauses, the timing of utterance and turn-taking issues are strictly functional to dialogic structures and scriptwriters' goals. Those specific features recur onscreen with a frequency capable of influencing and altering viewers' natural language awareness and usage (Kozloff, 2000; Richardson, 2010; Ayaß & Gerhardt, 2012). Nonetheless, the need for creating recognisable and *approvable* patterns in context though forces cinematic contents to a partial, limited and always stereotypical display. This procedure rises some significant issues to be discussed, such as the cultural role of sound/silence, gestures-in-talk, use of specific colours. Moreover, a further point concerning the insertion of polarising categories (heroes and villains, good and evil) is tackled by Robyn Wiegman in her article "Race, ethnicity, and film" in 2000:

> Across the three decades that now constitute the history of the study of stereotypes, we can trace the emergence of important issues about representation and difference, the political economy of the industry, spectatorship and identification, and, most importantly, the relationship between film and culture. (Hill & Church-Gibson, 2000, p. 159)

Consequently, such circumstances spotted one more query for the broadcasters over the years. How to survey the transmission of appropriate content-enriched messages to divergent audiences without the embarrassment of resulting in unsatisfying or—even worse—offensive content? Indeed, the problem is rooted in the past. In the very beginning of the twentieth century movie theatres offerings increased as they started proposing and showing a broader range of "fiction formats such as anarchic farces, crime stories, and melodramatic love stories". The consolidation of more and more authoritarian censorship policies followed, "motivated by anxieties about social consequences of the medium's immense popularity, especially with children and adolescents" (ibid., p. 201). After a few decades, the problem remains essential. The use of more democratic and demographic controllers nowadays aims at studying audiences' flow, share and appreciation indexes, which operate for the setting of "both negative constraints and positive requirements, with compliance monitored via a system of state-appointed regulatory authorities" (Kuhn, 2007, p. 115).

Today almost every broadcaster undergoes some norms to be respected and which vary from place to place. Anglophone countries, for instance, all substantially agree in respecting four primary objectives also sanctioned within the 2003 British *Communication Act*:

## 3 The Linguistic and Cultural Environment of Canadian Television    81

1. Social values concerning education, cultural identity;
2. Diversity via the support of tolerance-inclusive social behaviours towards minorities;
3. Quality, for the release of innovative and standardised products;
4. Range and balance (demanding displaying heterogeneous contents across different genres and formats) (ibid., p. 117).


# The Canadian Television Background

The already discussed mass mediatic aptitude to influencing the masses has long undergone some political perspectives. Those points of view often require some special attention to harness that capability, to funnel consumers towards designated orientations mostly involving the increase of national belonging and the growth of socio-behavioural education.

As for the best part of national entities globally, Canada's situation regarding broadcasting policies has a controversial history. Indeed, the first subject on the telecommunication scene was born in the mid-1920s and ascended to its solid form only in 1936, after the *Canadian Radio Broadcasting Commission*'s dismissal.[5] After such provision, the Government allowed creating an arm's length Crown Corporation known as *CBC* (Canadian Broadcasting Corporation, also known as the *Corpse*), which would have operated autonomously in the communicational interest. However, until a few decades later, *CBC* chiefs were directing a hegemonic broadcaster, which was not affected by any superior authority and was in the position of programming transmissions without supervisors to lead them or judge their results. Finally, this contingency of *CBC* acting as both "cop and competitor" (McPhail, 1986, p. 43) ended in 1958 when the Government promulgated a renewed overview on the matter through a *Canadian Broadcasting Act* that instituted the *Board of Broadcasting Governors* (BBG) for the regulation of broadcasters' functions, limits, and obligations. Since its creation, it was the first time *CBC* was openly subdued to one actual authority that dictated the pace. Ten years later, in 1968, subsequent political redrafts commanded the Board dismissal to create a brand new watchdog to guard Canadian media. The redesigned *Canadian Broadcasting Act* abolished the previous organ of control and founded the *Canadian Radio-television and Telecommunication Commission* (CRTC). *CRTC* updated the *CBC* mandate and assumed the task of carefully overseeing the telecommunication environment. Despite many responsibilities on technical matters, Canadian content, competitions, copyrights, and organisational standards kept on being prerogatives of Federal Government Departments until the extension of commission competence via the *CRTC Act* in 1976 (McClausand, 2009). However, the real overturn only occurred in 1991, when the latest version of the *Canadian Broadcasting Act* was enacted to amend its 1968 draft and the *CRTC Act*. Nevertheless, this new document was more restrictive than the previous one and immediately assured the country a public property of broadcasting corporations rather than private, along with a list of clauses denoting some major points affecting their programming to:

1. "Be predominantly and distinctively Canadian" [*Canadian Broadcasting Act*, S.C. 1991, c. 11, I: 3(m), (i)];
2. Transmit contents that would "reflect Canada and its regions to national and regional audiences" (ii);
3. "Actively contribute to the flow and exchange of cultural expression" (iii);
4. On the linguistic level, "be in English and in French, reflecting the different needs and circumstances of each official language community, including [...] linguistic minorities" (iv) and "strive to be of equivalent quality" (v) in both languages;
5. "Be made available throughout Canada" (vii) in the most efficient way;
6. And, most importantly, "contribute to shared national consciousness and identity" (vi) and "reflect the multicultural and multiracial nature of Canada" (viii) for the utter achievement of a pure feeling of Canadianness.

The given perspective urges this specific Canadianness sentiment (Beaty & Sullivan, 2006; Bredin et al., 2012) to stand out from the television kaleidoscopic background. Where Canada is "a country still in search of its modernist moment of national certainty" (Dorland &

# 3 The Linguistic and Cultural Environment of Canadian Television 83

Charland, 2002, p. 22), the characterising multifaceted attitude still struggles to find a univocal identity and a consciousness mustering people in a sole social body.

Considering that, the study of the Canadian television background and environment would not represent just an opportunity to retrieve potentially creative, innovative and sophisticated products to feed viewers with—rather than worn-out imitative ideas. It could also contribute to defining better the boundaries limiting the sight on florid (socio)cultural and linguistic *overtures* often blinded and daring not to encroach beyond generic "US-centric" (Bredin et al., 2012, p. 117) tendencies or internal discords:

> The first wave of histories and analyses of cultural policy in Canada tended to regard the government's own claims about the need for a strong national culture as simply platitudinous, if not fraudulent. The true function of cultural policy, scholars suggested, was to protect the dominant interests in a particular industry, or to produce the ideological gloss which rendered palatable the Canadian government's complicity in our economic subservience to the U.S. (Straw, 2002, p. 97)

US industry seems predominant in telecommunications in North America as much as in the rest of the world. As reported by *The New York Times* journalist Brian Stelter, 96.7 per cent of the entire US population owned a TV set in 2011. Moreover, even if it represented a 2 per cent fall compared with previous statistics (Stelter, 2011), television appeared (and still does) as the dominating mass media, granting the North American County some enormous visibility worldwide. By the late 1980s, the United States authoritarian personality—whose solidity is acknowledged and reinforced by the star system—already required around 75 per cent of US content and product exports for world television programs. Yet, during the early 1990s (Hoskins & McFayden, 1991), it became even more aggressive after the 9/11 attacks when:

> [A] delegation of high-level media executives [realised that] the entertainment industry could play a part in improving the image of the United States overseas.

> One of the central ideas was using 'soft power' by spreading American television and movies to foreign audiences, especially in the Muslim world, to help sway public opinion.
>
> There were few tangible results from the meeting [...]. But since then, the media companies have gotten what they wanted, even if the White House was not. In the last eight years, American pop culture, already popular, has boomed around the globe while opinions of America itself have soured. (Arango, 2008)

The hegemonic power paraded by US broadcasters somehow caught on whatever *environment* its seeds had been falling on over the years, strengthening their influence in the New World as much as in the Old one. Thanks to the fascination produced by the North American culture, whose charm appears way more effective than any other economic interests or political affiliations, US broadcasters continued pulling off accomplishments on the market. Hence "Batman is Batman, regardless of if Bush is in the White House or not", said Jeffrey Schlesinger, head of Internal Television at Warner Brothers (ibid.). Moreover, it is worth noting that despite the fact that Canada is a sovereign state with proper inner organisational power structures, rules and apparatuses, its history always reminds its citizens of a past, a present and a future of immigration and fragmentation. There, the governmental legitimacy does not coincide with the sharing of "a single cohesive culture" (Beaty & Sullivan, 2006, p. 9) within the same immense country, whose geography continually draws attention to several regional inner and outer idiosyncrasies (e.g., the Quebec situation related to a cultural, linguistic and political resistance for the recognition of its autonomy; see also Chap. 6). Then, Canada's multiculturism appears like the most reasonable compromise for permitting diverse and unique experiences to converge into one identical both physical and ideological milieu. In a similar context, "a person could consider themselves a Canadian on national terms, but culturally could be many kinds of 'hyphenated', cultural Canadian: Native-, French-, Indo-, Chinese-", (Collins, 1990, p. 26) and counting. On this track, the 'melting pot' aggregational model makes way for a 'mosaic' whose overview is given by myriads of tiny dissimilarities contributing to shade the whole social picture.

## 3 The Linguistic and Cultural Environment of Canadian Television     85

To that extent, of course, mass media play a vital role in being an active subject during the process of forming (sometimes *degenerationally* casting and diverting) a—possibly critical—consciousness. Media can access people's minds to seed ideas through their representational and simultaneously representative statuses. Moreover, the enhancement of new technologies and the consolidation of Canada's economy over the years have granted television to becoming the herald medium before the plateau of newspapers, journals and radios. Since the end of World War II, Canadians started buying TV sets that would be reached by US frequencies and thus programmes, which led to the already described nationalisation urgency of contents between the 1950s and 1960s by founding the CRTC (Fremeth, 2010). Also, 1952 is a milestone to something more: the introduction of cable television (Base, 2012). In the period 1965–1975 almost 60 per cent of Canadian houses had subscribed to cable; a percentage that rose even more by 1998 when, after further amelioration and the introduction of high-speed Internet connections, almost reached 70 per cent (ibid.) adhesion by users spending nowadays about 20 h/w watching (Fremeth, 2010). Accordingly, programmers have a great responsibility in carefully selecting products to be distributed via screens inside spectators' houses, where shows have not only to contemporaneously meet the taste of different individuals and families from coast to coast. They also participate in the inoculation of specific values and principles through the seductive fascination of television. However:

> [...] Private broadcasters CTV and Global purchase Canadian broadcast rights for popular American network shows and then showing them in simultaneous substitution. That means that Canadian broadcasters grab the signals from the networks at the same time as it airs in the United States but insert their own advertising and station identifiers. This dependency model is predicated on a rather self-serving claim to preserve Canadian values by ensuring that the invisible ownership structure behind the airing of any show remains Canadian. (Beaty & Sullivan, 2006, p. 41)

Indeed, despite the fundamental aim of media, cultural and national transmissions always succumb to the market's law. Thus, broadcasters have to deal with political and economic issues forcing them to choose among homegrown and foreign productions only in terms of share and audience appraisal rather than ideological motivations to *survive* the world of the networks. As a public corporation, *CBC* could optionally dam release cheaper United States contents and invest in some more expensive domestic productions. The broadcaster benefited from the support of different funding conduits like parliamentary appropriations—which in 2015–2016 equalled $1.027 billion, "representing 66% of the Corporation's total revenue and sources of funds"—advertising—second source of income reaching 16 per cent of funds—and subscription revenues—9 per cent—for becoming "more local, digital and financially sustainable" by 2020–2021.[6] However, private entities may only lean on the latter two options because lacking a Governmental financial bolster. Likewise, public broadcaster's diversified programme schedules often contrast the few local contents affordable by private networks and capable of capturing people's fancy. So, sports investments (Robert Sparks, 1992) flank a massive range of TV shows, news, documentaries, movies and TV series springing information and entertainment at any time. Indeed, for instance, in the 2002–2008 years, *CTV* spent about $253 million for purchasing and airing many hockey games (2002, 2008), the 2010 Vancouver Winter Olympics and the 2012 London Summer Olympics (invested in a partnership with Rogers Communications in 2004), and the 2006 Canadian Football League's Grey Cup game (Fremeth, 2010).

According to an overall perspective, one could deduce that private broadcasters have approximately had the same historical development and trend as their public rival, though in less time. *CTV* Television Network is indeed relatively younger than its antagonist and it officially debuted in July 1961. In its first year, the Network could immediately represent a hard bargain when its director, Spence Caldwell, signed an impressive agreement with *Bell Telephone*. He obtained to use the company's microwave circuits throughout the Windsor-to-Quebec City corridor at the cost of $11 million in annual payments (Gittins, 1999, p. 72) for the transmission of its (radio) signal. In addition to that, Caldwell also had nine 'second' television stations set by *BBG* in 1960–1961 in Calgary, Vancouver, Winnipeg, Toronto, Halifax, Montreal (one in English language and one in French), Ottawa, and Edmonton (ibid., pp. 7–8).

## 3 The Linguistic and Cultural Environment of Canadian Television   87

Moreover, just like *CBC*, *CTV*'s relationship with *BBG* involved issues concerning the number of transmitted materials. At the beginning of its story the channel could not fulfil the requirements of 10 h/w of broadcasting imposed by the Board. By the second year, transmissions rose from 8 to 14 h/w of taped programming. However, on the qualitative level, things were not perfect as well. Between 1966 and 1967, the chief of *CRTC*, Pierre Juneau, "wanted *CTV* to meet two [...] objectives: extending its service to sparsely settled areas and producing 'significant' Canadian content (Cancon) programs" (ibid., p. 95); a goal always underestimated by *CTV* directors since the broadcaster continued transmitting mainly foreign or *cheap* shows until the late 1970s, when about 90 pr cent of contents was still from the US. Once more, in perfect parallelism with the *Corpse*, the rebirth of the Network occurred at the end of the 1990s, when Ivan Fecan (CEO of *CTV* Television Network from 1998 to 2011) passed the 40 h/w of programming scheduled by his predecessor, John Cassaday, to 126 h/w, along with the insertion of five praised Canadian contemporary TV series, among which there were *Due South* (Canada: *CTV* & *CBS*, 1994–1999), *The City* (Canada: *CTV* & *Fiver*, 1999–2000) and *Power Play* (Canada: *CTV*, 1998–2000; ibid., p. 334).

Having dealt with the two leading examples of the industry—*CBC* as the major one, and *CTV* as its direct competitor—it seems necessary to mention the third party involved. While *CTV* released the first and the second TV series observed in the survey (*Flashpoint* and *Motive*) since their first season and episode, the third one, *19-2*, has a different background. It was transmitted on *CTV* only since 2017 after *Bravo!* had broadcast the first three seasons.

In 1983, Canadian television witnessed the launch of *C-Channel*, whose ambition was to transmit only cultural, artistic content in the form of pay-TV. However, those materials were strictly associable with the products that already made the *CBC* schedules for free. Thus, the channel never gained the number of subscribers necessary for survival. Only five months after that February 1 release, the underfinanced status and the restrictions dictated by *CRTC* led to the *C-Channel* epilogue (Robert Sparks, 1992; Plummer, 2012). Notwithstanding its demise, the purpose of the channel was intriguing; hence the Commission started

## 88    F. P. Gentile

looking forward to finding an alternative to that attempt. About ten years later, *CHUM Limited* finally proposed creating a brand new channel bearer of the same leaning. After preliminary assessments, *CRTC* licensed *CHUM* to launch *Bravo!* on February 14, 1994, "for a wide variety of programs having a general focus on the performing arts" (*CRTC* decision 94-281, § Programming). Disregarding the approval that allowed *Bravo!* to be on air since January 1, 1995, the brand was a (homonym) US creation. Aware of the temptation of fishing in the sea beyond the border, CRTC immediately listedsome limitations to be observed by *CHUM* and affecting the channel:

> [...] The licensee has made a commitment that U.S.-produced programs, whether from *Bravo* (U.S.) or the sources, will not make up more than 25% of drama offerings in the prime time on *Bravo!*.
> [...] In the first two years of operation, at least 40% of programs broadcast on *Bravo!*, during both the broadcast year and the evening broadcast period, will be Canadian. In the third and fourth years of the license term, the levels will increase to 50% overall during the broadcast year and 45% in the evening broadcast period. In the final two years of the term, the Canadian content will again increase, to 60% throughout the broadcast year, and 50% in the evening broadcast period. (Ibid.)

Such conditions bound the broadcaster throughout the duration of the license. Therefore, they assured Canadian television a substantial preponderance of domestic content in place of alien products. Nonetheless, the agreement also made up for some more exciting clauses. The deal related the legitimacy of the *Bravo!* foundation to the substantial investment of $3.6 million "in grants to Canadian artists, arts groups, and independent production companies" (ibid.). Such a payment was sanctioned to be made over the six years of the contract's validity so that national creativity would have felt supported, promoted and appraised by both media and audiences simultaneously. After the license expiration date had arrived, the contract was renovated; however, *CHUM*'s economic situation was not particularly florid. In June 2007, CRTC approved the operation. and *CTV Globemedia* exploited the acquisitional transaction of *Bravo!* from

# 3 The Linguistic and Cultural Environment of Canadian Television    89

*CHUM Limited* (Broadcasting decision CRTC 2007-165). Between 2010 and 2011, *Bell Canada Enterprise Inc. (BCE Inc.)* purchased 100 per cent of *CTV Globemedia* shares and renegotiated the original license after paying out *Bravo!* debts. The former passage from *CHUM* to *CTV Globemedia* had already involved some programming schedule modifications favouring a higher percentage of television dramas and movies, even if still saving some room for art shows and performing arts. However, the utter change of property through the acquisition of *CTV Globemedia* by *BCE* entailed a final transformation that erased 'cultural' assets, devoting the channel to pure entertainment via the sole transmission of TV series and movies. Consequently, later *BCE* rebranding plans advertised *Bravo!* to be renamed after *CTV Drama* by 2019 (Wong, 2018), and as we know it today.

It seems worthy to sketch out some of the main peculiarities of the contemporary Canadian products involved in the seriality of the crime genre.

## The 'Cancon' Contemporary Context

The reader may have already sensed the grasp of the Canadian television drama situation, while poring over the previous paragraph. Broadcasters' workings are about scheduling different businesses and airing plans for finding the best products that would reflect the requirements imposed by governmental decisions. Above all, they have to meet the public's taste as it represents the only valid parameter to comply with for commodification purposes. The audience's judgement is indeed one crucial aspect of any broadcaster's prosperity or failure. Moreover, in the first light of their stories, Stations did not have great disposal of live events in terms of both materials and technologies, which would have allowed the airing. As a consequence, the best part of television programmes consisted of taped contents to be displayed when needed. Such contingency implied not only the abuse of pre-recorded broadcast shows but also the consecration of TV series and movies, preferably in the form of drama (intended as fictional stories), although:

Up to 1951 you could say that television drama here lacked mobility [...]. But two important things did happen during this period. The first was the development of dramatized documentary of the kind associated principally with writers such as Robert Barr and Duncan Ross, who aimed at breaking up the action into many scenes helped by the introduction of film sequence. The second thing was the crime serial of the kind originated by Francis Durbridge. (Bluem & Manwell, 1967, p. 49)

A similar aura invested television production throughout the 1950s and 1960s decades. On the one hand, documentaries gave up the purely descriptive attitude by embracing the stylistic tradition inherited by Robert Barr's (1849–1912) verve of *The Idler*, where the author—in collaboration with Jerome K. Jerome—never hesitated to harshly expose inhibitions of the contemporary narratives mostly through the use of parody. On the other hand, Francis Durbridge's (1912–1998) perspective as a novelist, radio and television writer hardly ever left the biting features that distinguished the creation of the Paul Temple character. Amid the entire panorama, Temple represented a renewed, brilliant hero whose actions were finally supported by recent scene shooting techniques introductions. Such a positive trend of crime drama launched in these years led to its undisputed predominance on screens. Quoting Richard Sparks, "by the early 1970s, the cop show had entirely supplanted the Western as [the] dominant genre of narrative fiction on U.S. television, largely on the basis of its superior demographics" (Richard Sparks, 1992, p. 27). Indeed, argues Sparks, while other fictional narrative forms of entertainment continued to gather audience appraisal, crime stories success could count on the interest of a younger public that was also wider, more constant (in terms of TV viewing), and sparsely settled (ibid., pp. 27–28). Nevertheless, while the initial heritage of crime drama leant on the sole experience of those who devoted their lives to writing, the television content maturational process moved to another level over the following decade.

During the 1970s [...] the dominant debate [on cop series] here included a mix of Althusserian notions of police as ideological state apparatus, Barthesian concepts of the textual conversion of history into myth, and

## 3 The Linguistic and Cultural Environment of Canadian Television 91

> Gramscian notions of hegemony, as well as feminist critique of police and patriarchy within critical criminology. [...] But in the field of television studies this diffusion was significantly contained within the framework of critical (Marxist) theory, semiotics, structuralism, feminism and psychoanalysis. (Tulloch, 2000, p. 34)

It is thus clear that, starting from the 1970s, the observation of television products from the textual and narrative point of view was no longer enough. Further speculations took the examination of screen products beyond the lens of Philosophical-Media Studies, even summoning Althusser's censured epistemology about the involved mediatic conveyance of ideological contents as diverted by the Gramscian theory of hegemonic corruption of society by capitalism and strategic power dynamics. The twenty-year-period inclusive of the 1970s and 1980s assisted to the proliferation of the already mentioned process of stereotypisation of crime drama, where plot pivot happened to hinge upon social discrimination, political corruption and injustice. TV series became the playground of dissolution insofar as they tended to deal with police forces often bending the rules for the sake of the conventional motto that 'the ends justify the means', to conclude the case. Television got drenched with ideological connotations suggesting crime, violence and murder wherever one would direct their gaze, within a society struggling for the utter erasure of the evil and yet always winning minor battles which would let the *war* continue over and over the episodes (and seasons). Gender and sociological perspectives participated in the evaluation, as well. The majority of the series indeed used to depict situations which presupposed cops to be male, masculine, handsome and often womanisers against the habit of women who incarnate weakness and play secondary roles (see *The Sweeney*, UK: *ITV*, 1975–1978; *Magnum P.I.*, USA: *CBS*, 1980–1988; *Miami Vice*, USA: *NBC*, 1984–1989), along with much racial and ethnic prejudices (ibid., p. 45; see also Kellner, 1995) and generally lacking aesthetic representations of some specific social— and sociological—aspects of the world transposed. Although, some *virtuous* examples still appeared in the list of TV series in the reference period as subverting the schemes and undertaking different paths, at least about the female portrayal, where heroines turned into fortified, independent models capable of shattering down the glass ceiling that sealed them aside in the past (see *Charlie's Angels*, USA: *ABC*, 1976–1981; *Cagney and Lacey*, USA: *CBS*, 1982–1988). On the same trend, an increasing number of contemporary TV products seem to have chosen to represent also queer and transgender tones along with the rebuttal of merely domestic women (*CSI*, USA: *CBS*, 2000–2015; *Psych*, USA: *USA Network*, 2006–2014; *Rizzoli & Isles*, USA: *TNT*, 2010–2016), formerly "visually non-existent" (Jenner, 2016, p. 49).

Yet, 'cops and robbers' approaches would fascinate people mostly in their childhood and, as a consequence, nothing like stiff dichotomies contrasting absolute goodness with pure evil and vice versa would have limited credibility for an evolving public. The genre has only ever dealt with heinous facts that would have rendered a more plausible transposition of reality as possible. Of course, this transposition had to fit social customs, from time to time extending and moulding the definition of 'heinous' itself. This entire procedure eventually aimed at conquering people's attention, as the audience had to keep sitting in their couches and relate with blood, fear and death, pretending crime to be fun rather than dangerous.

Therefore, thinking of some peculiar TV series such as the "*CSI* franchise"—according to Deborah Jernyn's label—even though it shares more with the sci-fi industry than with "its TV crime drama predecessors" (Allen, 2007, p. 81 and ff.), it is also true that "America currently needs reassuring and the uber-professional teams that head the three *CSI* shows are unrelenting in their investigation on the minutiae of criminal evidence" (ibid., p. 9). The real power of television crime drama (even more than its literary *alter ego*) seems *purely* mythological, as:

> Myth encounters nothing but betrayal in language [...]. The elaboration of a second-order semiological system will enable myth to escape its dilemma [...]: it transforms history into nature. (Barthes, 1972, p. 128)

Thus, reading a book could, without doubt, enchant the readers and envelop them with its plots to the last page. However, any sheer linguistic description would likely never have the same protrusive inclination of the visual immediacy.

# Crime Genre and Television Seriality

In a like manner of the fortitude exhibited by the characterising visual immediacy of the television *medium*, the strong point of crime both as a genre and narrative mode lies in the harshness of the deeds it describes. Such aspect recurrently resides in the brutality of the images displayed. One prominent feature of this narrative consists of the enucleation of different detection modalities (Fig. 3.4). It could be possible to range from the *classic* tripartition among deduction/induction/abduction to the contrast between rational-scientific and irrational subjective, finally

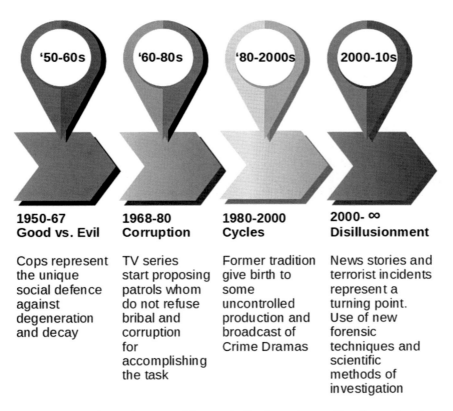

**Fig. 3.4** Detection TV transposition periodisation scheme (the figure is mine, based on Jenner [2016])

leading to an apical epiphany through "intuitive leap[s] of logic" (Jenner, 2016, pp. 15–17).

Nevertheless, investigation modalities and narrative styles and techniques are tightly dependent on the audiences' craving for the killings. Lucy F. Donaldson, qua expert in Film Studies, underlines that "violence and physical action are the main concern of the police series genre, which leads to an emphasis on the body, both as an object of violence and as a vehicle for the expression of action and effort" (Jacobs & Peacock, 2013, p. 210). The ubiquitous presence and recognition of bodies and corpses within the cinematic product frames is, once more, symptomatic of multimodal needs, which demand the coarse visual consistency to flank verbal communications and behaviours (see Bednarek, 2010, 2018, 2019; Piazza et al., 2011; Davis, 2021).

Such alternation of oral utterings with visual communication that implies gesture, gaze, etc., benefits from the assessment of "ideational metafunction[s]" (Bateman, 2008, p. 40), where viewers fire up dichotomies of "narrational" and "conceptual" visuals (Kress & van Leeuwen, 1996, pp. 73–75, 88–89). The said focuses are responsible for the mental representation of actions process—the former—and the implied classification and study of those for understanding visual contents—the latter. Also, ideational metafunctions appear in a tight relationship with Anthony Baldry and Paul J. Thibault's medium-specific "visual transitivity frames" operations (Baldry & Thibault, 2006, p. 122) and Terry D. Royce's "visual message elements"—VME (Royce, 2007, p. 73).

According to similar parallelism, the television content displays a combination of textual metafunctional elements that include different degrees of salience and framing, responsible for the narrative (visual) cohesion end coherence. Along with those aspects, televised products also emphasise an "interpersonal metafunction", putting audiences in cognitive connection with the materials administered to them (Bateman, 2008, pp. 41–42; also see Halliday & Hasan, 1976; Halliday, 1978, 1994, 2001 [1990], 2003; Halliday & Matthiessen, 2004), hence varying communication informativity degree (De Beaugrande & Dressler, 1994).

In the crime drama, spectators are not passive agents assisting the vicissitudes befalling the displayed characters since they actively participate in the narration. Primary understanding processes are started by the deed

# 3 The Linguistic and Cultural Environment of Canadian Television 95

implicatures' actual mental schematisation (crime, violence, murder, blood) that originates from a specific context (television, drama, fictional realm). After that, viewers implicitly establish a situational bond, through which they accept to undergo the rules imposed by the *medium* and tread the investigation path to the final solution. Also, they do that under the narrative mechanisms predisposed by the *sequences* (foreground, background, tight close-ups, sequential speed-ups or slow-downs, suspense, climax). Subsequently, audiences' eyes become inclusive parts of the aesthetic product and physically move all over the scene, both onscreen and inside the frame. The viewer, "represented by the camera, does not remain in one viewing position. He sees the action from both close-range and at a distance", based on shifts labelled by David Barker as "camera space" and "performer space" (Newcomb, 2007, p. 172). Additional aspects typical of television contents involve narration modalities, other than shooting techniques varying space angles to be framed.

Along with the camera and performer's space, it is possible to count as many plot organizational structures. On the one hand, they define a *centrifugal complexity* "[whose] richness is found in the complex web of interconnectivity forged across the social system rather than in the depth of any one individual's role in the narrative or psychological layers".

On the other hand, *centripetal complexity* is "where narrative moment pulls the action and characters inward towards a more cohesive centre" (Jacobs & Peacock, 2013, p. 52).

As a result of such procedures, narrative techniques in dramas and TV series could create less than hour-long and compact stories to adhering with genre formulas. Those formulas facilitate audiences to recognise their type and common point with other dramas, series or serials (centrifugal). Nonetheless, they could, instead, also present intricate and dense plots, whose details would rather build some distinctive features creating affiliation (centripetal). In the crime genre, the distinction between centrifugal and centripetal narration is the same as courses through TV series and serials. The former tends to have numerous episodes and a long legacy of seasons to be aired through the years. This creates a heterogeneous narration that focuses on the investigator's (or team/police station in which the investigator serves) to solve all the *different* criminal cases entrusted to him/her. The plot dynamics thus flow through the array of topics describing isolated felonies that require an identification and solution within the limited content-enriched space of single instalments, consisting in a row of sealed boxes to be stacked aside one after another on the shelves of the seasons (to that extent, see the related visual immediacy of *Cold Case*, USA: *CBS*, 2003–2010; *Castle*, USA: *ABC*, 2009–2016). An emblematic example of TV series analysed in this study is the *Flashpoint* one (see Chap. 4). Here, the three seasons observed recount the vicissitudes of a contemporary Toronto, where the Strategic Response Unit (SRU) led by sergeant Gregory Parker intervenes in situations involving terrorism, criminal law and negotiation procedures. All the episodes narrate their own stories, whose consequences bring along the following instalments of the seasons for coherence and consistency. The centrifugal role of the structure sustaining the series aims to create fascination through the hybrid deployment of crime and action genres within the single onscreen event and gradually to capture spectators' attention.

On the contrary, TV serials concentrate their communicative goal in creating affiliation and gathering viewers to be charmed and maintained *throughout*—not just during—the seasons. The narrative, centripetal mechanism here consists instead in the making of a series of interconnected episodes, which deal with crimes that need more than one episode to be solved, or, even better, propose isolated, small cases whose consequences (or premises) give birth to the main story starting from the pilot episode and coming to a conclusion only at the end of the last one (see *Criminal Minds*, USA: *CBS*, 2005–; *Dexter*, USA: *Showtime*, 2006–2013). Some functional examples of the 'serial narrative modality' are present in *Motive*'s third season (see Chap. 5). In Vancouver, the facts that lead to the death of one crucial character stretch from the first episode until the season finale, along with collateral cases and the related implicatures defining the entire story. However, *Motive*'s remaining seasons can be ascribed to the 'series model' (thus creating a hybrid product). Similarly, this 'model' structures the *19-2* (see Chap. 6) Montreal-based cop show— where annual broadcasts are all about one basic set of crimes to be solved, which also influence the following seasonal thematic narrations. The TV serial public is somehow urged not to miss any broadcast minutes to comprehend the plot thoroughly.

## 3 The Linguistic and Cultural Environment of Canadian Television

In light of that, one should ponder over the two described narrative modalities to construct a television crime drama with effective schematisation, avoiding neglecting any fundamental perspective. Yet, despite the neat narrative distinction between TV series and serials, the survey opts for using the former term as a general label attributable to the totality of the case studies reported in the further chapters, being TV 'series' the commonly accepted reference terminology in terms of television seriality. Based on said terminological level, the television series involved in the examination are also referred to as 'shows' in adherence to the broadly shared United States linguistic usage, to avoid redundancy. However, the term—adopted in the AmE to denote both TV series and other kinds of broadcast (such as *reality show, talk show*)—is employed here in its only synonymical relationship with the former type of onscreen transmission, and its use is exclusively associated with its singular significance (as collective noun inclusive of the entire product parts, even when recurring as 'shows') in lieu of its plural form as the equivalent of 'episodes' or 'instalments'.

Besides the described nomenclature, it is clear that (script-)writers of television crime dramas could realistically arrange worlds ruled by vices and moral dismantlement. There, power structures are embodied by gangsters who control and manipulate people at their convenience (Chandler, 1950). On the same level, ordinary men and women or teams of corporate professionals could suddenly rise as heroes above anonymous masses, fighting for what is right and—often unrealistically victorious—annihilating delinquency. However, the *enormous* creative difficulty is found in the fundamental thematic and narrative standardisation of materials affecting the television series via both the centrifugal and centripetal patterns and requirements just described. The 'bringing home the big result' mentality often forces broadcasters to adhere to mostly flattened expectations which—aiming at customer fidelisation—could produce the same object over and over again, with only different names:

> Anyone who has been channel flipping and stumbled over such shows as *StarGate SGI, Relic Hunter,* or *PSI Factor* is seeing the most abundant fruits of the Canadian television production sector. Very few of these shows have any kind of Canadian indicators, and most, like *Sue Thomas: FBEye,* are

clearly set in the United States. In many ways, these shows are logical outcomes of what producers in the United States call 'runaway productions'. (Beaty & Sullivan, 2006, p. 79)

The cultural dominion of the US lingering in the mass media influences Canadian television badly. Not only have Canada's productions lately been pale imitations of the competitors beyond the border. The country is still subdued to their economic strength as well. Indeed, US investors tend to relocate productions up North (especially in Vancouver) to lower the costs (Lederman, 2013): "the Canadian market is a 10th of the American one. But the cost of producing a quality product is the same, [ranging from] $2 million to $3 million" (Wong, 2017). Nonetheless, the situation seems to be changing, and Canada is nowadays affirming its authority concerning many genres, first of all, science fiction (ibid.), by specific "Cancon" requirements (Gittins, 1999, p. 95).

Notwithstanding a similar perspective, crime drama appraisal is crucial as well. Particularly, 2017 seems to have represented a watershed, definitely separating such a past *lacking personality* by a different present, enriched with a lot of brand new ideas contending for the leadership against other North American and online broadcasters such as *HBO* and *Netflix* (Wong, 2017). *CBC* and *CityTV* thrilled their public by launching 'irrevocably Canadian' TV series like *Pure* (Canada: *CBC*, *Super Channel* and *WGN America*, 2017–), *Bad Blood* (Canada: *CityTV*, 2017–) and *Cardinal* (Canada: *CTV*, 2017–; see also Yeo, 2018). Along with such examples, one tenacious topic of the Canadian genre is represented by *contemporary* fears (Fig. 3.4), which contemplate actual international politics mainly dictated by leader nations, such as the terrorist threat and the dread concerning foreigners, yet unexpected about the Canadian attitude (*The Border*, Canada: *CBC*, 2008–2010), or the everlasting corruption motif (*Intelligence*, Canada: *CBC*, 2006–2007; the show was cancelled after rumours associating its corruption and bribery themes with the Harper's government over that period; see Doyle, 2017). Furthermore, other productions differ from the shows mentioned above. They tend to relate to the consolidation of feelings of national belonging while proposing criminal investigations and murderous acts through the fascination of charming historical reconstructions (*The Murdoch Mysteries*,

## 3 The Linguistic and Cultural Environment of Canadian Television

Canada: *CityTV* and *CBC*, 2008–). When dealing with literature, one could speak about a diversity of genres, each having its peculiarities, formulaic elements, characterising features and narrative patterns, contributing to its success. Media, though, within this contemporary era of social-economy teem with creativity and products providing an environment that needs to be regulated by different sets of rules, which also involve copyright restrictions that contain the risk of plagiarism and define the property of particular contents:

> The term 'format' to which a great many definitions can be attributed, in the world of television is taken to mean a copyrighted programme whose license can be sold or leased to a foreign country. Throughout the eighties and nineties of the last century, European television networks were inundated by such formats, *The Big Brother* being perhaps the most well-known. (Hughes, 2017, p. viii)

What has been described so far flanks the acknowledgement that the best part of TV products has even had a North American matrix reaching the old Continent in its most *recent* history. Thus, the cop-show format can be identified by its crystallised narrative patterns, characters and themes common to the genre itself. The formulaic connotation of the crime drama requires a narrative stylistic scheme (centrifugal or centripetal), and the presence of symbolic fixed heroes and villains. The investigator comes along a murderer, one or more victims, some witnesses, and a series of cops, all stereotyping the incarnation of good purposes, evil intents, sacrifice, social values and morality, plus the efforts supportive of what is right, accordingly. The pace passing from one situation (and character's role) to the other is then utterly rendered by the "aestheticizing of crime" (Bargainnier, 1980, p. 7). The killings are introduced and subsequently dissected and reconstructed. They demand a detailed description of every clue and investigative progress for the final *deconsecration* of the murderous impiety via the resolution of the case and the figuring of the *mens rea* in the epilogue of the instalment. Although, despite the fixed elements, the framing slant and the cinematic techniques applied to the story are the very characterising aspects, distinguishing one TV series from the other in terms of structural features.

The *Flashpoint* format (produced by *Avamar Entertainment* and *Pink Sky Entertainment* and acquired by *ION Television* since 2012), for example, is different from the *Motive* one, which has a strictly procedural focus comprehensive of heroes who act within the station/crime-scene/morgue dimensions, and yet is comparable to its Australian sibling, *Rush* (Australia: *Network Ten*, produced by *Southern Star Entertainment*, 2008–2011), whose high specularity and fictional salience, centred onto the SRU (Strategic Response Unit) the former and the TR (Tactical Response) team the latter, allow to retrieve effective parallelisms between the two shows. The Canadian police enforcement protocols and hierarchical schemata are necessarily different from those employed in Australia, the US, Italy, France, even if the show's configuration dictates some irrevocable watermarks. Consequently, given the formula, every country (and production) must adapt and modulate the contents under its internal institutional organisation to render a plausible version of the relocated final televised product.

Indeed, the commercialisation criteria leading the market tend to make TV products internationally usable. The *Flashpoint* TV series was the first Canadian show aired in prime time in the US since *Due South*, having the American network *CBS* acquired the right to air the televised content beyond border since 2008 (*Channel Canada announcement*, 2008). On the same path, formats may also be purchased by different producers within the same country to reboot its original narration otherwise. *19-2*, for instance, is whitefly in the swarm of TV seriality, where the original Francophone version (*19-2* [*Dixneuf-Deux*], Canada: *Télévision de Radio-Canada*, produced by *Société Radio-Canada*, 2011–2015) was purchased by *CTV* in 2012 and aired on *Bravo!* in its adapted Anglophone version (*Sphere Media Plus, Echo Media*, and *Bell Media* productions, 2014–2017), which did involve an actual remake of the whole television product, and not more simplistic (and cheaper) dubbing or subtitling procedures of the linguistic adaptation. Together with the mediatic formula, the police format interest regards its relationship with real-life legislative frameworks. Those workplace situations must be reproduced within typical environments, mostly connected to deductive and descriptive patterns. The linguistics of the dialogues emulate cop interviews as "highly regulated form[s] of discourse that is structured

# 3 The Linguistic and Cultural Environment of Canadian Television 101

around legislative requirements" (Heydon, 2005, p. 4) and information-acquisition schemata adhering to standardised and routine procedures pertaining to the police talk (ibid., p. 51; Olanderwarju, 2009).

The following chapters provide the details of the TV series involved in the analysis. The examination sieves, one by one, each show via its respective multimodal corpus to present the peculiarities of onscreen natural language and transmitted *legal communication*, intended as a combination of a "non-verbal semiotic system [...], and a linguistic aspect" used to "negotiate meaning" (Gibbons, 2003, p. 9) within functional situations reproducing actual criminal and investigative events.

## Notes

1. 'Medium.' The Cambridge Dictionary. https://dictionary.cambridge.org/dictionary/english/medium (accessed 10/03/2018).
2. This very acceptation of 'mono-modal' is more related to the field of multimediality than multimodality. Newspapers and radio appear constrained in their written texts or voice, accordingly. Those channels certainly are, instead, multimodal. The former displays images and diverse font sizes and colours along with salient articles carrying contents (graphic dimension). The latter uses all the para-verbal expressiveness shades that implement verbality (plus the alternation of radio-news programmes with other entertainment broadcasts and music forms of communication).
3. Marshall McLuhan Official Site. FAQ section, edited by Eric McLuhan. https://marshallmcluhan.com/common-questions/ (accessed 04/08/2018).
4. Ferdinand De Saussure died in 1913. Three years later, two of his devotees—the scholars Charles Bally and Albert Sechehaye—published the notes they had gathered during their Professor's *Course de linguististique générale* in the homonym volume. Also, the year of publication was meaningful, as they chose to release the volume exactly one hundred years after Franz Bopp's *On the Conjugation System of Sanskrit in Comparison with that of Greek, Latin, Persian and Germanic* [*Über das Konjugationssystem der Sanskritsprache in Vergleichung mit jenem der griechischen, lateinischen, persischen und germanischen Sprache*].

5. CBC—Radio Canada. "Our story". http://www.cbc.radio-canada.ca/en/explore/our-history/ (accessed 06/10/2018).
6. CBC Corporate Plan Summary, 2016–2017 to 2020–2021. http://www.cbc.radio-canada.ca/_files/cbcrc/documents/corporate-plan/corporate-plan-summary-2016-2017-2020-2021.pdf (accessed 06/11/2018).

# References

Allen, M. (Ed.). (2007). *Reading CSI: Crime TV Under the Microscope*. I.B. Tauris.

Arango, T. (30/11/2008). World Falls for American Media, Even If It Sours on America. *The New York Times* [Online]. Retrieved October 5, 2018, from https://www.nytimes.com/2008/12/01/business/media/01soft.html

Ayaß, R., & Gerhardt, C. (Eds.). (2012). *The Appropriation of Media in Everyday Life*. John Benjamins Publishing Company.

Baldry, A., & Thibault, P. J. (2006). *Multimodal Transcription and Text Analysis: A Multimedia Toolkit and Course Book*. Equinox.

Bargainnier, E. F. (1980). *The Gentle Art of Murder: the Detective Fiction of Agatha Christie*. University of Wisconsin Press.

Barthes, R. (1972). *Mythologies*. The Noonday Press. Trans. A. Lavers. [Original Title: *Mythlogies*, 1972]. Retrieved June 13, 2018, from http://faculty.georgetown.edu/irvinem/theory/Barthes-MythToday-excerpt.pdf

Base, R. E. (12/03/2012). Cable Television. *The Canadian Encyclopedia*. Retrieved June 11, 2018, from http://www.thecanadianencyclopedia.ca/en/article/cable-television/

Bateman, J. A. (2008). *Multimodality and Genre*. Palgrave Macmillan.

BCE. News Releases. (09/12/2006a). Bell Globemedia Completes Takeover Bid for CHUM Limited. Retrieved June 12, 2018, from http://www.bce.ca/news-and-media/releases/show/bell-globemedia-completes-takeover-bid-for-chum-limited

BCE. News Releases. (10/30/2006b). Bell Globemedia Completes Acquisition of All Outstanding Shares of CHUM Limited. Retrieved June 12, 2018, from http://www.bce.ca/news-and-media/releases/show/bell-globemedia-completes-acquisition-of-all-outstanding-shares-of-chum-limited

Beaty, B., & Sullivan, R. (2006). *Canadian Television Today*. University of Calgary Press.

Bednarek, M. (2010). *The Language of Fictional Television: Drama and Identity*. Continuum.

## 3 The Linguistic and Cultural Environment of Canadian Television  103

Bednarek, M. (2018). *Language and Television Series. A Linguistic Approach to TV Dialogue*. Cambridge University Press.

Bednarek, M. (2019). *Creating Dialogue for TV: Screenwriters Talk Television*. Routledge.

Beers-Fägersten, K. (Ed.). (2016). *Watching TV with a Linguist*. Syracuse University Press.

Bluem, A. W., & Manwell, R. (1967). *Television: The Creative Experience. A Survey on Anglo-American Progress*. New York Hastings House.

Bredin, M., Henderson, S., & Matheson, S. A. (2012). *Canadian Television: Text and Context*. Wilfrid Laurier University Press.

*British Communications Act*. (2003). Retrieved March 8, 2018, from https://www.legislation.gov.uk/ukpga/2003/21/contents

Cambridge Dictionary. https://dictionary.cambridge.org/

*Canadian Broadcasting Act*, S.C. 1991, c. 11. Government of Canada. Justice Law Website. Retrieved June 10, 2018, from http://laws-lois.justice.gc.ca/PDF/B-9.01.pdf

Canadian Radio-Television and Telecommunication Commission. (1994). CRTC Decision 94-281. Retrieved June 10, 2018, from https://crtc.gc.ca/eng/archive/1994/DB94-281.htm

Canadian Radio-Television and Telecommunication Commission. (2007). Broadcasting Decision CRTC 2007-165. Retrieved June 10, 2018, from https://crtc.gc.ca/eng/archive/2007/db2007-165.htm

Carroll, J. B. (Ed.). (1956). *Language, Though and Reality: Selected Writings of Benjamin Lee Whorf*. MIT Press.

*CBC* Corporate Plan Summary 2016–2017 to 2020–2021. Retrieved June 11, 2018, from http://www.cbc.radio-canada.ca/_files/cbcrc/documents/corporate-plan/corporate-plan-summary-2016-2017-2020-2021.pdf

*CBC Radio Canada*. Our Story. Retrieved June 10, 2018, from http://www.cbc.radio-canada.ca/en/explore/our-history/

Chandler, R. (1950). *The Simple Art of Murder*. The Curtis Publishing Company.

Collins, R. (1990). *Culture, Communication, and National Identity: The Case of Canadian Television*. University of Toronto Press.

Dance, F. E. X., & Larson, C. E. (1976). *The Functions of Human Communication: A Theoretical Approach*. Holt, Rinehart and Winston.

Davis, M. (2021). The TV and Movies Corpora. *International Journal of Corpus Linguistics, 26*(1), 10–37.

De Beaugrande, R.-A., & Dressler, W. U. (1994). *Introduzione alla Linguistica Testuale*. Il Mulino. [Original Title: *Einführunh in die Textlinguistik*, 1981].

De Saussure, F. (1959 [1916]). *Course de linguistique générale*. Grande Biblioteque Payot. Retrieved March 8, 2021, from https://monoskop.org/images/f/f1/Saussure_Ferdinand_de_Cours_de_linguistique_generale_Edition_critique_1997.pdf

Dorland, M., & Charland, M. R. (2002). *Law, Rhetoric and Irony in the Formation of Canadian Civil Culture*. University of Toronto Press.

Doyle, J. (07/28/2017). John Doyle: Finally the Canadian Classic Intelligence Has Come to Netflix. *The Globe and Mail*. Retrieved June 14, 2018, from https://www.theglobeandmail.com/arts/television/john-doyle-finally-the-canadian-classic-intelligence-has-com e-to-netflix/article35830637/

Fremeth, H. (02/24/2010). Television. *The Canadian Encyclopedia*. Retrieved June 11, 2018, from http://www.thecanadianencyclopedia.ca/en/article/television/

Gibbons, J. (2003). *Forensic Linguistics. An Intriduction to Language in the Justice System*. Blackwell Pub.

Gittins, S. (1999). *CTV: The Television Wars*. Stoddart.

Granata, P. (2015). *Ecologia dei media. Protagonisti, scuole, concetti chiave*. Franco Angeli Editore.

Halliday, M. A. K. (1978). *Language as Social Semiotic: The Social Interpretation of Language and Meaning*. Edward Arnold.

Halliday, M. A. K. (1994). *An Introduction to Functional Grammar*. Edward Arnold.

Halliday, M. A. K. (2001 [1990]). New Ways of Meaning: The Challenge to Applied Linguistics. In A. Fill & P. Mühlhäusler (Eds.), *The Ecolinguistics Reader: Language, Ecology and Environment* (pp. 175–202). Continuum.

Halliday, M. A. K. (2003). *On Language and Linguistics* (Collected Works) (Vol. 3). Equinox.

Halliday, M. A. K., & Hasan, R. (1976). *Cohesion in English*. Longman.

Halliday, M. A. K., & Matthiessen, C. M. I. M. (2004). *An Introduction to Functional Grammar*. Edward Arnold.

Heydon, G. (2005). *The Language of Police Interviewing: A Critical Analysis*. Palgrave Macmillan.

Hill, J., & Church-Gibson, P. (Eds.). (2000). *Film Studies. Critical Approaches*. Oxford University Press.

Hoskins, C., & McFayden, S. (1991). The US Competitive Advantage in the Global Television Market: Is It Sustainable in the New Broadcasting Environment? *Canadian Journal of Communication, 16*(2), 207–224. Retrieved October 5, 2018, from https://cjc-online.ca/index.php/journal/article/view/602/508

## 3 The Linguistic and Cultural Environment of Canadian Television 105

Hughes, B. (2017). *Investigating Formats: The Transferral and Translation of Televised Productions in Italy and England*. Cambridge Scholars Publishing.

Jacobs, J., & Peacock, S. (Eds.). (2013). *Television Aesthetics and Style*. Bloomsbury Academic.

Jenner, M. (2016). *American TV Detective Dramas: Serial Investigation*. Palgrave Macmillan.

Kellner, D. (1995). *Media Culture: Cultural Studies, Identity and Politics Between the Modern and the Postmodern*. Routledge.

Kozloff, S. (2000). *Overhearing Film Dialogue*. University of California Press.

Kress, G., & van Leeuwen, T. (1996). *Reading Images: The Grammar of Visual Design*. Routledge.

Kuhn, R. (2007). *Politics and the Media in Britain*. Palgrave Macmillan.

Lamberti, E. (2012). *Marshall McLuhan's Mosaic: Probing the Literary Origins of Media Studies*. University of Toronto Press.

Lederman, M. (04/13/2013). How Canada Is Becoming the Sci-Fi Nation. *The Globe and Mail*. Retrieved June 14, 2018, from https://www.theglobeandmail.com/arts/television/how-canada-is-becoming-the-sci-fi-nation/article11157191/

Levinson, P. (1988). *Mind at Large: Knowing in the Technological Age*. JAI Press.

Levinson, P. (1997). *The Soft Edge. A Natural History and Future of Information Revolution*. Routledge.

McClausand, T. (02/25/2009). Canada Radio-Television and Telecommunication Commission. *Mapleleafweb*. Retrieved June 10, 2018, from https://www.mapleleafweb.com/features/canada-radio-television-and-telecommunications-commission.html

McLuhan, M. (1964). *Understanding Media. The Extensions of Man*. McGraw-Hill. Retrieved October 4, 2018, from http://robynbacken.com/text/nw_research.pdf

McLuhan, M. (1967; 2001). *Medium Is the Massage: An Inventory on Effects*. Gingko Press Inc.

McLuhan Official Site. FAQ Section. Ed. E. McLuhan. Retrieved April 8, 2018., from https://marshallmcluhan.com/common-questions/

McPhail, B. (1986). The Canadian Content Regulations and the Canadian Charter of Rights and Freedom. *Canadian Journal of Communication, 12*, 41–55. Retrieved June 10, 2018, from https://www.cjc-online.ca/index.php/journal/article/view/369/275

McQuail, D. (2010 [1983]). *Mass Communication Theory*. SAGE Pubns Ltd.

Nelson, R. (2007). *State of Play: Contemporary 'High-End' TV Drama*. Manchester University Press.

Newcomb, H. (Ed.). (2007). *Television. The Critical View*. Oxford University Press.

Ogden, C. K., & Richards, I. A. (2013 [1923]). *The Meaning of Meaning: A Study of the Influence of Language upon Thought and of the Science of Symbols*. Martino Fine Books.

Olandewarju, F. R. (2009). *Forensic Linguistics. An Introduction to the Study of Language and the Laws*. Lincom Europa.

Ong, W. J. (1962). *The Barbarian Within and Other Fugitive Essays and Studies*. Macmillan.

Ong, W. J. (1986). *Hopkins, the Self, and God*. University of Toronto Press.

Piazza, R., Bednarek, M., & Rossi, F. (Eds.). (2011). *Telecinematic Discourse. Approaches to the Language of Films and Television Series*. John Benjamins Publishing Company.

Plummer, K. (06/30/2012). Historicist: Post-Mortem of a Pay-TV Channel. The Brief Life of of C Channel Canada, Canada's Arts and Culture Pay-TV Service. *Torontoist*. Retrieved June 11, 2018, from https://torontoist.com/2012/06/historicist-post-mortem-of-a-pay-tv-channel/

Postman, N. (1970). The Reformed English Curriculum. In A. C. Eurich (Ed.), *High-School 1980: The Shape of the Future in American Secondary Education* (pp. 160–168). Pitman.

Richardson, K. (2010). *Television Dramatic Dialogue. A Sociolinguistic Study*. Oxford University Press.

Ricoeur, P. (1997). *Il conflitto delle interpretazioni*. Jaca Books. Trans. R. Balzarotti, F. Botturi, & G. Colombo. [Original Title: *Le Conflict de Interprétations. Essais d'Herménetique, I*, 1969].

Royce, T. D. (2007). Intersemiotic Complementarity: A Framework for Multimodal Discourse Analysis. In T. D. Royce & W. L. Bowcher (Eds.), *New Directions in the Analysis of Multimodal Discourse* (pp. 63–110). Lawrence Erlbaum Associates.

Sparks, Richard. (1992). *Television and the Drama of Crime. Moral Tales and the Place of Crime in Public Life*. Open University Press.

Sparks, Robert. (1992). 'Delivering the Male': Sports, Canadian Television, and the Making of TSN. *Canadian Journal of Communication, 17*(3), 319–342. Retrieved June 11, 2018, from https://cjc-online.ca/index.php/journal/article/view/678/584

## 3 The Linguistic and Cultural Environment of Canadian Television

Stelter, B. (05/03/2011). Ownership of TV Sets Falls in the US. *The New York Times* [Online]. Retrieved October 5, 2018, from https://www.nytimes.com/2011/05/03/business/media/03television.html

Straw, W. (2002). Dilemmas of Definition. In J. Nix & J. Sloniowski (Eds.), *Slippery Pastimes: Reading the Popular in Canadian Culture* (pp. 95–108). Wilfred Laurier University Press.

Thompson, J. (1995). *The Media and Modernity*. Polity Press.

Thompson, R. J. (2000). *The Story of Viewers for Quality Television. From Grassroots to Prime Time*. University of Syracuse.

Thomson, D. (2016). *Television: A Bibliography*. Thames and Hudson.

Tulloch, J. (2000). *Watching Television Audiences. Cultural Theories and Methods*. Arnold.

Wong, T. (12/24/2017). Who Says Canadian TV Is Dead? 2017 Was the Best Year Ever for Drama. *The Star*. Retrieved June 14, 2018, from https://www.thestar.com/entertainment/television/2017/12/24/who-says-canadian-tv-is-dead-2017-was-best-year-ever-for-drama.html

Wong, T. (06/07/2018). Klingos in Toronto? Get Set for the Pinewood Studios Tour. *The Star*. Retrieved June 11, 2018, from https://www.thestar.com/entertainment/television/2018/06/07/ctv-unveils-their-fall-programming-slate-for-2018.html

Yeo, D. (01/03/2018). Canadian TV Crime Drama. Cardinal Returns to Its Elements. *The Star*. Retrieved June 14, 2018, from https://www.thestar.com/entertainment/television/2018/01/03/canadian-tv-crime-drama-cardinal-returns-to-its-elements.html

# 4

# *Flashpoint* as in-Group Psychological and Action Narrative

When dealing with crime, different legal codes accordingly punishing diverse degrees of violations, and numerous types of related perpetrators correspond to many divisions of law enforcement areas (Dorland & Charland, 2002; Olandewarju, 2009; Brundson, 2010; Marmor, 2014). Nonetheless, large amounts of police force sectors exist, and television interests are well focused on the utter rendition of fascinating ones from the commodification perspective (Collins, 1990; O'Toole, 1994; Gittins, 1999; Creeber, 2006; Allen, 2007). Thus, crime drama genres operate at different narrative levels shifting from pure procedural aims to conveying of the catchy contents ascribable to cinematic action environments.

The case of the *Flashpoint* TV series thematic target well fits the action mentioned here. Its domain describes high-risk tasks to be solved by a specialised team of agents identified as one of the Strategic Response Units (SRUs) in Toronto, intervening in a whatsoever illegal situation that involves extreme contingencies, which cannot be properly handled by standard corps. Indeed, the agents of SRU are presented as officers who have received special training specifically designed to face critical situations. On the silver thread of the actual Toronto Police Service Emergency Task Force (ETF)—the Canadian equivalent of US

© The Author(s), under exclusive license to Springer Nature Switzerland AG 2021    **109**
F. P. Gentile, *Corpora, Corpses and Corps*,
https://doi.org/10.1007/978-3-030-78276-4_4

SWAT—they are equipped with tactical weapons and assembled into organised squads. Every member is identifiable because of his/her fixed role (e.g. team leader; negotiator; sniper; assaulters; bomb technician). Emulating actual ETF teams, the fictionalised *Flashpoint* version collocates the goup[1] inside an enormous headquarter (inclusive of briefing rooms, training areas, shooting range and garages to host special vehicles). Inside that fortress, officers wait for their calls, signalled via noisy alarms and loudspeaker dispatcher communications, to leave the place and travel the city towards the many locations requesting their presence.

Its eloquent title renders the thematic intent of the series observed here.

The figurative sense of 'flashpoint' as 'moment of truth' has landed natural language uses from a pre-dated sectorial origin belonging to Specialised Discourse. In physics, it indicates the point of explosion of an element when temperatures cause vapours to burn. Hence, the term secondarily permeated police language jargons to denote the very place where violence occurs, indicating another figurative (thus neologisation via metaphoric resemantisation) word for 'crisis'. Despite subtextual storylines evolving through the seasons for coherence reasons (also about characters' lives off-workplace to enrich them with *real-life* plausibility), the product is a 'series' because of its primary concern with singular episode-oriented developments. Such targets also support cinematically communicative modalities that tend to operate via expressive patterns that mould the linguistics and the language of the recount using intense rhythmic formulations that integrate verbal elements with the impressive salience of the visual channel (Kress & van Leeuwen, 1996; van Leeuwen, 2004; Adolphs & Carter, 2013).

## The Broadcast

The interest in the examination of *Flashpoint* derives from its thematic value. Nevertheless, it is also related to the productive path structuring the series and defining its existence. In truth, the project started in 2005 as part of a *CTV* initiative that exhorted film industry professionals to collaborate. People had to submit their scripts for the making of a two hours-length movie whose actual title should have been either *Sniper* or

## 4 *Flashpoint* as in-Group Psychological and Action... 111

*Critical Incident*, eventually preferring this latter option (Pender, 2007). The product was confirmed in 2007 thanks it its success and became a series entitled *Flashpoint*. The Canadian Companies *Pink Sky Entertainment* and *Avamar Entertainment* produced the series. Given the international demand, however, also *CTV Television Network* and the US *CBS Television Studios* participated in the co-production, establishing a "significant achievement for *CTV*'s development team and Canada's independent production community", said Susanne Boyce, former President Creative, Content and Channel, *CTV* Inc. (Wild, 2008). Indeed, along with Canadian producers, the resonance of *Flashpoint* beyond the border urged the North American broadcaster to purchase the rights to air the series on *CBS* too, in simulcast throughout the entire first season (2008, then only the fourth one in 2011 maintained the same criterion, while seasons 2, 3 and 5 did not), making the product the first in *CTV* history to be transmitted in prime time contemporaneously in Canada and US since *Due South—CTV* (Can.), *CBS*, (US), 1994–1999— (ibid.). In addition to that, the *Flashpoint* TV series seems to be the herald of a strong political and ideological connotation as well:

> The only non-Canadian actor that has ever been on *Flashpoint* is Amy Jo and she's actually in the process of getting her citizenship. She was living in Montreal when we cast her so it's a point of pride that we bring so many Canadian actors back up form Hollywood to guest star on *Flashpoint*. (Mark Ellis, interview; Barr, 2010)

TV investments must, then, respond to a crucial spirit of Canadianness. Consequently, the series results as a *pure* product whose North American idiosyncrasies derive from unclear relationships with United States politics. Economic policies have been wiped out through drastic erasure phenomena (as already described in Chap. 3). The TV sale does not solely include professionals (onscreen and behind cameras) from no other place than the Canadian territory. Indeed, it is one of the few to advertise it as an added value to be counterpoised to US hybrids. This nationalistic climate is without doubt influenced by real antagonisms against the Southern film industry located in Hollywood. Also, with reference to the cross-border US-to-Vancouver situation in the film industry (see Chaps.

## 112      F. P. Gentile

3 and 5), the ideological charge seems fitting, yet not perfectly coherent (Canadian regulations allow such dynamics of related financial incomings, and no *super partes* authorities impose them).

Nonetheless, the defect of form appears even more evident, given the overtly international distribution target. *Flashpoint* producers launched the said simulcast formula and then protracted it worldwide (*Alchemy Television* distributed the series in North America; *Tele München Group* sold it outside the continent). Still, suppose that those considerations could be shared on a superficial level. As stated by Mark Ellis himself, police units in Toronto operate differently from SWAT (ibid.). Yet, that dissimilarity should be mirrored coherently via many cinematic choices (including cast hirings) to build up some legitimate TV *payback*. Considering all the characters loitering Toronto—and other Canada's cinematographic poles—in LA, Chicago, New York and different US police department uniforms, the merchandising of a candidly Canadian product that could *invade* North America's televisions with Torontonians would only be fair.

## The *Flashpoint* Visual Narrative

Based on the "Canadian style" (Treble, 2013) rendition of its national identity, the *Flashpoint* corps is expressly inspired by real units intervening in tangible high-risk situations. It cannot be *just* as good fictionalisations of urban police divisions:

> "They are not a team that goes in first and asks questions later, which is how a lot of SWAT teams have been criticized", says Ellis. "The ETF is trained to physiologically profile the subject, to figure out what's brought them in this place, to see if they can negotiate them out safely and, at the same time, come up with a tactical plan should that fail." (Ibid.)

Consequently, despite the ubiquitous cinematic needs to mould dialogues and narrations through catchy angles only finalised at the success of the onscreen transmission, the monitored communicative events presented are not forged nor far-fetched. Plot-derived developments are

## 4 *Flashpoint* as in-Group Psychological and Action... 113

created after thorough consultations with—and interviews to—ETF agents. Of all, the pilot episode, *Scorpio* (*CTV*, July 11, 2008), calques the killing of Sugston Anthony Brookes—a 45-year-old hostage-taker shot by a tactical sniper outside Toronto Union Station on August 25, 2004 (Treble, 2008; see also Freeze et al., 2018; *CBC News*, September 17, 2004). Surprisingly enough, the series maintained the same crime scene location and the visual narration proposed by newspaper reporters and photographers at the time of the attack.

In addition to that, the actual representation of stories seems peculiar here as well. An intense *visual* salience (Kress & van Leeuwen, 1996; O'Halloran, 2004; Kress, 2010; Bednarek, 2010; Richardson, 2010)— emblematic of the medium observed here—recounts the *Flashpoint* Toronto prominence.

Nonetheless, observing the theme of the product examined here, one would notice an exciting discontinuity in narrative perspectives between the theme song and episodes. The 30"-length theme of the TV series (Fig. 4.1) is supposed to generally occur during a non-fixed moment between 5'–10' of the instalment, once the narrative context has been well premised (yet, it sporadically occurs even later in season 3, between 10'–15'). The rapid alternation of frames-per-second (the figure does not include all the frames) starts from the mute red and blue glittering of police sirens to signal the Crime Drama aim. Then, the screen gets blurred by a dazzling central halo surrounded by a dark smoky foreground. An alphanumeric cypher appears as if spectators were focusing on some indistinct object through a gunsight supported by angle sensors, which quickly decipher the code and let the 'FLASHPOINT' wording emerge (Fig. 3.1, frames 2–6).

The theme lists some of the series main characters in-action, accompanied by respective actors' names, to conclude the sum up via a slower collective sequence showing the entire geared-up team walking towards the viewer (frames 21–23).

Like an army of epic warriors, those characters majestically stride through a low and ample labyrinth of corridors in only a few milliseconds. Camera techniques cut their feet from the shots but include the ceiling—emphasising the oppressing horizontal dimension. The corps connotatively emerge from the darkness positively and gloriously, passing

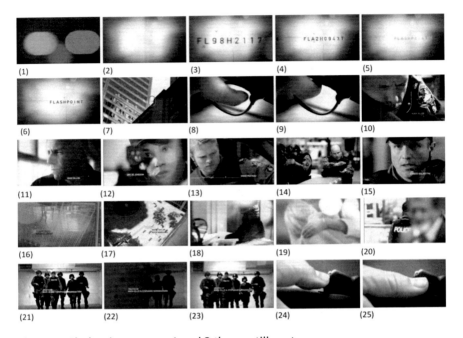

**Fig. 4.1** *Flashpoint*, seasons 1 and 2 theme still captures

through neon flickering lights and shadows (alternating out of focus to high-resolution frames). This 'help is on the way' metaphor is corroborated utilising the team's equipment visual impact.

Utterly dissimilar to ordinary cops in their standard blue shirts, the *Flashpoint* unit wears dull grey uniforms that remark the thick black of the bulletproof vests, weapons and kit bags supplying the commando with even more sensationalism. Police agents usually appear onscreen in their stereotypical blue shirt and black trousers uniform. They are provided with light equipment, mostly a handgun, baton, and a seldom worn easy-on bulletproof jacket. SRU, instead, only leaves headquarter after a long dressing rite. Putting on a solid vest and placing the gun in its thigh holster are just the first steps in the team's routine. The entire gear also includes heavy sniper rifles, machine guns, rams, bombs and grenades of various types, colossal shields and many other tools, turning those urban squads into some as strong as deadly legendary heroes.

## 4 *Flashpoint* as in-Group Psychological and Action...    115

Therefore, along with sirens, more weaponry hints disseminated in the theme reveal other bits of information about the series, like the sharp-shooter on the roof (frame 7, circled in red), or the detail of Ed's index finger checking its sensibility against the trigger (frames 8, 9) and the thumb removing the safety from the rifle, to get himself ready to shoot (frames 24, 25). The first frames of the theme establish the genre of the broadcast. The visual salience on the index and thumb (like the cover of a book) opens and closes the interlude of a narration where things happen amid superior eyes both threatening and protecting their targets. Unstoppable boots treading over shards, and weapons displayed as if they were inorganic prostheses of human limbs eventually determine the seriousness of the dangers in a *warlike* city.

The *Flashpoint* theme song duration equals the one of *19-2* (the interlude of *Motive* only lasts 3" and consists in the sole title CGI wording, thus is not considered here; see Chap. 5). However, a similar weaponry and gloomy violence display seem lessened in the Montreal product via the contrast with the 'deer' frame and the introspective focus on Nick while sitting on the locker-room bench. Conversely, Toronto does not know any wilderness, and the urban jungle is only preyed on by terrorists, whose TV viewers require the decimation. If the Anglophone rural-style Montreal deals with crimes ranging from the worst to the funniest, and Vancouver sketches itself like a murderous and fashion place, Toronto reveals—in *Flashpoint*—the most terrific sides of Canada's megacity. Yet, given the importance of narrating the urban site—since the political, social and ideological connotations to be related to choosing the fittest environment for specific cinematic goals (O'Halloran, 2004)—it is worth noting that explicit references to Toronto are disseminated all over the show. Significant details are retrievable within the TV series instalments, even in lower percentages in season 1 than in the second and—even more—third ones. The absence streak of reference to the city of Toronto dominated the *Flashpoint* theme song between 2008 and 2009—season 1—although it was broken in 2010 when the TV series presentation was changed. Nonetheless, nothing more than a single *non-iconic* (it does not trigger Toronto's immediate visual identification) frame of the skyline was inserted.

Along with the display of Metropolitan Toronto Police tags and logos over RMPs, flags and bags, spectators are delivered mentions of actual newspapers, like the *Toronto Star* or the purely fictional *Toronto Interpreter*, still rare toponym occurrences and, most importantly, emblematic panoramas of the city. 2008 and 2009 broadcasts demonstrate a growing display of recognisable urban areas *during* the transmissions. Indeed, suppose the theme song introduction does not significantly support imaging the city during the series presentation. In that case, the instalment narrations in seasons 1 and 2 are enriched with emblematic urban shots contextualising the event settings. However, in line with the filming strategy adopted in the first couple of seasons, 2010 instalments of *Flashpoint* remain highly evocative of Toronto's fabric.

Moreover, they implement the recognisability of the megacity hosting the show in the theme song. There, ten in thirteen episodes directly *open* via the contextualising overlook on Toronto. They employ some aerial filming strategies (Fig. 4.2), imaging famous downtown views, including *CN Tower* shots already present in seasons 1 and 2, emphatically taken from any possible angle and at different hours during the day.

This choice is crucial in terms of identifiability. As per the *CN Tower*, consistent part of the *Flashpoint* TV series was shot downtown, where massive tourist fluxes move all over the year. Other places outside the city

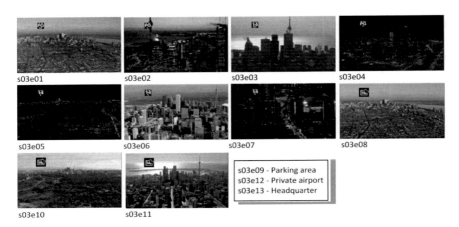

**Fig. 4.2** *Flashpoint*, season 3 episodes' opening frames

core involve isolated parking areas, private airports (see s03e09, 12), suburbs or close towns, and SRU Headquarter (see s03e13). This latter is often shown in its insides, rather than on the external façades or building structure (contrarily, carefully presented in s01e01, in the very beginning of the episode).

## The *Flashpoint Corpus* Structure

The *Flashpoint* product has an immense array of characterising expressive aspects deployed for the utter assemblage of such a television format, although the sole TV viewing of series instalments could not produce any valuable considerations. Thus, all the collectable pieces of information related to and deriving from *Flashpoint* demand their assimilation within a unique nucleus that would allow an all-inclusive examination. The said multimodal data are gathered into the *Flashpoint Corpus*. Here, they are observed through diverse lenses, whose focuses range from *purely* linguistic to other extra-linguistic ones on non-verbal and para-verbal communication aspects. Then, these elements are related to the synthetic process combining the linguistics of performed dialogues with speech peculiarities (e.g., rhythm and prosody), multidimensional language patterns (co-occurrence of mimics, gestures-in-talk, body language, proxemics), and cinematic techniques enhancing or funnelling narrative comprehensions (via soundtracks, ambient noises, visual salience and camera movements).

Nonetheless, the study does not target the framing of *one* precise code disregarding the others. Consequently, the goal of the present investigation—finalised at revealing the most significant expressive patterns of the product and the genre—is reckoned to be both descriptive and analytical. It proffers *all* the substantial and relevant (also in terms of statistical occurrence) communicative situations possibly comprehensive of TV series narrative modalities and interactive patterns including diverse codes, registers and channels, coherently with the recounting modes presupposed by media and in adherence to the multidisciplinary approach enounced in Chap. 2.

The decision to limit the contents to be evaluated to those retrieved in seasons 1, 2 and 3 of the series is strictly related to the motivations setting the boundaries of the *Motive Corpus* (see Chap. 5) and the *19-2 Corpus* (see Chap. 6) as well. On the one hand, the *Flashpoint* series has required a narrow range of analysis since possible coherence failures and transmission alterations potentially rising after season 3. Indeed, born as *CTV* creation, the product maintained its original broadcaster until 2011 (beginning of season 4) when *CTV* passed to *Bell Media* (see Chap. 3). The change implied many reasonable broadcasting policy modifications in both its fourth and fifth seasons (*Flashpoint* is the longer-lasting production among the three discussed in this survey), similar to the *19-2* case. Some other US counterparts also carried out a similar path to the one covered by Canadian broadcasters. *CBS Paramount Television* (2008–2009) became *CBS Television Studios* from 2009 to 2011 and then the larger *CBS Television Distribution* (2012–present), transmitting *Flashpoint* in North America concurrently with *Ion Television*.

On the other hand, like *Motive*, the number of episodes-per-season originates from other mismatches. If *19-2* scheduled ten instalments for each annual broadcast, and *Motive* programmed 13 (see Chaps. 5 and 6), *Flashpoint* did something more peculiar by arranging several shows in odd seasons (13 episodes in seasons 1, 3, 5), which was different from those aired in even seasons (18 episodes in seasons 2, 4), through a regular alternation. In light of that, the eventual fragmentation of the series and the exclusion of five random instalments is something that could not happen. This eventuality would generate bias aplenty (in terms of linguistic relevance, communication salience, selection criteria about the episodes to be erased from the corpus) and the broadcasting gaps characterising the *Flashpoint* series (discussed later). Therefore, premising that the thematically and communicatively coherent macro-structure of the season is a dominant discriminant compared to episodical narrations, the building of the *Flashpoint Corpus* has solely included the first three annual broadcasts (2008–2010), reckoning the instalment count discrepancy as secondary and not determining.

Likewise, in the other cases treated in Chaps. 4 and 5, the corpus assemblage required the perusal of circa 1804 minutes of transmission and ~210,892 spoken words to be transcribed into written dialogues (for works on spoken and written copora see Aijmer & Stenström, 2004; Baldry & Thibault, 2006; Adolphs & Carter, 2013; Rühleman, 2013) for

## 4 *Flashpoint* as in-Group Psychological and Action... 119

the actual parsing and assessment of its data. Once the collection of materials was terminated, the *Flashpoint Corpus* was POS-tagged—automated process—as required by praxis in this study (Example 4):

***Example 4 Flashpoint Corpus, Flashpoint, s02e02, min. 00:06:26–07:09***

| | |
|---|---|
| Irina: | [DT]This [VBZ]is [RB]not [JJ]right |
| Misha: | [VBZ]Is [PRP]it [JJ]right [IN]that [PRP$]your [NN]boy [VBZ]has [DT]no [NN]mama [DT]this [VBZ]is [WRB]why [PRP]you [VBP]do [DT]this [UH]Yes [IN]for [NNP]Leo |
| Irina: | [UH]Yes [IN]of [NN]course [CC]but |
| Misha: | [PRP]They [VBP]have [DT]a [NN]lot [PRP]We [VBP]take [DT]a [JJ]tiny [NN]bit [IN]With [PRP$]your [NN]share [PRP]you [VBP]can [VB]go [NN]home [VB]get [PRP$]your [NN]boy [VB]bring [PRP]him [RB]back [NNP]Irinushka [VB]look [IN]at [PRP]me [PRP]I [VBP]want [PRP]you [TO]to [VB]meet [PRP]him [JJS]very [JJ]much [PRP]I [VBP]know [PRP]he[VBZ]'s beautiful [JJR]like [PRP$]his [NN]mama [DT]a [NN]child [VBZ]is [DT]the [JJS]most [JJ]beautiful [NN]thing [IN]in [DT]the [NN]world [VBP]Am [PRP]I [JJ]right [JJ]Good [JJ]Good [NN]girl |

Nonetheless, it is now clear that grammatical labels attributed to single words are of no use to this study if considered alone, mainlybecause what one observes here is not a written text by its right. Indeed, similar texts of the spoken-to-written kind, deriving from transcription activities, tend to convey extra-linguistic meanings, which cannot be obtained just by syntactic readings of reported speeches. Therefore, part-of-speech specifications represent some auxiliary codes to be integrated into the broader compass of multimodal annotations. These further specifications include some already mentioned data about non-verbal features (e.g., tone, rhythm and prosody) and para-verbal aspects (e.g., visuals, music, gestures, filming techniques), which are typical of actual contexts of communication (Example 4.1):

**120**    **F. P. Gentile**

**Example 4.1 Flashpoint Corpus, Flashpoint, s02e02, min. 00:06:26–07:09**

Irina:     ((Russian accent Shakes head and speaks emotionally)) [DT]This [VBZ]is [RB]not^ [JJ]right↓

Misha:     ((Marked Russian accent)) [VBZ]Is [PRP]it [JJ]right [IN]that [PRP$]your [NN]bo:y [VBZ]has [DT]no [NN]mama^ (..) ((Camera shot moves onto Irina, then back to Misha)) [DT]this [VBZ]is [WRB]why[PRP]you [VBP]do [DT]this^=[UH]Yes (3') [IN]for [NNP]Leo

Irina:     [UH]Yes [IN]of [NN]course [CC]but-

Misha:     /[PRP]They [VBP]ha*ve [DT]a [NN]lo::t (..) ((Smirks)) [PRP]We [VBP]take [DT]a [JJ]tiny^ [NN]bi:t (..) ((Turns serious again)) [IN]With [PRP$]your [NN]share [PRP]you [VBP]can [VB]go [NN]home (.) [VB]get [PRP$]your [NN]bo:y=[VB]bring [PRP]him [RB]ba:c- (h) [NNP]Irinushka [VB]look [IN]at [PRP]me (..) [PRP]I [VBP]want [TO]to [VB]meet [PRP]him [JJS]very[JJ]much (3') [PRP]°I°⇒ ((maintaining the same whispered tone until the end of his speech)) [VBP]know [PRP]he[VBZ]'s bea:utiful[JJR]like [PRP$]his [NN]mama (..) ((Irina breathes, then hints a smile)) [DT]a [NN]child [VBZ]is [DT]the [JJS]most [JJ]beautiful [NN]thing [IN]in [DT]the [NN]world (..) [VBP]Am [PRP]I [JJ]right^ (..) ((She nods)) [JJ]Good (..) [JJ]Good [NN]gi:rl

Along with culture-bound names, Irina and Misha—which, however, would not mean anything per se in the multicultural Canadian territory— comments inserted in double brackets at the beginning of the reported dialogue signal the marked Russian accents of the speakers. A preliminary annotated observation of the exchange thus already adds some information useful to the reader to understand that those speakers are possibly migrants. Nonetheless, said feature does not derive from any misspellings or mispronunciations. Conversely, it is only associable with recognisable prosodic flows that would not be noted by linguistic examiners if not (in *some* cases) operating through a phonological transcription of the words composing the dialogue. As for the prosody, essential bits of information omitted by

## 4 *Flashpoint* as in-Group Psychological and Action... 121

POS tagging procedures circumvent the need for descriptive approaches to understanding the actual context, where any iteration occurs. Besides the deduction about the two characters being foreigners, one could only see the exchange's emotional nature after having witnessed it in person. Should such a contingency be impossible, the unique data conveying similar details would once more be the transcriber's comments (multimodal tag conventions follow Heydon, 2005).[2] Those expedients are adopted here to signal the woman speaking via a touched tone, then underlining the pauses alternated to the elocution pace, facial mimics—where smiles quickly turn into smirks and then into serious expressions—and whispered utterances. All these traits happen to be emphasised by camera movements and shooting strategies. Even here, however, the written report of extra-linguistic pieces of visual information could fail to transmit the quintessential aim of televised communicative intents.

The mentioned characteristics referring to the reported dialogue shall, then, submit to a multimodal analysis, which would be inclusive of all the contemplated communicative dimensions within a single examination (Table 4.1).

Every separation of sight data from linguistic features, useful information from emotional connotations, camera techniques from elocution rhythm would only produce a partial result incapable of transmitting a complete interpretation of the scenes. For example, if the annotation procedure renders Irina's emotional tone, her head movements shaking in denial associated with a close-up camera position pressing her to communicate even more. The atmosphere is of anxiety. Irina instead seems to be very worried about something possibly linked to her interlocutor's proposal (one could not know that yet). Her contrite expression is implemented by scared mimics determined by a motionless (almost petrified) look. Her disclosed lips are protruded downwards, and there is prominent muscular tension in the lower part of her visage and neck (min. 00:06:26). The line "<u>This</u> is not^ right↓" emits an enunciation with an initial flat tone that emphasises the grammatical determiner (<u>this</u>). However, this latter tends to increase in terms of elocutionary strength via a slight pitch raise on the negation (not^) to suddenly drop on the 'judgemental attitude' adjective (right↓). Such considerations funnel the idea of a dialogue on something either non-ethical, illegal or opposite to the woman's opinion and still originating massive concern in her mind.

## 122  F. P. Gentile

**Table 4.1** *Flashpoint*, s02e02. Multimodal annotation aligned with frames

| Frame/Min | Visual image | Kinesic action | Soundtrack | PhasesMetafunctions |
|---|---|---|---|---|
| 00:06:26 | MovA; CP: Shacky, CLU-OSS; VS> P: M; W; Ph; | Movt: Participant #1 shakes head; Tempo: Fast; | ST: Pressing rhythm; | A single phase setting the context emphasised by characters' emotional and whispered tone; EXP: Room + actors INT: viewer positioned very close (the entire dialogue is made of CLU shots), listening carefully and following characters' movements and gestures. The spectators' position changes from OSS to SV to highlight characters' facial expressions TEX: Single main phase. Narration slant: 1. convincing speech; 2. emotional connotation; 3. participant #2 takes participant #1 to cooperate despite not being sure; |
| | CP: CLU-SV; VS> P: M; | Movt: Participant #2 talks, Part. #1 shakes head; | ST: none; | |
| 00:06:35 | CLU-OSS; VS> P: M; W; | Movt: Participant #1 head mov. And facial expr.; | ST: Background pressing wind instruments; | |
| | CLU-SV; VS> P: M; | Movt: Participant #2 facial mimics; | ≈ | |
| | CLU-BV; VS> P: M; W; | Movt: Participant #1 hand mov., Part. #1 cries; | ≈ | |
| 00:06:56 | ≈ | ≈ | ≈ | |

### Dialogue

Irina: ((Russian accent Shakes head and speaks emotionally)) [DT]This [VBZ]is [RB] not^ [JJ]right↓

Misha: ((Marked Russian accent)) [VBZ]Is [PRP]it [JJ]right [IN]that [PRP$]your [NN] bo:y [VBZ]has [DT]no [NN]mama^ (..) ((Camera shot moves onto Irina, then back to Misha)) [DT]This [VBZ]is [WRB]why[PRP]you [VBP]do [DT]this^=[UH]Yes (3') [IN] for [NNP]Leo

Irina: [UH]Yes [IN]of [NN]course [CC]but-

Misha: /[PRP]They [VBP]ha*ve [DT]a [NN]lo::t (..) ((Smirks)) [PRP]We [VBP]take [DT]a [JJ]tiny^ [NN]bi:t (..) ((Turns serious again)) [IN]With [PRP$]your [NN]share [PRP]you [VBP]can [VB]go [NN]home (.) [VB]get [PRP$]your [NN]bo:y=[VB]bring [PRP]him [RB]ba:c- (h) [NNP]Irinushka [VB]look [IN]at [PRP]me (..) [PRP]I [VBP]want [TO]to [VB]meet [PRP]him [JJS]very[JJ]much (3') [PRP]°I°⇒ ((maintaining the same whispered tone until the end of his speech)) [VBP]know [PRP]he[VBZ]'s bea:utiful[JJR]like [PRP$]his [NN]mama (..) ((Irina breathes, then hints a smile)) [DT] a [NN]child [VBZ]is [DT]the [JJS]most [JJ]beautiful [NN]thing [IN]in [DT]the [NN] world (..) [VBP]Am [PRP]I [JJ]right^ (..) ((She nods)) [JJ]Good (..) [JJ]Good [NN]gi:rl

## 4 *Flashpoint* as in-Group Psychological and Action... 123

In the example, Misha is more self-confident than Irina. He, being aware of the communicative issues, conversely, behaves through a convincing attitude urging the woman to answer as he likes. The man's elocution rhythm is very straightforward, ignoring grammatical pauses where punctuation is supposed to occur, then stopping in some other parts of his speech to highlight the value of similar silences. At the end of Misha's first line ("This is <u>why</u> you do this^=Yes (3') for Leo"), he stresses the 'why' to put more emphasis on the motivations that have brought them to such a conversation, putting himself in a dominant position compared to the woman. The latching between "this" (whose pitch raise presupposes the presence of an exclamation mark) and "yes", not respecting punctuation norms, involves Misha's rhetoric strategies to guide Irina to experience guilt, without conceding her any time to reflect and answer. The following pause (3'), indeed, occurs right after the "yes", since once he has planted the seed of remorse, the man makes sure to let it blossom before persisting: "for Leo".

On a Textual Linguistics level (see De Beaugrande & Dressler, 1994 for details on the discipline), the woman's subdued role (see Simpson & Mayr, 2009) is not allowed any balking reply (her adversative clause is hushed by the man's interruption). It translates itself into the overwhelming preponderance of Misha's speech compared to hers. The man's discourse is full of 'affect' and 'appreciation' (Martin & White, 2005)[3] adjectives (from the reductive "a tiny^ bi:t" to the overuse of superlatives like "<u>very</u> much", "most bea:<u>utiful</u>" emphasised by empty pauses or syllable lengthening; plus the "Irinushka" nickname) since he knows the emotional ground of his words is the best key to crack Irina's mind and urge her to do as she is told. The narration of the man's speech proposes the same visual salience dedicated to the female character.

Visually, several close-up shots draw spectators' attention to Misha's facial mimics (smirks and serious expressions, alternated between pitching rises and whispered tones) and gestures. The very moment in which Misha holds Irina's face in his hands, he sees he has subjugated her, thus opts for a rewarding strategy as she nods a backchannel to his phatic question "Am I right^" (hence, "Good (..) Good gi:rl"). Two relevant musical accompaniments escort the entire sequence. The first involves the ending of the previous narration terminated into the observed scene.

The second one, adhering to both the gravity of the proposal and the just concluded dialogue, introduces a wind instrument pressing tone on the wake of its precedent soundtrack (besides a brief moment of silence determining the interval between the first and the second narration; see min. 00:06:28) implementing tension.

As anticipated, a mere linguistic (verbal) examination of naturally multilayered communicative events (though the awareness of TV contents being constructed and construed ad hoc) could never reach the interactive pattern descriptive completion. The model allows different individuals to share ideas and converse intransparent and cooperative ways. Therefore, the following paragraphs propose a multimodal study of the *Flashpoint* major communicative and expressive trends.

## Communication in the *Flashpoint* TV Series

The *Flashpoint* TV series is an interesting formula to be analysed, also in consideration of its main expressive patterns characterising the discourses adopted by its creators (§ Appendix) to convey plot-related contents fascinating spectators.

Like *19-2* (see Chap. 6) and dissimilar to *Motive* (see Chap. 5), numerous main protagonists' rallying characterises the TV product presented here. Seven fixed characters compose the initial Toronto squad (six men and one woman), intervening in astonishingly dangerous situations and keeping the peace. Breaking with US TV stereotypes, producers chose to cast two "follicly challenged 45-year-old Canadians" (Treble, 2008)— Enrico Colantoni and Hugh Dillon—as main protagonists of the series. They attributed them leading roles in the Strategic Response Unit and some familiar controversial issues, in contrast with the North American cliché of young and handsome single heroes contemporaneously caging the criminals and heart-breaching the ladies. The team leader is Sergeant Gregory Parker (Greg, starred by Enrico Colantoni), a 45-to-50-year-old white Canadian, who also handles the role of negotiator in most cases. He is often supported by his veteran colleague Edward (Ed, alias Hugh Dillon) Lane, a 45-to-50-year-old, white Canadian, expert tactical agent and sniper. A younger group of 35-to-40-year-old agents gathers around

## 4 *Flashpoint* as in-Group Psychological and Action...   125

the leaders as other primary protagonists of the series. Michelangelo Scarlatti (Spike) is an Italian-Canadian geek (no accents are attributed to his linguistic proficiency and the 'Italian-' characterisation of the cop is only rendered via scant cultural references, although his parents do speak with a marked inflection), who often puts his knowledge on explosives and computer technology expertise at the disposal of his colleagues to solve crises. Kevin Wordsworth (Wordy)—Ed's right-hand man—is represented as a resolute and tenacious fellow with particular preference to close-quarter combat. Juliana (Jules) Callaghan is the only woman having an active agent role in team 1—not in SRU—during the first season (although, no gender issues emerge in the *Flashpoint* TV series on that ground). Interpreted by Amy Jo Johnson, she is the sole non-Canadian performer acting in the show. Lewis (Lou) Young—Spikes' best friend— is the only non-Caucasian actor/character in the team (Commander is also African-American, although he is not a recurring character and his appearances on the scene are more like seldom cameos). Although no clear mentions of his ethnicity in the show, he supposedly mirrors the actual Jamaican origin of the professional acting his role (Mark Taylor); he is specialised in less-lethal weaponry, psychological profiling and bomb diffusion. Eventually, Samuel (Sam) Braddock is a former JTF2, with a relevant military familiar legacy. His traits (starred by David Paetkau), conversely to what has been said about Greg and Ed, remark the North American stereotype of a young pale Caucasian hero with blond hair and green eyes falling in love with the female beauty of the plot, Jules. Despite these main characters, other protagonists follow. Donna Sabine, Canadian, is the women's quota substituting Jules for a ten-episodes-break between seasons 1 and 2, as the main character is recovering from a gunshot wound.[4] Leah Kerns, a black Canadian, substitutes Lou after his demise since s02e10 (maintaining the ethnic visible contrast with the other squad members and implementing the number of women in the team). Even Sam, who joins the team in the first episode, in truth substitutes Roland (Rolie). However, after the replacement, the latter vanishes (thus not mentioned within the array of significant characters). Eventually one minor recurring name (often substituted by other colleagues) is Winnie, a mixed-ethnicity 35-to-40-year-old Canadian, working as SRU dispatcher from her headquarter position.[5]

126    F. P. Gentile

Besides the consistent number of protagonists (main heroes are accompanied by recurring characters as well) and the thematic rendition of series plots, the action genre never really jeopardises the crime drama attitude of the show, mostly facilitating the conveyance of psychological maturation along with procedural focuses. Characters are "emotionally invested in every case they run across. While they are figuring out a lethal solution to potentially defuse a difficult situation, they are at the same time trying to save the subject" (Kristine, 2008). Still, the recounting strategies concentrate on the Flashpoint protagonists' job-related burdens. In that case, such implicatures show themselves for what they are in their private lives as well, often distressing heroes' familiar statuses.

From the narrative point of view, it is clear that most screen products are characterised by similar recounting strategies aiming at emphasising specific actions or setting contexts for the rendition and the development of the stories. The informativity criterion in Textual Linguistics declares texts with higher degrees of clarity being less attention-seeking than others. On a three-step scale, narrations delivering expected pieces of information to their users—in a linear way—are granted the first step and represent communicative situations obtaining low interest from those requested to face them. On the contrary, other texts, which require more complex elaboration processes to pursue new understandings, climb on top of the scale, conquering the highest degrees of textual informativity (De Beaugrande & Dressler, 1994, pp. 157–179). Instructive texts, for instance, need to follow specific patterns similar to a linguistic application of the mathematical stochastic Markov chain, where bits of information occur one after another, paving the path to comprehension and avoiding any eventuality of intricacy.

Contrariwise, TV products (as much as literary texts) are supposed to reveal a *sadistic* attitude. Information learning has to be undertaken and concocted sideways, nurturing end-users with crumbs to stimulate their appetite instead of serving solutions right away. One leading recurring expedient that scriptwriters tend to adopt is the deployment of flashback leaps which discombobulate viewers (Fig. 4.3).

This strategy can maintain high informativity levels and grant the audience's interest. Of course, the same procedure may appear differently

## 4 *Flashpoint* as in-Group Psychological and Action... 127

**Fig. 4.3** *Flashpoint*, s01e01. Flashback narration

in diverse situations and according to one's purpose. In the case of the *Flashpoint* TV series, flashbacks are at the very beginning of each instalment, to—first—establish the recount context and—second—structure a characterising skeleton of its narrativity. In Fig. 4.3, it is possible to observe a peculiar type of time-lapse. Considering the first episode of the series, since emblematic of the entire product, actions start with the assailant visual salience while already facing SRU in a threatening manner and using a woman as a human shield. As the instalment speeds up, the viewer sees Ed being about to trigger his rifle and kill the hostage-taker. There, the camera shot suddenly shifts into the cop's gunsight (which is blurred), and actions reverse through the display of a euphemistically enormous quantity of episode-frames rewinding in just three seconds. Through a similar technique, viewers acquaint with the case when the criminal has already been located and linguistically engaged. They are linearly led to a climax point (the cop is instants away from ending the story), and eventually narration breaks down to start over.

Things move backwards at high-speed rates from when the agents arrive, to the hostage-taking, and then to a pleasant initial situation. As rewind terminates, the observer is required to cooperatively put his episodical awareness aside to witness other events happening earlier that same day (Fig. 4.3, the last frame reporting the wording 'two hours earlier'). In the knowledge that something will happen soon, the viewer curiously stands awaiting, while Wordy pulls over Ed's house singing, to go to work together with his colleague. After that, the instalment starts afresh from the flashback to the end of the story, with no further jumps.

The expressiveness of a similar strategy involves the dialogues of the series as well. Indeed, the narrative choice of starting *in media res* to secondarily recontextualise the situation, *forces* spectators to confront on the spot some linguistic and (generally) communicative levels. Events have escalated already at the beginning of the instalment. They require huge amounts of attention in the first place. Then, viewers can reflate a couple of minutes later via a placid, progressive salience meant to increase multiple times again by the end of the show (the flashback montage style is the same as the series theme song, and that creates a second narrative pause later on in the instalments, as said; see Fig. 4.1).

## Narrativity and Popularisation

Concerning statistical data (that are discussed more precisely in the final paragraph of this chapter), the 1804 minutes of the broadcast of the *Flashpoint* TV series correspond to a 7.6 per cent increase in terms of televised product, compared to *Motive's* 1677 minutes (see Chap. 5) on a pair with seasonal transmissions, also determined by the supernumerary five episodes of *Flashpoint* season 2 (2009; 18 against 13). Nonetheless, the 127 extra minutes only correspond to a 5.8 per cent increase in word conveyance. It means a decrement of ~1.6 per cent in terms of words per minute (WPM)—although written text word numbers do not mirror WPM counts, such association can be related to said calculation, given the transcribed nature of the *Flashpoint Corpus*. Considering similar data, one would immediately comprehend the enormous relevance of visual display over linguistic verbal usages, where instalment length growth seems not to correspond to elocution implementations. Consequently, one primary hypothesis ascribable to the observation of the series would affirm once more the validity of Mehrabian's equation (Chaps. 1 and 2) about the prevalence of extra-linguistic factors in lieu of mere verbal aspects in communication. Those factors, here labelled as 'multimodal features', include staged cinematic environments and narrative slants plus other dimensions like the non-verbal and the para-verbal ones.

## 4 *Flashpoint* as in-Group Psychological and Action... 129

Many of the languages involved onscreen are specialised communication. Varying from highly to less featured communication, content and knowledge, they may summon (Roelcke, 2010, p. 56-ff.):

- *General language lexicon* (as ordinary spoken or written interaction)— 'language', or 'discourse' as "language above the sentence or above the clause" (Stubbs, 1983, p. 1), thus 'speech';
- *Extra-specialised communication* (procedural knowledge and terminology originally belonging to a certain discipline, and then largely used in other both specialised and ordinary contexts). The concept is similar to Klein's *transdisciplinarity* (2013, p. 93);
- *Inter-specialised communication* (procedural knowledge and terminology that were borth to denote the thesaurus of a discipline, and then trickled down other specialised domains). This idea of *interdisciplinarity* is also shared by Bammer (2013, p. 8);
- *Intra-specialised communication* (consisting in procedural knowledge and terminology originated from a certain sectorial area and maintained within its expressive and communicative domain).

Those four levels rendition via either linguistic (verbal) or extra-linguitic (beyond verbiage, it includes visually or acoustically expressive content) modes to produce meaning. Nonetheless, TV environment cannot hazard and propose their spectators highly technified terminology or Expert-to-Expert interactions (unless specific needs require it). Every meaning would arrive blurred to its receivers at home. One recurrent procedure to funnel specialised knowledge undergoes the so-called 'popularisation' strategies (Grego, 2013; Garzone, 2020). This expertise massification goal generally works through five possible stages (Grego, 2013, p. 154), that can be retrieved in the present analysis, especially in the forms of:

- (over-)explanation, exemplification, simplification (see the vocative function, reiterating names and more rarely terms multiple times lo let receivers absorb them);
- argumentation (involving metalinguistic explanations or glossing);
- critical/social reference. This point may represent the fundament of the examination describing the TV series social models following some psychological speculations discussed further in the chapter.

## 130    F. P. Gentile

# The Vocative Function

The expressiveness of the series results in a blending of police procedural and action genres. Particular attention falls onthe psychological developments afflicting the characters' workplace and private lives and introspective schemata. Subsequently, the retrieval of word frequency lists and co-occurrence plots could produce incomplete results. Hence, in these paragraphs, the analysis benefits from the corpus computational statistical parsings, although a significant qualitative selection of specific passages is present. The televised sequences often rendition mute interactions where participants communicate through mimics, gestures, or the shooting technique simply narrates some storyline passages via camera movements, isolated frames, or even music and sounds. In light of that, verbal data about the *Flashpoint Corpus* might appear lacking essential aspects of communication and miss the comprehension of meaningful prosodic connotations.

On an introductory level, observing the noun frequency list (Table 4.2), it is worth noting the presence of some relevant elements. Although it could resemble a mere list of names, the linguistic salience that is given to the protagonists is also reflected through vocative functions related to recurrent mentions of their names or nicknames. This aspect reveals the necessity of presenting several characters onscreen, who constantly seek

**Table 4.2** *Flashpoint Corpus* noun frequency list

| RANK | NOUN | | RANK | NOUN | | RANK | NOUN | | RANK | NOUN | |
|---|---|---|---|---|---|---|---|---|---|---|---|
| 1 | GUY | [702] | 12 | GUN | [297] | 37 | CAR | [162] | 48 | JOB | [142] |
| 2 | RIGHT | [662] | 13 | THING | [277] | 38 | FRIEND | [162] | 49 | WIFE | [135] |
| 3 | TIME | [482] | 14 | ANYTHING | [272] | 39 | HOME | [161] | [...] | | |
| 4 | BOSS | [481] | 15 | POLICE | [255] | 40 | GREG | [156] | 54 | SERGEANT | [132] |
| 5 | WAY | [435] | 16 | HAND | [224] | 41 | SIR | [155] | [...] | | |
| 6 | SPIKE | [420] | 17 | ED | [222] | 42 | PLACE | [153] | 58 | OFFICER | [182] |
| 7 | TEAM | [379] | 18 | SUBJECT | [216] | 43 | GIRL | [146] | 59 | NIGHT | [127] |
| 8 | SAM | [378] | 19 | PEOPLE | [216] | 44 | SHOT | [146] | 60 | HOSTAGE | [123] |
| 9 | SOMETHING | [332] | [...] | | | 45 | ROOM | [146] | [...] | | |
| 10 | JULES | [302] | 35 | LIFE | [171] | 46 | PARKER | [144] | 63 | BOMB | [115] |
| 11 | KID | [302] | 36 | CALL | [164] | 47 | BABY | [143] | | | |

## 4 *Flashpoint* as in-Group Psychological and Action... **131**

verbal and visual contact with each other. The criminal environment proposed by the genre linguistically translates into "illocutionary acts" (Searle & Vanderveken, 1985, p. 60; see also Searle, 1969) checking the status of respective partners or summoning colleagues to dispatch the orders.

Condensed within position #40 of the table, one would quickly find Spike (rank 6, 420 count), Sam and Jules (rank 8, 378 count; rank 10, 302 count), Ed (rank 17, 222 count) and Greg (rank 40, 156 count), this latter associated to his surname as well only six entries further (Parker; rank 46, 144 count). Surprisingly enough, though, naming processes only work for five in seven members of the unit. Hence, Lewis is only 186th (47 count), almost doubling his substitutive officer, Leah, at rank 302 (30 count), and the same goes for Donna (rank 209, 49 count). Nonetheless, suppose heroes' temporary or definitive turnovers could justify a similar view. Lewis Young dies in the tenth episode of the second season, being substituted by Leah Kerns (yet his name is a lot more recurrent than hers); Donna Sabine replaces Jules between the finale of the first season and the beginning of the second one (for a few instalments). In that case, what appears motiveless is Wordsworth's absence in the reported table. Indeed, the man is mentioned 82 times, reaching position 98, nine ranks behind Winnie (#89, 96 count), who has a—recurring—more marginal role as a dispatcher.

To that extent, it is clear that had the verbal dimension had the same relevance of visual salience, name counts would have scored identical numbers in terms of the characters' visual display. The divergence between verbal vocatives and screen imaging is fundamental for the multimodal observation.

As premised, the minor verbal significance attributed to certain characters and events determines such contingency. However, those linguistic exchanges remain vital. Wordy (Wordsworth's nickname) is present in every episode of the forty-four examined here, and he carries out the same crucial tasks as those assigned to his colleagues (Table 4.3). Despite being involved in brief interactions as much as in long dialogues—and having a consistent number of lines as well—Wordy's name rarely occurs within the transcripts of the corpus. In opposition to Tables 4.2 and 4.3 this demonstrates how such a character is linguistically less relevant than some others (his name scores low count rates) but visually fundamental

**Table 4.3** *Flashpoint*, s03e07. Investigator's assessment multimodal annotation

| Frame/Min | | | |
|---|---|---|---|
|  |  |  |  |
| 00:12:00<br>MovA;<br>CP: Tracking, MS-SV;<br>VS> Interrog.; P: W; M; Ph;<br>Tempo: Fast;<br>ST: Reverber. music; | 00:12:03<br>Stationary;<br>CLU-SV;<br>VS> P: M; | 00:12:06<br>VS> P: W; | 00:12:08<br>CSU-FV;<br>VS> P: M; |
|  |  |  | |
| 00:12:12<br>CLU-OSS;<br>VS> P: M; W; | 00:12:16<br>MS-OSS;<br>VS> P: W; | 00:12:24<br>Tracking; SV;<br>VS> P: M; | 00:12:30<br>Stationary;<br>VS> P: W;<br>ST: Deep piano notes reverberate |
|  |  |  | |
| 00:12:35<br>Tracking;<br>MS-FV;<br>VS> P: M; | 00:36:41<br>Stationary;<br>VS> P: M;<br>ST: Music becomes lower; | 00:12:50<br>Tracking;<br>MS-FV/OSS;<br>VS> P: W; M; | 00:12:59<br>Stationary;<br>MS-FV;<br>VS> P: M; |
|  |  |  | |
| 00:13:05<br>Stationary; CLU-FV;<br>VS> P: W;<br>Tempo: Slow; | 00:13:08<br>CLU-FV/OSS;<br>VS> P: M; | 00:13:13<br>MS-FV/OSS;<br>VS> P: W;<br>AS: Papers; | 00:13:17<br>CLS-FV/OSS;<br>VS> P: W;<br>Tempo: Fast; |

**Dialogue**

*(continued)*

## 4 *Flashpoint* as in-Group Psychological and Action... 133

**Table 4.3** (continued)

| Frame/Min |
| --- |
| Investigator: Wait (..) This was (..) eight minutes in (..) ((Wordy nods)) Eight minutes since you entered the building and Ed Lane told you to stay |
| Wordsworth: /Yep* ((Nods again)) |
| Investigator: O:r (..) was^ it (.) Sergeant Parker |
| Wordsworth: Ed^ (.) We↓⇒ needed the crowd^ (.) contained ((Corrugated expression)) This is all in the transcript. |
| Investigator: ((Inquisitional tone)) Does=your=team leader have confidence↓⇒ in you |
| Wordsworth: ((Suspect gaze)) What do you mean^ |
| Investigator: Pursue an active shooter or babysit eyewitnesses (.) Ed=Lane=left=you behind |
| Wordsworth: Those witnesses were putting themselves and us ((Hand movements)) in danger (..) They needed to be evacuated |
| Investigator: Okay (.) I: get it (..) It was important to keep them safe so put a=trusted=officer o:n=it |
| Wordsworth: What is this (h) some solo version of good cop/bad cop^ |
| Investigator: (h) ((Chuckles softly)) Sorry^ (..) Old habit from the force |
| Wordsworth: Okay=Well (.) it's confusing ((Smiles)) |
| Investigator: You would've just made my old partner Brian very happy (..) ((Ample gestures bringing her closer to the table)) He thought it would trip up the bad guys if we sort of (.) ((hand gesture)) switched sides (.) mid-interrogation (..) I guess I (h) still do it |
| Wordsworth: It's hard (..) losing a partner |
| Investigator: What^ |
| Wordsworth: Wait (..) You said (..) it (.) would've made him happy (.) not it will (4′) ((She stares at him touched)) I'm (.) sorry ((Hand gesture)) I didn't mean to- ((Stops talking and looks at her)) |
| Investigator: .h ((Retreats, creating separation. Then restarts with a more pressing attitude than before)) So (..) what happened next^ (.) was=that=a=mistake^ |

for the development of the plots: his presence is constant. This name's scant vocative occurrence may link up to the character often being on the scene, already. Thus, Wordy's colleagues rarely need to specifically call him (he would notice if they talk to him via gaze and body language). From a sheer verbal investigation level, a similar idea would have not come out as the integration with image supports is once more crucial.

The Wordsworth character is a physical CQB expert (thus often involved in training sessions with his colleagues, instructing them on close combat skills), never lacking judgement and emotional aspects. As shown in Table 4.3, when involved in intense exchanges, the man alternates resolution to thoughtfulness to demonstrate his sensitive side (more examples will follow during the chapter to discuss other *Flashpoint* qualities).

Notwithstanding the inquisitional aim of the investigator's questions, in the instance proposed, Kevin stays lucid. He answers via a placid rhythm and keeps a low modulated vocal pitch. This practice transmits the man's calmness still emphasising significant words through slight intonation raises ("We↓⇒ needed the crowd^ (.) contained') and meaningful empty pauses ('Those witnesses were putting themselves <u>and</u> us ((Hand movements)) in <u>danger</u> (..) They needed to be <u>evacuated</u>"). The officer's utterances are straight and use plain language. They display a preference of passive voice referring to linguistic agents undergoing other people's actions or decisions ("We needed the crowd contained"; "They needed to be evacuated"). These said communicative pattern mirrors some more natural expressive ones lying behind police jargon. The investigator's attitude is judged too insistent by Wordy, who answers via a graduation 'focus softening' ("What is this (h) **some** solo **version of…**")[6] used to deflect the attention of his interlocutor from potential answers by belittling the value of the question itself. There, the investigator's cooperation (she smiles at his joke) causes the officer to lower his guard via an 'affect' attitude ("Okay. Well, it's **confusing**"), trying to establish an emotional connection between him and his addresser. The woman, however, pushes the interview back from her emotional barrier after a nth sympathetic comment ("It's **hard** losing a partner") through a WH- interjection "What?" that should have warned the man to back off. There, again, Kevin's trained skills in profiling put him back on an analytical track that lets him explain his conjectures ("You said it <u>would've made</u> him happy, not <u>it will</u>…"), reopening an old wound. The investigator, unwilling to show her weak side, terminates the emotional confrontation by re-creating separation through the interrogation formality via an even faster elocution pace.

The criticality and the seriousness of the narration, in Table 4.3, are rendered using just two camera positions and framing techniques. The stationary over-the-shoulder close-up shots deliver the intensity of the moment, as they press characters whenever visual salience should emphasise their tension, respectively. On the contrary, quicker tracking sequences transmit the interrogations' tennis-like rendition, made of questions and prompt replies. The camera hinges upon the table to slide from one character onto the other via frontal or side mid-shots, increasing the exchange rapidity. Dark lights with yellow neons on the background and reverberating deep notes contribute to implementing the pathos within a sombre inward-looking atmosphere.

Along with those communicative features, gestures play a relevant part in the interaction. When the two participants are sitting at the same table and leaning against their seat-backs, initial social space proxemic distance is supposed to occur because of their mutual willingness to create separation since their dichotomous roles. Although contrasted by some aggressive body language, Wordsworth's verbal calm urges him to approach his interviewer by solidly placing his elbows on the surface of the table and extending the neck towards the woman (min. 00:12:03). The action precedes a contrite facial expression (min. 00:12:12) that underlines his uneasiness. Yet, the woman's smile at his reaction brings him to a defusing comment ("What is this (h) some solo version of good cop/bad cop^") supported by a more *peaceful* posture. His shoulders are relaxed downwards, and his hands are clasped in front of him to signal an attentive attitude. After that, the two characters leave their seat-back to pitch forward, and the social space becomes personal: the symptom of an emotional channel being created. Still, the impracticability of becoming closer since the different tasks they are there to accomplish urges Wordy to retreat defensively (min. 00:13:08). The woman passes again to a cold social distance and resets her dominant role towards the addressee, starting over with more questions.

Table 4.2 highlights two more aspects. On the one hand, the noun frequency list displays relevant hierarchy-based terms (in light yellow), mostly defining two main *Flashpoint* features. There, the general 'police' (rank 15, 255 count) environment is contextualised via the precise SRU organisation. A leader emerges ('boss', rank 4, 481 count; 'Sergeant,' rank 54, 132 count) over the rest of the 'team' (rank 7, 379 count). However, the squad moves and acts as a single body whose brain is not simplistically Greg—as the individual with higher ranks—nor is it Ed—the team leader. It results out of a collective and cooperative entity aiming at succeeding in one common task.

## 136     F. P. Gentile

On the other hand, meaningful nouns (in dark grey) determine the best quantity of situations to be handled in the investigation. They are ascribable to the action domain and to the related weaponry lexical thesaurus ('gun,' rank 12, 297 count; 'subject,' rank 18, 216 count; 'shot,' rank 44, 146 count; 'hostage,' rank 60, 123 count; 'bomb,' rank 63, 115 count) that enhances the charm of the TV product.

## Tactics

Observing Table 4.4, the case that the SRU is supposed to face requires intense reasoning activities since every possible move has to be evaluated following its effects, pros and cons. Despite Ed Lane's role as team leader, the man is not taking decisions on his own. Some of his colleagues support him in-presence (Jules, Spike and Sam, while Greg and Wordy are approaching the subject and Lou is in the truck). The team cooperates to figuring out tactical choices to decrease percentages in terms of unwanted consequences. Lane, Scarlatti and Callaghan are on the same page since their long professional relationship—thus, they do not need to brainstorm with each other in this part of the assessment. Conversely, Braddock has only recently joined the squad, so he starts proposing solutions (also for narrative reasons increasing suspense, where no ideas seem adequate), showing off his soldier's proactive attitude and cold blood. In Sam's perspective, since the man is used to war contexts, the primary goal is to neutralise the enemy; thus, his troubleshooting schemata are less concerned with the implications his proposals would bear.

At first, the young agent interacts with his veteran colleague through a 'monogloss' engagement. He only portrays one subjective solution ("Let me shoot the gun^ (.) problem solved^"), underlined by vocal pitch rises on meaningful terms (^). In like manner, Sam tries to draw the listener's attention to those elements, also guided by the speaker's willingness to be on the front line ("Let **me** shoot..."; "**I** won't mi:ss"). With the same cooperative attitude described so far, Ed cares to answer him, explaining why shooting the gun is not advisable. Lane cuts short with a ('judgement'attitude) "too risky" that produces his interlocutor's insistence. Thus, the man recaps the matter more accurately to enlighten the

## 4 *Flashpoint* as in-Group Psychological and Action... 137

**Table 4.4** *Flashpoint*, s01e02. Professional discourse and sarcasm multimodal annotation

| Frame/Min | | | |
|---|---|---|---|
|  |  |  |  |
| 00:18:49<br>MovA;<br>CP: Tracking, CLU-FV;<br>VS> Command post; P: M; M; Ph;<br>ST: Percussions; | 00:18:52<br>≈<br>Tempo: Slow; | 00:18:56<br>CLS-FV;<br>VS> Monitor; P: M; M; | 00:19:00<br>CLS-SV;<br>VS> P: M; W; |
|  |  |  |  |
| 00:19:01<br>Tempo: Fast; | 00:19:04<br>Det.; VS> Monitor; Hospital plan; SP1<br>ST: Percussions plus reverberating notes; | 00:19:35<br>Shaky; CLS-SV.;<br>VS> Command post; Ed is in foreground, Sam in the background although speaking;<br>Tempo: slow; | 00:19:38<br>Ed is speaking now; |
|  |  |  |  |
| 00:19:41<br>MS-D;<br>VS> P: W;<br>SP2; | 00:19:43<br>MS-FV;<br>VS> P: W; M;<br>SP3; | 00:19:47<br>Stationary,<br>CLS-FV;<br>VS> P: M; M; Ph; | 00:19:58<br>≈ |

**Dialogue**

*(continued)*

# 138     F. P. Gentile

**Table 4.4** (continued)

| Frame/Min |
| --- |
| Lane: It's gotta be a less lethal option<br>Braddock: Let me shoot the gun^ (.) problem solved^<br>Lane: Too risky<br>Braddock: I <u>won't</u> ((Emphasised by gectures and eye movements)) mi:ss<br>Lane: Gun^ fragments (.) <u>c</u>ivilians (.) we don't get^ awa:y with collateral damage↓⇒ here Sam.<br>Scarlatti: We need to ((Body movements. Suddenly turns towards Sam)) isolate=him<br>[00:19:05–35]<br>Braddock: Why=don't=you=just <u>tase</u> his=a:ss<br>Lane: Muscle spasm he'll pull the trigger<br>Braddock: So we go in <u>hard</u> tactical<br>Lane: Yeah I was just gettin' at that (..) Look^⇒ (..) there's=something=I=need=you=to=do (..) All right (.) see these <u>stairs</u> here (..) ((Indicating on the map)) That's where we came in right^ (..) ((Sam follows carefully, nodding)) I want you to make a reverse entry (..) Go across this hallway (.) these doors here (.) I need you to go through=them↓ (..) Now be <u>careful</u> because that's a <u>big road</u> (..)I want you to cross it (..) ((Sam realises the situation)) I want you to make an entry into this Timmy's^ (.)=I'll=have a double double [...] |

interlocutor about his refusal. The procedure is operated via the uttering of a similarly ungrammatical sentence adhering to linguistically economic perspectives that require such exchanges to be brief and concise ("Gun^ fragments (.) civilians"), except for the subsequent gloss "we don't get^ awa:y with collateral damage↓⇒ here Sam". The final part of the sentence, pronounced via a descending tone, indicates the fading attention Ed has conceded to Sam. Notwithstanding Braddock's apparent arrogance, his linguistic behaviour transmits humbler slants, then. Once his leader has motivated his negation, the young man transforms the initial 'monogloss' engagement into a more conversational 'heterogloss' one (**"Why don't you just** tase his ass?"). Again, Lane formulates his answer using a double construction. The synthetic side ("Muscle spasm…") is secondarily expanded by a less technical explanation ("…he'll pull the trigger"). Pretended to be given to Sam, glosses are, in truth, useful to the TV series spectators to understand the terminological domains of the passages conveyed (e.g., gun fragments > Weaponry; muscle spasm > Anatomy) and their related plain language meanings.

## 4 *Flashpoint* as in-Group Psychological and Action... 139

On a visual level, the initial part of the exchange between Sam and Ed happens via scant cooperation. The former character adopts constant research for eye-contact feedback (mins. 00:18:52, 00:18:56, 00:19:38), but the latter is never returning it (often concentrated on the screen). However, despite Braddock's willingness to learn, his pressing behaviour upsets the team, which gives him disappointed and incredulous gazes (mins. 00:19:41–43). The very moment Lane establishes eye contact with Sam is to make the boy *believe* that he is being given personal attention and instructed on something crucial. Considering the terse moment, Sam misinterprets Ed's mendacious body language (attentively directed towards the officer) and falsely cooperative attitude. He listens closely to the words of his leader. Even in this case, Lane adopts hints of a formal register and terminological collocations. The linguistics of his lines emulate the *tactical*, technical discourse (e.g., "make a reverse entry"; "make an entry") to mock his younger colleague and put an end to his questions (by actually sending him out for coffee). The situation—and the functional misuse of specialised communication—is clear from the visual perusal of the sequence, because of the attitude displayed by the interlocutors and the bystanders' body/facial mimics.

Besides internal puns, the speaker's competence meets the visual salience of the framing strategies. The shooting techniques employed facilitate a professionally determined communication apt at evaluating the risks of the dangerous. Several detailed close shots focus either on the characters while assessing the environment and debating or on narrative minutiae like the building blueprints on the screen (min. 00:19:04), to study effective neutralising actions to be performed. On the same level, a slow tempo regulates the sequence pace to transmit the communicative relevance of the interaction to the spectator. The severe decisions are being taken with no need to hurry the participants up.

Nonetheless, the verbal dimension of the dialogue, associated with the slow rhythm, could misleadingly give viewers the idea of a relaxed context only *reporting* strategic opinions rather than mirroring the anxiety of a moment where thoughts are urged into *facts*. A constant soundtrack made of percussions and reverberating noises implements the rendition of the scene. Music increases the attention of the viewers, who await new plot developments to happen soon.

# 140    F. P. Gentile

## Weaponry Occurrence

Together with the communicative operations described in the previous paragraphs, the series' primary aim remains to transmit meaningful content focusing on the themes of the show. The police procedural point of view in *Flashpoint* results are indissolubly mixed with the action intensity. The SRU team is not concerned with any minor misdemeanours or crime scenes to be examined afterwards. Nor are its members at any rate worried about ongoing investigations that would suppose week- or month-long lucubrations finalised at the arrest of an *ordinary* perpetrator. Instead, every case here consists of a *Blitzkrieg* manoeuvre. The unit operates through a strategic assessment of the situation followed by the *immediate* real-time actualization. The plan has to utterly demolish illegal intents, which are reckoned to be critically harmful (e.g., hostage-taking; terroristic attacks; bombing or chemical threats; child abduction). Such fictional rendition credibility inevitably has to pass through a linguistic and visual expressiveness mirroring the context via specific reference systems (Table 4.5).

The equipment vocabulary demands extensive attention (Table 4.5). There is no mitigation in the verbal formulation of weaponry references except for functional abbreviations; nonetheless, the predominant communicative *stratum* remains the visual one. Generic hypernyms like 'gun' and 'rifle' are divided into separate subcategories. The individuals handling the terminology are professionally aware of the qualitative and structural distinctions existing among the reference objects. Hence, one would find 'handguns' (like pistols and revolvers, they have a short narrow rifled barrel causing bullets to spin, for longer ranges and accuracy), 'shotguns' (with longer and broader non-rifled barrels, useful in quarter combats, not for long-distance targets) and 'machine guns' (automatic, firing bullets as long as the trigger is pressed). The classification of weapons in *Flashpoint* is precise. Moreover, the subcategories that define the sphere of use of those tools increase via further passages from hypernyms to hyponyms exemplifying and contextualising them (e.g., 'beretta 40 cal.'; 'HKG3'; 'Luger'; Pug-nose 44 cal.'). Observing Table 4.5, one could also note remarkable differentiation between those weapons that the series labels as lethal and those called less- or non-lethal.

## 4 *Flashpoint* as in-Group Psychological and Action... 141

**Table 4.5** The *Flashpoint Corpus* weaponry lexicon

| WEAPONRY LEXICON | | | |
|---|---|---|---|
| POLICE LETHAL | POLICE NON-LETHAL | POL. DEFENS. / TOOLS | ACRONYM/PHRAS. |
| AUTOMATIC RIFLE | BATON | BIPOD | EXPLOSIVE ENTRY |
| BERETTA 40 cal. | CONCUSSIVE GRENADE | BODY ARMOUR | FULL VALUES CROSSWIND, RICOCHET RISK |
| BRAMBLER (double trigger rifle) | CS GAS | CUFFS | GUN FRAGMENTS |
| HKG3 | DDs (destructive devides) | INFRARED | MOA (Minute Of Angle) |
| MP5 SUB-MACHINE GUN | FLASHBANGS | RAMS | SYMPATHETIC FIRE |
| REMMY 700 | INFERNO (Sound Bomb) | RANGEFINDER | |
| 308 WINCHESTER | NON-PYROTECHNIC CS | RAPPELLING GEAR | |
| | PEPPER SPRAY | SCOPE | |
| | RUBBER BULLETS | SHIELD | |
| | TASER | THERMAL IMAGE SCOPE | |
| | | VEST | |
| **CRIMINAL/GENERIC** | | | |
| AMMO | FRAGMENTATION MINE | LAND MINE | RIFLE |
| AMMONIUM TRILODITE | GUN | (NON-/LESS-) LETHAL | SHOTGUN |
| BLAST MINE | HANDGUN | LUGER | WEAPONS |
| Cal.: 45; 50; 375 | IED (Improv. Explosive Device) | MACHINE-GUN | 380 ACP (Automatic Colt Pistol) |
| COLT | JURY (sl. Tautur Judge 410 cal.) | PHOSPHOROUS | |
| CR38 (Anti-Tank)/ BOUNCING MINE | KNIFE | PUG-NOSE 44 Cal. | |

Entries are disposed alphabetically and their order does not match occurrence ranks or their position in the corpus, plus repetitions are not reported and every term occurs once in Table 4.5

The list of deadly equipment used by SRU (and actual ETF as well) is accurate but short. Conversely, the other list is a bit longer. *Non-lethal* and *less-lethal* tools (any ammunition, even if dampened or made *safer*, remains potentially deadly and cannot be formally included within the 'non-lethal' domain) are here linguistically classified under the non-lethal one. This step is made to highlight the contrast with the strictly lethal category. Those other devices are not just less potent in terms of mortal risk (e.g., 'rubber bullets' in place of regular ones). Indeed, they display an apparent technological enhancement of the weapon industry finalised at producing supplies fitting any neutralising need required by police corps. Most of those weapons cause sensory deprivation (e.g., 'flashbangs' are blinding bombs; 'inferno' is a sound bomb; 'tasers' electrically paralyse subjects). They are adopted in situations where—for instance—perpetrators take human shields, and officers cannot risk hostages' lives, thus opting for other less radical solutions (also see Table 4.8 analysis for more considerations).

The narrative aim of *Flashpoint* focuses on the rendition of police officer preparation to assault, rather than on the actual criminal takeover (despite its spectacularization). Weaponry denotation procedures coincide with initial evaluative phases (hence the significant number of 'criminal/generic' weapons in Table 4.5). Routine lists of SRU equipments and—especially—gear tool statuses (e.g., 'vest'; 'shield'; 'rams'; 'cuffs'; 'bipod') have to be checked *before* acting to avoid possible and compromising malfunctions. In some parallelism with medieval champions and paladins taking care of their war-inventory before jousting or epically clashing in battles, the team inspects all the augmentations useful for the imminent action.

Along with the linguistic usage of a similar type of lexicon, narrative sequences play a relevant role that includes more complex verbal passages:

### Example 4.2 Flashpoint Corpus, Flashpoint, s02e01, min. 00:01:33–01:57

((Shooting range))

Lane:     ((To the officer training. Both men wearing cuffs because of the noise)) 3-0-A CAL (.) PROJECTILES AT 2750 FEET

## 4  *Flashpoint* as in-Group Psychological and Action...    143

PER <u>SECOND</u> (.) PROJECTILE WEIGHTS 168 GRAINS ((No pause)) <u>EYES</u> ((Hand gesture in direction of the aim, followed by head movement)) ON THE TARGET (..) ((shots at regular intervals are fired throughout the sequence. To another officer)) TARGET SIERRA AT 100 YARDS (.) USE STANDARD ATMOSPHERIC CONDITIONS AT SEA LEVEL (..) ((To Donna)) WHAT'S THE DROP AT 200 YARDS?

Sabine:   ((While shooting)) Drop↑⇒ at 200 yards (.) 3.8 inches

Lane:     DOUBLE THE WEIGHT OF THE PROJECTI:LE (.) WHAT'S THE DRO:P

Sabine:   ((Without distracting from the task)) 3.8↑⇒ inches (.) The drop^ is <u>constant</u>

Example 4.2 (see also Table 4.5, 'acronyms/phraseology') involves an interaction whose content is enriched not *just* by some terminological occurrences (e.g., projectile; grains; drop). Both a procedural aim and multiple specialised fields of knowledge to be conveyed also benefit from the instalment's linguistic construction.

On the one hand, the procedural perspective facilitates the contextualisation of the narration within the instructive dimension. Many cops are lined up within the shooting range in their respective compartments, facing their targets at a distance. Behind them, Ed Lane, as instructor, supervises their shooting rates, pressuring them with theoretical questions or peremptorily advising them employing regulatory norms ("eyes on the target"). The exchange (although more likely a monologue) presupposes very high tones because of the disturbing noise of shots being fired and the subsequent necessity of wearing ear protectors. Nonetheless, the instructor's rigour (formulates questions; gives orders without pausing; observes others' [re]actions and behaviours) suggests the intense discipline officers must undergo as well when dealing with firearms.

On the other hand, despite the interactive environment being the police procedural (and the training session) one, the passage's dialogic lines also reveal more than a single domain. The summons of measurement units (e.g., "grain"> weight, equalling 1/7000 pound; "yard", "inch"> size), and physics norms and terms ("standard atmospheric conditions at sea level"; "drop") tell spectators that firing a gun is not just a matter of good aim. Snipers must master some essential physics and mathematics knowledge. One of the most self-evident calculations a professional of this kind should perform before shooting, thus concerns the *Equations for a falling body*, to determine the correct trajectory one's bullet would trace along its path towards the target. Aware of the formula, and helped by more data presented by Ed ("calibre"—to determine drag coefficient: 30a; "speed": 2750 ft/s; mass: 168 grains; air density coefficient: the standard atmosphere at sea level; and range: 200 yds), Donna provides her instructor the result of such calculation (3.8 inches of deviation), also declaring other notions ("The drop^ is <u>constant</u>") when the supervisor changes the maths.

As said, the communicative value of weapon-inclusive sequences of narration—representing the most consistent part of the *Flashpoint* TV series episode contents—is not simply delivered by linguistically salient occurrences (Fig. 4.4). Instead, it is worth noting that the cinematic world knows very well that informative structures often take routes that diverge from the verbal dimension's approach, comprehending the immense power resulting from visually impressive displays. When naming a Luger, the narration aims at presenting an estranging factor before

**Fig. 4.4** *Flashpoint Corpus* weaponry display

the public, since the old-fashion nature of the gun employed in early twentieth-century (mostly between 1898 and 1948) war contexts, formally called Parabellum-Pistole. Without a doubt, people who have experienced some weaponry knowledge would appreciate that and understand the linguistically descriptive goal.

Contrariwise, those who do not have any acquaintance with pistols would miss the importance of the detail. Cops signalling a bomb about to explode would want to alarm the viewers because of the implicated dangers.

Wherefore, a man in the presence of an explosive device hardly ever would waste precious seconds to describe it for their audience instead of running away. *Saying* that there is a man with a gun is never like *showing* him (Fig. 4.4, frames 2, 3) using slow and detailed sequences, possibly supported by the presence of a hostage, or aiming the weapon directly towards the camera. In like manner, *announcing* the very spot where a mine is buried does not have the same clamour of *placing* a ticking dog-sized thing under the nose of an agent whose foot happens to be thereabouts stuck on a second mine (frame 8). The team *uttering* a 'we are here' via radio could never equal the dread of their geared-up *scenic bios* (frames 1, 9–12). In like manner, the linguistic occurrence of 'shield' cannot mirror its thickness and weight nor the scratches from the previous battles it has already won (frame 6). The language, in its verbal dimension, is undoubtedly a powerful tool. However, the television's real strength, as a medium, in these contexts revolves around the total tyranny of visual preciseness, where no verbal labels are as threatening as the crossed circular black hole onto the unaware target (frames 2, 5).

## Localisation Operations

Some more peculiar aspects seem relevant in *Flashpoint*. Like *19-2* (Chap. 6), this series often mentions toponymic street names (Table 4.6; Fig. 4.5) intersecting each other and useful for the localisation of subjects to be apprehended or witnesses to be fetched. Coherently with the typical Canadian vastness of space, Toronto streets are characterised by extensive lengths portraying hypothetically unlimited scenarios. For instance,

**Table 4.6** *Flashpoint Corpus* topnym list

| TOPNYMS [ST/BLVD/RUE/ALLEY/SQ] | | | |
|---|---|---|---|
| 1. ADELAIDE | 12. DANFORTH | 23. JUNCTION | 34. QUEEN |
| 2. AVENUE | 13. DUFFERIN | 24. KING | 35. QUEENSWAY |
| 3. BAY | 14. DUNDAS | 25. KIPLING | 36. RICHMOND |
| 4. BEECHMONT | 15. GERRARD | 26. LAWRENCE | 37. ROSEDALE |
| 5. BEVERLY | 16. GLOUCHESTER | 27. MARINA QUAY W. | 38. SAINT SIMON |
| 6. BLOOR | 17. GOLDWIN | 28. MATHESON | 39. SHUTEN |
| 7. BRIMLEY | 18. HYNES | 29. MONTROSE | 40. SPADINA |
| 8. BROCK | 19. JAMESON | 30. OSSINGTON | 41. VICTORIA |
| 9. CARLTON | 20. JANE | 31. PARADISE | 42. WELLESLEY |
| 10. COLLEGE | 21. JARVIS | 32. PARKDALE | 43. WELLINGTON |
| 11. COOPER | 22. JOHN | 33. PARLIAMENT | 44. YONGE |
| OTHER CITIES AND PROVINCES PLACE NAMES [ST/BLVD/RUE/ALLEY/SQ] | | | |
| 45. HAMILTON | 48. WOODBRIDGE | 51. MONTREAL | 54. BRITISH COMUMBIA |
| 46. MISSISSAUGA | 49. (NORTH) YORK | 52. ONTARIO | 55. CHICAGO |
| 47. REXDALE | 50. TORONTO | 53. MANITOBA | |

Entries order is alphabetical. Street names often recur in couples intersecting each other, although here they are listed individually for space reasons

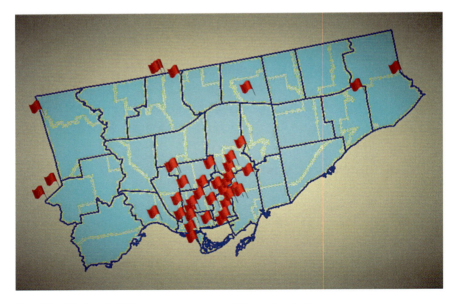

**Fig. 4.5** *Flashpoint Corpus* topnym map (figure is mine)

**Fig. 4.6** *Flashpoint*, s02e13, min. 00:02:17–18/00:30:18–21. Pursuit multimodal observation

Bloor Street is about sixteen miles long, stretching from the Don River Valley into Mississauga, from West to East. However, the longest street in Toronto is without doubt Yonge, running Northbound from Queen's Quay at the waterfront to the left of Queensville, about thirty-five miles further.

Subsequently, in the *Flashpoint* TV series, most urban area names are flagged through the individuation of the closest intersection to the crime scene (e.g., 'Yonge and Bloor'; 'King and John').

This level of clarity, not contemplating generalisations misplacing locative requirements, allows the examination to conclude that the city's bosom also coincides with the areas of significant interest in terms of narrative action (Fig. 4.5). Therefore, the relevance of Toronto downtown on screen permits the creation of a fully recognisable Canadian product, since extensively involving shooting procedures to be realised within the most known tourist hot spots (e.g., King St; Queen St; Bay St; Bloor St; Yonge St; waterfront locations). Given the high identifiability of those urban zones, significant amounts of end-users could read the Toronto map sketched by the series through their faithful mental representations of the toponyms as well, also given to the social, cultural and political implications of cities multimodal representations (Alias, 2004, p. 55).

The number of occurrences reported in Table 4.6 is also relevant. The percentage of street names relying on the Dispatcher's communication in the *Flashpoint Corpus* is minimal. Indeed, SRU is rarely connected to the perpetrator's chasing via itineraries that require a radio employee to coordinate multiple units within the same apprehension. Thus, the single occurrence of one precise location might be formulated (not all the episodes involve toponymic data) at the beginning of the instalment to determine where the intervention is required.

**148    F. P. Gentile**

No further communications with the Dispatcher include localisation information (unless being about criminal identification through personal and residential data). The team is mostly stationary in the single place where a subject has to be neutralised, and part of its task is to avoid break-outs. Even in those other cases, when the culprit manages to escape, the entire unit (never a single individual only; Fig. 4.6) performs the chase. The squad arrives on the scene (mins. 00:02:17–18; Toronto identity markers are notable), runs after the fugitives until their utter capture (mins. 00:30:18–21), and eventually leaves to headquarter all together. In terms of visual salience, the massive prominence of frames and sequences concentrating on the team (and its members individually) demonstrates it. Compared to that, the passages where the main subjects are the villains are relatively fewer and mostly functional for shifting from one narrative segment to another.

From a Corpus Linguistics perspective, when the focus of narration concentrates on the actions to be performed, locative specifications are only marginal. Thus, the attention allotted to the urban description is not linguistically relevant since already funnelled by image sequences (Fig. 4.6) corroborated by ambient noises inclusive of engine rumbles of acceleration, sirens and breaking screeches. In line with that, verbal dialogues maintain their cohesive thematic unity and carry on exchanges that prefer to gather around the planning of subjects' annihilation (renouncing to the superfluous proliferation of place names).

## The Psychological Communication Slant

The general communicative slant of *Flashpoint* (observed so far) makes its narrative peculiarities, above all, described through procedural praxes deployed by the tactical point of view that characterises the structure of the drama. On a superficial level, the show is made recognisable because of many determinant features that define the product's identity via its catchy format. The development of the plots is presented *in media res* in the very first seconds of the instalment. Then, the recount shutters firstly via the insertion of *initial* flashback strategies rewinding the facts to their origin. Secondly, because of the TV series theme song—by the tenth minute (often fifteenth in season 3)—letting the narration reflate considering its intense rhythm flow going on to the end.

On a more profound level, great relevance is given to the team's definition as an all-inclusive entity, still considering the importance of its members as singularities.

Nonetheless, observing the frequency count of some relevant nouns (Table 4.2, dark grey cells) related to their word sketch schemes, respectively, one more exciting point emerges. Meaningful terms—like 'subject', 'hostage' and 'bomb' (Table 4.7)—denote the presence of a significant thematic aspect: *crisis*.

Indeed, the *Flashpoint* TV series' fascinating atmosphere comes from the exorcism of real-world threats transposed on screen to be demolished. The genre is keen on general crimes to be solved, assassins to be found, and drug cartels to be wiped out. The Toronto series is even more involved, discussing other topics like the terroristic one, which does not deliver any person from its cruelty and stealthy unpredictability. Several monitored formulaic linguistic collocations narrate such a dark world. These associate the said meaningful lexical poles to frequent adjectival and nominal correlations (see Table 4.7) measuring dangers and informing on the seriousness of the situations (e.g., 'high-risk', 'armed', 'dangerous' + 'subject'; 'multiple', 'many', 'several' + 'hostage'; 'bomb' + 'threat', target').

Verb workings appear more effective than collocations. Those three instance nouns' abundant occurrence requires many verbal syntagms to link to them via S/O + V grammatical relationships. The best part of verbal interactions depends on the *numerous* members of the team—as protagonists. Given the professional context surrounding the actions, they tend to talk via hints of peers' specialised communication, thus preferring brief enunciations and concise structures often supported by formal expressions (Table 4.4). A similar standard would inevitably produce relevant quantities of passive voices and depersonalisations that would facilitate:

- the preponderance of the V + O order rather than S + V;
- mustering around verbs denoted by legal terminology values ('contain'; 'engage'; 'restrain'; 'secure'; 'extract'; 'escalate');

# 150    F. P. Gentile

**Table 4.7** *Flashpoint Corpus*, 'subject', 'hostage', 'bomb' word sketches

| SUBJECT, N. | | | |
|---|---|---|---|
| MODIFIERS OF 'S.' | VERBS WITH 'S.' AS OBJ. | V. WITH 'S.' AS SUBJ. | ADJ. PREDICATES OF 'S.' |
| POSSIBLE; PRIMARY; THIRD; **HIGH-RISK**; **ARMED**; UNARMED; **DANGEROUS**; MALE; MULTIPLE; SINGLE; MANY; NEW | **ARM**; **CONTAIN**; APPROACH; FLUSH; **PROVOKE**; **ENGAGE**; **RESTRAIN**; CHARACTERISE; **PROFILE**; **ARREST**; **PURSUE**; INTERRUPT; ASSUME; **LOCATE**; **ALERT**; CONFIRM; MEAN; REMEMBER; KNOW; BRING; **SHOOT**; THINK; LET; MAKE; GET; FIND; HAVE; ACQUIRE; **SECURE**; BE | **BARRICADE**; APPROACH; BE; **SHOOT**; HAVE; **LIE**; MOVE; COME; ABANDON; TEND; BUMP; **SURRENDER**; TERMINATE; **FLEE**; SCREAM; DECIDE; CARRY; **ESCALATE**; ENTER; SPEND; BELIEVE; SET; OPEN; STAY; MAKE; TELL; DO | **ARMED**; INACTIVE; CAUCASIAN; ABLE; **VOLATILE**; **UNACCOUNTED**; SECURE |

| HOSTAGE, N. | | | |
|---|---|---|---|
| MODIFIERS OF 'H.' | AND/OR + 'H.' | V. WITH 'H.' AS OBJ. | V. WITH 'H.' AS SUBJ. |
| **MULTIPLE**; PEOPLE; **MANY**; SECOND; PREGNANT; **SEVERAL**; **UNIDENTIFIED**; CIVILIAN; WOMAN; FEMALE; **ARMED**; POSSIBLE; OTHER | SITUATION; **GUNMAN**; CONCESISON; TAKER; **CRISIS**; **WEAPON**; **ROBBERY**; UNIT; MONEY; SUBJECT | HOLD; **KILL**; RESCUE; **GAG**; **HUMANISE**; EXTRACT; LOCATE; SECURE; THREATEN; CONFIRM; CLEAR; **HIT**; **SHOOT**; **SAVE**; TAKE; THINK; LET; HAVE; LOSE; KEEP; GET; BE | **ESCALATE**; SECURE; TURN; **LIVE**; **DIE**; TAKE; HAVE; BE |

| BOMB, N. | | | |
|---|---|---|---|
| N. MODIFIED BY 'B.' | MODIFIERS OF 'B.' | V. WITH 'B.' AS OBJ. | V. WITH 'B.' AS SUBJ. |
| **THREAT**; CALL; **SCARE**; **SHELTER**; TECHNICIAN; SWEEPS; **TECH**; GEAR; **KILLING**; TRUCK; **TARGET**; NUMBER; GUYS | THIRD; NECKLACE; SMOKE; **CHEMICAL**; **MULTIPLE**; COLLEGE; FOLLOW-UP; BOGUS; **LIVE**; **NEXT**; FIRST | **DEFUSE**; **PLANT**; **SET**; **BUILD**; **DISMANTLE**; PARK; **ASSEMBLE**; **DETONATE**; **DIFFUSE**; DELIVER; **LOCATE**; APPROACH; **TRIGGER**; MOVE; GIVE; **DROP**; TAKE; FIND; GET; **MAKE**; BE; DO; HAVE | **DESTROY**; **HIT**; GO OFF; NEED; HAVE; BE |

#### 4 *Flashpoint* as in-Group Psychological and Action... 151

- synonymic versus antonymic stratification (e.g., 'defuse' vs. 'plant', 'set', 'go off', 'diffuse', 'detonate'; 'dismantle', 'destroy' vs. 'make', 'build', 'assemble').

As known, however, the television milieu is not just verbal, and its multimodal communication happens to reveal various bits of information through different concurrent dimensions.

In *Flashpoint*, the linguistics of stone-cold assessments and decisions portrays resolute unbreakable men and women. There, the narrations indulge in the psychological implicatures connected to the scenarios lived by those Canadian heroes and perturbing them both professionally and personally. The 'bomb' cinematic context is one of the powerful ones set by Table 4.7. Table 4.8 reproposes it as one of the most emblematic sequences of the whole *Flashpoint* product. Dealing with officer Lewis Young's death after the explosion of a CR38 anti-tank bouncing mine (Table 4.5) identified by Sam, the episode—entitled *One Wrong Move*, s02e10, *CTV*, Sept. 25, 2009 (§ Appendix)—was selected via a qualitative evaluation adhering to its enormous expressiveness.

The episode counts ~5283 words on a statistical ground plus a frequency of 46 bomb-derived occurrences and other synonymic terms (20 count 'mine'; 3 count 'explosive'). Despite the instalment being about the bombing theme, related tokens' linguistic relevance is statistically found poor. However, the communicative power of the instalment does not come from verbal interactions. Indeed, the spoken dimension is only accessed in the initial part, during the first twelve seconds of the passage (actually lasting only 8").Still, the narrative phase terminates 1'40" later. While taking the bomb away from Lou's proximity, Spike's opening line addresses his colleagues. The man urges the team to hurry up to retrieve the items he needs. The Appraisal framework facilitates highlighting his talk's 'monogloss' initial statement ("**I** said...") emphasised by the passionate approach to the problem also through a vocal pitch raise and modulation ("Let's^⇒"). Scarlatti's tone is expressed as if he were the one in command, then immediately 'softened' by a more 'heterogloss' perspective entraining the entire group cooperation to succeed ("**we** need... **we** need"; "**we're** gonna do...").

**Table 4.8** *Flashpoint*, s02e10. Bomb explosion multimodal annotation

| Frame/Min | | | |
|---|---|---|---|
|  00:40:48 MovA; CP: Dolly, CLS-FV; VS> Bomb location; P: M; Ph; ST: Intense rhythm; Tempo: Fast; |  00:40:50 Shaky; CLU-SV; Tempo: Slow; |  00:40:54 Dolly; CLS-FV; Tempo: Fast; |  00:40:55 CLU-SV; Tempo: Slow; |
|  00:40:59 Dolly; CLU-FV; Tempo: Slow; |  00:41:02 Stationary; Det.; Tempo: Slow; AS: Click; | 00:41:03 Dolly; MS-FV; Tempo: Slow; AS: Deflagration; |  00:41:04 Shaky; Det.-D; Tempo: Fast; |
|  00:41:06 Tracking; CLS-SV; Off-Focus; Tempo: Slow; |  00:41:08 Very shaky; CLU-SV; AS: Deflagration echoing noise; |  00:41:09 ECLU-SV; Foregroud focus; AS/ST: Absent; | 00:41:12 CU-in; SV; |
|  00:41:15 AS: Muffled tinnitus; |  00:41:17 ≈ |  00:41:19 AS: Muffled tinnitus; ST: String instruments; |  00:41:21 Shaky; CLU-SV; |
|  00:41:24 |  00:41:26 | 00:41:28 |  00:41:47 |

*(continued)*

## 4  *Flashpoint* as in-Group Psychological and Action...    153

**Table 4.8** (continued)

| Frame/Min | | | |
|---|---|---|---|
| Tracking; | ≈ | Shaky; MS-BV; VS> Participant leaving the scene; | CLU-FV; |
| 00:42:02 | 00:42:13 | 00:42:18 | 00:42:28 |
| EWS-BV/FV; Ph2; VS> P: M; M; M; W; M; | Shaky; WS-FV; VS> P: M; M; | CLS-FV/SV; | Dolly; CLS to EWS-FV; ST: Acute piano notes playing *Flashpoint* theme (very slow rhythm); |

| **Dialogue** |
|---|
| Scarlatti: Let's^⇒go (.) I said we need a shield=we need <u>water</u>=oka:y (.) ((Lou tuns crying. Spike's voice is heard through the earpiece)) We're↑⇒ gonna do a <u>weight</u> transfer |
| Young: ((Emotional tone)) Spike^ |
| Scarlatti: Yeah↑ bud (..) ((Lou remains silent)) <u>Lou</u>^ |
| Young: It's gonna be o:kay |
| Scarlatti: ((Barely heard, off-screen)) °Lou° |

Conversely, Lewis's interruption and reassuring tone ("it's gonna be **o:kay**") could be interpreted as either an 'affect' attitude as it could be related to the emotional expressiveness or "reacting to behaviour" (Martin & White, 2005, pp. 42–43) or 'focus softening' manifestations that aim to "downscale"(ibid., p. 138) and relieve the situation.

The man aims at taking his friend's feet back on solid ground to let him realise what is about to happen. Hence—to confirm the interpretation—Spike evokes his partner's name twice. The first time his tone is jubilant and proactive as always; the second time, the name is barely heard ("°Lou°"), as if Scarlatti were exhaling, once understood officer Young's decision (min 00:40:59). Scarlatti's weak whisper blurs in the sound of the deflagration, heard at a distance as Lou deliberately removes

**154**   **F. P. Gentile**

his foot from the mine (mins. 00:41:02–04) to impede Michelangelo to come back and risk his own life in that impossible rescue.

Nonetheless, Spike's last enunciation is also the final verbal information of the scene. From 40'49" to 42'28", the rest of the sequence is only narrated through the tragedy's visual iconicity. Breaking once more with the victorious US tradition, the Canadian product proposes a realistic gravity, where heroes are not always shinily grinning after their battles, and some of them fall along the path to save some others, who remain alive and yet crushed from the friendly loss. The brief echo of the explosion roar and the subsequent muffled whistle of tinnitus are the only elements supporting the sequence, implemented by some instrumental emphasis finally turning into languid piano music that plays the *Flashpoint* theme first notes to conclude the instalment. The moving and acute piano notes resounding in the final seconds of the episode communicate with the spectators to dismiss them and let the characters grieve in solitude. Along with them and the almost imperceptible reverberation, silence (meant as lack of words) is the dominant hero.

The initial visual shift from Spike's busy MSs and CLSs to Lou's emotional and calming CLUs is interrupted by the former character's realisation of the situation (he suddenly slows down, losing his typical smile; min. 00:40:59). The latter's foot detail being removed from the mine in self-sacrifice (min. 00:41:02) follows. There starts the most powerful sequence of the entire show. Between 41'06" and 41'19", viewers assist to thirteen seconds of great silence narrating Michelangelo Scarlatti's inner torment. The bomb deflagration has pushed Lewis's body away among fragments and pebbles, and Spike has not seen that because the whole scene has happened behind him. However, the man seems to observe the event mentally, and the deafening thunder of the device gets translated into his *unspeakable* cry. The ruckus is so chaotic that even the camera goes off-focus. The sequence moves from the detonation frame's stationary position towards Spike's face, to focus again and approach closer and closer (from close shot to close-up, and from close-up to extreme close-up with a final cut-in) as his horrified expression turns into dry tears. Facial mimics transmit some unbearable suffering. The first incredulous expression tends the nerves to their limits until the man cannot make it anymore and summons his hands to outroot the pain in a desperate grasp.

Lou's "it's gonna be o:kay" turns into his death, and from there on, everything about the sequence is described through complex oxymorons. The clamour of the bomb is heard in the background and immediately turns into its ghostly echo.

Similarly, Spikes' shout remains suffocated in his uvula as much as his tears can only imaginarily gush. The unit's active slant petrifies all the men and women in the surrounding area. The group mentality shatters into individualistic solipsism (Sam even leaves the place in discomfort; min. 00:41:28). Once come to his senses, Greg, as team leader, steps forward to reach his colleague kneeling on the ground helpless where, in a sympathetic hug, the pieces to be put back together seem to belong to the soul of the friend that is still living, and not to the one that has just passed.

Along with music and soundtrack, frame alternation complies with a slow tempo giving characters the right time to manage the death and viewers to appreciatea narration that no words could have expressed more significantly.

The example reported in Table 4.8 is undoubtedly related to the series' emotional characterisation. It aims at presenting its heroes through intragroup relationships that reach beyond the merely professional ones, and establish sincere and consolidated co-dependencies via some familiar-like bonds. Suppose the TV series observation at issue allows the retrieval of specific passages of specialised knowledge—like police discourse and weaponry terminology—disseminated all over the corpus more often through a popularised manner. In that case, other communicative linguistic and extra-linguistic traits combine to transmit content-enriched meanings. Here, the psychological slant plays a pivotal role in the utter construction of interactive dynamics.

## Psychology and Profiling

Many psychology hypotheses defining group structures find application in the *Flashpoint Corpus*, and theoretical formulations seem to *transcode into linguistic data* via some primary interactive modalities between the participants involved. The narrative focus somehow blends the

## 156   F. P. Gentile

differentiation between 'primary' and 'secondary' groups set by the American sociologist Charles Cooley in 1909 and then redefined by his colleague Pitirim Sokorin as counterpoising 'familiar' to 'contractual' relationships (Sokorin, 1937). Indeed, the Strategic Response Unit, as workplace *équipe*, should correspond to the second type, where impersonal relationships are necessary for the reaching of common goals through the assignment of stiff and labelling roles. Anyhow, the very tight bonds that exist between group members (possibly because of the fundamental life-protecting mutual aims) alter the rigorous normative classification and include preferential solid interpersonal relationships increasing the internal cohesion of the assembly (Example 4.3):

**Example 4.3 Flashpoint Corpus, Flashpoint, s02e11, min. 00:06:08–07:07**

| | |
|---|---|
| Parker: | ((Enters the briefing room. Some are already inside)) Go:od <u>morning</u> team one |
| Kerns: | Morning ((Spike enters, stares at Leah for a second, then goes the other way around the table. She notes that)) |
| Parker: | Barring any ca:lls^ (.) it's gonna be a <u>light</u> day (..) No warrants until this afternoon so I'm thinking we're gonna patrol ((Everybody sits)) You okay with that Eddie^ |
| Lane: | ((Observes the briefing room situation and faces)) Yup↑ (..) Yup^⇒ good with tha:t |
| Parker: | °Good° (1') ((To Leah, indicating her with his arm)) Leah Kerns (..) First day=welcome ((She nods with a smile)) We're gonna take it <u>easy</u> (.) today=and-a: I'm sure (.) you remember everyone from the recruiting trials ((In turn, everybody nods a cold welcome)) (2') So I^ won't (..) embarrass you with any speeches |
| Kerns: | ((Smiling)) Can I say something^ |
| Parker: | ((Everybody looks at her)) ((4' later)) Floor's yours ((Nods, then sits. She raises)) |
| Kerns: | Thank you for choosing me (..) I know why I'm here (..) You're down a guy and I'm replacing him ((Team members' sad faces)) (3') Don't hate me for it (..) Firefighting=unit=I |

## 4 Flashpoint as in-Group Psychological and Action... 157

>  served=with we lost one of ours so (.) I (..) know what that's
>  like ((More sad faces)) (..) If you wanna talk about it^
> Callaghan: /We're* good ((Firmly))

The same obstinacy shown towards Sam in his first day with the team (Table 4.4) is demonstrated to Leah, as she joins the SRU in replacement of the now-dead Lewis (Example 4.3). Group members enter the briefing room with a smile that vanishes the second they see officer Kerns sitting. They stare at her uncomfortably and take place at the table as distant as they can from the woman cop. Parker's welcome is quite formal and aloof. Despite his good manners, the man tries to keep it short, preventing Kerns from speaking, since he seems to know the possible reactions of his colleagues ("So I^ won't (..) embarrass you with any speeches", followed by a 4' pause after Leah's insistence). As the woman raises, the others' gazes become impatient, and when she tries to express her empathy for the misfortune freshly occurred, she gets hushes. There, a linguistic behaviour apt at preserving the original cohesion of the *closed* aggregation transmits the psychologically recalcitrant attitude pressing the SRU to assimilate their friend's death prematurely, mostly through Jules Callaghan's manifest emotional retreat ("/We're* good").

Nonetheless, precisely like Braddock's case, the professionally determined group's formal structure prevails, and Leah breaches through to join the team in no time. The training processes associate the team with designed preparations. Similar to congregational implications, these processes also determine peculiar multiskilled and multiproficient attitudes that blur the boundaries among compartmented roles (facilitating creating an organic entity). The rigorous standardised organogram of professionally related hierarchies and abilities tends to align all the group members within unitary qualifications. In like manner, another colleague of the squad can substitute the individual without affecting the result's quality. There, a more homogeneous bottom-up levelling (towards a highly-specialised perspective, and not from a ground-oriented flattening point of view) of group skills erases role label:

**158**    F. P. Gentile

*Example 4.4 Flashpoint Corpus, Flashpoint, s01e01, min. 00:07:03–33/18:35–41*

Lane:  ALPHA (..) Wordy^⇒ 1 Spike 2 Lou 3 (..) Wordy (.) you man the ra:m ((Wordy extends his arm for the win, although maintaining an unmoved face)) Rolie you head up bravo^ […] 5 (.) 6 (..) Spi:ke Dds and flashbangs ((Spike mimes an explosion with voice and hands)) (..) Lou↓⇒ (..) less lethal

Young:  ((In protest)) °Wha-° (..) Again↑ ((Nodding at Ed from behind))

Parker:  /And*^⇒I shall negotiate should the need ar:ise (..) Snipers (..) Ed (.) you're Sierra two: (..) ((Ed looks at Jules)) Jules (.) you're Sierra one ((She nods with a falsely neutral, but happy, smile)) (3') Mr. La:ne^

Lane:  Absolutely (..) Absolutely (..) Spread the wealth (..) ((To Jules, teasing her)) °Is°⇒ it Jules' Day^

Callaghan:  ((Mocking)) Every day is Jules' Day

Lane:  ((Ready to shoot)) Sierra one in position

Young:  ((Via radio, from the truck)) Sa:rge (..) sierra one's position was compromised (..) ((Articulating carefully)) Sierra two (.) is now sierra one

Example 4.4 reports the assignment of roles in the subsequent intervention. In light of the comprehensive set of abilities at the disposal of those cops, team leaders decide time after time what individual to charge with which task. Ed is the one that attributes code names (numbers from 1 to 6) and first subdivisions. Wordy loves using heavy tools, and Spike likes explosives. Hence, they gladly accept the team leader's decisions assigning them the rams and the flashbangs accordingly. However, Lou wants action as well, and, as he acknowledges getting less-lethal weapons again, he protests. Greg and Ed both foresee the cop's reaction. Lane firstly tones down his initially loud and clear speech to deflect the listener's attention from his words ("ALPHA (..) Wordy^ […] (..) **Lou↓⇒ (..) less-lethal**"). Secondly, Greg terminates Lou's reply, since the assignment is not supposed to be a dialogue, and continues Ed's job to relieve his colleague from the burden ("/And*^…"), although somehow revenging

# 4 *Flashpoint* as in-Group Psychological and Action... 159

Young's bad luck giving officer Lane the charge of the *secondary* sniper. Ed—maturely—accepts the situation via a cooperative 'appreciation' attitude ("**Absolutely** (..) **Absolutely** (..)"), except teasing Jules for her related fortune. Nevertheless, once on the scene, schemes change and, as Callaghan's position appears compromised, Ed *ex abrupto* becomes "Sierra 1" again.

Internal role-repartition appeal determines group entitativity under social and cultural variable factors influencing the individuals (Campbell, 1958). Thus, verbality announces such unconscious statuses using:

- a chuffed expression greeting the task (Example 4.4; Wordy and Spike's feedbacks);
- deluded externalisations hoping for unrealised better options (Lou's response);
- or competitive challenges (Jules and Ed teasing each other).

Such versatility, however, is not transposed (if not in seldom occasions) in the member/leader approach. Again, coherently with the *familiar* view, where brothers and sisters (team members) are supposed to acknowledge and hopefully legitimise their parents' guidance, this *professional* entity presupposes of two chief persons' presence. Greg is the Sergeant, and he is the one with more in-field experience. His tender and confident personality could allow the observation to identify him with the 'mother' stereotypically. Ed, the team-leader, has practically the same authority as Greg but inferior rank; he is also resolute and rough—like a 'father' cliché:

***Example 4.5 Flashpoint Corpus, Flashpoint, s01e03, min. 00:13:37–52***

| | |
|---|---|
| Lane: | Alpha^ team (.) we're switching up (..) Sam, you're gonna be 3 I'm gonna take lead entry |
| Braddock: | ((Discussing)) We're changing the ta:c plan^ |
| Lane: | /Tac plan* is a thing of beauty=Let's go (1') ((Greg gives encouragement pat to them as they pass by)) Jules (.) Spike (.) drop us off (.) roof=side |
| Braddock: | ((Continues)) Why^ |

| Lane: | Because when=you're <u>democratically</u> elected=team=leader you get to make ((Turns towards Sam while walking)) autocratic decisions (.) Let's go |
| --- | --- |

Suppose the members of the SRU-group can play the part of each other in terms of acting roles. In that case, some other tasks only are the appanage of a few. Despite being open to debate when necessary, the decision-making process is only handled by actual and formal guides, whose duty is to continually assess the evolving situation and evaluate eventual plan changes (Example 4.5).

Such authority is compulsory in a formal group structure that requires no second opinions, nor would explanation needs be elicited. In Example 4.5, the team member's insistence is peremptorily replied via a resolute statement ("Because when=you're **democratically** elected=team=leader you get to make **autocratic decisions**"). This utterance recalls fundamental leadership efficiency schemata focusing on the best—autocratic—management in place of other less effective styles—democratic, or even laissez-faire modalities (Lewin et al., 1939)—in certain *climatic* occasions.

The preliminary determination of the crime presupposes the communication to *all* law enforcement units of the sensible data related to the perpetrator.

In Table 4.9, the initial three-way process performed by ordinary officers—when they get informed of a criminal's presence within the area they are patrolling—is shown. The visual salience on the assaulter first focuses on his visage to let the viewers fix the man's trait in their mind. The criminal looks contrite, forced to inexpressiveness. The mimics tense up the nerves in his face faking a relaxed attitude (e.g., wrinkling forehead, eyebrow line lowered, semi-disclosed mouth with strained temporo mandibular joints). A wide-shot-framed peculiar gait speeds up as he proceedes through the crowd, although gripping the arms crossed on his chest to hide something.

In this phase, police procedural protocol verbal formulation flanks the visual narration. A radio communication keys in the muffled *description* of the suspect. There, the police language terminology blends with actual specialised discourse formality. Linguistic economy requirements allow the erasure of subject elements. This practice also facilitates

## 4 *Flashpoint* as in-Group Psychological and Action... 161

**Table 4.9** *Flashpoint*, s01e01. Culprit identification multimodal annotation

| Frame/Min | Visual image | Kinesic action | Soundtrack | Phases and Metafunctions |
|---|---|---|---|---|
| 00:09:16 | MovA; CP: Tracking/ Shaky;CLS-FV; VS> Street; P: M; Ph; | Movt: Participant #1 walking Tempo: Slow; | AS: Crowd; ST: Theme song fading; | A single phase setting the context. The criminal passes by a cop, who recognises him |
| 00:09:21 | WS-FV/BV VS> P: M (perp); M (cop); Crowd; | ≈ | AS: Crowd; | EXP: Crowded street |
| 00:09:25 | ≈ | ≈ | ≈ | INT: viewer close-ups the assaulter to focus first on his face, then on his gait amid the crowd. |
| 00:09:26 | ≈ | Movt: Participant #2 notes the man; | ≈ | Sudden wide shot to emphasise on the cop noting the man. Further close shot showing the engagement |
| 00:09:31 | MS-BV; VS> P: M; | Movt: Participant #1 turns back; Tempo: Fast; | AS: Crowd; ST: Low wind instrument notes; | TEX: Theme-rheme alternation: 1. description; 2. identification; 3. engagement; |
| 00:09:32 | CLS-BV/FV; VS> P: M; M; | Movt: Participants extract the gun; | AS: Crowd; Screams; ST: Low wind instrument notes; | |

**Dialogue**

Radio: ((Communication barely audible, disturbed by music and ambient noises)) °Suspect°⇒ is <u>flagged</u> (..) Alpha (..) Seen fleeing vicinity (.) exiting First York (..) Ma:le (.) white (.) 40s (.) blue jacket (.) heavy-set (..) 10-64 (..) Repeat 10-64 ((The man passes by a cop who notes him and follows him with his hand on his gun, ready to extract it))
Cop: ((They aim the gun at each other)) DROP YOUR WEAPON^

## 162    F. P. Gentile

ungrammatical usages (e.g., "Seen fleeing vicinity (.) exiting First York"; "Male, white…") of verbs lacking prepositional dependencies, pronouns and proper tense constructions (e.g., "seen fleeing vicinity", instead of '**was / has been** seen fleeing **in [the]** vicinity'; "Male, white, 40s…", instead of '**He is** male, white, **in his** 40s,…'). For the same reason, the grammatical subject of the description is deployed in the most informative position of the speech—and thus referencing all the subsequent clauses by omission—although deprived of its determinative article. The intense adjectival display in Table 4.9 is also related to a procedural pattern. Those syntactic elements do not play the role of mere connoted *qualifiers* as in everyday language situations. Handled by cops, they become terminological *identifiers* denoting the person of interest via a rigorously formulated string that tells data about gender, ethnicity, age and more supportive details like wardrobe, gait and body size. Once the description has ended, the warning continues with a final police code, "10-64", extensively limiting the motivations connected to the suspect's pursue, as 'Message for Local Delivery—Crime in Progress' (also see Chap. 6).[7]

The second and third steps of *identification* and *engagement* follow the linguistic radio communication. The precise details about the suspect let the cop recognise him and immediately intervene. There, a perlocutionary speech (the shouted "DROP YOUR WEAPON" authoritatively orders the addressee to 'surrender') preceded a performative act (extracting the weapon and aiming it at the criminal). After that, other communicative dimensions change. The wide-shot technique narrating the sequence suddenly turns again into close shots expressing the urgency of the situation via a tracking camera always chasing the culprit from the back (to eventually show the mutual cop-and-criminal threat, having each other at gunpoint). On the acoustic level, the original ambient noises are hushed by a startled cry of a woman seeing the gun, indicating the beginning of a tension-building moment implemented by low wind instrument notes. Despite the subject's hurried pace, the sequence is recounted by a slow tempo permitting the narrative need for displaying the cop to surpass the man, turn back, recognise him and attempt the apprehension. The foreseeable engagement is scanned via a faster rhythm

## 4  *Flashpoint* as in-Group Psychological and Action...     163

pressing the two participants to fight—following their respective roles of the status-quo protector (the former) and social-order subverter (the latter)—helped out by said music supports.

Nonetheless, suppose the fundamental of police interventions require similar approaches. In that case, the protagonists' team starring the *Flashpoint* TV series concentrates on the Strategic Response to critical situations, which demand alternative actions for the utter annihilation of the implied risks. Consequently, the psychological slant remains crucial for planning a safe and legal modus operandi that does not presuppose the capitulation of the subjects (exploited when no other solutions work) but the primary extinguishment of their evil intents. Those tactics, within the television environment observable throughout *Flashpoint*, are mostly carried out via two emblematic stages: *profiling* and *negotiation*:

### Example 4.6 Flashpoint Corpus, Flashpoint, s01e01, min. 00:17:45–50

| | |
|---|---|
| Parker: | Hey, Doc, what're ya thinking? |
| Dr. Luria: | ((Via rario)) First impression^ (..) <u>Not</u> ((Shakes her head)) substance^ issues (.) He's in <u>full-on tunnel</u> vision=I'm=thinking ((Watching CCTV footage form the crime scene)) multiple stressors |

### Example 4.7  Flashpoint  Corpus,  Flashpoint,  s01e02,  min. 00:19:11–22/21:14–19

| | |
|---|---|
| Dr. Luria: | ((From the car, via telephone)) Good morning (.) Luria here |
| Callaghan: | Morning Doc (..) Subject is Jack^⇒ Swanson (..) in↓ transition from <u>red</u> to yellow (.) he's responsive to Stockholm |
| Dr. Luria: | ((Nods astonished)) No flies on you↑ guy:s |
| Callaghan: | So we're=looking=at=impaired=cognitive=function=and=ir ritability |
| Dr. Luria: | ((Via telephone, although she nods at every term to emphasize it)) Emotional volatility (.) impulsiveness ((Scene cuts into a different phase)) |

164  F. P. Gentile

The science of 'criminal profiling' (Bartol, 2002; Singh & Mittal, 2016) is often referred to in consideration of its many branches ranging from 'behavioural', 'psychological', 'criminal personality' or 'offender', and eventually 'crime scene' *profiling strategies* of the investigative analysis (Palermo & Kocsis, 2004; Turvey, 2003). The latter disciplines focus on the implications between the victimology and the assailant schemata—like verbal threats, weaponry display, physical presence escalating to aggression (Hazelwood et al., 1991). Conversely, the former two types prefer cognitive examinations of the subjects' conscious or unconscious communicative reactions to certain *stimuli*. Examples 4.6 and 4.7 are both apt at establishing potential mental conditions or unbalanced statuses demonstrated by the persons of interest to understand how to launch communicative attempts without distressing them. Indeed, similar sciences—also appanage of Special Services of Investigative Bureaus worldwide—are good at sketching outfitting portraits of serial offenders.

Nevertheless, difficulties in profiling methodologies arise when specialists have to perform analyses on unique cases about individuals who cannot be associated with any MO pattern or scheme. In Example 4.6, the psychology specialist underlines her "first **impression^**" (followed by a further reiteration "…=I'm=thinking…") via a vocal pitch raise on the second word to emphasise the conjectural nature of her hypothesis. Then, she formulates the diagnoses of PTSD afflicting the subject due to "multiple stressors" (once seen the man's behaviours through CCTV). The subject seems unresponsive to any communicative *stimuli* since auditory exclusion co-occurs with loss of peripheral perception and spasmodic gestures (Levote, 2012) that indicate a severe disorder. Dr Luria's closing statement confirms results via high graduation 'force' employing positioning-strengthening adjectival uses (e.g., "**full-on** tunnel vision=…").

The same methodology is proffered in instance 4.7. The clinical report obtained from profiling techniques indicates 'impaired cognitive functions', 'irritability', 'emotional volatility' and 'impulsiveness'. Once retrieved in the observed subject's behaviours, they prove the psychological theorisations right and proceed with the correct construction of a phatic channel of interaction. On the same trend, the psychological *perspective,*

## 4 *Flashpoint* as in-Group Psychological and Action... **165**

combined with the formulation of interactive *strategies*, assumes the organisation of profiles in adherence to linguistic points of control to be categorised. To design communication blueprints in want of a given output, in fact, profilers on both legal sides—medical specialist Luria and SRU tactical—need psychological *labels* rigidly defining the suspect (e.g., "Subject is Jack^⇒ Swanson (..) **in↓transition from <u>red</u> to yellow**"; see also "[the suspect is] clearly=**progressing=from <u>assaultive</u> to grievous bodily <u>harm</u>**", *Flashpoint*, s01e01, min. 00:31:32):

### *Example 4.8 Flashpoint Corpus, Flashpoint, s01e02, min. 00:15:28–50*

| | |
|---|---|
| Parker: | ((To the hostage-taker, while keeping a hand on the shoulder of the agent covering him)) It's all right (.) these guys are with me (.) They don't move unless ((Nodding)) I^⇒ say so↓ […] It's^⇒ my: job to <u>help you</u> and I want to make sure no one gets hurt↑ |
| Gunman: | I↑⇒ want you to <u>back</u> off |
| Parker: | Can't do that Jack (.) We're gonna stay right here (2') Is it all right if I call you Ja:ck^ (.) My name's Greg |
| Gunman: | Hey↑⇒ I mean it |
| Parker: | Let's just talk (.) okay^ |

### *Example 4.9 Flashpoint Corpus, Flashpoint, s01e02, min. 00:16:46–50/21:14–19*

| | |
|---|---|
| Braddock: | We already know why the perp's here |
| Lane: | ((Checking CCTV)) He's↓⇒ a <u>subject</u> (.) not a pe:rp |
| Braddock: | He's a guy with a gun^ ((Smirks)) |
| Callaghan: | ((Turns towards Sam, while on the phone)) He's a father^ in trouble |
| Lane: | ((Without looking at the agent, but conscious of his disappointment)) You ask questions Sa:m (.) you show him that you're listening |

The final step eventually is about *negotiation*. Having assessed the mental status of the criminals, the one in charge (in most cases Greg) tries to latch a communicative bond with them showing sympathy for their situation and letting them believe they are on their side (to peacefully guide their surrender). Indeed, the prime notion of negotiation deals with the avoidance of 'judgemental' attitudes compromising the interactive channel's balance (Example 4.9). Sam's 'appreciation' is uttered through a connoted prejudiced jargon ("perp"). Ed and Jules intervene to clarify the procedure for him. Together with a long list of rules (e.g., "Negotiating 101: Never lie to the subject", *Flashpoint*, s01e02, min. 00:21:01), the basics of said practice forbid users to construct preconceived and biased ideas of the individuals with whom they dialogue. Indeed, every person's acts move following some hidden reasons to be found (Example 4.9; "He's a guy with a gun^ / He's a father^ in trouble").

Like a sort of practical application of Game Theory, negotiation procedures require participants to make a move one after the other, in turn, to conclude a match that is hopefully ending with the good side's checkmate on the bad one. In the *game*, all the parts renounce something as much as they obtain something else along the communicative path. In that light, the agents' attitude has to appear cooperative to the subject (Example 4.8; also Example 4.7, "responsive to Stockholm"). Thus, the negotiator needs to carry out his task using a constant tone, which has to be clear and reassuring, never submissive nor too authoritative. In Example 4.8, Greg utters his lines with no hesitation and through gestural hints subconsciously funnelling bits of information into the receiver's mind. While talking, the man maintains his smile and relaxed posture throughout the exchange, even when he has to refuse the subject's "back off" order. A similar body language slant would open a conversational situation where the two Parts could declare their goals. However, a subject could misinterpret Greg's confident approach (also underlined by his posture, behind another officer in full gear covering him, with a hand on his shoulder) as a challenge.

For this reason—from the Appraisal framework stance—the negotiator makes his statements in an attempt to calm his addressee via the cooperative perspective. The strategy is linguistically emphasised by endorsing 'affect' attitude and 'lower' levels of graduation force ("It's **all right**"; "let's **just** talk"), and positive declarations ("It's my job **to help you**"). Along with such linguistic occurrences, the man continually attempts to reinforce the phatic channel with the subject ("Is it all right if I call you Ja:ck^ (.) My name's Greg") to create some empathy and induce the receiver out of the situation through a collaboratively responsive behaviour.

# The *Flashpoint Corpus* Results

The *Flashpoint Corpus* counts ~210,892 tokens (already deprived of empty words) and ~2586 word-types in a ratio of 1/81.55 between new terms and their associated reiterative pattern (via full or partial repetition). A similar 1.23 per cent count in the types/tokens fraction indicates a shallow variation rate in comparison to the corpus lexical density. Separating those data about each season, also considering the different amounts of episodes in seasons 1 and 3, statistical counts undergo different results compared to season 2. Considering the massive gap between *Flashpoint*'s second season and the more even first and third ones, token variation—that is ~87,619 (2009) against ~58,681 (2008) and ~64,592 (2010)—seems to flatten on the differentiation of the types—approximately 4892 (2009) against ~4058 (2008) and ~4393 (2010). The average ratio of seasonal tokens/types variation, indeed, would reach 6.33 per cent, in place of an overall 1.23 per cent, implying a type turnover of one new term in 15.80 repetitions (instead of one in 81.55) and 5.1 per cent raise of vocabulary heterogeneity (Table 4.10).

**Table 4.10** The *Flashpoint Corpus* results

| FLASHPOINT CORPUS [SEASONS 1 TO 3 > (2008–2010)] | | | |
|---|---|---|---|
| Tokens (T) | Types (t) | | FpC T/t ratio |
| ~210,892 | ~2586 | | **1/81.55 (1.23%)** |
| SEASON 1 (2008) T/t | SEASON 2 (2009) T/t | SEASON 3 (2010) T/t | AVG $(T_1 + T_2 + T_3) / (t_1 + t_2 + t_3)$ |
| 1/58.681 (1.71%) | 1/87,619 (1.14%) | 1/64,592 (1.55%) | **1/15.80 (6.33%)** |
| VOCABULARY HETEROGENEITY (AVG T/t vs. *FpC* T/t) | | | |
| **+5.1%** differentiation | | | |

Nonetheless, if similar statistical separation could work for other products, the *Flashpoint* TV series presents a more organic structure. Production timetables in the three years 2008–2010 were defined through a more relaxed programming schedule expanding transmission periods. The first season premiered July 11, 2008, and finished February 13, 2009—seven months—and the second one only forebore about a week to start, on-air between February 27 and November 20, of the same year (during nine months). Almost a half-year later, the third season premiered July 16, 2010, and went on until February 6, 2011 (lasting the same seven month-period of season 1; moreover, seasons 4 and 5 got aired via a similar pattern, although not included in the current study). Suppose the TV products surveyed in the following chapters could find a compartmented approach coherent. In that case, the *Flashpoint Corpus*—given the linear *mise en scène* programme—could, without doubt, result as a single non-separate collection of data to be analysed with no inner interruptions or discontinuities in terms of staging time and themes.

In *Flashpoint*, the token/type ratio count statistically highlights the great attention paid by producers and scriptwriters on the florid linguistic and terminological thesaurus to be adopted within the seasonal broadcasts. Such attention has been levelled down over the years, employing some coherently designed expressive structures and peculiarities characterising the series and causing a homogenisation of content via iterative, discursive and dialogic schemata. The said narrow range of lexical choices also mirrors the linguistically and thematically specific set of narrations. These structures often focus on critical situations resolved via a procedural *iter* that remains unaltered episode after episode. In a "centripetal complexity" vortex (Jacobs & Peacock, 2013, p. 52; see also Chap. 3), every show is made a *revival* of another. Along with the themes discussed, the cinematic techniques characterising the series operate through crystallised formulae. Every instalment opens in *media res* towards an escalating breakdown originating a narrative climax that suddenly gets defused through flashback rewinding strategies which scan salient frames backwards hours before the situation started (Fig. 4.3). On the silver thread of flashbacks, minutes after a similar expedient display, a second climax shatters because of the insertion of the TV series theme song (Fig. 4.1), used to pause the narration and let viewers reflate after the intense

## 4 *Flashpoint* as in-Group Psychological and Action... 169

presentation of facts soaring up rapidly (between 5'–10' in seasons 1 and 2, and between 10'–15' in season 3). The first section of the instalment works like some teaser clutching spectators' appeal. The second one serves as an introduction or contextualisation for the subsequent happenings. Yet, as soon as the *Flashpoint* theme song is over, the actual episode development is launched, focusing on the operative activities of its protagonists hastening throughout the show to peacefully and safely fizzle out the risky circumstances.

The serial juxtaposition of other expressive modes supporting of cinematic techniques mostly delivers the said alternation of tension and calm. Sound effects play a relevant role in the flashback. They signal every image framed on screen via the rustle of photograph-like chaotic browsing. Likewise, in the theme song, they act through a peculiar music-and-jingle branding the TV product. The said acoustic interludes emphasise rhythmic narrative pauses, but they also appear significant in the larger part of the episodes (from the theme song conclusion to the end of the show). Interludes underline meaningful situations and culminate (almost every time in the forty-four instalments observed) with a musical recount narrating the episode's final sequences using famous Anglophone song refrains or stanzas harmoniously fading in association with the visual dimension.

Along with some descriptive choices, the *Flashpoint* setting geographic localisation also contributes to conditioning the series rendition. The decision of picking Toronto as the ideal environment for the product is emblematic, given the general aim depicting strongly Canadian connoted features on screen, meant to break with USA-centric traditions for a broader plateau of receivers. Many television productions have moved to Canada's major city lately—i.e., *The Bridge*, Canada: *CTV*, 2010; *Cracked*, Canada: *CBC Television*, 2013; *Rookie Blue*, Canada and USA: *Global/ABC*, 2010–2015—electing Toronto as the perfect milieu for police procedural. However, *Flashpoint's* peculiarity inspired by actual Emergency Task Force (ETF) operations interrupts the US consolidated legacy of SWAT-based TV series even more clearly. The pure action of North American genre philosophy 'shoot first, think later' (Carveth & Arp, 2015) is decidedly counterpoised to the Canadian culture of "ask [a] question [and show] you are

## 170   F. P. Gentile

listening" (Example 4.9), through an intensely communicative police procedural proposal. Albeit, the serious dangers connected with the series themes imply the narrative need for associating toponymic occurrences determining the urban radar of significant events (Table 4.6 and Fig. 4.5) with other semantic fields.

On the communicative ground, verb occurrences are peculiar. Imperative modes and action verbs denoting brutality or legitimate use of force are commonly expected in similar contexts. Instead, the *Flashpoint* peacekeeping philosophy vividly prefers mitigating modes and forms urging criminals to sympathetic cooperation more than simplistically ordering the surrender (and 'action verbs' are solidly contrasted by 'negotiation verbs'). Anyhow, imperatives and peremptory iterations do recur here. For the best part, they concern copula verbs (via the intense use of auxiliary verbs) under linguistic economy strategies that prefer nominalisation or verbal elision phenomena for a fast elocution pace.

Moreover, the series dedicates great attention to certain domains monopolising linguistic and extra-linguistic levels of expressiveness. On the one hand, the law enforcement slant mainly derives from the definite unitary sense of team-work of the SRU—passing through slightly displayed bureaucratic rigour, intense training sessions (Example 4.2), and high-risk interventions. Its active stages are extensively ascribed to the florid usage of the weaponry vocabulary and terminology (Table 4.5), and, most importantly, to the ubiquitous iconicity of deadly devices (Fig. 4.4). Therefore, despite the preciseness of the linguistic data funnelled within the series, the most expressive degrees of informativity and semantic salience are the appanages of the extra-linguistic dimensions. Those features can develop plot-related facts via visual, acoustic and cinematic techniques showing relevant events rather than reporting them for a more immediate reception and assimilation of the content.

On the other hand, verbal features seem irrelevant in many passages of the corpus compared to other non-verbal and para-verbal aspects associated with emotion conveyance (Table 4.8). Yet, it is worth noting that linguistically meaningful dialogues help define a secondary thematic core of the *Flashpoint* series. Action is crucial for the resolution of issues and the neutralisation of threats. Yet, the psychological perspective represents

## 4 *Flashpoint* as in-Group Psychological and Action... 171

the igniter of all the mental processes and schemata responsible for apical lucubrations to be actualised in a three-way pattern of *thought-plan-action*, narratively mirrored by *description-identification-engagement* modes (Table 4.9). Here, as said, verbs are an essential element for the examination. They are deployed for the oral enunciation and explanation of tactic strategies, despite their prominent copula usages, or cooperation/negotiation connoted aims.

In comparison to the verbal dimension, the para-verbal observation of the scenes (especially on the visual level) produces an oxymoronic contrast. The iconic assessment of the SRU scenic bios displays a consistent number of soldiers geared up from head to toe, ready to assault criminals and utterly dismantle terroristic threats for good. Nonetheless, the gigantic display of guns, bombs, tools and weapons of any sort (e.g., Figs. 4.1, 4.3 and 4.4) confidently handled by those men and women in raid formation gets annihilated by their 'talkative' attitude. Their professional behaviours confine the task force's mediatically charming combat skills to a secondary role via a different kind of performativity. Here, dialogic narrations (Table 4.4; examples from 4.7 to 4.9) surpass action.

Considering the emphatic relevance of team-focused situations, the *équipe*, as a single entity, or its members—accordingly—are determinant for the instalment happy ending. From that perspective, the lens of psychology—whether they define the social in-/out-goup separation (Sokorin, 1937; Lewin et al., 1939; Campbell, 1958; Singh & Mittal, 2016) or police profiling techniques (Hazelwood et al., 1991; Bartol, 2002; Turvey, 2003; Palermo & Kocsis, 2004; Levote, 2012)—can sketch the product's boundaries of fundamental social behaviours that range from *in-group dynamics* (Examples 4.3, 4.4 and 4.5) to *labelling procedures* denoting mental associations and comportment schemes summing up individuals' categorisations (Examples 4.6 and 4.7). Those same psychological references define the basis of Negotiation strategies. Together with Tactical approaches (plus weaponry lexicon and strategic planning), they result as the most significant communicative spheres of the *Flashpoint Corpus*, through preferential fast-track iconic deliveries secondarily formulated by respective verbal enunciations glossing or expanding the narrative bubbles.

# Notes

1. Despite the narrative focus on a single team, other units are mentioned or referred to in the series, seldom cooperating with the main one.
2. The corpus is not merely based on straight TV series scripts. It comes from an extensive qualitative transcript activity inclusive of POS tags and other essential prosodic annotations implementing the collected data's informativity levels.
3. All the labels about appraisal framework evaluations—here as in the following chapters—reference J.R. Martin and P.R.R. White (2005)
4. Although plot developments justify Jules' absence because of the gunshot wound, Amy Jo Johnson took a break due to maternity leave in real life. The actress was already an expectant mother when she started filming *Flashpoint*, and her status was camouflaged as far as possible thanks to the uniforms and vests she had to wear all the time throughout the shootings (Goldman, 2008).
5. The actress also starred in another TV serial analysed in this study. Tattiawna Jones indeed interpreted the fixed character of Amelie De Grace in *19-2* from 2014 to 2017 (her character was killed in the show).
6. Bold is mine for emphasis throughout the manuscript.
7. Police Radar Information Center. 'Police 10 codes'. https://copradar.com/tencodes/ (accessed June 19, 2019).

# References

Adolphs, S., & Carter, R. (2013). *Spoken Corpus Linguistics: From Monomodal to Multimodal*. Routledge.

Aijmer, K., & Stenström, A.-B. (Eds.). (2004). *Discourse Patterns in Spoken and Written Corpora*. John Benjamins Publishing Company.

Alias, S. (2004). A Semiotic Study of Singapore's Orchard Road and Marriott Hotel. In K. O'Halloran (Ed.), *Multimodal Discourse Analysis. Systemic Functional Perspectives* (pp. 55–84). Continuum.

Allen, M. (Ed.). (2007). *Reading CSI: Crime TV under the Microscope*. I.B. Tauris.

Baldry, A., & Thibault, P. J. (2006). *Multimodal Transcription and Text Analysis: A Multimedia Toolkit and Course Book*. Equinox.

Bammer, G. (2013). *Disciplining Interdisciplinarity Integration and Implementation Sciences for Researching Complex Real-World Problems.* Australian University Press.

Barr, M. (2010, July 16). Interview: The Creators of *Flashpoint. Film School Rejects.* Retrieved May 3, 2019, from https://filmschoolrejects.com/interview-the-creators-of-flashpoint-2c6b71d6f587/

Bartol, C. R. (2002). *Criminal Behaviour: A Psychological Approach.* Prentice Hall.

Bednarek, M. (2010). *The Language of Fictional Television: Drama and Identity.* Continuum.

Brundson, C. (2010). *Law and Order.* Palgrave Macmillan.

Campbell, D. (1958). Common Fate, Similarity, and Other Indices of the Status of Persons as Social Entities. *Behavioral Science, 3*, 14–25. Retrieved May 15, 2019, from https://onlinelibrary.wiley.com/doi/pdf/10.1002/bs.3830030103

Carveth, R., & Arp, R. (Eds.). (2015). *Justified and Philosophy: Shoot First, Think Later.* Open Court.

*CBC News.* (2004, September 17). Officer Who Shot Toronto Hostage-Tacker Cleared. Retrieved May 6, 2019, from https://www.cbc.ca/news/canada/officer-who-shot-toronto-hostage-taker-cleared-1.497501

Collins, R. (1990). *Culture, Communication, and National Identity: The Case of Canadian Television.* University of Toronto Press.

Creeber, G. (Ed.). (2006). *Tele-Visions. An Introduction to Studying Television.* British Film Institute.

De Beaugrande, R.-A., & Dressler, W. U. (1994). *Introduzione alla Linguistica Testuale.* Il Mulino. [Original Title: *Einführunh in die Textlinguistik,* 1981].

Dorland, M., & Charland, M. R. (2002). *Law, Rhetoric and Irony in the Formation of Canadian Civil Culture.* University of Toronto Press.

*Flashpoint.* CTV. Toronto. July 11, 2008–February 6, 2011.

Freeze, C., Gray, J., & Pooley, E.. ([2004] 2018, April 21). 49 Minutes of Terror and Tragedy in Toronto. *The Globe and Mail.* Retrieved May 6, 2019, from https://www.theglobeandmail.com/news/national/49-minutes-of-terror-and-tragedy-intoronto/article1140356/

Garzone, G. (2020). *Specialised Communication and Popularisation in English.* Carocci.

Gittins, S. (1999). *CTV: The Television Wars.* Stoddart.

Goldman, E. (2008, July 10). Amy Jo Johnson in the *Flashpoint. IGN.* Retrieved May 8, 2019, from https://www.ign.com/articles/2008/07/10/amy-jo-johnson-in-the-flashpoint?page=1

**174**    **F. P. Gentile**

Grego, K. (2013). *The Physics You Buy in Supermarkets*. Writing Science for the General Public: The Case of Stephen Hawking. In S. Kermas & T. Christinsen (Eds.), *The Popularization of Specialised Discourse and Knowledge across Communities and Cultures* (pp. 149–172). EDIPUGLIA (off print). Retrieved March 9, 2021, from https://core.ac.uk/download/pdf/187907774.pdf

Hazelwood, R., Reboussin, R., Warren, J. I., & Wright, J. A. (1991). Prediction of Rapist Type and Violence from Verbal, Physical and Sexual Scales. *Journal of Interpersonal Violence, 6*(1), 55–67.

Heydon, G. (2005). *The Language of Police Interviewing: A Critical Analysis*. Palgrave Macmillan.

Jacobs, J., & Peacock, S. (Eds.). (2013). *Television Aesthetics and Style*. Bloomsbury Academic.

Klein, J. T. (2013). The Transdisciplinary Moment(um). *Integral Review, 2*(9), 189–199.

Kress, G. (2010). *Multimodality. A Social Semantic Approach to Contemporary Communication*. Routledge.

Kress, G., & van Leeuwen, T. (1996). *Reading Images: The Grammar of Visual Design*. Routledge.

Kristine, D. (2008, July 11). Cop Drama *Flashpoint* Explores Human Costs of Heroism. *Blog Critics* (archived). Retrieved May 8, 2019, from https://web.archive.org/web/20080718124735/http://blogcritics.org/archives/2008/07/11/001823.php

Levote, D. (2012, August 25). Criminologia. Fisiologia e psicologia delle aggressioni violente. *Crime List. Approfondimenti di Intelligence*. Retrieved June 19, 2019, from http://www.crimelist.it/index.php/analisi/criminologia/818-fisiologia-e-psicologia-nelle-aggressioni-violente

Lewin, K., Lippit, R., & White, R. K. (1939). Patterns of Aggressive Behavior in Experimentally Created "Social Climates". *Journal of Social Psychology, 10*(2), 269–299. Retrieved May 15, 2019, from https://tu-dresden.de/mn/psychologie/ipep/lehrlern/ressourcen/dateien/lehre/lehramt/lehrveranstaltungen/Lehrer_Schueler_Interaktion_SS_2011/Lewin_1939_original.pdf?lang=en

Marmor, A. (2014). *The Language of Law*. Oxford University Press.

Martin, J. R., & White, P. R. R. (2005). *The Language of Evaluation. Appraisal in English*. Palgrave Macmillan.

O'Halloran, K. L. (Ed.). (2004). *Multimodal Discourse Analysis. Systemic Functional Perspectives*. Continuum.

O'Toole, M. (1994). *The Language of Displayed Art*. Leicester University Press.

Olandewarju, F. R. (2009). *Forensic Linguistics. An Introduction to the Study of Language and the Laws*. Lincom Europa.

Palermo, G. B., & Kocsis, R. M. (2004). *Offender Profiling. An Introduction to the Sociopsychological Analysis of Violent Crimes*. Charles C. Thomas Publisher.

Pender, T. N. (2007, July 20). Cop Action in the Works for CTV. *Playback*. Retrieved May 3, 2019, from http://playbackonline.ca/2007/07/20/critical-20070720/

*Police Radar Information Center*. Police 10 Codes. Retrieved June 19, 2019., from https://copradar.com/tencodes/

Richardson, K. (2010). *Television Dramatic Dialogue. A Sociolinguistic Study*. Oxford University Press.

Roelcke, T. (2010). *Fachsprachen*. Erich Shmidt.

Rühleman, C. (2013). *Narrative in English Conversation: A Corpus Analysis of Storytelling*. Cambridge University Press.

Searle, J. (1969). *Speech Acts. An Essay in the Philosophy of Language*. Cambridge University Press.

Searle, J., & Vanderveken, D. (1985). *Foundations of Illocutionary Logic*. Cambridge University Press.

Simpson, P., & Mayr, A. (2009). *Language and Power*. Routledge.

Singh, T., & Mittal, S. (2016). Psychological Profiling in Criminal Investigation: An Overview. *Journal of Human Behaviour and Development, 3*, 17–21.

Sokorin, P. A. (1937). *Social and Cultural Dynamics*. Digital Library India [online resourse]. Retrieved May 15, 2019, from https://archive.org/details/in.ernet.dli.2015.46550/page/n301

Stubbs, M. (1983). *Discourse Analysis. The Sociolinguistic Analysis of Natural Language*. University of Chicago Press.

Treble, P. (2008, July 7). A Series Inspired by a T.O. Sniper. *Maclean's*. Retrieved May 6, 2019, from http://archive.macleans.ca/article/2008/7/7/a-series-inspired-by-a-to-sniper

Treble, P. ([2008] 2013, December 16). TV: New Cop Drama *Flashpoint. The Canadian Encyclopedia*. Retrieved May 6, 2019, from https://www.thecanadianencyclopedia.ca/en/article/tv-new-cop-drama-flashpoint

Turvey, B. E. (2003). *Criminal Profiling: An Introduction to Behavioural Evidence Analysis*. Academic Press.

van Leeuwen, T. (2004). Ten Reasons Why Linguists Should Pay Attention to Visual Communication. In P. LeVine & R. Scollon (Eds.), *Discourse and*

*Technology. Multimodal Discourse Analysis* (pp. 7–19). Georgetown University Press.

Wild, D. (2008, January 29). CTV Serial *Flashpoint* Picked Up by CBS for U.S. Broadcast. *TV, eh?* Retrieved May 3, 2019, from https://www.tv-eh.com/2008/01/29/ctv-series-flashpoint-picked-up-by-cbs-for-us-broadcast/

# 5

## The *Motive* 'Whydunit' Television Hybrid

The word 'serial', used as an adjective (mostly related to verbs and amid the array of other possible occurrence contexts), refers to what is "used in sequence to form a construction".[1] As a noun associated with media discourse, it defines "a story or a play appearing in regular instalments on television or radio or in a magazine" (ibid.). Subsequently, the development of a single and consolidated behaviour or pattern is in slight contrast with the 'series' signification as "[several] events, objects or people of a similar or related kind coming one after another".[2] By this last definition, serial events correspond to the cause–effect scheme of a single story. A series of facts—although the possibility of being as much consequential—is not necessarily related to a unique pattern but a similar format. Such differentiation reflects a diverse narrative rendition on a television context, which associates the *series* muster of stand-alone episodes with a *serial* concatenate collection of instalments sharing the same silver thread to making a cinematic multi editor project (MEP).

© The Author(s), under exclusive license to Springer Nature Switzerland AG 2021  **177**
F. P. Gentile, *Corpora, Corpses and Corps*,
https://doi.org/10.1007/978-3-030-78276-4_5

178  **F. P. Gentile**

## The Broadcast

The *Motive* TV show is engaging precisely because of its miscellaneous attitude as it differs from other television products in its fascination and formal narrative consistency. The product appears as a hybrid TV crime drama. It skilfully switches from the series structure of the first two seasons (the second one is already hybrid) to the third one of an utterly serial stylistic narration. Then it shifts back to the series modality in its fourth season (not discussed here). These changes also match fluctuations between either "centrifugal" and "centripetal complexity" (Jacobs & Peacock, 2013: 52) of its narrative.

Through a more generalisable cinematic scheme, the first season (2013) deals with a *broader* contextual introduction setting characters and preparing the audience to witness the show and its broadcast techniques, along with the actual narrative display of single criminal events to be investigated. In this case, every vicissitude is a singularity, packed solo and stashed in its related slot inside the ample seasonal ensemble. The second annual televised product (2014) is different from the one that has preceded it. Events are separate and unconnected with each other, despite their rhematic plot aiming at developing the characters' interpersonal attitudes that determine a subtextual expansion of collateral happenings, which are secondary to the main thematic structure. Those same structures affect the narration, surrounding the 'series' configuration with a diaphanous halo introducing the 'serial' slant. The third season starts recapping the events in-between second-year content and the present (in 2015). It reports direct consequences of some mentioned interpersonal clashes and introduces a pivotal murder that acts as a gigantic narrative phase. The subsequent instalments almost act like extensive subphases stretching towards the finale for the culprit's implied discovery and punishment. The macro-thematic bubble premiering the penultimate annual broadcast of *Motive* establishes the limits of a *static* recount. Detail after detail and killing after killing, the plot mesmerises the spectator. It demonstrates how the entire 2015 show reconnects to the assassin appearing in the first episode and performing his deeds to erase the traces.

Notwithstanding *Motive*'s hybridity (series ↔ serial), it is hereafter labelled 'series' for ease of reference, since the predominance of such mode over the other.

## The *Motive* Narrative Core

Here, the examination aims to assemble the show's linguistics with its several communication qualities. It is already evident in its very title. In association with the series narrative perspective, 'motive' could represent the leitmotif framing the context. Natural language usages of the word put it in a synonymic relationship with other equivalents such as *reason* or *cause*. Anyhow, it has its specialised and terminological value, which seems to be very relevant. Legal discourse shapes the environment set by the criminal-fictional milieu recounting deadly events. The investigation follows. Therefore, the 'motive'—from the Latin 'motivus', meaning 'moving'—actually is the triggering purpose leading a killer to commit unlawful deeds (murders). It is the intention *moving* the action. Moreover, the title contextualisation seems fundamental. The name introduces the series audience to a police procedural dimension (unlike the *Flashpoint* one, which sets the critical stage requiring tactical squad interventions; Chap. 3). This TV show is about the a posteriori homicide department investigative approach to retrieving heinous individuals once they *have accomplished* their irreparable harm. Therefore, the title reveals further details about the narrative attitude, where the protagonists are not keen on pedestrian tasks aiming at *preventing* the making of whatsoever violation. They are contrarily and posthumously intervening on already acknowledged, brutal crime scenes to study available pieces of evidence. There, reconstructive and deductive procedures would serve to catch the murderers.

Of course, the motivations behind their conduct deserve particular attention. It is already clear that the best part of the depicted scenarios could involve indoor office jobs along with minor external tasks (discussed in the following paragraphs).

180 F. P. Gentile

The connotation of the series setting (because of Vancouver's value in terms of geographical position and investment power deriving from its film industry activity) is not the sole primary concern of television. On economic and political grounds, the commodification of contents is essential for product identifiability. Hence, the Broadcaster aims to convey paramount Canadian linguistic and cultural markers (Collins, 1990; Dorland & Charland, 2002; Bredin et al., 2012; see Chap. 3) on national and international scales (Gittins, 1999; Beaty & Sullivan, 2006). For this reason, "set in Vancouver in the same way *Rookie Blue* is set in Toronto—very subtly, so as not to confuse or turn off American viewer's—*ABC's* newly imported crime drama, *Motive*, offers a common Canadian trade-off" (Hale, 2013; see also Lowry, 2016). Indeed, one predominant criterion for similar productions remains the satisfaction of the spectators' tastes through the proposal of catchy narrations, which create affiliation. This perspective stays fundamental for audiences worldwide, even when the Broadcaster and specific media policies urge the transmission of connoted features strictly marking out format and localization praxes.

The *Motive* Vancouver peculiarly mirrors the Canadian format camouflaged as a West Coast North America production. That is to preserve the economic interests of the geographical area from the mediatic perspective. The "longstanding, stable and competitive tax incentives and government support, and a community that nurtures creativity", transforms the place into "the ideal location for any Film or TV production", as reported by the *Vancouver Economic Commission* (n.d.).[3] Hence, the Vancouver Film Industry has to consider constructing an aseptic environment where both Canadian and US TV series and movies might be set and plausibly narrated.

Notwithstanding such requirements, every product also has to be markedly identifiable via the insertion of particular narrative and cinematic signals determining its (national) target as much as its cultural source, without annoying receivers. In *Motive*, every episode of the show is rich in distinctive traits. They contribute to render the narrative aim of Canadianness through the multimodal conveyance of significant plot events in association with recognisable elements of the megacity, such as the Lions Gate Bridge, postcard-style shots of the Canada Place waterfront or skyline, and further details like the small shoulder patches on cop uniforms calquing the Vancouver police logo (they are all present in the series).

As explained, *CTV* (Canadian) and *ABC* (US) viewers can consequently relate to the *Motive* product criminological interest regardless of their backgrounds and enjoy its episodes, yet simultaneously detecting the nationally determined environment that the TV series has occupied.

The identity marker deployment procedure throughout the instalments, however, does not unexpectedly mirror the show intro structure as one central element of characterisation. *Motive*'s theme choice is a sombre and minimal visual strategy that does not indulge the common "Cancon" (Gittins, 1999: 95) attention-seeking and iconic expectations either on the visual level or on the acoustic one. The entire intro only lasts three seconds (more like a brief interlude). It consists of the 'motive' uppercase wording carved on a black foreground, with the night-time city skyscraper lights flowing behind the wording transparency. At the same time, it comes into focus instants before fading in bright, to move to the first frame of narration that kicks off the episode. The introduction is too short to contemplate some music or a jingle corroborating the show openings, resulting in the diaphanous tinnitus of a suspense-ish reverberation.

In consideration of such preliminary observations, a multimodal study of the *Motive Corpus* endorses the quest of those main linguistic strategies, narrative techniques and stylistic patterns, which screenplay writers underwent to build up their creation via the consistent integration of natural linguistic and extra-linguistic situations. Here, the visually appraisable content immediacy of *core* expressiveness stands tall over the verbal dimension. Everyday language and professional contexts of knowledge, discourse and terminology co-occur—or alternate—to render that. As already explained with the *Flashpoint Corpus* (Chap. 4), the investigation initially concentrates on the results regarding the *Motive Corpus* multimodal modes of communication solo, to determine the most sensible amounts of data characterising this corpus itself. Secondarily, the evidence collected will constitute a final contrastive analysis to egress the Canadian TV crime drama genre symptomatic qualities. The comparison includes both structural and communicative levels and the related divergent features. These aspects are inferable thanks to the utter comparison of the currently perused corpus with those obtained from the Montreal and Toronto shows.

## The *Motive Corpus* Structure

The TV series evaluation serves the actual assessment of content-enriched data. Such *perceived* information is then 'translated' into some *tangible* proofs, for the effective classification and description. The observation of the related communicative features has to pass through the necessary step collecting all the possible bits of information within a single (extra-)linguistic thesaurus (Aijmer & Stenström, 2004; Adolphs & Carter, 2013). The *Motive Corpus* resulting from the procedure above is considered as a whole. However, as a blending of series and serial mediatic patterns, the case study would undoubtedly cause some quirks in thematic diversification (discussed in the following paragraphs), hence possibly in terms of linguistic *spectra* amplitude.

Like the analytical range limitations explained in Chap. 4, the *Motive*'s coherence issues regard some focus deflections. The particular *CTV* product concentrates on its *whydunnit* slant. There, the evolving narrative perspective flattens from the series to serial modes. This shift intensely contributes to reshaping the textual, descriptive, linguistic and, generally, multimodal storyline communication of each season. Nonetheless, it might cause some points of discontinuity in the retrieved data statistical relevance—given by the narrow thematic range of the content. On a merely linguistic level (of *natural* language), it could represent a problem.

Contrarily, a similar screen-play tendency does not represent a bias. Indeed, television observation fundamental awareness includes monitored expressive patterns (Durovicova & Newman, 2010; Wildfeuer, 2016) designed to emulate ordinary communicative events through fictionalised and *artificial* modes (Trudgill, 2000; Bednarek, 2010, 2018, 2019; Richardson, 2010; Piazza et al., 2011; Eco, 2016; see Chap. 2). Part of the methodological statement reflects the purpose of describing TV crime seriality main patterns under the multimodal communication lens. Consequently, the said thematic channels assimilate part of the expressively productive process moulding the medium language (Baldry & Thibault, 2001, 2006; Bateman & Schmidt, 2012). Here, the narrative disparity considers the examination carried

## 5 The *Motive* 'Whydunit' Television Hybrid    183

out and senses it as a crucial discriminant to be pondered over when assessing the thematic and linguistic diversification rates in narrative and iterative topic redundancy.

The three chosen TV series seasons then rally together to constitute the multimodal *Motive Corpus* body.

The first step towards structuring the analysable materials included retrieving the episodes. The televised broadcasts described in the previous chapter count forty-four instalments (with a differentiation between the thirteen episodes of odd seasons plus eighteen of the even one; Chap. 4). Instead, the *Motive Corpus* comprehends thirty-nine episodes (thirteen per season) that the researcher has firstly transcribed to harness linguistic and cultural data into their respective written, tangible form (Aijmer & Stenström, 2004). The conspicuous amount of dialogic sequences and interactive exchanges gathered via linear script rendition makes the linguistic statistics of ~200,574 words reunited within a complete transcription task of about 1677-minute length of the broadcast. The subsequent tagging procedure of the *Motive Corpus* follows:

### Example 5  *Motive Corpus, Motive, s03e01, min. 00:21:45–59*

Maria: [PRP]You[VB]'ve [VBN]been [VBG]talking [IN]to [NNP]Dale [NNP]Barbizan

London: [EX]Those [CD]five [NN]men [VB]are [RB]not [DT]the [RB]only [NNS]ones [TO]to [VB]die [IN]because [IN]of [PRP$]my [NN]father [POS]'s [NN]greed

Maria: [RB]Even [IN]if [WP]what [PRP]you[VB]'re [VBG]saying [VBZ]is [JJ]true [WRB]how [VB]do [PRP]you [VB]expect [TO]to [VB]prove [DT]any [IN]of [PRP]it [PRP$]Your [NN]father[VBZ]'s [RB]not [JJ]stupid [NNP]L. [PRP]You [MD]wo[RB]n't [VB]find [WP]what [PRP]you[VB]'re [VBG]looking [IN]for [IN]on [PRP$]his [NN]laptop [RB]Now [VB]get [RP]out [IN]of [RB]here [IN]before [PRP]he [VBZ]catches [PRP]you

184　F. P. Gentile

The said operation contributes to the more straightforward interpretability of the corpus grammar, nonetheless the readability of the written linguistic passages is inevitably compromised by the overwhelming fragmentation of the sentences due to the tags. Moreover, besides the said visual flaw, software quantitative syntactic evaluations lack exactitude here and there. Thus, they require qualitative adjustments due to the wrongful assessment of the phrastic elements automatedly parsed. The uppercase "L" followed by the dot, for example, derives from the speaker's interlocutor's habit to spelling out names by their initials, phonetically /ɛl/. However, the woman also writes names that way, and "London" becomes "El" in her notebook. The parser surprisingly tagged the said case as the correct singular proper noun a human analyst would know [PRP], and it did not mistake the punctuation mark for a full stop.

Nonetheless, a *simpler* grammatical case such as the 'to' particle often happens to be by default marked '[TO]'. Instead, the Penn Treebank's theoretical basis assigns the particle that exact label only when referring to the infinitive mode verbal conjugation. Otherwise 'to' must classify as '[IN]' for a preposition or subordinating conjunction, or '[RP]' shortening for the particle associated with phrasal verbs, accordingly. The POS tagging operation by itself is insufficient for the utter description and the consequential examination of the corpus neither on a purely linguistic level, or (and much less) on a multimodal one. For this reason, the conclusion of the tagging process involved a markup intervention. That procedure defined the oral-to-written communicative intension (since the analytical perusal) forms of uttering belonging to the *Motive Corpus*. Here, adjunct multimodal symbols (Heydon, 2005; see also Adolphs & Carter, 2013) codify changes of rhythm, prosodic variations, pauses and further annotations commenting on the scenes:

### Example 5.1 Motive Corpus, Motive, s03e01, min. 00:21:45–59

Maria:　　((Approaches the table with concern)) [PRP]You↑⇒[VB]'ve [VBN]been　　[VBG]talking　　[IN]to　　[NNP]Dale [NNP]Barbiza:n^

## 5 The *Motive* 'Whydunit' Television Hybrid 185

London:  [EX]Those^⇒[CD]five  [NN]men↓⇒[VB]are  [RB]not [DT]the [RB]only [NNS]ones [TO]to [VB]die [IN]because [IN]of [PRP$]my [NN]father [POS]'s [NN]greed

Maria:  ((Piano  music  accompanying  the  dialogue)) [RB]°Even°⇒[IN]if [WP]what [PRP]you[VB]'re [VBG]saying [VBZ]is [JJ]true (.) [WRB]how [VB]do [PRP]you [VB]expect [TO]to [VB]pro:ve [DT]any [IN]=of [PRP]=it^ (.) [PRP$]Your [NN]father [VBZ]'s [RB]no:t [JJ]stupid (.) [NNP]=L.  (..)  [PRP]=You  [MD]wo[RB]n't [VB]find[WP]what  [PRP]you[VB]'re  [VBG]looking [IN]for [IN]on [PRP$]his [NN]laptop .h [RB]Now (.) ((Turns around to check whether anybody is coming. London is very upset by hearing that)) [VB]get [RP]out[IN]of [RB]here [IN]before [PRP]he [VBZ]catches [PRP]you

Such additional metadata would undoubtedly contribute to defining the higher degree of comprehension of the corpus linguistic usages associated with emotional transparency connotation specks. If lacking annotation symbols, the reported dialogue would read as a flat exchange, whose informativity was on users to guess thanks to little details. Such facilitated communicative conveyance, instead, immediately renders the enormous emotionality unfurled onto the scene. The more the interaction proceeds, the tenser the elocution rhythm gets. The onscreen iterative construction prefers latchings of long single- or multiple-sentence word-streaks (see the '='mark). Those verbal episodes culminate with an audible in-breath ('.h') where the speaker needs to reflate after having spat out her concern at once, then pauses just a microsecond and restarts talking at the same pace.

Corpus linguistics analysis would merely report the sentences. Oppositely, the example reading describes London being in trouble and introduces Maria as a friend who has come to help. The characters' names' enclosure also indicates their gender, which adds metadata useful to the final examination. Nonetheless, thanks to the multimodal annotation, the user would see the woman's support potently, almost to force the younger girl to realise the consequences of her purpose. To that extent, Maria sets numerous control situation points throughout the dialogue imposing her dominant role, as some Jiminy Cricket. She mostly uses resolved vocal pitch risings (↑), maintained constant until the end of her formulations (⇒). This strategy reads as a warning to London. Contrarily, the girl does not accept the paramount linguistics of Maria's speech. Replies involve slight tone-ups (^), followed *ex abrupto* by a vocal pitch lowering and modulation (↓⇒) when London understands the situational confidentiality and the need for keeping it quiet. In some Game Theory non-cooperative pattern (Myerson, 1991), individuals pressure their interactions by self-enforcing in a dynamic turn-taking of one person's control to the other's (Simpson & Mayr, 2009). Maria answers London's stubbornness with a further almost-whispered line. However, the woman enunciates at once. She makes no pauses, except for the physiologic in-breath ("…his laptop **.h** Now **(.)** get out of…"). Although Maria's tone gets lower and lower, the key to interpreting this expressive situation is not speech volume.

Indeed, Maria's uttering rhythm displays a relentless intensity, which allows the woman to establish a final situational control that squelches London's recalcitrant attitude and drives the girl to a silent final ponderation. A prime multimodal annotation has added some information to the *Motive Corpus*. The alignment of linguistic data with metalinguistic symbols already makes it multimodal, regardless of any audio or visual further supports. Considering that, the building procedure is over. Such marks fundamentally contribute to some comprehension and observation *stadia* of the research. Also, iconic assistances proffered by image flowing and shooting techniques burst the cinematic content interpretability.

Furthermore, some visual descriptions refer to the dialogic sequence for integrating (transcribed) linguistic data with the para- and non-verbal elements involved in multimodal communication. The example provided in Table 5.1, for instance, validates the speculations presented above after the annotated symbolic pieces of information. More precisely, the concern expressed during the dialogue distinctly reflects Maria's non-verbal body language in the initial frame and her prosodic peculiarities. Tone and pace assist the *spontaneous* movement towards the desk that London is sitting at to reduce the gap. Her left arm stretches to reach the desk surface and beat upon it with her fingertips emphasises that, as solidly making a point. London's facial expression is a manifest reaction to this behaviour. Her ajar lips and squinting eyes transmit scepticism. Still,

| Min./Description[a] | Visual image | Kinesic action | Soundtrack | Phases and metafunctions |
|---|---|---|---|---|
| 00:21:45 Dark backlit dining room. Huge window on the background (day-time). London (white dress) is sitting at the desk; Maria (dark suit) arrives | NmovA; CP: Stationary, EWS-BV; VS room; P: W; W; Ph; | Movt: Participant #1 gestures; Tempo: Fast; | ST: Piano music (acute tone); | A single phase setting the context (London's father's office), implemented by two subphases emphasising characters' concern about the theme introduced in the phase; |
| 00:21:48 London's foreground (facial mimics) | MovA; CP: Tracking, CLS-OSS; VS P: W; W; SP1; | Movt: Participant #2 gestures and stands up; | ≈ | EXP: Room + actors INT: Viewer positioned close the far wall of the room (extremely wide shot); introduction of subphases at close distance (CLS), following characters' movements and gestures. |
| 00:21:50 Maria's foreground (facial mimics) | NmovA; CP: Shaky, CLS-FV; VS P: W; SP2; | Movt: Participant #1 talks; head mov.; Tempo: Slow; | AS: Dull noise; ST: Piano music (acute tone); | The spectators' position changes, getting closer to participant via OSS: They take part in the scene, eavesdropping dialogues right next to the speakers |
| 00:21:54 London's foreground (facial mimics) | CP: Shaky, CSL-OSS; VS P: W; W; SP1, SP2; | Movt: Participant #2 head mov.; Tempo: Slow; | ST: Piano music (deep notes); | TEX: Main phase (Ph) introducing a theme, which is explicated through SP1 and 2. |
| 00:21:56 Maria's foreground (quick lateral head movement [check]) | ≈ | Movt: Participant #1 ample head mov.; Tempo: Hurried; | ≈ | Narration slant: 1. Secrecy and conspiracy; |
| 00:21:59 London (FV) stands up to confront Maria (OSS) | MovA: CP: Tracking, shaky, CLS-SV; VS P: W; W; SP2, SP1; | Movt: Participant #1 head mov., participant #2 leaving; | AS: Footsteps of part. #2 leaving; ST: Piano music (acute plus deep notes); | 2. Information appraisal; concern; 3. Participants' non-cooperation; |

Dialogue

Maria: ((approaches the table with concern)) [PRP]you↑⇒[VB]'ve [VBN]been [VBG]talking [IN]to [NNP]dale [NNP]Barbiza:n^

London: [EX]those^⇒[CD]five [NN]men↓⇒[VB]are [RB]not [DT]the [RB]only [NNS]Jones [TO]to [VB]die [IN]because [IN]of [PRP$]my [NN]father [POS]'s [NN]greed

Maria: ((piano music accompanying the dialogue)) [RB]°even°⇒[IN]if [WP]what [PRP]you[VB]'re [VBG]saying [VBZ]is [JJ]true (.) [WRB]how [VB]do [PRP] you [VB]expect [TO]to [VB]pro:Ve [DT]any [IN]=of [PRP]=it^ (.) [PRP$]your [NN]father [VBZ]'s [RB]no:t [JJ]stupid (.) [NNP]=L. (..) [PRP]=you [MD]wo[RB] n't [VB]find[WP]what [PRP]you[VB]'re [VBG]looking [IN]for [IN]on [PRP$]his [NN]laptop. h [RB]now (.) ((turns around to check whether anybody is coming. London is very upset by hearing that)) [VB]get [RP]out[IN]of [RB]here [IN]before [PRP]he [PRP]he [VBZ]catches [PRP]you

[a]Chapter 5 tables have no images due to copyright restrictions imposed by Lark Productions and Fundation Features. Frame descriptions substitute still captures

**188**     F. P. Gentile

Maria's dominating role is inferable following the proxemics of the two characters. On the horizontal dimension, their interpersonal distance moves from *social*—at the beginning of the scene—to *personal* (almost *intimate*), during the exchange exploitation (Hall, 1966). The woman never retreats. When London stands up to decidedly contrast Maria's words, the younger character underlines a friendly-to-dominant manifestation of non-verbal power attitude on the grounds of the vertical dimension. Nonetheless, the elder doesn't give in and remains steady:

> [...] High power individuals (or more precisely: those high in verticality of any type), compared to low power ones, have more open body positions (arms and legs), maintain closer interpersonal distance (when sitting or standing next to someone) speak more loudly and interrupt others more often. Noteworthy, *no* differences in smiling and in the amount of gazing between high and low power individuals emerged. (Hall & Knapp, 2013: 616)

Maria's confident approach is evident. It diverges from London's submissive posture, with narrow shoulders and her back slightly arched forwards while sitting. Hence, the former's "visual dominance" (ibid.) shows bald. However, the difference between those women is not over. The scenic para-verbal eloquence also emerges thanks to the cinematic shooting techniques, which confirm the controlling verbal and non-verbal role of one character towards the other. Indeed, "L." is initially filmed via an up-to-bottom mid-shot or medium close-up perspective. That seems to tame her attitude. Oppositely, Maria's camera shots are always bottom-up or frontal wide-shots. The technique contributes to inoculating into the viewers' minds a first, prime identification of the latter as the dominant individual in the dialogue, standing taller over the observer's viewpoint (Table 5.1, mins 00:21:45–56). Nonetheless, once this interpretation key has solidly conditioned the spectators' perception, London can rise and stand opposite her. Here, the techniques change into over-shoulder-shots or shifting frontal close-ups, framing participants' faces only. However, even if camera angles focus on the protagonists with similar perspectives and the room they are in is quite dark—despite its amplitude—Maria's visage is always clearly brighter than London's, almost overshadowed by the penumbra. Similarly, the entire scenic rendition plays with more light contrasts. The sequence is set in a commodious dining room (Table 5.1, min. 00:21:45). It is day-time and a bright beam illuminates the room naturally. Nonetheless, camera positions are backlit to create an oxymoronic darkness shadowing the characters (even the table lamp is on). That informs the spectators about the secrecy of this intimate encounter.

When physicality is not enough, one character's predominance surfaces through subtle, suggestive narratively iconic mechanisms adding connoted details to the linguistic aspects, and providing some important extra information. It is worth noting that the darkness overwhelming London's face is only one of the features communicating her faltering certainty. The girl's synthetic utterances help it. In comparison, Maria's long sentences spell through a dogged rhythm. Some piano music notes accompany her voice. They start acute as to lead to a climactic exchange. Then, sounds turn lower and more profound when the tension musts hustle the character's initial non-cooperative attitude. Several ambient dull noises implement the rendition and signal other people's presence in the house, with the subsequent need for secrecy.

*Motive* forms a (hybrid) collection of linguistic and metalinguistic data worth studying under the lens of multimodality. The following paragraphs offer a descriptive examination of the main communicative aspects of the series. A possibly more comprehensive observational *spectrum* also includes a few factors and interactive milieus, which were absent or not classified as sensibly relevant in Chap. 4.

## The *Motive* TV Series Language(s)

The *Motive*'s debate originates from the narrative focus of the TV series itself, which conditions the linguistic and communicative rendition of its plots. On the one hand, one finds that the crime drama procedural aspect, generally stereotyped by the *whodunnit?* perspective (Gentile, 2015: 21), become *whydunnit?* (LeChevallier, 2013), here. The show articulation mainly concerns shifting from perpetrators' individuation to the causes unleashing a murderous rage against their victims.

The said peculiarity is evident in the initial sequences of the *Motive* instalments. Surprisingly, every episode (even those of the third season *serial* structure) starts with a preliminary introduction of both the assassin and the assassinee's ordinary lives. The overall contextualisation of the character's personality, ethnicity, gender, age, habits or daily routine lasts a few seconds not to waste precious time. Suddenly, the narration freezes. That facilitates a tracking close-up shot of the person of interest. A characterising uppercase label 'KILLER' or 'VICTIM' appears beneath his/her face. Immediately after police discovers the corpse and detectives arrive on the scene, the a posteriori recount starts.

The pilot episode ('Creeping Tom'. *Motive*. CTV, Vancouver. Feb. 3, 2013) is already emblematic, chacarterising the rest of the series narrative, as well. Extrapolating the said described contextualisation, it sets the motivational pattern of the subsequent cinematic narrations and police procedural investigations. Here, the narration through linguistic data, such as dialogic passages or interactive exchanges is mandatorily secondary to the visual salience. Surrounded by ambient noises and other people's shouts and cries, the killer (no *verbal* mention of his role, though) emerges as the slender drummer in a band that parades during a football match. Despite his role as a member of a closed *social* group of individuals, camera techniques emphasise his solitude via slow dolly movements framing his *stiff* body or squirming face deriving from bullies' misdemeanours towards him coming from the bleachers on top of his head. The suspense simmered in the initial seconds of the storyline is, then, *ex abrupto* shattered. The camera's slow motion swiftly stops to focus on the boy's face using a Lo-fi filtered shot enhancing dark contrasts behind the subject (this latter stands more evidently out of the background, yet surrounded by a grey-to-black halo). A dull echoing noise accompanies the visual rendition, silencing any other background sound and contemporaneously determining the appearance of the 'KILLER' black wording in a still image lasting a few milliseconds (min. 00:01:01).

Once the killer's narration finishes, the narrative phase cuts into another one of the same duration: a man is in a bar late-night, where a stereo is playing loud music. He entertains his friends with karaoke, singing the 1982 *Hit Me with the Best Shot* by the American artist Pat Benatar. Despite the low relevance of isolated linguistic exchanges, what communicates something about the subject is again the multimodal representation of verbal interactions tightly bound to cheers, laughter, visual dancing, and singing, depicting the inclusive and friendly atmosphere of amusement. The man is surrounded by people who like him while having fun, which creates the best cinematic opportunity to turn the person into a body. Indeed, the initial tracking camera movements following the character amid the crowd and varying from close shots to close-ups (min. 00:01:14; min. 00:00:25) gradually decelerate, losing proximity with the protagonist. The narration's fast tempo originally coincided with the song rhythm. It becomes slower as soon as the character distances the camera via an over-shoulder-shot (OSS). The scene suggests a sudden loss of contact between the protagonist and his closer acquaintances, that coincides with the spectators' eyes. Thus, he loses the viewer's *protection*, as well. The shot gets ampler, and the OSS angle shifts into a slight bottom-up perspective as if observing the man from a lower level. At the same time, he has somehow risen (like the exposure of a sacrificial lamb). At that moment, the image freezes again, and the same dull noise heard to mark out the killer reverberates to label the 'VICTIM' (min. 00:01:46). This time photography opts for a blue filter dimming background extras and having the protagonist emerge brighter, associated with a pure-white but scratched wording, which is symptomatic of the unhappy ending.

A similar structure impedes spectators from fancying themselves into misleading lucubrations and contorted second thoughts to search for a *mens rea*. The narration communicativeness gets distorted by the apical increase of informativity rates. It implies the utter defusing of any climax chances in each preliminary instalment part. The *Motive* TV series lacks generalisable stereotypical schemata leading to the criminal discovery at the end of the recount. Yet, its narrative style—which proposes the immediate revelation of the culprit—needs to appeal differently. Language struggles through the deductive research stress, more interested in apprehending the links between the perpetrator and the murdered person via a highly descriptive expressive tendency, which often shifts from the investigative pathos to the catchy irony of certain situations. An example of that is the unaware victim's portrayal while singing *Hit Me with the Best Shot* during the sequence preceding the one where his request has been satisfied, and he is found dead. There, also music choices and ambient sounds display great narrative relevance.

## The Characters' Portrayal

The deflection of focus towards the Vancouver homicide department hierarchical skeleton and routine investigative organisation permits users to pore over the major interaction schemata undertaken by the involved officers, whenever they get assigned a case and launch their enquiries. Moreover, being the show about assassinations only, the examination can foreseeably guess the *intrusion* of some specialised discourses and terminology (on the linguistic level) simultaneously occurring in their original shape and popularised form (Grego, 2013; Garzone, 2020). The medical or the legal ones, to name two of the most recurrent sectorial languages in TV crime dramas, balance the relationship between the events and the conveyance of specialised knowledge (through the medium visual iconicity). The *Flashpoint* case study relates the vicissitudes happening to a team of patrols/tactical agents in their working hours as much as in their civilian habits. Instead, the *Motive Corpus* theme openly deals with in- and out-door detectives' job assignments excluding relevant narrative passages on the characters' civilian practices. Private-life events seldom show up to attribute credibility to the fictional heroes only: the main focus stays on police tasks. In the *Motive Corpus*, significant dialogues occur between partners (in close parallelism with *Flashpoint*; see Chap. 4), and laypeople have a voice only when referred to as witnesses to be questioned.

Register shifts and discourse style changes are not utterly relevant here.

The Vancouver mediatic representation proposed in the series synthetically concentrates on a handful of protagonists, whose narration never detaches from its jurisdiction. The only character allowed to bring some of her private life on screen, is detective Angie Flynn. She occasionally buys herself some spare time to deal with her son, Manny, once home after working. More generally, the total amount of people inhabiting *Motive*'s dangerous and eerie world only counts four/five fixed characters, all belonging to law enforcement offices. The actual heroine of the series, as mentioned, is detective Angie Flynn—a Caucasian woman, 40-to-45-years-old, a single parent, known for her subtle sarcasm and masculine attitude. Her acute insightfulness shares the spotlight with Oscar Vega—Angie's work partner, a Latino,

45-to-50-years-old. The man has a US background related to his expensive Ivy League Education and a familiar controversial legacy ideologically mismatching his industrialist father's economic power. However, his mother's professionalism as a neurosurgeon could be associated with Vega's medical fundamental knowledge.

The formula fiction of crime (Cawelty, 1977; Gentile, 2015) shows, then, requires some newly inducted cops coming up beside veterans to learn the job. Brian Lucas is a freshly graduated detective with a financial crime division past. He is 30-to-40-years-old, Canadian, characterised by a certain naiveté, which happens to be even more evident opposite Angie and Oscar's experience. Right beside the three leading detectives, another central role is Betty Rogers who is 40-to-45-years-old. She works as a medical examiner, decidedly sympathising with Angie whenever this latter character needs emotional and professional support in light of their loyal and mutual friendship. Sergeant Boyd Bloom, 40-to-50-years-old and Black Canadian, covers the last fixed role. Mark Cross, a Caucasian 35-to-40-years-old, substitutes Boyd since season 2 as team commander when he becomes superintendent of investigation (declassed from 'fixed' to 'recurring' character after the first season).

Some recurring characters are still relatively relevant. Manny (in seasons 1 and 2, absent in the third one) is Angie's adolescent son who does not know anything about his father's identity. Officer Wendy Sung is a season 2 rookie having a little flirt with Brian Lucas. Samantha Turner—the prosecutor—has a liaison with Mark Cross throughout season 2; her death is the pivotal narrative expedient to resolve the seasonal itchy case. Other individuals play significant roles during the third annual broadcast only, given the serial narrative modality focusing on some facts and crimes attributable or ascribable to them. Neville Montgomery, Henry Guenther and Maria Snow all link to London Montgomery's death.

The characters' private life events do not *extensively* regard the series. However, scriptwriting accurately profiles them from a psychological and interpersonal dimension, whose resolution contributes to shaping and solidifying those individuals' plausibility and credibility through the TV screens.

Some interesting pieces of information in *Motive* evidence peculiar and particularised expressive aspects of communication. They include linguistic/verbal, visual, non-verbal and para-verbal layers, identifying every individual according to its interactive and performative strengths. As discussed, the television as a medium mostly conveys pieces of information via a primary visual ground. This aspect communicates data about the characters' age, gender, social role, etc. One immediate detail, then, is represented by the dress code adopted on the set. In dichotomous contrast with *Flashpoint* (Chap. 4), *Motive*'s heroes do not parade before the public in scary uniforms or are armed to the teeth. The Vancouver product oppositely shows off elegantly dressed detectives used to accessing the crime scenes wearing slim coats and loafers or pantsuits as much as the intriguing pathologist in miniskirt and heels under whatever weather. In like manner, weapons are rarely present and, even when they appear on screen, shots are never actually fired: in line with the procedural slant of the TV series, the show majorly indulges with the interrogatories.

It is also worth noting the prominent position of gender issues in the observed series. Women seem to be the depositary of social and professional powers. Besides the thematic crime list, that is analysed further, the narration mostly focuses on Angie's deductions, hypotheses and dialogues, which constantly outclass her colleagues' as much as superior's authority and mental skills. The only man capable of managing Angie's vitality is Oscar, although with (maybe just *because* of his) peaceful manners and intents, never trying to engage in social, professional nor gender supremacy fights. Together with Angie's attitude, Dr Roger's mastery of the medical profession and her key role as coroner, ensure the female gender its essential presence within the series. In the other corpora analysed in the survey, femininity remains a minority (meant as characters' gender and not in terms of discrimination or disparity of treatments). These and other relevant features of the *Motive* TV series are part of the following paragraphs via the multimodal perusal of the corpus.

## Procedural Language: The *Whydunnit* Reconstructive Approach to Homicides

The *Motive Corpus* is expected to show some linguistic peculiarities. Those traits should evidence a preponderance of some descriptive and expressive schemata rendering the main recounting structure of the television product (Buckland, 2004; Davis, 2021) already on the statistical ground offered by the computational parsing approach (Biber, 2012; Kübler & Zinsmeiter, 2015; Calabrese, 2019). Given the series' explicative title, interactive dynamics represent one significant aspect of the plot articulation. They underline the investigative inquiry goal through a mostly anaphoric reconstructive procedure a posteriori referring to and referencing something, which has taken place before. Such an approach would serve the functional building of storyline events nervously shifting backwards and forwards, from present to past situations and then again to the present via flashback strategies blended up with dialogically salient exchanges used as a constant narrative mechanism. Specific linguistic usages confirm such operation. Locative, temporal and interrogative pronouns and adverbs grant the corpus its multilayered dimension in terms of the diversified moments of action presented (Table 5.2).

Accordingly, based on the frequency count observation of the wordlist (Table 5.2), it is evident how fundamental grammatical elements *mathematically* enhance the internal coherence of the series descriptive modes. Function words like personal/possessive pronouns and isolated prepositions not related to phrasal verbs do not belong in the Table. WH-determiners, -pronouns and -adverbs (in order, rank 15, 'what'; rank 60, 'why'; rank 64, 'how'; rank 72, 'when'; rank 74, 'who'; rank 87, 'where') cover prominent positions. They set an escalating relevance classification from the factual reporting point of view. Essential information is bound to the precise apprehension of the happening or the contextualisation of facts (*what?*; Table 5.3), followed by the *ensemble* of remaining variables to be solved. Considering Tables 5.2 and 5.3, one would undoubtedly read such usage consistency through certain determiner occurrence levels (also mirrored by the related plot sketch remarkably displaying the employment of the given words).

The 'what' 1842 count occur throughout the corpus with picks, but no blanks: a strongpoint indicating the lack of narrative deflections within the entire three-year period production, always maintaining the same expressive focus. Nonetheless, verbs *consecutio temporum* concordances are symptomatic as well. Focusing on those occurrences, one would notice the prevalence of auxiliary verbs (Table 5.4) highly above any other. They mostly conjugate as past tense forms like present/past perfect

## 196     F. P. Gentile

**Table 5.2** *Motive Corpus* word frequency list

| Rank | Word | Rank | Word | Rank | Word | Rank | Word |
|---|---|---|---|---|---|---|---|
| [...] | | [...] | | 62 | WANT [578] | [...] | |
| 6 | THAT [3519] | 27 | Have[1346] | 63 | HAD [578] | 87 | **WHERE** [359] |
| [...] | | [...] | | 64 | HOW [573] | 88 | THANK [358] |
| 12 | **Do**[2142] | 38 | **BE** [889] | [...] | | [...] | |
| [...] | | 39 | OKAY [886] | 72 | **WHEN** [469] | 93 | MAYBE [330] |
| 15 | **WHAT** [1842] | [...] | | 73 | TIME [469] | [...] | |
| [...] | | 42 | THERE [849] | 74 | WHO [468] | 132 | DETECTIVE[213] |
| 18 | THIS [1620] | [...] | | [...] | | 133 | PLEASE [209] |
| [...] | | 50 | HERE [750] | 76 | NOW [448] | 134 | THANKS [209] |
| 23 | YEAH [1491] | [...] | | 77 | THEN [425] | 135 | HOME [204] |
| 24 | KNOW [1449] | 60 | WHY[597] | 78 | GOOD [415] | 136 | BEFORE [202] |
| 25 | **DID**[1414] | 61 | WERE[584] | 79 | BEEN[410] | 137 | MURDER[198] |

**Table 5.3** *Motive Corpus* "what" word sketch

| WHAT, WH-DET, PRON [WORDLIST > DETERMINER, PRONOUN; RANK 15 – 1,842 COUNT] | |
|---|---|
| **RANK** | **CONCORDANCE LIST** |
| 1 | SLEEPING IN THE SPARE ROOM. OR SO SHE SAYS. WHAT? IT HAPPENS. YEAH, IT HAPPENS |
| 2 | MAKE SURE YOU GET HER HANDS, PLEASE. SO, WHATSUBJECT DID GLENN TEACH? |
| 4 | VICTIM'S INSIDE, DR. ROGERS. HMM. WHAT TIME DID MR. MARTIN COME HOME? UM, 10:00? |
| 19 | I DON'T KNOW, HE LOOKED RUSSIAN. WHATWERE YOU DOING AT THE PARK SO LATE? |
| 54 | TIME THAT YOU SPOKE WITH TIFFANY? MONDAY NIGHT. ANDWHAT HAPPENED MONDAY? |
| 57 | TELL ME EXACTLYWHAT YOU WERE DOING THE NIGHT TIFFANY WAS KILLED |
| 1556 | RUSHED TO THE HOSPITAL AND NEVEL LET HER SIDE. IS THATWHATHE TOLD YOU? YES. NO |
| 1557 | I WENT TO SEE HER AROUND 8:30, HE WASN'T THERE. WHATTIME DID HE ARRIVE? |
| 1837 | I FOUND THE COP. THE ONE NEVILLE PAID TO LIE ABOUTWHAT HE DID TO YOU |
| WHAT OCCURRENCE PLOT | |

## 5 The *Motive* 'Whydunit' Television Hybrid

**Table 5.4** *Motive Corpus* verb frequency list

| RANK | VERB | | RANK | VERB | | RANK | VERB | | RANK | VERB | |
|---|---|---|---|---|---|---|---|---|---|---|---|
| 1 | BE | [12,963] | 14 | FIND | [529] | 27 | LIKE | [235] | 40 | LOVE | [142] |
| 2 | DO | [4,174] | 15 | NEED | [470] | 28 | WORK | [227] | 41 | CHECK | [140] |
| 3 | HAVE | [2,999] | 16 | LOOK | [462] | 29 | ASK | [225] | 42 | BELIEVE | [136] |
| 4 | GET | [1,675] | 17 | MAKE | [460] | 30 | GONNA | [224] | 43 | LISTEN | [135] |
| 5 | KNOW | [1,662] | 18 | LET | [385] | 31 | HAPPEN | [209] | 44 | MEET | [129] |
| 6 | GO | [1,360] | 19 | TALK | [381] | 32 | HELP | [190] | 45 | START | [128] |
| 7 | THINK | [916] | 20 | KILL | [361] | 33 | WAIT | [186] | 46 | STOP | [125] |
| 8 | WANT | [790] | 21 | THANK | [359] | 34 | KEEP | [184] | 47 | FEEL | [119] |
| 9 | SEE | [732] | 22 | CALL | [312] | 35 | HEAR | [181] | 48 | LIE | [119] |
| 10 | TELL | [690] | 23 | MEAN | [296] | 36 | USE | [174] | 49 | PAY | [114] |
| 11 | SAY | [672] | 24 | GIVE | [294] | 37 | PUT | [164] | 50 | REMEMBER | [109] |
| 12 | COME | [638] | 25 | TRY | [276] | 38 | RUN | [144] | 51 | GUESS | [108] |
| 13 | TAKE | [568] | 26 | LEAVE | [257] | 39 | DIE | [142] | | | |

simple and continuous (Tables 5.2 and 5.3). Consequently, verbal patterns concentrate on both the action and the temporal gap, indicating whether its consequences are still relevant for the investigation. Once more, the syntax emphasises the great concern with time relations and performative consequentiality of events. That could help either the descriptive development of the onscreen rendition and the case connected resolution.

The *whydunnit* reconstructive perspective acts within the deductive path to collect crucial evidence. Detectives tessellate bits of information in the utter mental recreation of the murder. Consequently, the statistical observation of the *Motive* verb frequency list (Table 5.4) raises more points. Such a parsing appears strictly to verbal syntagms expressing sensory or perceptive relations. Knowledge access (voiced by the equivalent verb 'to know', rank 5) is often tightly close to conjectural patterns (e.g., rank 7, 'think'). There, its ponderative schemata mostly depend on the self-consciousness of the agent performing the action (in light grey: rank 42, 'believe'; rank 47, 'feel'; rank 51, 'guess') or on its visual and auditive activations (rank 9, 'see'; rank 16, 'look'; rank 35, 'hear'; rank 43 'listen') towards the context.

**198     F. P. Gentile**

Similar data might also link to the rates of actual performative verbs filling in the chart first 51 positions (Table 5.4). Coherently with the sensory/perceptive speculation, entries bind to the *oral* dimension (rank 10, 'tell'; rank 11, 'say'; rank 19 'talk'; rank 22, 'call'; rank 29, 'ask'). They accordingly relate to the police agent (who should 'check'—rank 41—any entry), or to the interviewed individual (possibly shifting from cooperative behaviours about requests to 'remember'—rank 50—the happening, to the possibly non-cooperative confabulatory forgery of lying—rank 48). Eventually, it is not surprising that core positions of the table highlight 'kill' (rank 20) and 'die' (rank 39), whose continual recurrence (and uttering) mirrors the linguistic characterisation of the examined TV series as well as the other examples provided.

The emblematic enunciation "let's forget about <u>who</u> (..) and focus on <u>why:</u>" by Angie Flynn (*Motive*, s01e02, min. 00:28:23–27), reflects the cinematic recount of the reconstructive approach. This dominant strategy references the observed series' philosophy, following the actual transmission of content-enriched dialogically and visually significant exchanges. It aims at a crablike analysis of facts sized via a backwards-oriented re*construction* of stories.

Some peculiar elements in Table 5.5 confirm that main verbal occurrences, in terms of a phrastic display, serve information evaluation dynamics mostly oriented to communicate emotional statements that underline the value of professional remarks. Dr Rogers should be the only specialist allowed to detail the scene, although detective Vega regularly intervenes transforming the coroner's report more into a dialogue. Despite the apparent disparity of expertise levels between the two participants, the 'heterogloss' engagement structures the exchange. It announces the doctor's cooperative behaviour towards her colleague and friend Oscar, allowing the detective to comment on anything she says with no hierarchical superimpositions (or positions of linguistic control/dominance) that the context would however permit. Thus, the "so **you're thinking**…" opening of Vega's utterance, implying a partial observation, only remarks Betty's perspective. It is not a hostile formulation. Thus, the medical examiner's negation gently replies to the remark, followed by the same construction referencing Vega's question in a spiral pattern adjusting the focus ("*No*, the head wound […] [Vega makes another question]

## 5 The *Motive* 'Whydunit' Television Hybrid     199

**Table 5.5** *Motive*, s03e07. Medical examination multimodal observation

| Min./Description | Visual image | Kinesic action | Soundtrack | Phases and metafunctions |
|---|---|---|---|---|
| 00:12:44 Corpse's bruised face detail. Medical examiner's gloved index ponting | NmovA; CP: Stationary, CLS-FV; VS morgue; P: W; W; SP1; | Movt: Participant #1 gestures; Tempo: Fast; | ST: Violin (acute tone); | A single phase setting the context in the morgue after the corpse examination, introduced by one rhematic subphase implementing sensationalism; EXP: Morgue + actors (one corpse) INT: Viewer close-ups the corpse to observe it, then steps back behind Dr. Roger's or Det. Vega's shoulder accordingly; sudden distance camera position framing the entire room TEX: Rheme-theme juxtaposition. Narration slant: 1. Details of the body facial wounds; 2. Information appraisal; 3. Participants' personal remarks; |
| 00:12:46 Medical examiner ALC via detective's OSS. The room is enlightened by turquoise dissection room LED lights. Dr. rogers wears a violet scrub suit; det. Vega wears a dark suit | NmovA; CP: Shaky, CLS-OSS; VS P: W; M; Ph; | Movt: Participant #1 gestures; head mov.; | ≈ | |
| 00:12:47 Vega's CLS (facial mimics) checking the body | VS P: M; W; | Movt: Participant #2 talks; head mov.; | ST: Violin (deep piano notes are introduced); | |
| 00:12:50 Dr. Rogers CLS (facial mimics; backchannel) | CP: Stationary shaky, CSL-OSS; VS P: W; M; | Movt: Participant #1 head mov.; | ≈ | |
| 00:12:58 Dissection room SW. Dr. Rogers is next to the corpse (gesture-in-talk); Vega holds ont the table with his left arm | CP: Shacky, D-BV; VS P: W; M; W; | Movt: Participant #2 facial expr. | ST: Violin (acute note); | |
| 00:13:06 Rogers' gesture-in-talk; Vega's left arm moves towards his ear while his head tilts downwards | ≈ | Movt: Participant #1 gestures; participant #2 gestures; | ≈ | |

*(continued)*

**Table 5.5** (continued)

| Min./Description | Visual image | Kinesic action | Soundtrack | Phases and metafunctions |
|---|---|---|---|---|
| Dialogue | | | | |

Rogers: Judging^ <u>by</u> the shape of the <u>wound</u> I^⇒'d say she was clubbed↓
Vega: So=you're=thinking=what^=the=murder=weapon could be:: a=<u>bottl</u>-
Rogers: No (.) .h the^⇒ head wound bled <u>profusely</u> (.) but the blow wasn↓⇒'t strong enough to kill her (..) <u>that</u> and the lividity .h ((establishes eye-contact with Oscar)) she^=was alive^ when she went in the freezer^
Vega: So=wh- did=she <u>froze</u> to=death^ was=she <u>conscious</u>^
Rogers: No I think the blow was strong enough to knock her o:Ut (.) and there was no evidence that she tried to <u>escape</u> (..) so I'm pretty sure her death↓⇒ was painless
Vega: That's a small mercy: [...]

*I think that*…"). On the 'graduation' level, Rogers' use of the specialised discourse (more medical discourse features follow in the next paragraphs) transmits her competent enunciation through a combination of 'focus softening' plus 'sharpening' strategies (and 'force raise': "…bled <u>profusely</u>…"). These aim to communicate emotional neutrality in place of possible and unwanted connotations via crystallised formulae. The less undoubtful and subjective "judging by…" contrasts the peremptory "there was no evidence…" as the statement proceeds positioning (Hyland, 2005: 175–176; Chap. 2). Once more, Betty's professionalism emerges in comparison to Oscar's basic knowledge of medicine. The man is decidedly as keen as his friend on the abuse of attitude 'appreciation' patterns about grieving ("That's a small mercy") or death, which reads as *his* professional bias. Vega's locutory tendency urges mental schemata to work through the same spiral of 'heteroglossia'. He continually gets back to what his interlocutor affirms ("So you…"; "So what…")—which is something typical of the deductive method proposed in *Motive*.

On the prosodic level, the difference between the two speakers is even more evident. Betty Rogers handles her elocution well, spelling out most words of her lines correctly. However, a flattening rhythm occurs, also modulating her regular tone with the intrusion of some low intonation rises (^) and vocal pitch decrements (↓) on words to be gravely stressed. Her sentences tend to show acute episodical alterations whenever the character expresses her opinion or reports crucial pieces of information ("Judging^ <u>by</u>…"; "I^d say she…"). The same thing occurs for

## 5 The *Motive* 'Whydunit' Television Hybrid    201

terminological emphasis ("<u>wound</u>"; "bled <u>profusely</u>"; "…tried to <u>escape</u>"). Nonetheless, these features solidly oppose other different prosodic peculiarities where emotions corroborate communication. They describe other information types like the modalities of one's death ("I^'d say she was clubbed↓"; "the blow wasn↓⇒'t strong enough…"; "her death↓⇒ was painless"). Such formulations articulate through many audible in-breaths (.h) supposed to indicate urgency, haste or concern.

If similar linguistic aspects to outline the expressive proficiency of one area of professionalism—like the medical one—some less accurate interactive techniques mark out the other sphere depicted in the sequence. Indeed, notwithstanding the educational background profiling the character, Oscar Vega—as a detective—adopts some linguistic traits, which appear entirely dissimilar from Dr Rogers'. His speech often happens to be on a low modulated standard tone that requires higher attention levels. It affects understandability. His discourses frequently involve intense word flows (=) coagulating multiple separate syntagms almost into single phonic strings, not respecting punctuation norms. The first part of the spoken sentence, '*So, you're thinking what? The murder weapon could be a bottle?*', is pronounced like being univerbalised. There are no pauses—either grammatical or physiological—where the question mark should be. The transcription, then, follows like "So=you're=thinking=what^=the=murder=we apon could be::=a=<u>bottl</u>-". Along with that, one would also notice the graphic sign determining the adoption of elision phenomena ("**bottl-**"; "So **wh-** did she…") and the emphatic glottal stop pronunciation of 'bottle' (/bɒʔl/ in place of /bɒtəl/) employed in the tautosyllabic phonetic voiceless ending of the word. The asymmetric enunciation patterns of the said speakers also extensively render subjective focuses harnessing their respective communication aims. In light of her medical expertise, Betty Rogers knows how information-delivery needs to flow to facilitate clarity. She is aware that the specialised lexicon in her speech could blur the addressee's reception. Thus, the woman carefully spells out every word also highlighting important contents via voice modulations, due to the significant value she attributes to such data. On the contrary, linguistic frills are unimportant to Oscar Vega at the time, because he, as detective, only needs crucial bits of information disregarding emotional connotations involving sympathy. The rapidity of his elocution merely slowing down on sporadic but precise words reveals his intentions. Vega tends to cut short any descriptive additions. He only cares to concentrate on the details (like the weapon possibly being a bottle or the victim being conscious when shut in the freezer), since those are the elements he has to consider when pressing charges against the apprehended assailant. Personal remarks are only allowed once the learning process is over ("That's a small mercy").

Besides verbal communication and non-verbal aspects related to the described prosodic peculiarities, other major expressive features in *Motive* are visual. The non-verbal charge of the characters' body language immediately measures the scenic narrative salience. It starts with Betty Rogers' finger indicating the freezing burns over the victim (min. 00:12:44), followed by close shots onto the participants' facial expressions while having their dialogue. In the case of *intra-specialised* formal language (Roelcke, 2010: 56-ff), gestures are superfluous or inappropriate. Oppositely, as the technicality of the discourse decreases towards lower specialised communication like *inter-specialised* (when Rogers explains to Vega the evidence found on the corpse) and *general lexicon* (ibid.) gestures support the exchange. Body posture alternations and ample arm movements emphasise verbal dynamics being recounted orally. Camera cut-ins focusing on the index finger scanning the victim's body serve as denotative remarks that transmit to the spectators the urgency and the relevance of the details one's hand is pointing at. A similar situation occurs when sequence passages display hands that move towards the speakers' face in a plausibly protective attitude, as to reveal one's uncomfortable mood or reaction to any (extra-) linguistic stimulus (see Vega in Table 5.5, mins 00:12:58–13:06). These movements are already epressive per se, utterly anticipating the verbal clarity by means of *immediate object* (Eco, 2016: 23–32) transparency.

On the one hand, the Doctor is focused. She is down-looking, with pursed lips and raised eyebrows (min. 00:12:46), while briefing detective Vega. Her body stays neutral and uncommunicative in the first part of the exchange, concerning terminological and professional data transmission. However, gestures are required when she has to gloss her report due to understandability reasons (min. 00:12:58–13:06) and mostly involving right arm ample open movements. On the other hand, Oscar's concentration is even more evident. The same corrugated eyebrows and pursed lips of the medical examiner are present on his face too. Hand movements assist as he adjusts his glasses for a better focus (min.

00:12:47). A shaky body posture culminates the performance. His head tilts downwards, followed by the left arm-raise to scratch his ear in thoughtfulness while hearing the details of the woman's demise (min. 00:12:58–13:06). A final left arm concludes the scene, lowering over the close metal piece of furniture to lean on it while Vega makes his remark ("That's a small mercy") as if the news overwhelmingly weakened him.

Like visual salience, acoustic features contribute to setting the atmosphere as well. An unidentified fiddle melody accompanies the scene. Its sparse, acute notes feebly raise to increase the narrative pathos of the recount when medical examiner Rogers is speaking. Suddenly, more profound piano melody remarks that detective Vega is latching his colleague's talk to formulate his questions. As a result, instruments seem to portray participants separately, and also in relation to their gender. The acoustic breakdown is displacing, unbalanced by the instrument alternation even if playing very delicately.

## Interrogation Room Talks

The features described in the previous paragraph well integrate camera movement tempo and frame cuts in diverse environments other than the obituary. The same goes for the relevance of the dialogue (verbality) and the rhythmic aspects, creating an all-inclusive context reaching the spectators. The vivid expressiveness of linguistic data is important. Nonetheless, the verbal dimension does not reflect the actual gathering and subsequent understanding of every shade of the multimodal televised narrative patterns. It compulsorily requires the simultaneous (although unconscious) acquisition of multilayered informative structures comprehensive of all the collateral *strata*.

Yet, it is also worth noting that the medium per se proffers a prevalence of fast-track visual insight *stimuli*. They stand out over other acquisitional processes, letting users access the informative content whenever they encounter a narratively consistent creation (Table 5.6).

Plots recount stories set in the present. However, they continuously shift through the *timeline* to recover concluded events, which effectively reflect their consequences onto current situations. It presupposes the presence of a fragmented scheme shattering the *storyline* into unmatching shards masterfully reordered to compose a renewed looking-glass whose

**Table 5.6** *Motive*, s02e11. Interrogatory flashback narration and multimodal observation

| Min./Description | | | |
|---|---|---|---|
| 00:36:22<br>Flynn's CLS (facial mimics: Incredulous + body language: Prone forwards, steady elbows on the desk); weak lights NmovA;<br>CP: Shaky, MS-OSS;<br>VS interrogatory room; P: W; M; Ph1;<br>ST: Drum&Bass deep rhythm; tempo: Fast; | 00:36:25<br>Subjects #2,3 SV (facial mimics: Attentive)<br>CP: CLS-SV;<br>VS P: M; W;<br><br>00:36:26<br>Flynn's CLS (facial mimics: Scoffing-to-provocative)<br>CP: MS-FV;<br>VS P: W; | 00:36:28<br>Subject #3 CLS (facial mimics: Oppositional)<br>CP: CLS-OSS;<br>VS P: W; W; SP1.1;<br>AS: Flashback noise;<br><br>00:36:29<br>Proof detail<br>CP: Stationary, Det.;<br>VS evidence; SP1.2; | 00:36:31<br>Subject #3 detail (ear + pearl earring)<br>MovA;<br>CP: Shaky, Det.;<br>VS car; P: W; Ph2;<br>ST: Drum&Bass deep rhythm; |
| 00:36:33<br>Flashback #1: Subjects #3,4 in a car (dark lights)<br>MovA;<br>CP: Tracking, CLU-S/FV;<br>VS P: W; M;<br>AS: VoiceOver; | 00:36:41<br>Flashback #2: Subject #3 talking<br>NmovA;<br>CP: Tracking, MS-OSS;<br>VS room; P: W; M; Ph3;<br>ST: Drum&Bass deep rhythm; | 00:36:44<br>Subject #2 OSS (facial mimics: Worried)<br>CP: Shaky, CLS-BV;<br>VS P: W; M;<br>00:36:52<br>MovA;CP: Shaky, Det.;<br>VS car; P: M; W; SP2.1;<br>AS: Hands touching; | 00:36:58<br>Subject #4 (facial mimics: Threatening)<br>NmovA;<br>CP: Tracking, CLU-OSS;<br>VS P: M; W; Ph2;<br>ST: Drum&Bass deep rhythm; |
| 00:37:02<br>O/I: Car windshield; subjects #3,4 arguing<br>MovA;<br>CP: Stationary, D-O/I;<br>VS P: W; M;<br>AS: Flashback noise; | 00:37:07<br>Flashforward (present); subject #3 (facial mimics: Oppositional)<br>MovA;<br>CP: Dolly, CLU-FV;<br>VS interrogatory room; P: W; SP1.1; | 00:37:14<br>Flynn's MS (handling papers)<br>MovA;<br>CP: Tracking, MS-OSS;<br>VS P: W; M; Ph1;<br>AS: Paper rustle; | 00:37:15<br>MovA;CP: Det.;<br>VS warrant; P: W; SP1.3;<br>AS: VoiceOver;<br><br>00:37:17<br>Subject #3 (facial mimics: Provocative-to-upset)<br>NmovA;<br>CP: Shaky, CLU-OSS;<br>VS P: W; M; Ph1; |

*(continued)*

# 5 The *Motive* 'Whydunit' Television Hybrid 205

**Table 5.6** continued

| Min./Description |
| --- |

| Dialogue |
| --- |
| Flynn: <u>Do</u>=you=know=wh<u>ere</u>=it might be^ |
| Bryce: Why↓⇒ the <u>heck</u>=would=we^ <u>know</u> what=Joey=did=with=it^ |
| Flynn: Because I think you're ly:Ing ((nods with sarcasm)) |
| ((flashback #1)) |
| Bryce: ((his voice is voiced over the flashback sequence)) °we°⇒ could always kill him (.) would solve all our problems |
| ((flashback #2)) |
| Erin: °there°⇒'s (..) another way .h |
| Bryce: h.h <u>N:o</u> h.h |
| Erin: h °you°⇒ saw the way he <u>looked</u>=at=me: |
| ((flashback #3: Night-time. Erin and the victim are in the car again. His hand is on the |
| Gear; she grabs it and moves it on her thigh. He meets her gaze, then they kiss)) |
| ((present: Interrogatory room)) |
| Erin: ((nasal voice, as if holding back her tears)) you↓⇒ don't know what you're talking about |
| Flynn: We:Ll (..) we=got^=a=<u>warrant</u> (.) to search your <u>hous</u>- |
| Vega: Yeah=we=find=that=other=earring we're=gonna=know=that=you=guys =are lyi:Ng |

sharp edges of the different pieces leave many blank spaces revealing the ghost of the original skeleton. Amid those empties, the lights from the past glare through the surface. Truth arises again via the utter reconstruction of facts. From the cinematic point of view, similar magic comes from adopting flashback expedients that quantitative linguistic parsings cannot identify. Thus, they require a qualitative selection of significant examples whose strategic position allows scriptwriters to move from one place (e.g., the Interrogatory Room, now) to the other (e.g., the crime scene, while the murder occurred). This narrative strategy puzzles out all the steps leading to the deed performance and the case final resolution in non-linear, strictly coherent ways.

In Table 5.6, interactions are seemingly not consistent with a decisive suspect interrogatory escorting the *Motive* TV series audience to Bryce's confession in the next scene (not included in the instance, since what determines his strong-will collapse happens here). Oscar Vega's elocution speed (as discussed in Table 5.5) also belongs to detective Angie Flynn. In her initial question, "Do=you=know=where=it might be^", she operates a flattening tone underlining the inquisitorial attitude (emphasis on the auxiliary introducing the "Do", and on the WH- determiner signalling the locative clause, "where"). However, the sentence is a little slower and more accurate than her partner's when remarking her feelings through a sarcastic facial expression (min. 00:36:26, "Because I think you're ly:ing"). Notwithstanding similar linguistic peculiarities, nothing about those reiterative exclamations on lying would ever lead to a confession, though. So, how to explain the interviewed character giving up? The answer to that query lies in the metalinguistic information labelled as 'transcriber's annotation' and descriptive of the scene. Those data indicate the insertion of three different timelines within the same recount. Yet, the story splits into four narrative sections whose dialogues (ten lines performed in 55") refer to only two. The sequence's first and last three lines relate to the detectives-to-suspects phase (present). Conversely, the remaining four belong to the orchestration of the crime (in the past) in phase 3. The only linker connecting and mediating the two diverging narratives is the second phase representing a more recent past between the planning of the assassination and the interview.

Visually, the police station room dark lights mirror the sombre inwardness of the three characters accused. Also, lights deeply reflect the participants' intimate feelings. Nonetheless, they contrast with the murder-planning phase atmosphere that is even gloomier and the morbid shadows covering the car in phase two. Bryce's stone-cold proposal of killing the man who is blackmailing him and his friends comes after Erin's perspective of giving herself to this latter individual to salvage the others. The former character's emotional negation replies to his friend's proposal, almost breathless at hearing the idea (see the deep out- and in-breaths both before and after the "N:o"). Bryce's final decision is unexplained through the dialogue. The next, entirely *silent* (in terms of spoken interaction) flashback returns to phase two. It shows Erin succumbing to her coercer's will in his car, seconds before the camera shot fades into the interrogation room to conclude the scene.

In Table 5.6, nothing is verbally clear. Still, the whole happening is perfectly understandable because of the usage of visual communication. The detail shot of the earring evidence fires up memories that ignite the imaging of pre-dated events throughout the suspects' secret meetings. A pressing drum-and-bass deep soundtrack backs up the narration, imposing the urgent and preoccupying pace, only hushed by the warrant's rustling, which terminates the suspense (the confession arrives only at the last moment). The exponential expressiveness of the cinematic visual content surpasses the verbal language power. The recurrent *oral* negations ("Why↓⇒ the <u>heck</u>=would=we^ <u>know</u> what=Joey=did=with=it^"; "You↓⇒ don't know what you're talking about") affirmed by the characters neither correspond to their contrite and passionate *mimics* nor the image display narrating the situation. As a result, linguistic assessments are secondary compared to the immediacy and actual trustworthiness of what the eyes can see. That sanctions the paramount role of iconic strategies (of body language contradicting spoken discourse) over uttered formulations on a multimodal perspective (Nelson, 2007: 11).

## The Crime Scene Dialogues

The expository modes of the TV Crime Drama emerge as correlated with the alternation of deductive and inductive methodologies adopted by law enforcement members to identify the crime (Centini, 2010). Still, the broadcast observed in this chapter has also made room for the assimilation of one more approach. Retroduction (or abduction), counterpoising rational and scientific objectives to irrational, subjective thoughts working via "intuitive leap[s] of logic" (Jenner, 2016: 16), takes the investigators to a final guess representing a moment of epiphany. The subjectivity of the said retroductive praxis represents a consistent quality of the *Motive Corpus* reconstructive slant. The abundance of perception verbs (Table 5.4) solidly contributes to grant that perspectival linchpin that shapes characters' traits and lets them attain apical solutions.

Table 5.4 observations can compare the series dialogic sequences like in Example 5.2. Also, they apply to Tables 5.5 and 5.6 verbs concerning emotional remarks and the use of sarcasm. Thus, the examination would facilitate reading some linguistic and expressive peculiarities characterising the individuals performing their respective acting roles onscreen. The *Motive* TV series highlights some communicative qualities of its heroes to funnel the construction of a connoted *spectrum* capable of portraying each of them. Those traits calque some subjective iterative preferential modes,

**208**    **F. P. Gentile**

### Example 5.2  Motive Corpus, Motive, s01e01, min. 00:10:53–00:11:25]

Flynn:   ((Voice heard through the crawl space, softened by the boy's pants, and the clatters, plus external shouts from the agents)) °She=didn't=kill=her=husba^nd°

Vega:   ((Noise interferences continue)) Come=on <u>Ange</u> (.) she=r eported=the=body (.) <u>and</u> they=were=alone in=the=house

Flynn:   So^⇒ what are you saying^ She=kno:cked=<u>off</u>=her=hubby:=an d=scrawled=so:mething=on=the= wa:ll to <u>throw</u> us <u>off</u>^

Vega:   Yeah=why=no:-^

Flynn:   N:o (.) She <u>is</u> hiding=something (..) But=she=didn't=kill=h er=husband

Vega:   Oh let me guess you can feel her pa:in ((teasing her via a fake incredulous expression))

Flynn:   No^ (..) Okay yes^ (..) When she was=talking=about=how=ever yone=loves=him I could see the <u>warmth</u> in=her=eyes (.) ((Gestures stretching her arm towards him)) You could <u>see</u> tha-

Vega:   *No/ (.) no (..) All I saw was the blood=all=<u>over</u>=<u>her</u>

Flynn:   From <u>hugging</u> ((mimicking a low and stiff hug)) her=dead=hus band=in=a=fit=of=grief

Vega:   *Which/ she did to cover=the=spray when she <u>bludgeoned</u>=him=to=death^

Flyn:   *You're <u>such</u> a/ <u>romantic</u>^ (.) And <u>still</u> single^

Vega:   *You know Angie/ all I'm saying is <u>maybe</u> it's time we=start=embracing the <u>facts</u> and not rejecting the obvious^

thus triggering linguistic tags identifying the characters. The spectators could use those tags to affiliate certain recognisable elocutions with the protagonists pronouncing them. The instance above includes the exchange between detectives Angie Flynn and Oscar Vega while inspecting the house of the murder. There, they discuss their respective conjectures.

Regarding the appraisal framework linguistic evaluation (Martin & White, 2005), the nature of the dialogue presupposes 'heteroglossia' when engaging the communication since both participants handle their counterpart's position in turn to explain theirs. However, on a graduation 'focus' point of view, Angie's 'sharp' tone ("She=didn't=kill=her=husba^nd") based on intuition 'softens' as it clashes against Oscar Vega's rationality, becoming less confident ("No^—pause—Okay Yes^"). Yet—through her vacillation—the 'force' of her speech, as conversely as unexpectedly, undergoes an increase. It passes from 'lower' scores ("and=scrawled=**so:mething**=on= the= wa:ll to <u>throw</u> us <u>off</u>^") to a confident 'raise' ("**You could <u>see</u> tha-**") that betrays the essential reliability she feels regarding her instinct. Likewise, Oscar's initial lines show a 'sharp' and 'risen focus' ("Come on Ange..."; "Oh let me guess..."; "All I saw was...") in vain, aiming to awake his colleague from daydreams. Instead, it terminates in a 'lower' and 'softened' ("All I'm saying is <u>maybe</u> it's time we...") parodic reflection of Angie's relentless irony via the use of a docile and yet sarcastic 'judgemental' attitude ("...start=**embracing the <u>facts</u>** and not rejecting the **obvious**^").

The two characters' prosody and elocution pace are very straightforward and dense. However, some more peculiarities are strictly notable within those instants where their speeches slow down or pause to emphasise certain phrastic elements. On the one hand, detective Flynn's uttering often seems to mock other people's ideas whenever she disagrees, via the employment of slight vocal pitch raises (^) complementary to her eloquent fastness of articulation. A similar aspect, conjoined to the report of those unfitting concepts utilising lengthening episodes of sparse polysyllabic words, produces fluctuating sentences emulating lullaby-ish enunciations. The expedient wants to discredit other ideas' credibility ("So^⇒ what are you saying^ She=kno:cked=<u>off</u>=her=hubby:=and=scra wled=so:mething=on=the=wa:ll to <u>throw</u> us <u>off</u>^"). Conversely, the assertive underlining of various lexical features supports her theses ("I could see the <u>warmth</u> in=her=eyes (.) You could <u>see</u> tha-"), pinpointed by supportive gestures (Example 5.2—*Motive*, s01e01, mins. 00:11:11–15).

On the other hand, Oscar Vega is a pragmatic. His speech is condensed and synthetic (besides the terse rhythm, his sentences are often quite short). Moreover, the man uses a rigorous grammar whenever needed to validate his remarks. Paratactic ("Come=on <u>Ange</u> (.) she=reported=the=body (.) <u>and</u> they=were=alone in=the=house") to hypotactic shifts ("*Which/ she did to cover=the=spray when she <u>bludgeoned</u>=him=to=death^") transmit the consistency and the transparency of his thoughts. Indeed, the character of Angie Flynn is linguistically recognisable for her passionate, emotional bond improving her senses ("Vega: Let me guess, you can feel her pain. / Flynn: No. Okay, yes. [...] I could see the warmth in her eyes..."). Instead, Vega's rational roughness acts as a constant anchor to reality ("...maybe it's time we start embracing the facts and not rejecting the obvious"). Its task is to spoil and remind colleagues—as much as spectators—of the show's fictional dimension (helped by significant non-verbal implements like scoffing facial mimics and hand gestures accenting what he says; Example 5.2—*Motive*, s01e01, mins. 00:11:11-17-25). Once established that the female officer's performative and communicative roles are the creative *spirit* in force with the righteous, the *male* officer *incarnates* solid professionalism.

Besides them, two principal individuals remain the greenhorn and the helper:

### Example 5.3 *Motive Corpus, Motive, s02e10, min. 00:22:30–00:23:00*

Lucas: ((Arrives while Flynn and Vega at at sitting at Flynn's desks)) Hey^⇒ guys

Vega: What=do=you=go:t^

Lucas: Weirdness^ (.) I looked into the <u>boat rental</u> (.) ((confidently leans on the piece of furniture next to the desk, handling a folder)) For all <u>we</u> know (.) John=just=liked=to=fish^ (.) So I tried=to=go=back=a=little=further          to          see          if he'd=ever=rented=a=boat^ befo:re

Flynn: ((Stretches her arms while listening)) Mm-hmm

Vega: I'm sensing a <u>shoe</u> about to dro:p

Lucas: ((Carefully placing the folder on the desk, though through an ample movement revealing satisfaction)) All of John's credit cards are all only a year old=Same=with=his= bank=accounts

Vega: ((Background chats. He checks the documents in it)) Oh and they're all joint with his wife <u>Jennifer</u>

Flynn: ((Focused expression)) Mm-hmm

Lucas: Yeah and it gets better=I=dug=a=little <u>deeper</u> (..) and^⇒ (.) there's <u>no</u> record (.) of= a=John Rivera=beyond a year ago (..) It↓⇒'s like he didn't exi:st

## 5 The *Motive* 'Whydunit' Television Hybrid 211

The former of those two positions is detective Brian Lucas'. In comparison with the protagonists, he represents the *hand* of the Homicide Department, always managing the paperwork fetch and carry. He phone-calls witnesses, schedules appointments, and checks suspects' alibis. Lucas also controls IT investigations delving into people's records and personal data concerning their financial statuses (Example 5.3), due to his professional background and computer skills. Because of this initially marginal role, the detective's speech is not highly characterised. His lines are often quite pragmatic and limited to reporting facts and new pieces of evidence to be submitted to Vega and Flynn's (and Rogers') attention. The young man is a newbie at homicides, thus his capabilities are often narratively dampened. Nevertheless, Angie and Oscar only like provoking Brian rather than disrespecting him, still without affecting his proactive attitude ("So I tried=to=go=back=a= little=further to see if…").

His inexperience appears connected to an intrinsic desire to show off and blend socially and professionally within the department. As a consequence, his speech frequently recurs to 'monogloss' engagement features. He unilaterally presents his hypotheses or, more generally, his work in contrast with common knowledge ("**I** looked into … For all <u>we</u> know … **So I** tried to … **I** dug…"). Such constructions also reflect the use of 'appreciation' attitude lexical choices, underlined by the insertion of empty pauses, expressing personal aesthetic judgements rather than denotative qualities demanded by specialised and formal discourses ("Vega: What=do=you=go:t^ / Lucas: **Weirdness**^…"). There, he takes care to transmit the relevance of his tasks even more transparently via the vivid support given by graduation 'force raise' deployments ("I tried to go back **a little further**… Yeah and **it gets better**. I dug **a little deeper** and…"). Those occurrences support the insertion of asymmetric information delivery as well when the attention moves from the intense work accomplished by the young man to the not as much surprising results communicated via 'focus softenings' preceded by longer pauses or co-occurring with intonation drops ("…ago (..) **It's like** he didn't exi:st"):

In contrast to detectives, the latter character, here labelled as the *helper*, corresponds to the medical examiner Rogers.

## 212    F. P. Gentile

### Example 5.4 *Motive Corpus, Motive, s01e03, min. 00:02:09–31*

Vega: Would=you look at tha:t^ (..) ((uncovers the corpse to retrieve the victim's wallet from his jacket inside pocket, pretending to have found it casually)) °O::h°⇒=dear (.) ((with fatigued tone)) look at that Angie (.) Look=what=happened=here ((covers the corpse again)) (…) His^ wallet fell out

Flynn: Let me see that (.) ((focusing on the victim's ID)) Scott Hayward (.) Born in '86 (.) That's an unrestricted cla:ss-three:

Rogers: ((Arriving on the scene. Camera tracking mid shot moves onto the character, who is walking slowly towards them with her eyes aiming at Vega)) Have you^ been putting your ha:nds all over my body:^

Vega: ((Flynn chuckles)) No ma'am (.) no (..) Not without permission

Rogers: ((Hints at a smile)) Permission to °back°⇒ awa:y


Everyday language is always present within the dialogues where she is involved. However, her linguistic peculiarities associate the character with terminological and specialised discourse conveyance (employing both technical and popularised aspects). The amount of information at Betty's disposal often reveals crucial details about the murders to solve. Nonetheless, the woman frequently takes advantage of possible polysemous expressions related to her job to make fun of her friends or ambiguously tease some of them (Example 5.4). In the example reported above, Vega's misdemeanour of searching the victim in want of his wallet without waiting for the woman-coroner to arrive causes a reprimand, once the gaze the man was sure to have escaped turns into Betty's recalcitrant voice. The multimodal scenic rendition of the context collocates Dr Rogers' utterance first heard off-camera. Meanwhile, the frame visual salience remains on Oscar. It slides onto the stylish gait of the forensic expert only secondarily, via tracking technique. The character's silhouette emerges striding

## 5 The *Motive* 'Whydunit' Television Hybrid 213

unhurriedly in Flynn and Vega's direction, self-confident. She always wears a tight and posh dress that does not match the cold weather as perceived by the two detectives, who fasten themselves into their coats.

The atmosphere narrated by cinematic expedients corroborates the linguistic relevance of Betty Rogers' ambiguous line ("Have you^ been putting your ha:nds all over <u>my</u> body:^"). Her facial mimics underline that through a prosodic flattening between the exclamatory (objectively denoting facts) and the interrogatory formulation (checking Vega's spirit), midway between a sharp comment and an intriguing proposal. The continuation of the dialogue also reveals the existence of marks signalling linguistic control situations of hierarchically prominent speakers over less relevant ones in terms of social, political and professional charge. Oscar Vega's reply, "No ma'am (.) no (..) <u>Not</u> without permission" (with many pauses and a final emphasis on the third negation) anticipates the peremptory "Permission to °back°⇒ awa:y". Different professional areas of conversation among the participants participate in the exchange. Example 5.4 displays the procedural praxis of investigative processes (thus its related specialised context), where primary detective characters should await forensic experts' formal decision before contaminating the crime scene. Yet, a power stratification pattern surfacing here demonstrates some cooperative attitudes on behalf of the interacting persons since guided by the common goal of apprehending the killer.

Thus, the dominance exerted by the medical examiner is received as it is by the addressee (the detective) and answered through an ironic response. Still, despite the friendly relationship between the male officer and female forensics, this latter protagonist manages the more substantial professional preponderance over the other. Control linguistically reaffirms via the termination of dialogic exchanges employing a closing remark. Betty politely dismisses (see the almost whispered tone) superfluous people from proximity before performing the scientific examination of the body.

In the *Flashpoint Corpus*, characters adhere to recognisable expressive patterns, although the team-minded unit tends to flatten personal idiolects for a standardised and uniformed expressiveness (see Chap. 4). Likewise, in *Motive*, the protagonists equally respect peculiar communicative traits that distinguish each of them. Moreover, as explained in the

## 214     F. P. Gentile

examples, some fixed roles emerge as expected. Nonetheless, in *Flashpoint*, there are two formally recognised leaders cooperating with the rest of the corps members. Instead, *Motive* opts for a subtler consecration of the main heroes. It does not exalt distinguishing professional *qualities* but the potent *personalities*, especially when it belongs to charismatic women (see Angie Flynn and Betty Rogers).

## Who's Killing the Killstreak?

Along with its different narrative, *Motive* also breaks with North American traditional TV stereotypes, where the characters' inter-gender relationships are usually schematic. Despite the dominant protagonist's sex, his/her charismatic attitude urges him/her through *inter pares* flirtations on the workplace, seasoning the plots with collateral gossip-like developments. For example, in *Flashpoint*, the heartbreaking role is attributed to male characters (i.e., Sam gently winning Jules' love; see Chap. 4). The *Motive* TV hybrid subverts those schemata and proposes a femme fatale (Dr Rogers) that frequently and self-confidently provokes her male colleagues via explicit or allusive friendly comments.

Forensic narrative aspects, as said, represent one determinant peculiarity of the *Motive* TV series (and, in general, of *most* crime dramas). A voyeuristic concern centred on the characters' personal-sexual dimension representation transplants into the morbid attention regarding death and its accurate description. The *Motive* show has no fundamental—and generic—infractions during the episodes (given the 'monothematic' slant of the product). It adumbrates every potential offence with the assassinations' substantial hegemony (Tables 5.7, 5.8, and 5.9).

The *Motive Corpus* contains a broad range of ferocious impieties. The mediated television modes deliver them to viewers via a recognisable pattern that would distract users' sensibility from the act's cruelty to harness it towards the interest in the guilty mind's ephemeral research. The overall outlook on the series allows us to read the scriptwriters' plans from different perspectives. Still, the most relevant observations would include thematic and gender approaches. On a thematic level, the 'cause of death' column in Tables 5.7, 5.8 and 5.9 shows the recurrence of a handful of

## 5 The *Motive* 'Whydunit' Television Hybrid     215

**Table 5.7**   *Motive* TV series, season 1, killers and victims report

| SEASON 1 | | | |
|---|---|---|---|
| EP. | KILLER'S SOC. ENVIRON. | VICTIM'S SOC. ENVIRON. | CAUSE OF DEATH |
| 1 | BOY; THIEF | MAN; HIGH-SCHOOL TEACHER | BLUDGEONED TO DEATH |
| 2 | MAN; MAYORAL CANDIDATE | GIRL; HIGH-SCHOOL STUD. | HIT-AND-RUN |
| 3 | MAN; CUSTOMS COP | YOUNG MAN;LIMOUSINE DRIVER | GUN-SHOT |
| 4 | WOMAN; STORE CLERK | MAN; LAWYER | STABBED TO DEATH (S2) |
| 5 | WOMAN; STORE CLERK | MAN; HEALTH GURU | ELECTROCUTED |
| 6 | MAN; AA | MAN; BROKER | ASPHYXIATION |
| 7 | WOMAN; PEDIATRIC SURGEOS | MAN; SHOP OWNER | LACERATION TO THE ARTERY |
| 8 | MAN; CONTRACTOR | YOUNG MAN; POST. GRAD. STUD. | HARD BEATING; SUFFOCATION |
| 9 | WOMAN; ART WANNABE | WOMAN; ART ENTHUSIAST | VINTAGE GUN-SHOT |
| 10 | MAN; JUST FIRED FROM WORKPL. | MAN; PRIEST | MULTIPLE WEAPONS (S2,3) |
| 11 | MAN; VICT.'S DISABLED BROTHER | MAN; EX BOXEUR | STABBED TO DEATH |
| 12 | WOMAN; FAMILY WOMAN | YOUNG MAN; BUSINESS MAN | POISONED (S2) |
| 13 | BOY; TEENAGER | BOY; TEENAGER | EXSANGUINATION VIA STAB WOUND |

**Table 5.8**   *Motive* TV series, season 2, killers and victims report

| SEASON 2 | | | |
|---|---|---|---|
| EP. | KILLER'S SOC. ENVIRON. | VICTIM'S SOC. ENVIRON. | CAUSE OF DEATH |
| 1 | MAN; PHOTOGRAPHER | MAN; N.D. | FALSE SUICIDE |
| 2 | WOMAN; DANCE TEACHER | YOUNG MAN; N.D. | GUN-SHOT |
| 3 | WOMAN; FAMILY WOMAN | MAN; EX-SOLDIER | MISTAKEN IDENTITY CASUALTY |
| 4 | WOMAN; CONSTRUCT. WORKER | MAN; CORONER | STABBED TO DEATH (S1) |
| 5 | BOY; TEENAGER | GIRL; TEENAGER | HEAD BLUNT-FORCE TRAUMA |
| 6 | WOMAN; WEB DESIGNER | MAN; BARTENDER | STABBED TO DEATH |
| 7 | MAN; PARAMEDIC | MAN; SKYDIVER | DRUGGED VICT. TO SIMULATE ACCIDENT |
| 8 | MAN; HOME-CARE NURSE | YOUNG MAN; N.D. | STAGED SCENE; VICT. IS BRAIN DEAD |
| 9 | YOUNG WOMAN; N.D. | WOMAN; DINER OWNER | EXPLOSION |
| 10 | WOMAN; NANNY, IMMIGRANT | MAN; BUSINESSMAN, IMMIGRANT | TRAMPLED BY HIS HORSE |
| 11 | 3 MAN + 1 WOMAN | MAN; REAL ESTATE AGENT | MULTIPLE GUN-SHOTS (S1,3) |
| 12 | MAN; CHEM. TEACHER | WOMAN; AUTHOR | POISONED (S1) |
| 13 | MAN; COP | WOMAN; PROSECUTOR | STRANGULATION |

## 216 F. P. Gentile

**Table 5.9** *Motive* TV series, season 3, killers and victims report

| SEASON 3 | | | |
|---|---|---|---|
| EP. | KILLER'S SOC. ENVIRON. | VICTIM'S SOC. ENVIRON. | CAUSE OF DEATH |
| 1 | MAN; VICTIM'S ACQUAINTANCE | WOMAN; N.D. | POISONED |
| 2 | WOMAN; N.D. | WOMAN; BUSINESS WOMAN | POISONED; SUFFOCATED |
| 3 | YOUNG WOMAN; BUSINESS W. | MAN; DIVING INSTRUCTOR | POISONED; SUFFOCATED |
| 4 | MAN; N.D. | MAN; N.D. | MASSACRED BODY; VICT.'S DAUGHTER ABDUCT. |
| 5 | WOMAN; FLORIST | MAN; CRIMINAL | STAGED GUNFIGHT |
| 6 | BOY; TEENAGER | YOUNG MAN; GRAFFITI WRITER | DEATH BY IMPACT |
| 7 | MAN; N.D. | WOMAN; CHEF | BEATEN AND FROZEN TO DEATH |
| 8 | MAN; BUSINESSMAN | WOMAN; FORTUNE TELLER | STABBING; STRANGULATION; MUMMIFICATION |
| 9 | YOUNG WOMAN; BLOGGER | WOMAN; PHOTOGR. ASSISTANT | SINGLE STAB WOUND TO THE BACK |
| 10 | WOMAN; CLUB OWNER | WOMAN AND MAN; BUSINESSPEO. | MASSACRE, POISONING |
| 11 | MAN; GAMBLER | MAN; GAMBLING HOUSE OWNER | MULTIPLE GUN-SHOTS (S1,2) |
| 12 | MAN; CLERK | MAN; CLERK | SUFFOCATED |
| 13 | MAN; BUSINESSMAN | WOMAN; BUSINESSWOMAN | STAGED SUIC. VIA DEFENETRATION |

modalities. The most significant ones seem to involve murders carried out through a scene staging—in dark grey—doctored to make the victims appear suicidal or accidental casualties. They predominantly occur in seasons 2 (where a similar narration is adopted for five in thirteen episodes, thus 38.5 per cent of killings) and three in season 1.

Nonetheless, the thematic examination also allows for understanding the product language,[4] in consideration of the explicit narrative style. Violent descriptions, displays, and interactions (about cases of murder implying beating, stabbing, strangulation, gunfight) outnumber other less raw events (e.g., episodes of poisoning)—in light grey. The case counts ~thirty deployments in thirty-nine instalments, in a ratio of 77 per cent versus 23 per cent (circa, since the borderline nature of at least two episodes where multiple causes of death co-occur). The communicative impact of sequences showing manslaughters and massacres (in orange) is different from the retrieval of lifeless *untouched* bodies, yet expressing diverse discursive models. Intoxications determine the *simplistic* and almost immediate reading of the coroner's exams. Instead, the human chunk extirpation from their corporeal, vital integrity summons two divergent *de-* and *re-compositiory* activities. The acts linguistically and visually perform onscreen via a narrative language connotedly (since the sensational target lurking behind the prime death display) taking note of the demise, and then denotatively (because of the expert's arrival and scientific observation) struggling to put the pieces back together. This final event parodies the attempt to revive the dead in adherence to the *whydunnit's* reconstructive schemata.

On the other hand, the adoption of good and evil dichotomies presupposes victims about to die and killers ready to slay. The gender perspective applied to the observation of the series operates via a four-way model pairing men and women in the Russian roulette of the fiction:

1. Woman (killer) Woman (victim): 1 (S1) + 1 (S2) + 2 (S3); total: 4.
2. Woman (killer) Man (victim): 4 (S1) + 5 (S2) + 3 (S3); total: 12.
3. Man (killer) Woman (victim): 2 (S1) + 3 (S2) + 4 (S3); total: 9.
4. Man (killer) Man (victim): 6 (S1) + 4 (S2) + 4 (S3); total: 14.

Similar statistics, together with the perusal of the Tables 5.7, 5.8 and 5.9 surprisingly reveal a stable pattern showing how all the three analysed seasons propose the same 61.5 per cent male killers (eight men and five women) contrasted by different rates in terms of the victims' gender—84.6 per cent male in season 1 (eleven men and two women), 69.2 per cent male in season 2 (nine men and four women), 53.8 per cent male in season 3 (seven men and six women)—confirming the preference of the male-killer/male-victim cliché (average: 61.5 per cent/69.2 per cent) over the others, as well as the less adopted woman-killer/woman-victim one (average: 48.5 per cent/30.8 per cent). The series' gender-focused appraisal would favour the still strong chauvinism of the social models broadcast by television. They encourage receptive schemes to have a propensity for associating violence and danger with male physicality, while prudence and safety are purely feminine. However, the murder trend of the thirty-nine cases examined here displays a substantial narrative equivalence between either the cruel assassination method (43.6 per cent male; 33.3 per cent female) and *non-violent* deeds (12.8 per cent male; 10.3 per cent female) among man and women, though showing the slight prevalence of male actions in both categories.

The social and cultural environments reported associate individuals to business affairs as if the series were sketching some parallelism correlating money interests to the abomination of the homicide. Also—considering the proverbial threat of culture over power—the educational sphere is present. It involves teenagers (six, divided into four boys—three of whom are killers—and two girls—both victims) and teachers or private course instructors (five, divided into four men—50 per cent killers, 50 per cent victims—and one woman—who is stereotypically represented via the delicate charm of a dance teacher, although making herself a relentless killer).

The same speculation stated about thematic features is ostensibly valid to this latter issue. The compound multilayered language translates different expressive channels and pieces of information and encompasses gender representation within the criminological suggestion.

# The *Motive* Forensics: Language, Discourse and Terminology

Television, as a medium, maintains its communicative vividness through the conveyance of visually catchy data. Therefore, users are called 'viewers' or 'spectators' because of the primary relationship they establish with mediated contents via the use of sight, etymologically speaking. All of this aside, in line with the *Flashpoint* analysis (see Chap. 4), the linguistic exchanges in *Motive* are undoubtedly relevant in terms of informativity. Despite its powerful charge, the sole iconicity is not sufficient to transmit every shade of the televised contents.

The adoption of highly intuitive imaging techniques may compensate for the lack of verbal interaction significance. The show opts for a more balanced equilibrium, synthesising what is uttered with what is viewed. Indeed, the series adopts different types of P2P communication (cops dealing with lawyers and doctors or facing investigative areas that involve competence in statistics or finances) instead of monotonous and limiting cop-to-cop dialogues. Professionals belonging to diverse sectors then handle terminological and discoursal constructions to render their sentences formal and effective. Given the contextual domains, talks range

## 5 The *Motive* 'Whydunit' Television Hybrid    219

from district to crime scene, from public places to morgue, and more (and often pairing precision and promptness with the observed reality clarity and transparency).

Every episode of the series consists of the presentation of a rigidly structured narrative scheme. It proposes a very brief and silent interlude that functions as a theme for the show, only displaying its title wording. The subsequent sudden beginning of the story frames both the killer and the victim. The a posteriori presentation of the crime scene sequence follows to serve as the contextualising operation finalised at launching the investigation (also enriched with flashbacks; Table 5.6). The structure of the instalment, however, stretches beyond that. Once presented with the case, spectators assist to the ingress of detectives Flynn and Vega, starting their non-cohesive dialogues midway between briefing procedures and chitchats (Example 5.2) generally to meet Lucas, whom frequently happens to be there before them. Step by step—in a loop-like circuit—the plot passes through different communicative, visual and linguistic stages articulated within a crystallised order presupposing:

1. The police procedural reconstructive approach—Example 5.2;
2. Passages of medical discourse via preliminary observations validated by further examination reports and terminological remarks;
3. Police procedural conjectures and hypotheses concerning the case resolution and identifying possible suspects;
4. Intrusions from IT and finances knowledge under investigative needs;
5. Crucial legal contexts involved in the interrogation phases and recurring when formalising the arrest of criminals.

Considering the *Motive Corpus* noun word list (Table 5.10), it is worth noting the presence of meaningful words to be ascribed to the mentioned domains. Within the first fifty entries of the table, some crucial elements manifest the police procedural aim of the TV sell-off, again. Hence, the Example 5.2 commentary compares the said conjectural discourse with its thematic range anew. Angie and Oscar pettifog about their initial theories via different perspective graduation intensities. Some of the most exciting nouns belonging to the crime drama environment (highlighted in dark grey) have law enforcement as a core role in the series. 'Murder' (rank 14) immediately precedes 'detective' (rank 15). The linguistically salient occurrences of 'killer' (rank 36) and 'body' (rank 49) contour the 'case' (rank 40) as the essential factors making up the story.

However, those participants in the plot articulation (along with other terms) set the insufferable burden of the *Motive*'s *fil rouge*, tracking a linear string guiding the narration (in bold):

1. Some unnoticed murder is performed;
2. The act involves a killer to have attacked and a victim to have died;
3. Police arrive afterwards to discover the body;
4. The realisation of death starts investigative concerns.

Yet, the police-procedural-oriented reading of terminological occurrences in Table 5.10 allows retrieving one more thematic pattern about the deductive (as much as inductive and mediatic) approach.

Focusing on the 'victim' word sketch (Table 5.11) concerning its position in the noun word list (Table 5.10), it is inferable that the utmost leads beaten by officers (within the TV fictional context but plausibly in real life too) refer to the person's inner group of acquaintances. Thus, the occurrence of the term (rank 29, 151 count) appears close to 'man' (gender-related discussions on victims and killers have already been provided). It also precedes domestically associable nouns like 'wife' (rank 37), 'mom' (rank 38; although 'mother' only reaches position 104), 'father' (rank 50; which, conversely to 'mom/mother' is more frequent than 'dad', rank 87) 'husband' (rank 52), the hypernym 'family' (rank 55) and more ('son', #66; 'daughter', #99). These pieces of information reveal possible data about deceased peoples' ages and social statuses, preferentially chosen by television producers for storyline constructions. 'Victim' (Table 5.11) mostly appears as the direct object of verbs relating to the misdemeanours it underwent (e.g., strangle; bash; stab; beat). More rarely, it is the grammatical subject performing the action. Indeed, when 'victim' is not a direct object, it occurs in the indirect object position. Prepositional phrases galore emphasise the communication via the

## 5 The *Motive* 'Whydunit' Television Hybrid    221

**Table 5.10** *Motive Corpus*, noun frequency list

| Rank | Noun | Rank | Noun | Rank | Noun | Rank | Noun |
|---|---|---|---|---|---|---|---|
| 1 | TIME [506] | 18 | EVERYTHING [179] | 36 | KILLER [143] | 48 | COURSE [122] |
| 2 | SOMETHING [330] | 19 | PHONE [177] | 37 | WIFE [137] | 49 | BODY [122] |
| 3 | NIGHT [324] | 20 | NAME [177] | 38 | MOM [136] | 50 | FATHER [119] |
| 4 | ANYTHING [315] | [...] | | 39 | MORNING [135] | 51 | CALL [119] |
| [...] | | 28 | WORK [152] | 40 | CASE [134] | 52 | HUSBAND [116] |
| 14 | MURDER [198] | 29 | VICTIM [151] | [...] | | [...] | |
| 15 | DETECTIVE [193] | 30 | MAN [148] | 45 | QUESTION [128] | 55 | FAMILY [111] |
| 16 | NOTHING [182] | 31 | POLICE [146] | 46 | WEEK [127] | [...] | |
| 17 | MONEY [179] | [...] | | 47 | ANYONE [125] | 67 | DEATH [96] |

combination of the 'victim' syntagm with other participants in the action, who possibly undergo an interrogation due to their communal relationships. Moreover, the noun often is the possessor of an ample array of items (used with the Saxon genitive of prepositional addition). The case represents the procedural need for examining every belonging or data attributable to the victim (e.g., *V.'s* + purse; office; phone; name). Here, the investigative interaction immediacy denotes the proximity of police procedural discourse to natural language praxes (despite the occurrence of sparse terminology). Also, it distances from obvious affiliation to the legal discourse via the adoption of short premodifying patterns in place of not relevant post-modification phenomena (which is instead a typical feature of the language of law).

## The Medical Communication Supports

Following the series' instalment narrative path, wherefore not through a rate count view, the next communicative domain spectators would encounter is the medical forensic one. Notwithstanding the narrative dominance of police procedural interactions facilitating the

## 222  F. P. Gentile

**Table 5.11**  *Motive Corpus*, "victim" word sketch

| Victim, N. [Wordlist nouns; Rank 29—151 Count] | |
|---|---|
| Rank | Concordance list |
| 1 | WHERE'S THE VICTIM? |
| 2 | VICTIM'S INSIDE, DR ROGERS |
| 3 | THE VICTIM MIGHT NOT HAVE SEEN HIS ATTACKER COMING IN THE DARK |
| 4 | THE LETHAL BLOW, THE VICTIM'S WIFE HEARS HIM SHOUTING FROM THE SPARE ROOM |
| 8 | VICTIM'S INJURIES ARE CONSISTENT WITH BEING STRUCK BY A VEHICLE MOVING AT A HIGH RATE SPEED |

| MODIFIERS OF "V." | MODIFIED BY "V." | V. WITH "V." AS O. | V. WITH "V." AS S. | "V." AND/ OR... |
|---|---|---|---|---|
| INTENDED; Motel; BURN; HIT-AND-RUN; GUNSHOT; HOMICIDE; Room; WHOLE; OTHER | SERVICE "V." + [NNP] | STRANGLE; CRUCIFY; QUOTE; BASH; STAB; PLACE; UNDERSTAND; BEAT; BLAME; CONVINCE; ROB; MATCH; SHOOT; KNOW; BRING; MEAN; HEAR; SAY; BE; KILL; FIND; HAVE | LEAK; RECEIVE; STALK; BLEED; SHARE; HAND; MEET; DRIVE; BREAK; BE; LEAVE; HAVE; DO; GET; GO | KILLER; Weekend; "V." + [NNP] |
| PREP. PHRASES | ADJ. PRED. OF "V." | "V.'S" [POS] | POSS. OF "V." | PRON. POSSESSORS |
| TO + "V."; ON + "V."; WITH + "V."; OF + "V."; LIKE + "V."; "V." + WITH; FOR + "V."; ABOUT + "V."; FROM + "V."; NEAR + "V." | NEXT; AFRAID; FEMALE; CAUCASIAN; ALIVE; HIGH | WIFE; BELONGING; PURSE; PRINT; FAMILY; OFFICE; HOUSE; PHONE; STUDENT; CO-WORKER; INSIDE; PARACHUTE; STATE; LUNG; FINANCIAL; CALENDAR; INJURY; FATHER; SISTER; MOTHER; NAME; CAR | LUCAS; OSCAR | Our; THEIR; Your; HIS |

# 5 The *Motive* 'Whydunit' Television Hybrid    223

understandability of dramatised recounts, medicine covers a crucial and consistent expressive portion in *Motive*.

The preliminary medical examiner analysis is competently delivered on the spot when she first arrives on the scene to check the victim. However, following its suppositious nature (and the cinematic need to protract actions throughout the episodes), it is limited to denotative guessing of the cause of death to be confirmed secondarily using a more accurate dissection (Table 5.12).

The case reported above offers an excellent example of medical discourse usage within the context arranged by TV needs on a linguistic level. Considering the high level of formality construed by the character's performance, a linguistic appraisal framework approach here would presumably fail an unbiased examination of the report because of its analytical requirements mandatorily assigning stiff 'engagement', 'attitude' and 'graduation' labels to discourse passages. The report-reading benefits from a clear voice and neutral and unemotional prosody—it does not involve positioning because of its strictly factual value.

Nonetheless, those aspects contrast the *emotional* and *hushed* parenthetical reprimand that Betty ("°Don°⇒'t do that") cautiously utters. She warns Angie about the situational formality (as if some other characters were supervising the pathologist's conduct), as detective mocks the procedural seriousness through a fleeing "Hi" on the microphone, once the doctor has announced her friend's colleague and recorded it (min. 00:08.47).

The textual dimension of the discourse reveals its spoken-to-written structure. The reporting aim urges introductory sentences to be concise. Linguistic economy formulation norms require straightforward, simple entries to provide essential data as headings. The case number is useful for classification needs ("12-AB5465"). More examples follow, like the patient's personal information, the examination phase description (initial) and the naming of the expert carrying it out, plus eventual collateral notes ("Detective Angie Flynn is present") specified before proceeding. After that, during the textual reading, the pathologist visually checks every mentioned detail to match the actual damages observable on the victim's corpse (also useful to the cinematic comprehension of the scene by the TV viewers). Subsequently, this part of the speech gets terminated

## 224   F. P. Gentile

**Table 5.12** *Motive*, s01e02. Medical report multimodal observation

| Min./Description | Visual image | Kinesic action | Soundtrack | Phases and metafunctions |
|---|---|---|---|---|
| 00:08:35 Dissecion room; turquoise LED lights. Dr. Rogers wears her white coat; she switches on a voice recorder hanging above the body | MovA; CP: Tracking, MS-FV; VS morgue; P: W; Ph; | Movt: Participant grabs the microphone; Tempo: Slow; | AS: Microphone clicks; step; | |
| 00:08:39 She starts reading the autopsic report; CLS | NmovA; CP: Shaky; | Movt: Participant reading; | AS: None; | A single phase setting the context in the morgue during the examination formal record. |
| 00:08:41 Dissection room WS; Flynn is sitting on a stool next to Rogers and the corpse | CP: Shaky, D-FV; VS P: W; W; | ≈ | AS: Chair clatters; | Three subphases implement the narration: Two of them focus on the corpse; a third one concentrates on Detective Flynn checking doctor's remarks on the corpse |
| 00:08:47 CLS; Flynn stretches towards the microphone while Dr. Rogers (out of focus) is reading | MovA: CP: Tracking shaky, MS-FV; | Movt: Participant stands up; | AS: Chair clatters; step; | |

*(continued)*

## 5 The *Motive* 'Whydunit' Television Hybrid     225

**Table 5.12** (continued)

| Min./Description | Visual image | Kinesic action | Soundtrack | Phases and metafunctions |
|---|---|---|---|---|
| 00:08:48-52 Dr. Rogers visual salience | CP: Tracking, MS-FV; + CP: Shaky; VS P: W; | Movt: Part. #1 turns back; part. #2 sits and slides back; Part#1 reading; | AS: Step; chair clatters; wheels; + AS: None; | EXP: Morgue + actors (one corpse) |
| 00:08:58 Corpse CLS-SV | CP: Tracking, Det.; VS: Corpse; SP1; | Movt: Tracking camera shot; | ST: Feeble reverberat. Note; | |
| 0:08:59-09:01 Dr. Rogers checking the body; Corpse detail: Right leg open wound (exposed bone) | CP: Shaky; VS P: W; + CP: Tracking, Det.; VS: Corpse; SP2; | Movt: Participant reading; + Movt: Tracking camera shot; | ≈ | NT: Viewer positioned distantly. It only approaches to rapidly focus on the corpse twice, but mostly concentrates onto the doctor via front view sequences |
| 00:09:06 Flynn CLS (body language + facial mimics: Peepin to check the body from the distance) | CP: Shaky, CLS-FV; VS P. W; SP3; | Movt: Part. Peeping; | ST: None; | TEX: Theme-rheme-theme order. The phase introduces rhematic details about the corpse multiple times. Narration slant: 1. Procedural routine; 2. Forensic report |

*(continued)*

**Table 5.12** (continued)

| Min./Description | Visual image | Kinesic action | Soundtrack | Phases and metafunctions |
|---|---|---|---|---|
| 00:09:08-13 Dr. Rogers concludes; She switched of the voice recorder | CP: Shaky; VS P: W; + MovA; CP: Tracking, MS-FV; VS morgue; P: W; Ph; | Movt: Participant reading; + Movt: Participant grabs the microphone; Tempo: Slow; | ≈ + AS: Microphone clicks; | |

Dialogue
Rogers: ((starts recording)) .h case^⇒ number (.) 12 (.) AB5465 .h Ti:Ffany: Green<u>wood</u> initial=examination (.) Dr. Betty Rogers Detective Angie Flynn (.) is present.
Flynn: ((stands up and approaches the microphone)) hi
Rogers: °Don°⇒'t do that
Flynn: °Wha:t°
Rogers: .h victim^⇒<u>is</u> Caucasian (.) female .h multiple abrasions (..) <u>compound</u> fractures ((slows down her uttering pace)) of the <u>left femur</u> (.) <u>right humerus</u> (.) <u>and</u> the <u>ilium</u> (..) X-ray:s <u>show</u> breaks^ in ribs 3 through 8^ and impact impression on right^ thi:Gh (..) Victim's^⇒ injuries are consistent with being ((emphasis via sudden head nod)) <u>struck</u> by a vehicle moving↓⇒ at=a=high=rate=of speed ((turns off the microphone))
Flynn: /whoa^ (.) wait a minute* [...]

without closing remarks or conclusions, emphasising the sheer, informative skeleton of a medical report.

Additionally, the syntactic observation of Dr Rogers' utterances in Table 5.12 shows several medical discourse peculiarities (Daniele & Garzone, 2016). Her lines address an E2E specialisation level. She adopts a technically constructed communication that informs another (abstract, since the recording) individual having an even disciplinary proficiency. Thus, Betty's formulations surpass the P2P quickness and disregard the presence of a non-professional listener, who could miss fragments of her speech. On the overall perspective, Betty's discourse spells via depersonification linguistic procedures enacted through the performative agent's erasure. The coroner's role is never mentioned, and, similarly, personal pronouns do not appear. The doctor's emotional neutrality and laconism contribute to increasing formality rates. Verbal occurrences within the enunciation are quite limited and confined to a mere copula function ("the victim **is** Caucasian…") if not inclusive of sight-related meanings used to validate descriptions ("x-ray **shows** breaks in…"). Wherever one could spot any verbal alterations or omissions, the prominence of dense nominal structures substitutes predicates through class-changes via post-modification and phraseology ("being struck by"; "are consistent with"). It enhances the crystallisation of specific patterns or verb nominalisations ("…impact **impression** on…").

From the lexical point of view, other significant omissions involve the conveyance of adjectival chains. Their terminological preciseness conflates them and the nouns they premodify. It originates consistent content-enriched specialised polyrhematics ("multiple + abrasions"; "compound + fractures"). Formal register increases influence preposi-tional dependence choices and determinative article sacrifices ("…shows breaks **in** the ribs 3 **through** 8"; "…impact impression **on** right thigh"). In other cases, they generate suppletivism episodes ("**vehicle**" instead of 'car'; "**at a high rate of speed**" for 'fast'). Eventually, one more peculiarity of medical language reflects aniso-morphism (Gualdo & Telve, 2011). Similar to suppletivism, it con-cerns the substitution of ordinary words and exoteric terms with their esoteric equivalents, frequently preferring those which have Greek or Latin matrices. They may reference sensible damages ("**abrasion**", from Latin *abradĕre* meaning 'scrape'; "**fracture**", from Latin *fractus* meaning 'broken [bone]') or anatomic parts ("**femur**", Lat. for 'thigh-bone'; "**humerus**", Lat. for 'arm bone'; "**ilium**" or 'pelvic bone' Lat. for 'hip bone'), to name a few.

Non- and para-verbality tell Dr Rogers to utter her lines almost irre-spective of any punctuation marks. Her constant and distinctly audible voice always follows a deep in-breath, somehow signalling to the viewers the effort of managing such a technical discourse. This narrative strata-gem draws the spectators' attention onto the speech due to its intricacy. Evident prosodic emphasis highlights any hints of terminological occur-rences. The visual salience flows slowly to allow receivers to perceive all the bits of information they need. The microphone initial and final clicks

**228**   F. P. Gentile

***Example 5.5  Motive Corpus, Motive, s03e02, min. 00:38:22–56***

| | |
|---|---|
| Lucas: | Here's=an=investment=statement that you provided Erica Grey. |
| Flynn: | Why didn't you <u>tell</u> us she was your client^ |
| Lucas: | Because this is a work of fiction (..) You're hiding behind^ a legitimate job at <u>Hillridge</u> (.) but you're running a <u>Ponzi scheme</u>=on=the=si:de (..) You're paying one client's return with another client's money and skimming 20% off the top for yourself |
| Flynn: | Ye:ah |
| Stephanie: | (h) .h <u>I</u>: take^ (.) a reasonable: (.) commission ba:sed (.) on my (.) experti::se (.) and <u>level</u> (.) ((turns towards Flynn, raising her eyebrows)) of service:: ((emphatically hisses /s/ final sound)) |
| Lucas: | Return is directly correlated to risk (.) .h US^ treasury is offering 0.6% on a two^-year note and you are <u>promising</u> a no-risk return (.) <u>2,000%</u> higher^ |
| Flynn: | Erica figured it out though^ (.) didn't she^ ((Dolly. Flashback starts)) |

are a great help, indicating the specialised communicative context beginning and ending. Nevertheless, this visual and acoustic iconicity mainly focuses on the medical examiner Rogers, while performing her text, and with only a little time dedicated to actual body injury displays (mins. 00:08:58, 00:09:01) or the secondary listener's curious attitude (mins. 00:08:41) and gaze (min. 00:09:06).

## IT and Finances

Following crime drama language permeance, many communication and knowledge areas trickle down the *Motive* TV series' porous expressive boundaries. It originates *intrusions* from diverse professional codes

## 5 The *Motive* 'Whydunit' Television Hybrid 229

useful to the narration. For instance, hints of financials (not discourse, properly) show up when inquiries involve investigating suspects' economic status. As said, many cases, deal with business and trades (Tables 5.7, 5.8, 5.9), also because of the recurrent presence of 'money' (Table 5.10; noun word list: rank 17, 179 count) throughout the corpus. Suppose a similar language is necessary for storyline developments, given the complexity of economics discourses. The broadcast product seemingly opts for the sole communicative contextualisation of such areas of expertise. It leaves aside any elaborate linguistic pattern to propose knowledge bubbles included in some formal interactions like interrogatories.

Example 5.5 presents the ongoing dialogue's central theme reflecting a monetary motive to have brought the questioned woman to kill. The intricacy of economics is known to the characters in the scene as well. Thus, the woman takes for granted her counterparts' ignorance on the matter, hoping to get away with her crime (Brian shows the suspect an investment statement: she supposedly wonders whether they can even read it; min. 00:38:22). However, detective Lucas immediately unveils his advanced proficiency. He spoils the "Ponzi scheme" orchestrated by the woman to illegally profit from her clients' investments via a detailed mathematical calculation. Despite the scant terminological count, this limited example reveals some lexicon determining the presence of specialisation degrees. Indeed, even though of lower percentages than medical discourse, one could note the conveyance of polyrhematics. Premodifying bounds (e.g., "**investment** + statement") determine such linguistic cases, together with other *usual* terms that belong to the financial environment and related to premodifiers as well (e.g., 'investment' [1] '**return**'; [2] '**risk**'; [1 + 2] "**no-risk return**"). Moreover, given the mathematics- and statistics-based nature of the language of economics, numbers and symbols are frequent. They mostly occur in the form of percentages ("20%"; "0.6%"; "2000%"), often aligned with collocation patterns inclusive of one head meaning-carrier noun/verb pre- or postmodified by adjectival ("**reasonable** commission") or adverbial determiners ("**directly** correlated **to** [risk]"). Other terms of higher technicality (e.g., "two-year note", from "Treasury note"), then, pair with widespread organs of control (e.g., "**US Treasury**") and typical theoretic speculations labelled through eponymic tags (e.g., "**Ponzi scheme**", for the model invented by Italian-immigrant crook Charles Ponzi at twentieth-century first light).

## The Legal Context Crystallised Praxis

Some relevant examples also regard legal communication conveyance, though there are evident differences (Example 5.5 and Table 5.13). Given its extensive diffusion, the legal discourse is one of the most controversial languages precisely because of its labile boundaries. It consists of vast amounts of praxis terms and terms stabilised in use. Hence, its lexical thesaurus confines are blurred, as they tend to blend their terminological pertinence with particular natural language expressive patterns.

Mathematics, economics and medicine (this latter plausibly included in the array of hard sciences with the former two) have a solid crust, which generally allows recognising their respective terminological affinity. Conversely, Law (as soft science related to humanities) is less pragmatic. Its intricacy lies in densely connected postmodifying hypotactic and paratactic relationships altering the English language syntheticism. Nonetheless, such a discourse certainly has ample terminological stratifications associable with its linguistic domain only.

The conveyance of similar lexical basis, along with the said syntactically complex aggregations, in the television context—despite the fundamental thematic proximity with the crime drama genre—would produce turmoil into receivers, thus generating useless focuses on the comprehension of the language rather than on plot developments. Medical discourse fascination opposes professionalism-narrating strategies. Similar to the economics communication case, they tend to present sectorial content via the association of significant dialogues. Visual and audible modes always support to make those contexts even more expressive than the purely verbal dimension.

## 5 The *Motive* 'Whydunit' Television Hybrid     231

**Table 5.13**  *Motive*, s01e04. Detectives' vs. lawyers' authority multimodal

| Frame/Min | | | |
|---|---|---|---|
| 00:21:48 | Specular sliding sequence 00:21:58—00:22:09 | | 00:22:16-18-23-25 |
| Interrogation room (penumbra); interrogatee (CLU-BV) + detectives at the desk (WS-FV): Flynn is writing NmovA; CP: Shaky, W/ MS-BV; VS interrogatory room; Ph; tempo: Slow; | Left side of the screen: Interrogatee tilting back his head towards his lawyer (facial mimics: Provocative) CP: CLS-SV; VS P: M; M; | CP: CLU +SV-OSS-BV; VS P: M; M / W; M Movt #1: Focus on lawyer; Movt #2: Finger movement;Right side of the screen: Detectives watching the lawyer and his client talking (facial mimics: Scoffing) CP: CLS-SV; VS P: W; M; | Frames filming the Interrogatee and Flynn, in turn (final Flynn's accuse) |
| 00:22:31 Vega drinks; Flynn reads the documents CP: MS-SV; VS P: W; M; AS: Papers; | 00:22:40 Interrogatee (CLU-BV) + detectives at the desk (WS-FV): Flynn and Vega are waiting (body language: Vega relaxed; Flynn has clasped hands) CP: Shaky, W/ MS-BV; VS interrogatory room; ST: String instruments; | 00:22:43 Movt: Lawyer peeps into the scene to reach his client's ear; | 00:22:49-23:04 Interrogatee turns towards the lawyer (he nods); Interrogatee (CLU-BV) + detectives at the desk (WS-FV): Flynn and Vega move CP:CLS-SV; VSP:M;M; CP: Shaky, W/ MS-BV VS interrogation room |
| Dialogue | | | |

*(continued)*

## 232    F. P. Gentile

**Table 5.13** (continued)

| Frame/Min |
| --- |

Flynn: Mr. Mitchell recently negotiated a:: (.) <u>merger</u> (.) between your construction firm and a national competitor correct^

Carlin: So^

Vega: For the record (.) that's a ye:s^

Carlin: ((slightly nods)) <u>yes</u>:^

Flynn: ((checking papers)) even <u>I</u> can see by these numbers (.) you=kind=of=got <u>screwed</u> in the deal

Carlin: For the record (.) define <u>screwed</u>

Vega: *you=know/ looking <u>past</u> the=mandated=audit and=the=sale=of=assets=on=hand there's a (..) <u>whale</u>^ of=a=non-compete agreement^

Flynn: Ouch (..) somebody bent ove:r

Lawyer: May <u>I</u> remind <u>you</u> detectives (.) my client is here to be <u>questioned</u> (.) not in<u>sul</u>ted

Flynn: My Ba:d (..) I'm sorry .h (.) but Jack^ (.) you busted a=few=heads=along= the=way=to=get=what= you=want ri:Ght^

Lawyer: ((VoiceOver, while camera is on Carlin)) <u>allegedly</u>

Flynn: °yeah° (..) ((pointing her finger towards the lawyer while looking at the suspect,. Then turns towrds the lawyer)) ventriloquism (.) that=is=a=really=neat^=trick (.) Let's^⇒ just take a little <u>stroll</u> down↓⇒ memory lane (..) <u>ex:Tortion</u> (.) attempted^=bribery of=a=civic=offi:Cial (.) aggravated assau:Lt

Lawyer: *yeah none/ of=which my client was <u>ever</u> convicted=of

Flynn: *so::/ (.) you've never=threatened (.) Mitchell's life^ (..) think↓⇒ carefully before you answer tha-((lawyer whispering in Carlin's ear))

Carlin: °It's°⇒ all right (..) yeah (..) ((to detectives)) maybe the deal wasn't the greatest=but (.) in this <u>economy</u> (.) even <u>I</u> have to settle=for=what=I=can=get^

Flynn: So you didn't say ((reporting suspect's words)) if you don't make me happy, you and your family won't live to regret it^

Vega: Which you know (.) aside from the lousy grammar (.) pretty much sounds like a death <u>threat</u>

Carlin: I don't know (..) people say a lot of things (..) Doesn't mean you have to take 'em <u>literally</u>

Flynn: °right°^ like when I say 15 to 20 (.) it might actually be:: <u>12</u> to 15^ (..) but↓⇒ what's a few years between friends right^

Carlin: ((smirks)) (h) all right^ (..) all right […]

## Observation

In Example 5.5 and Table 5.13, the attestation of legal communication parades through the powerful cinematic transposition of emblematic situations like questioning. The narration salience corresponds to intense dialogues. The locutory and perlocutory pressing pace intimidate suspects, whom spectators already know to be guilty, thus enjoying those individuals' moments of crisis. Also, if language appears not to be crucial, procedural schemata maintain their relevance. Detectives' discourse strength pursues the suspects' surrender via a formal confession within specific contexts, and hierarchically determined interactive exchanges render that. Question addressees often have no time to answer. The very moment in which one speaker terminates his/her enquiry, the other *tackles* with more interrogatives or even provides conjectural accusing answers (Example 5.5) to carry on the goal. Very frequently, questions and answers are semantically irrelevant (see Flynn's lines in Example 5.5). They merely serve to increase the cinematic rhythmic scansion of the sequence to create a conversationally viscous flow, supportive of decisive *visual displays* of nailing proofs placed under the culprits' eyes (Table 5.6 and Example 5.5).

Similar communication events reproduce the characters' personalities and profiles recreated onscreen.

The situation described so far is, without doubt, deployed when suspects happen to be ordinary, lower-class individuals or influential people represented via their weaknesses, for narrative reasons. Nevertheless, suppose criminals are requested to mirror social plagues like corruption and abuse. In that case, their image is indeed stronger. Their power physically personifies in the lawyer right behind or next to them. As the *voice* of their consciousness—or the choking grip of the status quo—lawyers protect their clients. They openly speak in others' place (Table 5.13) or whisper in their ears the permission to answer a question or to reveal the right details without putting themselves in jeopardy (min. 00:22:43).

Furthermore, lawyers' competence is sufficient to eradicate a whole allegation via the uttering of a *single* term (Table 5.13, line 11: "<u>allegedly</u>"). That could impressively discredit detectives' work, who—instead—must play a pivotal role in the broadcast. Hence, the presence

## 234   F. P. Gentile

(or better, the absence) of legal professionals inside interrogation rooms is also a reminder indicating to audiences the fictional milieu of the TV series.

On the same trend, rigid crystallised procedures should compulsorily set the *iter* followed by law enforcement agents on the occasion of police interrogations. Yet, they seem to vanish in the cinematic rendition (for reasons of time and costs), which automatically bypass stable bureaucracy to bestow more relevance to prominent heroes. Televised interrogations often cut short elements like the reiteration of subjects' personal data, the statement of their civilian rights to refuse to answer in the absence of a lawyer, and the repetition of alleged criminal activities' spacial and temporal information (see also Heydon, 2005: 51). Scriptwriters only keep those aspects when they have relevance in the plot articulation; otherwise, they disposable.

On TV, the suspects' arrest leads to immediately slamming them into dark and cold rooms. Detectives have them wait indefinite amounts of time before rushing in. Then cops suddenly irrupt, loudly shut the door and commence shooting face-to-face questions in a solo rendezvous to get the desired confessions. Lawyers and bureaucracy are left behind. Consequently, the *Motive* product (extensible to the entire genre format screenplays) constructs indissoluble links to the unfaithful remodulation of situations that dominate media transmission. In many cases, those representations would unquestionably result as procedurally illegal in real-life environments.

## The *Motive Corpus* Results

This chapter concentrated on the *Motive* TV series and has not include the other two corpora final comparisons (yet). Therefore, the *Motive Corpus* partial examination highlighted some linguistic observations integrated with non-linguistic data. They concerned the narrative, descriptive and broadcasting techniques adopted to rendition its contents for a targeted audience. The statistical results show a count of ~200,574 words followed by a substantial 5.8 per cent decrement once the corpus is deprived of empty words. Such an update counts ~188,988-word tokens, representing the total occurrence frequency of ~2734-word types. Those cyphers relationship leads to a 1.45 per cent ratio determining a lexical variation of one new word/term every 69.13 repetitions (Table 5.14).

The overall mathematical operations depend on a massive collection of data, which is not organic at all. It includes three macro-groups (the TV series seasons) divided into thirteen smaller textual bodies making the single instalment transcriptions. Indeed, observing the *Motive* TV series seasons individually, one could note a stable increase of word tokens from 2013 to 2015—from ~59,994 to ~66,545. The trend is inversely proportional to the word types variation in reference years, passing from the ~4642 of the first season to a 1.62 per cent slight reduction of ~4567 in the third one (however significant, since related to a higher number of tokens), determining an average 7.28 per cent tokens/types ratio. Such diverse quotients signal a relationship of circa 1/13.74, connected to the insertion of new words or terms with their respective partial or full repetitive occurrence (5.83 times higher than the *Motive Corpus* overall data; Table 5.14).

Numbers demonstrate how the three different seasons per se use an extensive vocabulary which contributes to casting the entire series language. However, all annual broadcast *ensembles* possibly use a coherent lexical choice criterion that affects the thesaurus heterogeneity in variation rates. The linguistic preferences tend to repropose the same linguistic formulations over the years and adapt the same reiterative vocabulary through diverse plot exploitations, affecting statistical portrayals.

**Table 5.14** The *Motive Corpus* results

| Motive Corpus [Seasons 1 to 3 (2013–2015)] | | | |
| --- | --- | --- | --- |
| Tokens (T) | Types (t) | MotC T/t ratio | |
| ~188,988 | ~2734 | **1/69.13 (1.45%)** | |
| Season 1 (2013) T/t | Season 2 (2014) T/t | Season 3 (2015) T/t | Avg $(T_1 + T_2 + T_3) / (t_1 + t_2 + t_3)$ |
| 1/59.994 (1.67%) | 1/63,267 (1.59%) | 1/66,545 (1.50%) | **1/13.74 (7.28%)** |
| Vocabulary heterogeneity (Avg T/t vs.MotC T/t) **+5.83%** differentiation | | | |

The linguistic *monotony* of the *Motive Corpus* corresponds to the thematic uniformity of the series. The *Flashpoint* florid differentiation centred on the approach to diverse threats ranging from kidnapping to bomb diffusion and terroristic attacks (see Chap. 4). Instead, *Motive's* heroes belong to the narrow reality of the homicide department. Accordingly, detectives Flynn, Vega and Lucas—and Dr Rogers even more—do not search the streets in want of a felon to fine or arrest them for *any* crime. They do not wander the city to keep it under control. These characters only leave their offices to reach an already acknowledged crime scene, as much as they only travel the town to fetch some namely identified witnesses for questioning procedures. Such a description well fits some linguistic deficiencies of the corpus. Pedestrian tasks are assignments of no interest to the officers of the Vancouver televised transposition. Hence, the impossiblility to tracking down the exact location of the many assassinations presented during the *mise en scène* over the 2013–2015 three-year period of broadcast analysed.

On an oral (verbal) dimension, the hypothetical toponym list of urban places mentioned and connected to the crimes would only count a few entries (altogether: 1. 'Broadway' Street; 2. 'Oak' Street; 3. an unidentified 'Canal Street'; 4. 'Cambie' Street; 5. '22nd' Street; 6. 'Larkin' toponym). Oppositely, the best part of the communicative aspect is visual immediacy. Even in this case, the city is only recognisable for those spectators who know its emblematic buildings and monuments. Like other locations, the name of 'Vancouver' itself has one occurrence only, in season 1 (2013).

The British Columbia product is undoubtedly Canadian, considering the narration style—very talkative and lacking that brutality that distinguishes the US productions from any other par excellence (see Chap. 4). Moreover, the televised linguistic accent seldom manifests peculiar linguistic phenomena, like the Canadian raising on diphthongs and other features, naturally performed by the actors.

However, suppose the series disseminates some sparse recognisable traits. In that case, the best part is well camouflaged, in a deflection play that aims to dissimulate the Canadianness spirit in want of some anonymous narrativity. The said contingency could represent business interest requisites seeking to produce TV merchandise traded internationally and

# 5 The *Motive* 'Whydunit' Television Hybrid    237

through a diaphanous Canadian label—which would appear indeed—without limiting beyond border fruitions and sociocultural extendable assimilations.

On the communicative level, *Motive* shows some interesting peculiarities. The dominant slant of the polarising thematic structure of the *whydunnit* visually and linguistically shapes the series expressivity through the reconstructive narration lens.

On a linguistic level, such characterisation mirrors the prevalence of terms associable with the legal environment. This vocabulary often determines deadly factors launching lucubrations to retrieving dangerous persons of interest and more affiliated hypotheses (Tables 5.2, 5.7, 5.8, 5.9 and 5.10). Also, it involves competent emulations of specialised discourse patterns whenever needed (Tables 5.12, 5.13 and Example 5.5). The occurrence of relevant nouns accompanies significant rates of verbal conjugation forms. They mostly adopt present perfect tenses to signal the flashback-oriented linguistic and thematic focuses recounting accomplished homicidal performances parallel with present-tense investigations (Table 5.4).

Visual strategies render the same perspective. Scenes alternate flashback digressions to flashforward come-backs within single dialogic sequences to emphasise recount dynamics that evolve in time. Narrative slants and stories change thanks to fresh mental associations and turning table evidential discoveries. The series visual peculiarity reveals both the victim's and the killer's identity in the initial seconds of every instalment. The factor multimodally cooperates with the product communicative efficacy. Besides the wording appearance, labelling individuals according to their respective roles of 'good' or 'evil' character (Table 5.2), means everyone is linguistically profiled. Heroes and antiheroes all have specific expressive features and connoted attributions of body language and gestural characteristics, like Vega's pressing prosody or Flynn's sarcasm and uneasiness (Example 5.2 and Table 5.12). Cinematic techniques vividly support the said communicative aspects through camera movements and cuts, emphasising attitudes and behaviours or urging the viewer to observe the scenarios under precise and monitored points of view.

# Notes

1. 'Serial'. The Oxford Living Dictionaries [online resource]. https://en.oxforddictionaries.com/definition/serial (accessed Jan. 24, 2019).
2. 'Series'. Ibid. https://en.oxforddictionaries.com/definition/series (accessed Jan. 24, 2019).
3. Vancouver Economic Commission. 'Film and television production'. https://www.vancouvereconomic.com/film-television/ (accessed May 9, 2019).
4. Multimodally intended as a blend of linguistic and extra-linguistic features consisting of visual salience, soundtrack/ambient noises, cinematic techniques, and merely verbal aspects.

# References

Adolphs, S., & Carter, R. (2013). *Spoken Corpus Linguistics: From Monomodal to Multimodal.* Routledge.

Aijmer, K., & Stenström, A.-B. (Eds.). (2004). *Discourse Patterns in Spoken and Written Corpora.* John Benjamins Publishing Company.

Baldry, A., & Thibault, P. J. (2001). Towards multimodal corpora. In G. Aston & L. Burnard (Eds.), *Corpora in the Description and Teaching of English-Papers from the 5th ESSE Conference* (pp. 87–102). Cooperativa Libraria Universitaria Editrice Bologna.

Baldry, A., & Thibault, P. J. (2006). *Multimodal Transcription and Text Analysis: A Multimedia Toolkit and Course Book.* Equinox.

Bateman, J. A., & Schmidt, K. H. (2012). *Multimodal Film Analysis. How Films Mean.* Routledge.

Beaty, B., & Sullivan, R. (2006). *Canadian Television Today.* University of Calgary Press.

Bednarek, M. (2010). *The Language of Fictional Television: Drama and Identity.* Continuum.

Bednarek, M. (2018). *Language and Television Series. A Linguistic Approach to TV Dialogue.* Cambridge University Press.

Bednarek, M. (2019). *Creating Dialogue for TV: Screenwriters Talk Television.* Routledge.

Biber, D. (2012). Corpus-based and Corpus-Driven Analyses of Language Variation and Use. In B. Heine & H. Narrog (Eds.), *The Oxford Handbook of Linguistic Analysis* (pp. 160–191). Oxford University Press.

Bredin, M., Henderson, S., & Matheson, S. A. (2012). *Canadian Television: Text and Context*. Wilfrid Laurier University Press.

Buckland, W. (2004). Film Semiotics. In T. Miller & R. Stam (Eds.), *A Companion to Film Theory*. Blackwell Companions in Cultural Studies. Blackwell.

Calabrese, R. (2019). *Patterns of English through History, Art and Literature*. Tangram Edizioni Scientifiche.

Cawelty, J. G. (1977). *Adventure, Mystery and Romance: Formula Stories as Art and Popular Culture*. University of Chicago Press.

Centini, M. (2010). *La criminologia. Comportamenti criminali e tecniche di indagine*. Xenia.

Collins, R. (1990). *Culture, Communication, and National Identity: The Case of Canadian Television*. University of Toronto Press.

Daniele, F., & Garzone, G. (2016). Communicating Medicine. *Popularizing Medicine*. Carocci.

Davis, M. (2021). The TV and Movies Corpora. *International Journal of Corpus Linguistics, 26*(1), 10–37.

Dorland, M., & Charland, M. R. (2002). *Law, Rhetoric and Irony in the Formation of Canadian Civil Culture*. University of Toronto Press.

Durovicova, N., & Newman, K. (Eds.). (2010). *World Cinemas, Transnational Perspectives*. Routledge.

Eco, U. (2016). *Lector in Fabula*. Bompiani.

English Oxford Living Dictionaries. (n.d.). https://en.oxforddictionaries.com/

Garzone, G. (2020). *Specialised Communication and Popularisation in English*. Carocci.

Gentile, F. P. (2015). *La linguistica del delitto. Maureen Jennings e il caso di 'Poor Tom is Cold', tra formulaicità e traduzione*. Tangram Edizioni Scientifiche.

Gittins, S. (1999). *CTV: The Television Wars*. Stoddart.

Grego, K. (2013). The physics you buy in supermarkets. Writing scence for the general public: the case of Stephen Hawking. In S. Kermas and T. Christinsen (Eds.). *The Popularization of Specialised Discourse and Knowledge across Communities and Cultures* (pp. 149–72). EDIPUGLIA (off print). (accessed March 9, 2021).

Gualdo, R., & Telve, S. (2011). *I Linguaggi Specialistici dell'Italiano*. Carocci.

Hale, M. (2013). Who Cares Who Did It? Why Is More the issue. *The New York Times*. Retrieved January, 24, 2019, from https://www.nytimes.com/2013/05/20/arts/television/motive-new-crime-drama-on-abc.html

Hall, E. T. (1966 [1990]). *The Hidden Dimension*. Anchor Books Edition.

Hall, J. A., & Knapp, M. L. (Eds.). (2013). *Nonverbal Communication*. De Gruyter Mouton.

Heydon, G. (2005). *The Language of Police Interviewing: A Critical Analysis*. Palgrave Macmillan.

Hyland, K. (2005). *Metadiscourse. Exploring Interaction in Writing*. Continuum.

Jacobs, J., & Peacock, S. (Eds.). (2013). *Television Aesthetics and Style*. Bloomsbury Academic.

Jenner, M. (2016). *American TV Detective Dramas: Serial Investigation*. Palgrave Macmillan.

Kübler, S., & Zinsmeiter, K. (2015). *Corpus Linguistics and Linguistically Automated Corpora*. Bloomsbury Academic.

LeChevallier, M. (2013). Review. Motive: Season One. *Slant Magazine*. Retrieved January 28, 2019, from https://www.slantmagazine.com/tv/motive-season-one/

Lowry, B. (2016). TV Reviev: '£Motive'. Variety. Retrieved January 25, 2019, from https://variety.com/2013/tv/reviews/tv-review-motive-1200481254/

Martin, J. R., & White, P. R. R. (2005). *The Language of Evaluation. Appraisal in English*. Palgrave Macmillan.

*Motive*. (n.d.). CTV. Vancouver. February 3, 2013–June 7, 2015.

Myerson, B. R. (1991). *Game Theory: Analysis of Conflict*. Harvard University Press.

Nelson, R. (2007). *State of Play: Contemporary 'High-End' TV Drama*. Manchester University Press.

Piazza, R., Bednarek, M., & Rossi, F. (Eds.). (2011). *Telecinematic Discourse. Approaches to the Language of Films and Television Series*. John Benjamins Publishing Company.

Richardson, K. (2010). *Television Dramatic Dialogue. A Sociolinguistic Study*. Oxford University Press.

Roelcke, T. (2010). *Fachsprachen*. Erich Shmidt.

Simpson, P., & Mayr, A. (2009). *Language and Power*. Routledge.

Trudgill, P. (2000). *Sociolinguistics. An Introduction to Language and Society*. Penguins Book.

Vancouver Economic Commission. (n.d.). Film and Television Production. Retrieved May 9, 2019, from https://www.vancouvereconomic.com/film-television/

Wildfeuer, J. (2016 [2014]). *Film Discourse Interpretation. Towards a New Paradigm for Multimodal Film Analysis*. Routledge.

# 6

# The *19-2* Anglified Police Procedural *Noir*

The *19-2* crime drama represents a peculiar case as a Canadian police procedural television serial. Set in contemporary Montreal, its study's interest is cultural- and linguistic-adaptive because of its narrative. The terminological point of view is also fundamental, as it emerges already in the title. On the one hand, such a televised product distinguishes itself from the other two shows described in Chaps. 4 and 5 since its format was not born as an Anglophone one. The original was a Francophone production focusing on the Québécois law enforcement environment. As formulated by Safeyaton Alias:

> Cities are more than a place to live, to work or to play in. As people observe the city while they move through it, the city serves as a political and social statement, and in some cases, symbolizes and encompasses the achievement and political prowess of the country's ruling elite. (O'Halloran, 2004, p. 55)

Thus, the *Dix Neuf-Deux* original aired intermittently for three seasons between 2011 and 2015. Anyhow, its 'adaptation' (ordered between 2012 and 2013) utterly subdued the authentic Francophone sociocultural context. This process resolved more into a cultural rebuttal rather than a more simplistic content reboot—via some "anglo-*phony*-sation" of the current and existing Montreal production (Gentile, 2020,

---

© The Author(s), under exclusive license to Springer Nature Switzerland AG 2021     **241**
F. P. Gentile, *Corpora, Corpses and Corps*,
https://doi.org/10.1007/978-3-030-78276-4_6

242    F. P. Gentile

p. 180). The *Dix Neuf-Deux* statement meant the televised large-scale diffusion of a representative social and political rendering of the less spread Franco-Québécois reality via generalisable Canadian-Anglophone media, and the *19-2* version contributed to distorting such perception. Francophone political and official charges were by praxis renamed after their Anglophone equivalents. That annihilated de facto the authority of the French-speaking Montreal (/mɔ̃ʁeal/), juxtaposed to its—Americanised—Canadian-English alter ego (/mʌntriːˈɒl/). Thus, the cinematic scheme substituted its former community's language (and possibly its linguistic community) and subverted the original ideological power fostering the show. The *stance* eventually transmuted into a prominently Anglophone homogenising society with sparse Francophone, considered but not necessarily relevant, minorities instead of vis-à-vis-ing a more likely reflection of the Canadian linguistic, cultural mosaic.

As a consequence, this brand new crime show premiered on the English-speaking Canadian broadcaster, *Bravo!*—on the same narrative path as its US homonym—in 2014. It lasted until 2017 (this last year it was moved on to *CTV*)—and with an number of seasons outnumbering the original (four against three). Thus, the process created an adaptation devouring and outstanding the adapted product, left in the audience's memory oblivion. This modification gave up the former acting crew, decided by *CBC* after shooting a pilot episode.[1] Also, every hint of the Francophone language was solidly eradicated and then supplanted through the ubiquitous and improbable insertion of the Anglophone communicative code. It produced "a racially diverse, English-speaking police force [which] is clearly something that Montrealers have only experienced on TV" (Carpenter, 2016).[2] The format purchase involved a more consistent amount of money investments in the serial compared to what some direct and faster dubbing, subtitling or voiceover procedures would require. However, the effort befell executive producer Jocelyn Deschênes' strong desire to portray the Québécois milieu significantly. "Montreal hasn't been shown that much on English-Canadian TV and it's a very cinematic city. They really want us to show Montreal from angles that we've never seen" (Brendan, 2012), she explained. The situation forged a nonexistent sociocultural communicative context. Such a case could be a potential bias bribing the televised scenario trustworthiness, thus distorting the show's linguistic expressiveness and reliability (Gentile, 2020). Nonetheless, the present research does not have any sociological pretence. It does not want to depict social statistics or any demographic and political statuses and feelings towards the police forces patrolling the Québécois urban boundaries. Hence, this potential controversy does not represent a crucial hurdle. The multimodal analysis of the *19-2* TV serial has its very goal in understanding the main features and linguistic expedients adopted by (English-speaking) scriptwriters to structure an adequate and fitting (both natural and specialised) communication within a commonly acknowledged Francophone environment. Anyhow, this milieu allows the spectators not to care about such a contradiction. It fascinates them with its narration—instead—funnelling the plausibility of the natural and popularised linguistic knowledge assimilability.

On the other hand, the investigative goal approaches the consistency of the police talk (Dorland & Charland, 2002; Heydon, 2005; Pozzo, 2005; Olanrewaju, 2009; Brundson, 2010; Marmor, 2014; Moorti & Cuklaz, 2017; Roufa, 2019). The specialised communication conveyed on screen can immediately be sensed through the observation of the TV serial title. Hyphenated numbers identify the name of the drama. They do not stand for a casual date, a fraction, or any randomised numerical choice. Contrarily, the ciphered code renders the preciseness of the label. It recurs in the Montreal police force to denote the exact area of the pertinence of patrols, in this case, precinct 19, plus the digit(s) assigned to the car that the scheduled cops are driving, number 2. It is worth noting that the filming location is a real decommissioned Montreal police station (Oswald, 2016).

Serial observation examines the shades of the linguistic spectrum. Structured throughout the iterative patterns construed within the said television product, they list and describe the primary and most communicative contexts simultaneously ranging from everyday language to specialised discourse. Popularisation events (Grego, 2013) deal with the law, medicine, economics jargon, and so forth. Thus, the *19-2* ambivalent string is not only the immediate and effective identifying code associated with a specific radio motor patrol (RMP). By extension, it also denotes the duo onboard (Table 6.1), synthesised and encoded in a chain of numbers and symbols according to the known principle of linguistic economy. That is one of the typical specialised language strategies investigated in this chapter.

Indeed, the results not only intend to provide the statistics of one preponderant channel rather than another. They plan to measure the specialised discourses or knowledge relevance comparable and co-occurring, with common language dialogical or descriptive situations.

The intra-analytical research (within the corpus, to observe the expressive change from one season to the other) precedes the inter-analytical examination (the *19-2 Corpus* contrasting the *Flashpoint Corpus* and the *Motive Corpus*). They proffer the chance of assessing different cinematically produced linguistic situations in- and out-of-context. The diverse narrative perspectival schemata retrieved will demonstrate the actual blendability of the English language transmitted onscreen and its array of usages. The deployment of visual and iconic frames of narration acts as the leading communicative agent of the broadcast (Table 6.1). It facilitates the overall comprehension, the harmonious coexistence and simultaneous alternation of the codes with which sight and sound are associated.

## The *19-2 Corpus* Structure

The following step of the research required the assemblage of all the linguistic and dialogic materials involved in the analysis. The investigation observed the single series' main peculiarities and then controlled them with the other series ones as a whole (after a primary contrastive phase). The recognition of the boundaries within which the survey has to operate was fundamental. To that extent, considering the different length of the

**Table 6.1** *19-2* TV series intro frames description

| (Frame)/Descrip. | | | | Phases and metafuntions |
|---|---|---|---|---|
| (1) Dark bluish filter; MovA; CP: Tracking; panorama VS > Montreal skyline; Ph1; AS: TV series theme | (2) MovA; CP: Tracking; MS VS > RMP: M;M;; SP1(1); AS: TV series theme | (3) MovA; CP: Tracking; WS VS > Stitches; eagles flying; SP2(1); AS: TV series theme | (4) MovA; CP: Tracking; Det. VS > Index + gun trigger; Montreal skyline sliding in the negative space; SP3(1); AS: TV series theme | EXP: City + indoor INT: One long tracking sequence. SP1 to SP3 refer to Ph1 (city narration). SP4 to SP7 refer to Ph2 (indoor secrecy). Ph3,4,5 last instants: no subphases. Viewer position:mid-distance/close up (details): pressuring visual narration. |
| (5) MovA; CP: Tracking; MS VS > Nacked woman's spine; Male hand caressing > W;M;Ph2; AS: TV series theme | (6) MovA; CP: Tracking; CLU VS > Locker room: M; SP4(2); AS: TV series theme | (7) MovA; CP: Tracking; VS > Glass pane shatters; CGI; Ph3; AS: TV series theme | (8) MovA; CP: Tracking; MS VS > Locker room; Nick sitting on the bench > M; SP5(2); AS: TV series theme | TEX: Theme-rheme loop. Phases introduce rhematic details: 1. City; 2. Patrols; 3. Eagles/wounds; 4. Weapons; 5. Sexuality; 6. Intimacy/tension; 7. Wilderness |
| (9) MovA; CP: Tracking; Det. VS > Hands with bullets in their palms;SP6(2); AS: TV series theme | (10) MovA; CP: Tracking; CLU VS > Deer; Ph4; AS: TV series theme | (11) MovA; CP: Tracking; CLU VS > Locker room; Benn (facial mimics + body language: tension); SP7(2); AS: TV series theme | (12) MovA; CP: Tracking; CLU-MS VS > Nick's vest; '19-2' wording > M; Ph5; AS: TV series theme | |

three TV shows (in terms of seasons and episodes per season), the *19-2 Corpus* size had to roughly match the bulk of the other two (see Chaps. 4 and 5). Subsequently, the study did not *entirely* observe any of the three mediatic products. Indeed, no examination criteria could have justifiably limited the subjective picking or rejecting of a given episode rather than another. Therefore, all data scaled to each other.

As already noted, the *Flashpoint* TV series (*CTV*, 2008–2012; Chap. 4) counts five seasons, and the *Motive* hybrid (*CTV*, 2013–2016: Chap. 5) counts four. Some disparities with the *19-2* serial (*Bravo!*, 2014–2016; *CTV* 2017, three plus one) emerge. As a consequence, there were a few contingencies to be acknowledged for the alignment.

*Motive* and *19-2* are shorter. They disallowed the research to ponder over the whole *Flashpoint* transmission (whose production peculiarities also interfered in the decisional process). Consequently, the primary condition was to establish the survey of a maximum of four annual broadcasts per series. Yet, this step was problematic, too. Indeed, while (the first four seasons of) *Motive* and *Flashpoint* aired on *CTV*, *19-2* shared their same broadcaster in its sole final transmission (2017). This latter serial premiered on *Bravo!*, where it continued for three years before moving. That possibly implicated a change of register and narrative style, which could have altered the serial overall linguistic connotation. Potential differences may have related to both *Bravo!* and *CTV* diverse production and broadcasting policies or requirements. Thus, the parsing of the entire *19-2* product could have originated internal (narrative and linguistic) incoherences. Giving prominence to the channel could have taken the research to consider *CTV* transmissions only in the analysis (thus one season per series). However, the study would have deflected itself towards the *CTV* modes of communication, disregarding the primary and more complex aim of—instead—describing the linguistic codes conveyed by the *genre* and not by a single television company. The final choice urged to consider the broadcaster without being limited by its influence.

The best option was to examine three annual programming schedules per TV series to grant the corpora an appraisable size. It would also have avoided an inner lack of cohesion and incoherence created by missing potential internal references. Consequentially, the assemblage of the multimodal materials related to the *19-2* TV serial regards its first three seasons (and thus evidently and definitively conditions the bulk of the *Flashpoint* and *Motive* corpora, resulting in the actual product determining the range of the comprehensive examination). The initial corpus construction stage involved retrieving written texts and corpus constitutive linguistic data that the researcher would have synchronised with visual data afterwards. This step required the transcription of dialogic exchanges of thirty episodes. They lasted 42-to-45 minutes each, for a total amount of ~1260 minutes of transcription and counted ~112,387 words.

Once the transcription task was over (Baldry & Thibault, 2001, 2006; Aijmer & Stenström, 2004; Adolphs & Carter, 2013; Calabrese, 2019), the corpus underwent a POS tagging parsing. It added part-of-speech metadata (Penn Treebank POS tagging standards) to the written text (reported hereafter in light grey, included in square brackets), outlining the basic grammar of the sentences formulated via the television medium and checking syntactic peculiarities:

### Example 6 *19-2 Corpus, 19-2, s02e07, min. 00:15:24–33*

Nick:  [DT]The [NN]gun[VBZ]'s [RB]still [RB]there
Ben:   [HM]Mhm    [RB]Then    [RB]again    [IN]at    [CD]7 [RB]PM[WP]What [DT]the [NN]fuck
Nick:  [WP]What [PRP]It[VBZ]'s [RB]still [RB]there
Ben:   [PRP]It [VBD]moved

POS tagging software is not infallible (Garside, 1987; Leech et al., 1994; Garside & Smith, 1997). Automatic labelling sometimes could fail, requiring the researcher's proofreading and intervention wherever computer misinterpret the linguistic data they process. In this particular case, for example, the abbreviation of the third singular person of the verb 'to be' in the exclamation "The gun's still there" (not in "It's still there") was mistaken for an English possessive. Software tagged it as [POS] in place of [VBZ]. The modification of such an error was manual. Casualties like that sometimes occur with interjections and backchannels. The exemplified "Mhm", although foreseen within the list of parts of speech, is labelled incorrectly. The current [HM] tag was initially confused with a singular proper noun [NNP], possibly because of the

## 248  F. P. Gentile

misleading initial capitol 'M' at the sentence beginning, attributed to the interjection during the transcription process.

Then, the *19-2 Corpus* qualitatively integrated other linguistic metadata coming from multimodal annotation symbols. They facilitate iterative situation reading comprehension in terms of para-verbal and prosodic aspects of communication. Indeed, the written mode lacks sound data (tone, rhythm, etc.) and surrounding noises (all nonverbal information). The descriptive information insertion assisted the initial POS tag-supported dialogic transcription of the scenes displayed onscreen. It consisted of the transcriber's comments on what could be seen or noticed beyond the mere reading (in double round brackets; Table 6.2).

Moreover, due to the transcription nature, no punctuation marks occur. This absence keeps the written rendition neutral and prevents any arbitrary prosodic interpretation that the transcriber could have mislabelled due to verbal-acting performances (where pause-lengths not necessarily correspond to commas and full stops anytime). Thus, the punctuation and the rhythm of dialogic exchanges only appear through the multimodal signals '(.)', '(..)', or '(n° of seconds)', reporting breaks as much as exclamation and question marks are mostly associable with vocal pitch alterations lacking subsequent tone modulations:

### Example 6.1  19-2 Corpus, 19-2, s02e07, min. 00:15:24–33

Nick:  [DT]°The°⇒[NN]gun[VBZ]'s [RB]still [EX]the:re

Ben:  ((Ben moves the cursor through the screen and selects another frame)) [HM]Mhm (.) ((footsteps on the background. Clicks of the mouse)) [RB]°Then°⇒[RB]again [IN]at [CD]7 [RB]PM (..) [WP]What [DT]the [NN]fuck^ ((The camera shot moves from Ben to Nick's face and then to the computer screen))

Nick:  [WP]What^ [PRP]It[VBZ]'s↓⇒[RB]still [EX]there

Ben:  ((Shakes his head)) [PRP]It^⇒[VBD]moved ((They both look at the screen))

Through a similar annotation, one perceives the grammar that structures the sentences—which is informal and essential in the example. Yet, s/he also sizes the prosodic peculiarities depending on the scene displayed

## 6 The *19-2* Anglified Police Procedural *Noir*    249

**Table 6.2** *19-2*, s02e07. Evidence tampering footage multimodal annotation aligned with frames

| Min./Description[a] | Visual image | Kinesic action | Soundtrack | Phases and metafunctions |
|---|---|---|---|---|
| 00:15:24 Monitor detail showing evidence room | NmovA; CP: Stationary, CLS-FV; VS: Computer frames; Ph + SP; | Movt: Footage frames are processed; Tempo: slow; | AS: footsteps, clicks of the mouse; ST: carillon-like music; | One phase establishing the narrative slant, implemented by two subphases emphasising tools support for the cinematic communication rendition EXP: Actor + tools INT: viewer positioned as a third agent participating in the scene, alternately focusing on the screen or on one's face from behind other's TEX: Hyperthematic single phase expressing 1. concern; doubt; suspect; 2. information appraisal through forensic computational analysis |
| 00:15:25 OSS-SV: Ben at the computer (clicking the mouse); Nick watches | CP: Stationary, CLS-LV VS > P: M; M; Ph; | Movt: Participants' head movements; Tempo: slow; | ≈ | |
| 00:15:28 Monitor detail showing evidence room (noise [photography]) | CP: Stationary, CLS-FV VS: Computer frames; SP1; | Movt: frame sequence slowdown; Tempo: slow; | ≈ | |
| 00:15:31 Ben and Nick checing the video (facial mimics: incredulous) | CP: Stationary, CLS-LV VS > P: M; M; Ph; | Movt: Participants look at each other; Tempo: slow; | ≈ | |
| 00:15:32–33 Camera cuts from Nick's OSS-SV to Ben's, to focus on Nick's facial expression (glimpse + realisation) | ≈ | ≈ | ≈ | |

*(continued)*

250  F. P. Gentile

**Table 6.2** (continued)

| Min./Description[a] | Visual image | Kinesic action | Soundtrack | Phases and metafunctions |
|---|---|---|---|---|
| **Dialogue** | | | | |

Nick: [DT]°The°⇒[NN]gun[VBZ]'s [RB]still [EX]the:re
Ben: ((Ben moves the cursor through the screen and selects another frame))
  [HM]Mhm (.) [RB]°Then°⇒[RB]again [IN]at [CD]7[RB]p.m. (..) [WP]What [DT]
  the [NN]fuck^ ((The camera shot moves from Ben to Nick's face and then
  towards the computer screen))
Nick: [WP]What^ [PRP]It[VBZ]'s↓⇒[RB]still [EX]there
Ben: ((Shakes his head)) [PRP]It^⇒[VBD]moved ((They both look at the screen))

[a]This chapter tables have no images due to copyright restrictions. Despite Sphere Media openness, it has not been possible to finalise an agreement to use its visual materials. Therefore, frame descriptions substitute still captures

and setting the communicative context. Nick's tone down (°word°) vocal modulation (⇒) would suggest some whispered uttering perfectly coherent with louder surrounding noises such as footsteps or the very relevant clicks of the mouse unfolding the truth to the two incredulous cops. Ben's as whispered answer and Nick's next vocal pitch lowering (↓) and modulation (⇒) confirm this interpretation. Moreover, the syllable lengthening in the adverb "there" emphasises further prosodic observations on Nick's insistence about not seeing anything odd (/ðər/ becomes /ðə:r/). It underlines Ben's assertive remarks (preceded by two pauses, one shorter (.) than the other (..)) followed by low rise intonation events (^) when he finds something in the footages.

The annotated reading of the dialogue is undoubtedly useful to multimodal comprehension. It is also worth noting that bits of information are still missing for the riddle's complete deciphering. Something is now clearly happening. Yet, one would know that the two characters on the scene are in a confabulatory-ish mode opposite to a computer, watching footages connected to some suspect gun.

The annotated corpus had to fully benefit from some additional requirements to let users evaluate and study language-in-context locutionary events. To that extent, after the qualitative alignment of the tagged and annotated script with respective image sequences, the multimodal corpus would eventually be ready for a final investigation. The exemplified scenario depicts the protagonists while carrying out a task, which is illicit or has to stay secret for some reasons. Also, whatever their goal, the computer is an essential element here (Norris, 2004; Scollon & LeVine, 2004). A similar deduction comes from merging linguistic data and metadata, in turn, integrated with more information. The whispering tone (tonal, prosodic) is one of the primary interpretation keys. The cautious attitude displayed by heroes' hunched backs makes body language visual nonverbal communication (Lund, 2007; Pinar-Sanz, 2015). Eventually, the wary and frowning expression and disclosed lips render the characters' focused facial mimics via close shot camera position.

Language is not a univocal communicative code as it would rather be the sum of multiple layers of expressiveness (Royce, 2007; Kress, 2010; Swain, 2010). Consequently, the written text (resulting from the sole verbal transcription) is no longer sufficient for the utmost description of interactive situations where information exchanges are involved. Many aspects exponentially implement communication, like background, landscape and setting collateral evidence that (visually) define the context. Thus, building the *19-2*—multimodal—*Corpus* clears how peculiar linguistics (speech acts) significantly coexist with para- and non-verbal features (e.g., prosody, rhythm, body language, gestural and behavioural approaches). Audible noises and soundtracks also play a vital role in the scenes. However, they would fall outside the analytical range of classical corpus linguistics observations. The thematic plot of the exemplified episode (Table 6.2) deals with the apprehension of an underage-prostitution panderer, who gets away with his crime thanks to some unidentified bribed accessory. In the scene, Ben and Nick suspect a mole complicit. Ambient noises thoroughly accompany a gloomy tension-building carillon-like music to increase pathos. Audio-supports tessellate all the narrative elements and measure the relevance of such circumstances with even more crimes involving paedophilia and abuses dirtying law enforcement corps.

It is worth noting that the technical limits of multimodal parsers are today still challenging to solve. The best part of the analysis requires intense qualitative examinations and mark-up procedures for correctly labelling extra-linguistic data and synchronising them with the linguistic aspects that quantitative results could fail to individuate. Consequently, the discriminating factor fetching relevant instances for the ease of the research maintains its fundamental corpus linguistics-bound approach under percentages and word-frequency presentations. Salient cases, then, answer statistical targets where linguistic materials correspond to occurrence and collocation lists. At the same time, those data integrate extra-linguistic features, whose goal is to demonstrate the prominence, the communicativeness and the higher understandability of iconic contents over *minor* verbal ones (Mehrabian, 1972; see Chap. 2).

## The Broadcast

The TV serial under examination is about the narration of routine on-duty episodes of given cops (Nick, Ben and their team) belonging to a Montreal precinct, along with the implications that their working days reflect onto their private life off-duty.

The main cast counts fifteen characters—ten fixed cops plus three occasional agents from Internal Investigation departments, one caseworker and one boy. They are ten men and five women, divided into seven degrees of authority in working/social positions. Indeed, a commander—Gendron, male, Caucasian, 40-to-50-years-old—leads the precinct to which cops belong. Sergeant Houle, a 40-to-50-year-old Hispanic male, is substituted by Sergeant Suarez from season 3, who has similar visible minority traits and age. The team includes seven more officers. These are five males and two females, all 35-to-45-years-old except for one man, the rookie, presumably in his late thirties (and substituted by a character with the same peculiarities from season 3). They are all white-Caucasian except for three: Nick, the protagonist, is Black-Jamaican; Tyler is Canadian African-American (no exact ethnicity information is given); Beatrice is Vietnamese.

Inspector Latendresse is a 35-to-45-year-old female character. The three internal investigation officers are two men and a woman, all 40-to-50-years-old. Despite the slight age difference, those four actors are all white-Caucasian.

Eventually, the caseworker, Amelie, is a 35-to-45-year-old mixed ethnicity woman, and the boy, Theo, a male, Canadian-Jamaican, a 10-to-15-year-old individual.

Plot plausibility also provides details about the protagonists' personal life and sexual orientation influencing their working place. Theo is Nick Barron and his ex-wife Isabelle Latendresse's son. The woman occasionally receives unreturned attention from Marcel Gendron. Audrey Pouliot, one of the agents, is in a relationship with Nick, terminating once the man starts dating investigator Elise Roberge. J.M. Brouillard, another cop, is a violent man who beats his wife (Justine); Tyler Joseph has serious drinking issues. Ben Chartier, the second protagonist, falls in love with Amelie de Grace, Nick's half-sister. Eventually, Beatrice Hamelin, the Vietnamese patrol, is often referred to for her homosexuality.

## The *19-2* Expressive Spectum

The pieces of information about ethnicity, age, sexual orientations and relationships given in the previous paragraph contribute to sketching the serial sociolinguistic aspects. In line with that, the examples that follow propose some everyday, ordinary language and specialised discourses, terminology and procedural codes coexisting. These linguistic blends signal diverse interactive contexts whenever the protagonists' interlocutors change, whether they are colleagues (with formal situations diverging from informal ones) or lay people (mostly citizens).

Indeed, the following paragraphs delve into the main linguistic and communicative traits of *19-2*, characterised by a narrative police-procedural approach tending to emphasise relevant dialogic contexts where cops interact within a P2P dynamic (see Chap. 2). Second in line, after cop interaction patterns, the investigative layer develops multiple plot sub-narrations implementing each character's personal and psychological profile. This event narrows the mediatic gap between the viewer and the fictional hero via the creation of an emotional filter connecting them through the screen. In light of a similar choice, most of the linguistic constructs employed in the serial are easily understandable, supplanting the use of specialised 'language' with the conveyance of a more fitting 'discourse'—as "*language* above the sentence or above the clause" (Stubbs, 1983, p. 1). 'Communication' incorporates a blending of verbal, non-verbal, and para-verbal behavioural and non-behavioural attitudes establishing phatic relationships among several interlocutors (Lund, 2007; Kress, 2010; Knight, 2011).

The televised product expressive context professionalism, here, detaches from the sole grammatical rigour typical of the linguistic method. Instead, it prefers discoursal interactions. The sparse terminology co-occurs with jargon and plain exchanges (Sykes, 1958; Devlin, 1996; Mayr, 2012; Roufa, 2019) contextualised in informal or formal situations (Cavagnoli, 2007; Scott-Phillips, 2015) from a popularisation slant (Grego, 2013; Bednarek, 2010; Davis, 2021). The medium iconic clarity transfers specific knowledge even in those exchanges lacking structured and highly explicative dialogic fabric (Newcomb, 2007; Moore, 2010; Richardson, 2010; Kress & van Leeuwen, 2011; Piazza et al., 2011; Hall & Knapp, 2013).

The verbal stage cooperates with TV serial visual iconicity to relate to those intrinsic aspects communicated by the images (non-verbality). Through a similar observation, age, gender, social class and the unexpected ethnic differentiation are relevant in the Montreal serial. Once more, the dress code is essential for the interpretation of the administered contents. Slightly similar to *Flashpoint* (Chap. 4), cops in *19-2* prominently parade before the public in their uniforms. However, they wear the regular blue-shirt and black trousers, irrevocably correlated with thick black vests with the visible 'POLICE' tag on the back even when they are inside the station (Tables 6.4 and 6.6). The bulletproof jacket has a slot for the considerable transceiver mouthpiece positioned on the left shoulder; a belt includes augmentations like baton, flashlight, cuffs and gun. Utterly dissimilar to *Motive* (Chap. 5), *19-2* patrols do not wear elegant suits, except for a limited number of detectives (e.g., Latendresse, Roberge).

## 6 The *19-2* Anglified Police Procedural *Noir*   255

Nonetheless, the Montreal-based product—gorier than its Toronto counterpart—counts less weaponry heterogeneity but many more shootings and killings. The *Flashpoint* Strategic Response Unit *appears* scary for their gears (still, they come to talk at the end of the day). Instead, the *19-2* agents *are* terrific in their prompt willingness to engage in a fight. They often lend themselves to violence and frequently succumb to that, like the rootless aggression perpetrated against agent Audrey Pouliot (e.g., s01e09) or Nick and Harvey's reckless abandon to answer a possible break-in that costs this latter character his physical and mental health (e.g., s01e01).

## Procedural Language: Authority

Workplace central dialogues set interactions both inside the station and patrolling the streets. Thus, the police force milieu appears as one rigidly structured organisation where hierarchies predispose a standardised chain—or better pyramidal pattern—where responsibilities, the power of decisions and command authority become looser as one descends to the lower levels. Also, observing the *19-2* verb word list (Table 6.3), it is foreseeably clear that the top positions belong to

**Table 6.3** *19-2 Corpus* verb word list

| Rank | Verb | Rank | Verb | Rank | Verb | Rank | Verb |
|---|---|---|---|---|---|---|---|
| 1 | BE [8220] | 12 | SAY [382] | 23 | WANNA [194] | 34 | LEAVE [122] |
| 2 | DO [2801] | 13 | LET [382] | 24 | THANK [192] | [...] | |
| 3 | HAVE [1383] | 14 | TAKE [380] | 25 | HAPPEN [175] | 40 | BRING [95] |
| 4 | GET [1325] | 15 | THINK [377] | 26 | STOP [168] | 41 | MOVE [95] |
| 5 | GO [1005] | 16 | WANT [361] | 27 | FIND [165] | 42 | KILL [94] |
| 6 | KNOW [933] | 17 | TELL [302] | 28 | HEAR [162] | 43 | LISTEN [84] |
| 7 | COME [624] | 18 | FUCK [283] | 29 | GIVE [162] | 44 | SHUT [83] |
| 8 | GONNA [486] | 19 | PUT [224] | 30 | CALL [146] | 45 | RUN [81] |
| 9 | SEE [445] | 20 | MAKE [221] | 31 | KEEP [141] | 46 | WAIT [80] |
| 10 | NEED [408] | 21 | TALK [212] | 32 | TRY [129] | 47 | SHOW [79] |
| 11 | LOOK [391] | 22 | GONNA [198] | 33 | STAY [126] | 48 | SHOOT [78] |

auxiliaries (ranks from 1 to 4, with 13,729 total occurrences: 60 per cent 'to be', 21 per cent 'to do', 10 per cent 'to have', 9 per cent 'to get'), and many other common-use verbs occur within the first fifty positions. They include colloquialisms deriving from accepted standardised forms (e.g., rank 5, 'to go' > rank 8, 'gonna'; rank 16, 'to want' > rank 23, 'wanna') and verbal premodification for reference nouns in swearing collocations (e.g., rank 18, 'to fuck' > fucking + gun/pig/asshole; some + fucked up + way of...). Some other relevant verbs are performative. They use the imperative form to express speech acts whose "directive" illocutionary force (Searle & Vanderveken, 1985, p. 60; see also Searle, 1969) synthesises their linguistics—verbal mood—and activates features—orders. It leads the hearer to behave according to the bits of information given by the speaker.

The instance verb 'to stay' (rank 33) is associable with utterances like "*stay* back! Back up, back up! Back Off!" or "*stay* with me, Julien!" (Example 6.3, Table 6.11). The former use is in a synonymic relationship with phrasal verbs changing the meaning of 'to back', indicating the addresser's intent of creating separation between him and the addressee. Still, placing himself in a prominent position compared to the hearer, the speaker has the listener to obey without any objections, avoiding unwanted consequences. The latter 'stay' implies a connoted usage of the verb in its 'remain' acceptation. It empathetically binds the cop, as the speaker, and the listener, as the stabbing victim. Here, phatic communication has produced two different perlocutionary responses by conveying a similar illocutionary act delivered via as many aims facilitating the receivers' performativity, accordingly (the observation is valid for the verb 'to put', rank 19, as well).

To that extent, such aspects of language and speech summarise more examples of hierarchical interactive patterns, where different participants embody different linguistic and behavioural roles, calquing real life contexts (Simpson & Mayr, 2009). Almost every character has his/her idiolect or characterising expressive routines displayed within formal dialogues as well as informal *rendez-vous*. Such episodes especially occur within the law enforcement context of communication.

Consequently, one emerging trend of the examination immediately surfaces for the utter definition or the ranks. They establish stiff Textual Linguistics situations of control denoting a vertical scansion of the military social scale division proper. For example, the verb 'to listen', position 43, displays intense 'force' (in terms of appraisal framework labels; see Martin & White, 2005).

However, the *19-2* TV serial offers several interaction degrees or levels that the speakers exert in different hierarchically controlled situations. Although useful for the analysis, the examples do not report POS tagging information for readability reasons; nonetheless, they maintain the multimodal annotation symbols.

On the one hand, in Table 6.4, Sergeant Houle is the speaker controlling the verbal and contextual situation. He reads directives and assignments as he scheduled them and without anyone questioning his decisions. The appraisal framework observation allows to contextualisethe utterance pattern. It displays ego-targeting predominance based on 'monogloss' engagements (e.g., rank 33, 'to keep' > "I'm *keeping* 19-4 for you"). A 'focus-sharpening' graduation (e.g., rank 43, 'to listen' > "*Listen up!*") turns 'softer' when informing his female interlocutor about her colleague's situation (e.g., "Tyler's *expected* back tomorrow *or* the day after"). Once more, the speech act illocutionary 'force' triggers a communicative event where the man plays the orator's paramount role. A broad plateau of listeners shall cooperatively receive prearranged pieces of information and execute the tasks. On a prosodic level, Houle's tone is always firm, mostly flat and straightforward. Sporadic low rises of intonation (^) or emphasis (<u>word</u>) in his speech highlight particularly relevant (to him) sentence elements. Such events surface whenever the participants' attention seems to decrease because of some naive jousting or chitchats. There, the man pauses to restart his monologue in a more vivid attention-seeking tone.

On the other hand, a level of interaction different from the Sergeant-to-cop one is cop-to-cop communication. It depicts colloquial and comradely exchanges, enriched with coloured expressions and harsh remarks or, sometimes, flirty comments outlining the body of patrols like an immature group of on-duty individuals held off by the superior authority of the man assigning tasks. Yet, the 'egocentricity' of some members sometimes escapes Houle's restrictive approaches. They complain about decisions coming from the top or subjectively favouring one colleague instead of the other (similarly to what occurs in *Flashpoint*, although the different respect for the authority; Chap. 4, Example 4.4). In Table 6.4,

**Table 6.4** *19-2*, s01e05. Police briefing multimodal observation

| Min./Description | Visual image | Kinesic action | Soundtrack | Phases and metafunctions |
|---|---|---|---|---|
| 00:11:56 Bright photography. WS Briefing room. All cops sitting. Sergent is the head of the table | NmovA; CP: Stationary, WS-FV; VS > Briefing room; All; Ph; | Movt: Folder slides along the table; Houle starts reading, listeners fidget on their chairs; Tempo: Fast; | AS: Ambient noise; | One phase establishing the narrative slant, implemented by nine subphases emphasising characters' moods and reactions concerning the theme introduced in the main phase for the cinematic communication rendition |
| 00:11:59 OSS-SV: Audry's smiling profile visual salience while Houle reads orders, next to her | CP: Stationary, CLS-LV VS > P: M; F; SP1; | Movt: Participants' head movements and facial expressions; Tempo: Slow; | AS: None; | EXP: Room + actors INT: viewer positioned opposite the table to supervise the scene and covering a role similar to the dominant character but silent, or aside/over the shoulder of other participants, as witness |
| 00:12:01 MS-FV: Nick winks back at Audry (facial mimics) | CP: Stationary, OSS/MS-FV VS > P: M; F; SP2; | Movt: Male participant winks, female participant smiles; Tempo: Slow; | AS: Ambient noise; Off-screen participant's voice; | |
| 00:12:05 SV: Colleages (facial mimics) | CP: Slight tilt + change of focus, CLS-LV VS > P: M; M; SP3; | Movt: Male participant raises his head; Tempo: Fast; | AS: Ambient noise; Off-screen participant's voice; Chuckles; | TEX: Hyperthematic single phase expressing |
| 00:12:09 OSS-MS: Commander watches the briefing from the other side of the door window (background). Houle notices | ≈ VS > P: M; M; F; SP4 | Movt: Male participant #1 nods while reading, male participant #2 appears beyond the door with his arms crossed; Tempo: Slow; | AS: Ambient noise; | 1. hierarchical organisation; orders; 2. information appraisal through formal reading; 3. participants' (lack of) cooperation while listening; 4. authoritarian non-participant influencing the scene; tension-building narration |

| | | | |
|---|---|---|---|
| 00:12:16–24<br>MS: JM + Beatrice. Huole's orders; she nods; JM comments; Beatrice nudges him without watching (verbal interaction + body language response) | CP: Slides towards the Hearer + CLU + CLS-FV<br>VS > P:M; M; F;<br>Ph + SP1; SP2; SP5;<br><br>CP: P: M > CLS-FV;<br>F > CLS-FV;<br>M > CLS-FV;<br>SP6; | Movt: Male participant read; female participant raises head, glimpses around, nods;<br>Tempo: Fast;<br>Movt: Participants head-nods; elbow;<br>Tempo: Fast; | AS: Ambient noise; Off-screen participant's voice; |
| 00:12:26<br>Audry's unvoiced reply to JM's joke (exageerated facial mimics) | CP: Stationary, CLS-FV;<br>SP6 + SP7 | Movt: Head-nod and hyper-articulated mouth expression;<br>Tempo: Slow; | ≈ |
| 00:12:31–32<br>Nick and Santorini's eye contact;<br>Audry turns towards them looking down (facial mimics: jealousy) | CP: Stationary, MCS-FV;<br>SP8;<br><br>CP: CLS-SV;<br>SP9 | Movt: Participants looks each other in the eyes;<br>Tempo: Fast;<br>Movt: female participant side look;<br>Tempo: Fast; | AS: Ambient noise; Off-screen participant's voice; |
| 00:12:34<br>WS Briefing ends. Sergent leaves | MovA;<br>CP: Stationary, WS-FV;<br>VS > Briefing room; All;<br>Ph; | Movt: Male prticipant #1 stands up, others follow;<br>Tempo: Fast; | AS: Ambient noise; |

**Dialogue**

Houle: Listen^⇒ up (.) Bourassa Nadeau 19-9 (..) Lunch will be at 11:00 (..) <u>Vince</u>, you will be 19-6 with Pouliot, lunch at noon

JM: //What^* (.) Ro:okielu:ck

Vince: You knowI got it baby! (h) ((background murmured cackles))

Houle: (..) ((Gendron is looking at him from beyond the window pane of the door with a severe expression and Houle notices it)) .h Beatrice hmm (.) Tyler's expected back <u>tomorrow</u> or the day after (.) I'm keeping 19-4 for yo:u (.) JM traffic (.) solo.

JM: You know what^ (.) That's all right (.) It'll give us a little time to let <u>tension</u> build (.) let things just simmer ((Beatrice nudges him without stopping taking notes)) (.) you know what I mean^

Houle: OK (.) OK (..) Barron due for qualification on the range (.) After that 19-2 with Santorini (..) ((Nick glances Santorini, then camera shot moves onto Audrey's face which is looking at them disappointed)) That's it folks^ Take care of each other out there

**260**     **F. P. Gentile**

JM's disrespectful remark interrupts the Sergeant ("//What^*?") with a fluctuating—informal—rhythm. He jokes on Vince's fate via a 'judgemental attitude' (e.g., "Rookie *luck*!"), since the newbie is not only planned to couple with the beautiful Audrey, he is also allowed the cosiest timetable for lunch.

As already described, the reading of merely written (transcribed) data values would not have allowed the utter comprehension of the exchange. The *19-2 Corpus* verb word list has offered relevant material about verbal syntagms and other occurrences of the same class. Conversely, it seems inadequate to describe the total expressiveness of the related contexts. Even disregarding the actual meaning of the uttered words, Table 6.4 shows a scene where the rhythmic pace explicated by the multimodal symbology and annotation is eloquent. Non-verbal and para-verbal data communicate pieces of information that surpass pure verbality. They grant the spectator some preliminary understanding of the sequence yet overlooking its linguistic features to focus on the extra-linguistic ones. A character overtakes the others for his influent presence. Houle shades his speech with pauses and vocal pitch fluctuations, expressing emphasis or disappointment, where latching or overlapping utterances and comments happen. It builds a dialogic scene where a closed group of individuals is cooperatively interacting under the command of said character. Nonetheless, the context is even more unambiguous if *read* via its visual ground.

More elements stand out after aligning the example with images. The same readability criterion that justified the POS tags removal induced the research to display a qualitative selection of frames extrapolated from the multimodal software analytical support. Observing such captures, one would perceive the strength of the "perlocutionary effect" (Austin, 1962; Searle, 1979) performed by two characters, whose presence within the scene is crucial. Audrey's magnificent mimic expressiveness represents the non-verbal communication that launches Nick's body language response (he winks at her after receiving a seductive smile). JM's verbal emphatic flirtation displays 'focus-softening' graduation and 'heterogloss' engagements in search of backchannels (e.g., "It will give us *a little time to* let the tension build [...], *you know what I mean?*").[3] Seen that, Houle's speech pauses as well to get in control of the situation again. Nonetheless, it is once more Audrey's para-verbal attitude to end the cop's inappropriate *excursus*. She replies to his joke via a mimicked and broad, *unvoiced*, 'I know' (with emphasis on both words through syllable lengthening calquing an /' a::ɪ:'nə:ʊ::/ in place of regular /' aɪ'nəʊ/; Table 6.4, frame 00:12:26). After the pairing is over, Nick and Santorini's *non-verbal communication* (they look for each other's eye contact; see Ekman & Friesen, 1969; Burgoon et al., 1996; Hall & Knapp, 2013) anticipate the colleague's *non-verbal behaviour* (Audrey's glance of jealousy closes the meeting right before the Sergeant stands up to leave; the differentiation between non-verbal 'communication' and 'behaviour' is explained in Fig. 2.3; see also Kendon, 1987; Richmond et al., 1991; Rimé & Schiaratura, 1991; Moore, 2010; Knight, 2011).

Commander Gendron's performativity is one more element of disturbance in the scene. The man is not even inside the room where the briefing takes place. He remains outside, staring at sergeant Houle from the back throughout the assembly. His facial expression tells dissatisfaction; the upper part of the body (the only visible across the door window-pane) is straight upright and his arms crossed. Again, the perlocutionary act transmitted by the commander's body language immediately informs Houle about something unpleasant as he notices the silhouette. That causes a further pause in his speech—longer than expected—and even a clear out-breath (marked as '.h') right before addressing Beatrice. Such contingency leads the speculation to establish one more authoritative control position, letting observers understand the pyramidal vertex in precinct 19 through a similar unvoiced and contactless commander-to-sergeant communication (this latter expecting a reprimand as soon as he finishes the briefing).

Beyond the examination described so far, the linguistic observation of the example also allows to focus on a clause level (extendable to the discursive stage as well) concerning the opening sentence: "[VB]Listen [IN]up [NNP]Bourassa [NNP]Nadeau [CD]19[SYM]-[CD]9". POS tagging metadata disclose sentence samples, which could also appear

## 262 F. P. Gentile

ungrammatical. Houle's uttering "Bourassa, Nadeau, 19-9" has no verbal syntagm. The "Vince, you will be 19-6 with Pouliot" uttering identifies the agents' couple with a code.

## Misdemeanours Citywide

Cases like Table 6.4 involve the mentioned linguistic economy as the "primary principle that governs our entire individual and collective behaviour of all sorts, including our behaviour of our language" (Zipf, 1949, p. viii). Sometimes speakers may construe discourses, willing to save time and efforts. They structure nominal sentences lacking verbs or conveying meanings through rhetoric images such as personifications and synecdoches.

Nevertheless, in like manner, they also avoid losing or jeopardising the message transmission clarity, thanks to the channel created and shared by those who participate in the conversation.

The linguistic economy criterion is more common than one might assume, and many contextual informative cases adopt it. Indeed, the omission of significant but dispensable syntactic elements throughout sentence formulation processes for conciseness needs is not only typical of contexts where speakers give directives. However, in the police discourse, those features are commonplace within the instructive and descriptive nominal strings. They serve to figure out persons of interest's somatic traits, gait specificities, or other exclusive qualities, determining their individuation. Indeed, considering the *19-2 Corpus* adjective word list (Table 6.5), one would notice the recurrence of common-use attributes. These qualifiers assess reality according to 'judgemental' and connoted modalities. The related collocational patterns and phraseology (e.g., rank 1, 'good' > 'good to see you', 'good luck/morning') appear in contrasting couples reaching similar scores (e.g., 'right' 90 count vs 'wrong' 56 ones at ranks 7 and 18 respectively). Nevertheless, the military context also takes advantage of adjectival usages to express some sharp terminology, precisely and denotatively referring to specific situations of said domain. The adjective 'clear', in rank 28 ("Team One, we're all clear? Team One? Shot Fired!") serves to check the cops' *situation*—whether

## 6 The *19-2* Anglified Police Procedural *Noir*    263

**Table 6.5** *19-2 Corpus* adjective word list

| Rank | Adjective | Rank | Adjective | Rank | Adjective | Rank | Adjective |
|---|---|---|---|---|---|---|---|
| 1 | GOOD [434] | [...] | | 28 | CLEAR [37] | 46 | FEW [24] |
| 2 | OK [160] | 18 | WRONG [56] | [...] | | 47 | COOL [23] |
| 3 | SORRY [115] | 19 | EASY [47] | 37 | SERIOUS [28] | 48 | AFRAID [23] |
| 4 | LITTLE [99] | 20 | NEW [47] | 38 | DRUNK [27] | 49 | HARD [23] |
| 5 | OKAY [99] | 21 | READY [43] | 39 | STUPID [27] | 50 | HAPPY [22] |
| 6 | NICE [94] | 22 | NEXT [42] | 40 | ENOUGH [27] | 51 | **CLEAN** [21] |
| 7 | RIGHT [90] | 23 | DEAD [41] | 41 | LATE [26] | [...] | |
| 8 | SURE [87] | 24 | SAME [40] | 42 | ONLY [26] | 58 | TRUE [18] |
| 9 | LAST [78] | 25 | WHOLE [39] | 43 | WHITE [26] | 59 | SAFE [18] |
| 10 | BIG [72] | 26 | OWN [38] | 44 | FULL [25] | 60 | SPECIAL [18] |
| 11 | BAD [68] | 27 | BLACK [38] | 45 | SICK [24] | | |

they have been hit in the gunfight—and not the *understandability* of the related utterance. Oppositely, rank 51 ("It was a clean shot") denotes the *unobstructed* path to the target, not a pristine bullet. Similar communication also affects adjectival-nominal strings (e.g., rank 23, 'dead' > "19-2, we have a *dead body, female, overdose*. Hold the scene") useful to determine the crime scene together with its relevant details.

To that extent, the attributes that label individuals following their ethnicity fit law enforcement descriptive needs, too. They apply to suspects or persons of interest (e.g., rank 27, 'black' > "Black male wearing a white hoodie and a ball cap! In pursuit in the alley off Tupper"), rendered even more transparent through the multimodal dimension.

In Table 6.6, the speaker utters a linear *terminological* chain constituted by nouns and adjectives abstaining from adding verbal elements: "*white* male, 5′10″, brown coat, red hat, uses a knife". Subsequently, some more aspects of the language of law enforcement seem relevant. The linguistic economy is often present for conciseness reasons. It saves time or space in sentence constructions, also being immediately and effectively informative through the avoidance of redundant phrastic elements

**Table 6.6** *19-2*, s01e01. Culprit description multimodal observation

| Min./Description | Visual image | Kinesic action | Soundtrack | Phases and metafunctions |
|---|---|---|---|---|
| 00:07:11 Bright photography. Briefing room. All cops sitting | MovA; CP: Stationary, WS-SV; VS > Briefing room; All; Ph1; | Movt: Two newly arrived participants sit down joining the others; Tempo: Fast; | AS: Participant chuckles; ambient noise; | Two phases establishing establishing the narrative slant (one inside the briefing room; one in the street), implemented by three subphases emphasising characters' concerns about the theme introduced in the main phase and consolidated in the second one for the cinematic communication rendition |
| 00:07:13–14 Sequence cuts onto Ben's and Nick's CLS in turn (one opposite the other) | NmovA; CP: Sliding, CLS-FV VS > P: M; SP1; CP: Stationary, CLS-FV VS > P: M; SP2; | Movt: Camera slides; participant's facial expresison; Tempo: Fast; | AS: Off-screen participant's voice; | EXP: Room + street + actors INT: viewer positioned at the far corner of the table; camera shots alternating wide view to individual close-ups taken from the same position at the table. |
| 00:07:17–20–22 Houle visual salience (facial expression + body language); CUT: Suspect's tracking phase; CUT: Houle's visual salience | CP: Shaky, CLS-FV VS > P: M; SP3; MovA; CP: Shaky + dolly, CLS-BV VS > P: M; Ph2 NmovA; CP: Stationary, CLS-FV VS > P:M; SP3; | Movt: Male participant head movements; Tempo: Fast; Movt: Male participant walking; Tempo: Slow; Movt: Head nods; Tempo: Fast; | AS: Ambient noise; AS: Random noise; Off-screen participant's voice; AS: Random noise; | The spectators have their own position which remains stable throughout the sequence: they are part of the team (within the narration) TEX: Thematic main phase (Ph1) introducing a rheme, which becomes the new theme (Ph2). Narration slant: 1. orders; informative structure; 2. information appraisal; concern; 3. environmental contextualisation supporting descriptions |

**Dialogue**

Houle: ((Ben and the Sergeant join the rest of the team at the briefing table)) <u>Chartier</u>^⇒, you will be ridi:ng (.) 19-2 with Barron. (..) Two^⇒ more armed robberies last night, (.) a dep and a gas station. Same^⇒ story as last week, white male, 5'10", brown co:at, (.) red hat, (.) uses a knife.

(Grice, 1981, 1989) whenever speakers need communicative urgency. Such rapidity mostly prefers premodifiers piling up and compressing information within single nominal strings. This procedure allows users to bypass possibly complex syntax complicating sentences via potential paratactic or hypotactic bonds. The adjectival use of the example reported is also crucial. When dealing with specialised communication, profanes often think of a term as a puzzling, utterly intricate and obscure word whose meaning is esoterically disclosed to a restricted range of experts or professionals and doomed to remain unintended by laypeople. However, the utmost terminological quality of monoreferenciality represents a denotative vocabulary characteristic associating one word with a single and univocal signification, which is not mandatorily a noun. Some of the most relevant, informative and precise contents in police descriptions have a very quibbling adjectival usage, which is not avoidable in light of such perspective. It appears unquestionably necessary for the final depiction of the targeted image. Despite the military context, which the police belong, said terminological values have quite a broad application. Whether they are suspects or generic citizens, persons of interest belong to a consumerist society with different habits, tastes, and economic possibilities.

Consequently, police descriptions (and the discourse) often have to face diverse domains and get easily contaminated by other terminologies or lexical *thesauri*, which they have to assimilate. Indeed, the physical description involves some sociological knowledge backgrounds, along with other linguistic areas galore. Cops shall label wanted individuals according to their ethnicity (and yet following plain language requirements). They must acknowledge the fashion register when providing specificities about the suspects' wardrobe. The example's generic brown coat could have been a Duffel coat or a jacket; the red hat, a balaclava or a white and red polka-dot beret, etc. Automotive competence is also essential when in pursuit of a driving criminal. The agents have to detail the warning with the colour, the brand and the model of the vehicle they chase.

On a multimodal level, the great relevance given to the suspect's linguistic portrayal follows (in terms of milliseconds) and mirrors its visual rendition (Table 6.6, frame 00:07:20). The sequence starts from Sergeant's foreground—framed via a shaky shot, using a technique where camera operators hold the device in their hands with an unsteady image. That is recurrently employed to bestow authenticity to the scene (reproducing a natural gaze's slight movements due to one's gait). Houle is speaking his regular and flat tone, maintained on a modulated low rise attention-capturing intonation from the beginning to the end of his line. The sole camera relocation cuts onto the criminal worriedly treading the street while being described, then the objective shifts back onto Houle. The perpetrator sequence transmits to viewers the actual overwhelming feeling of being hunted. The calm voice of the cop oxymoronically contrasts the man's walk—in the foreground, framed continuously from behind (as if running away) and eventually turning his face backwards (as if he were checking not to be followed) to cross the spectators' glance. Likewise, the narrative pace cuts the sequence adhering to a fast tempo, which only decelerates when showing the suspect via said modality (see Table 6.4). The rapid narration slows down in precise shots to emphasise their content. Sergeant's prosody is also peculiar. His rhythm is very straightforward and calm, although the empty pauses he takes are meaningful in communicativeness (Table 6.6). The first one is physiologic when changing the subject of his speech from Ben's assignment to the crime. The second and third moments of silence—measured in milliseconds—however, are different. The former is *mediatic*, separating the suspect's descriptive elements (passing from SP3 to Ph2, frames 00:06:17–20). It concedes the images enough time to flow ("…brown co:at, (.) red hat…"), like the emphasis set by the syllable lengthening of "coat" (/kəʊt/ becomes /kəʊ:t/), which would otherwise have no reasons to occur. Instead, the last pause is a discoursal expedient. It draws the viewers' attention back to the sergeant's speech ("…red hat, (.) uses a knife") as the camera shot returns onto the cop (from SP3 to Ph2, and then back to SP3 of the main phase, Ph1). Such a filming strategy informs his listeners about the weapon's striking detail, which, however, is not shown yet. Together with prosody, discourse register changes contribute to underline facts. The rest of Houle's description is aseptic, emotionless, flat and concordant with the nominal style of police language. Oppositely, this time a *verb* follows the pause. Expressing the implied danger ("*uses* a knife"), it interrupts the formality of the discourse to emotively warn the colleagues: the criminal does not just *have* a blade; he is apt at *wielding* it.

## 6 The *19-2* Anglified Police Procedural *Noir*

Other than similar features, one (expectedly and) persistent aspect observable within the TV *serial* is the occurrence of many unlawful deeds mentioned in the episodes and constituting a remarkable collection of legal terminology. On the whole, it is possible to list at least six macro-categories dividing all the crimes eminently recurring throughout TV serial *Corpus* (Table 6.7, the order is alphabetic), sketching out a thematic pattern as well. Nonetheless, when handled by cops patrolling the streets, law enforcement discourses irrevocably suppose speakers to formulate their communications formally (e.g., informing the station about alleged crimes; asking for back-ups). The subsequent linguistic pattern always hankers for clarity, employing syntactic locative indirect object conveyances determining the very area where officers are wanted to intervene (Example 6.2):

### Example 6.2 *19-2 Corpus, 19-2, s03e03, min. 00:15:54–16:20*

Dispatcher: ((Male voice)) Robbery 2<u>400</u>=Boyer (.) black^ suspect (.) in a blue hoodie^ (.) running south on foot (.) He's armed ((Audrey is driving carefully observing the street))

Tyler: ((Picks up the radio)) I'm right there

Radio: ((Camera shot stays in Tyler's car. Female voice)) 19-37 (.) we're coming down <u>St</u>-Urbain

Tyler: I^⇒ got=him I: got=him (6.5) ((drumming music and sirens. Tyler is driving holding a hand on his shoulder rai-dio mic-on key)) I got him 19-4 (.) I got a visual= He's in the <u>al</u>ley between Brébeuf and De la Ro:che=I'm in pursuit

Radio: ((Tyler's car I/O camera shot. Male voice)) 19-7 we're=<u>on</u> De la Ro:che-

Coherently with similar specifications, the long list of crimes reported within the *19-2 Corpus* mirrors as many urban parts of the city where misdemeanours are reported and managed (Table 6.8, the order is alphabetic). In adherence to that consideration, the Montreal fabric presented by such a broadcast could represent a geographic narration tracking the hotspots where on-screen actions take place (Fig. 6.1). It sets the limits within which all the agents of precinct 19 operate. Therefore, the most

**Table 6.7** *19-2 Corpus* crimes classification

| Generic | Violent/Deadly | Traffic | Domestic | Sexual | W/I police department |
|---|---|---|---|---|---|
| AMBER ALERT | ACCIDENTAL DEATH | A HIT AND RUN | BREAK IN | DISTRIBUTION OF CHILD PORNOGRAPHY | BRUTALITY CHARGES |
| (RESISTING) ARREST | ARMED ROBBERY | CARJACKING | (NOISE) COMPLAINT | HARASS AND BELITTLE | CHARGES |
| CARELESS DISCHARGE | ASSAULT (AGGRAVATED— WITH FURTHER CHARGES PENDING) | (MULTIPLE VEHICLE) COLLISION | DISTURBANCE | INDECENT EXPOSURE | CHARGES WITH NEGLECT |
| (FRAUDULENT 911) CALL | (DEAD) BODIES | CRASH | DOMESTIC DISPUTE (POSSIBLY VIOLENT) | PEDOPHILE | CIVILIAN CASUALTY |
| CHILD ABDUCTED | BUSTS OF (MULTIPLE) SHOT(S) FIRED | INCIDENT | HOME INVASION | PROSTITUTING CHILDREN | CORRUPTION |
| CHILD IN A CAR | FATALITY | JAYWALKER/-ING | INTRUDER | PROSTITUTION | EXCESSIVE FORCE |
| CITATION | FIGHT IN PROGRESS | OPEN FIRE HYDRANT | | RAPE | FLAG |
| CRIME | FIRE | TICKET | | SEX OFFENDER | JUVELILES |
| MINOR UNDER DISTRESS | GANG VIOLENCE | TRAFFIC CONTROL | | SEXUAL ASSAULT | LEAKING INFORMATION TO ORGANISED CRIME |
| MISSING | HOMICIDE | WRECK | | SEXUAL HARASSMENT | OFFICER NOT RESPONDING |

## 6 The *19-2* Anglified Police Procedural *Noir* — 269

| | |
|---|---|
| MANSLAUGHTER | SEXUAL MISCONDUCT |
| MURDER | SEXUAL OFFENSES INVOLVING MINORS |
| SERIAL ARSONIST | SOLICITING |
| SHOOTER/-ING | |
| STABBING (VICTIM) | |
| SUICIDE | |
| | |
| POSSESSION (WITH INTENT) | ORGANISED CRIME CASES TANKED |
| PROWLER | PAYROLL ROBBERY |
| RECKLESS ENDANGERMENT | PRIORS |
| RELIGIOUS INTOLERANCE | RECORD |
| ROBBERY/THEFT | WILLFUL MISCONDUCT |
| VANDALISM | WARNING |
| WARRANT | |

## 270 F. P. Gentile

**Table 6.8** *19-2 Corpus* toponym list

| TOPNYMS [ST/BLVD/RUE/ALLEY/SQ] | | | |
|---|---|---|---|
| 1. ALEXANDRE-DE-SEVE | 26. DELORME | 51. LONGUEUIL | 76. ROUIN |
| 2. BEACONSFIELD | 27. DEPANNEUR | 52. MAISONNEUVE | 77. SANGUINET |
| 3. BEAUDRY EAST | 28. DORIN | 53. MARSEILLE | 78. SHAWINIGAN |
| 4. BEAUBIEN | 29. DORION | 54. MASSON | 79. SHERBROOKE |
| 5. BEAUMONT | 30. DULUTH | 55. MILL STREET | 80. ST. ANTOINE |
| 6. BERNARD | 31. DUROCHER | 56. MONTREAL NORTH | 81. ST. CATHERINE |
| 7. BLAKE STREET | 32. FABRE | 57. MORIN HEIGHTS | 82. ST. COLUMBAN |
| 8.BORDEAUX | 33. FLAUBERT | 58. NAZARETH | 83. ST. DENIS |
| 8. BOSENCOURS | 34. FORTUNE | 59. OLD PORT | 84. ST. DOMINIQUE |
| 10. BOYER | 35. FULLUM | 60. ONTARIO | 85. ST. FRANCIS |
| 11. BREBEUF | 36. GRENVILLE | 61. OTTAWA | 86. ST. ISIDORE |
| 12. CABOT | 37. GRIFFINTOWN | 62. OUILLETTE | 87. ST. JACQUES |
| 13. CASTRO | 38. HAIG | 63. PALAIS DE CONGRES | 88. ST. LAURENT |
| 14. CHAMP DE MARS | 39. HOCHELAGA | 64. PANETPA | 89. ST. MARC |
| 15. CHATEAUGUAY | 40. JACQUES CARTIER BRG. | 65. PAPINEAU | 90. ST. MICHEL |
| 16. CHICOUTIMI | 41. JEAN-TALON | 66. PEEL | 91. ST. URBAIN |
| 17. CLARK | 42. JOHNSON PARK | 67. PIE-IX | 92. ST. ZOTIQUE |
| 18. COLBERT | 43. KENT PARK | 68. PLACE D'ARMES | 93. VALLEYFIELD |
| 19. COUTES-DES-NEIGES | 44. LA FONTANE | 69. PLACE DU MARCHÉ | 94. VICTORIA SQ |
| 20. D'IBERVILLE | 45. LA GAUCHETIERE | 70. PLESSIS | 95. VIGER SQ |
| 21. DE LORMIER | 46. LACHUTE | 71. POINTE-ST. CLAIRE | 96. VILLE D'ANJOU |
| 22. DE LA ROCHE | 47. LAPRAIRIE | 72. PRINCE LOUIS BVD | 97. VILLE MARIE TUNNEL |
| 23. DEL ALCORES | 48. LAURIER PARK | 73. RACHEL | 98. VILLE ST. LAURENT |
| 24. DEL CAMINO | 49. LAVAL | 74. RENE LAVESQUE | 99. VILLE ST. PIERRE |
| 25. DECARIE | 50. LOGAN | 75. RIMOUSKI | 100. WEST ISLAND |
| | | | 101. WESTMOUNT |

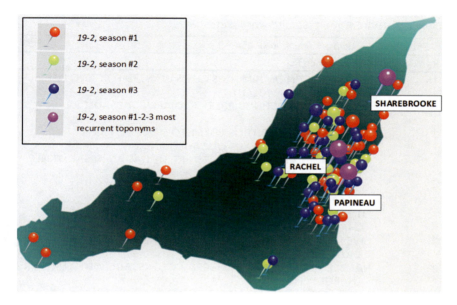

**Fig. 6.1** *19-2 Corpus* City of Montreal topnym map (figure is mine)

intense areas range from Westmount (South) to Tétreaultville (North), and from Saint Leonard and Villeray (West) to the St. Laurence River (East), sizing the actual city places fictionally recounted by the serial.

Despite the series Anglophone aim, the abundance of Francophone toponyms reveals to the area its actual Québécois soul. Yet, focusing once more on verbality, Table 6.7 includes a virtual terminological bank describing a considerable range of misconducts, deeds and codes, which law has legislated upon and police is supposed to monitor.

The escalating importance of such actions (on the legal ground) often adheres to condensation processes merging multiple violations in one felony from a concordance plot point of view. For example, the generic 'assault' is different from 'aggravated assault', yet way milder than 'aggravated assault with further charges pending' (Table 6.9). Moreover, the high level of technicality and formality also reveals the formulation context. Indeed, colleagues patrolling the streets generally have a straightforward (in-presence) channel (see also Example 6.2). Denotative behaviours

272     F. P. Gentile

**Table 6.9** *19-2 Corpus*, "assault" word sketch

| ASSAULT, N. [WORD LIST > NOUNS; RANK 454—9 COUNT] | |
|---|---|
| Rank | Concordance list |
| 1 | GET A BULLETIN ON HIM. THIS GUY'S WANTED FOR TWO OTHER **ASSAULTS**. HE'S VIOLENT |
| 2 | HOW ABOUT RESISTING ARREST AND ARMED**ASSAULT**ON AN OFFICER? |
| 3 | CHARLES ALLEN LEIGHT OF TORONTO HAS TWO PRIOR CONVICTIONS FOR SEXUAL**ASSAULT**, AND HIS … |
| 4 | BLACK BALL CAP, BLACK SWEATSHIRT. HE HAS AN **ASSAULT**RIFLE. 19-24 ON BEAUMARCH |
| 5 | CLEMENT. **ASSAULT**, POSSESSION, POSSESSION WITH INTENT, WEAPONS. THEY'RE COUSINS |
| 6 | I UNDERSTAND THAT THE CROWN IS WILLING TO DROP THE CHARGE OF**ASSAULT**ON A PEACE OFFICER |
| 7 | GIVE IT UP, WILL YOU? STOP RESISTING! HEY, THAT'S **ASSAULT**! SHUT THE FUCK UP! … |
| 8 | HAS BEEN CHARGED WITH AGGRAVATED**ASSAULT**WITH FURTHER CHARGES PENDING |
| 9 | YEAH, I GUESS. THE GUY DID ELEVEN MONTHS FOR**ASSAULT**. I MEAN IT'S THE ONLY … |

| MODIFIERS OF "A." | MODIFIED BY "A." | V. WITH "A." AS O. | "A." AND/OR … | PREP. PHRASES |
|---|---|---|---|---|
| SEXUAL; ARMED; OTHER | RIFLE; POSSESSION | AGGRAVATE(-ed); BE (conjugated) | POSSESSION; ARREST | FOR + "A."; "A." + ON; OF + "A."; "A." + WITH |

facilitate multimodal communicative approaches. When they are side by side, agents use gestures to point at something or someone, in conjunction with locutionary—visual sensory verbs in their imperative mode—or illocutionary acts—interjections. Contrarily, the preciseness of the listed labels and main collocation combinations show some evident preferences. Premodification opts for:

- past participles or adjectival usages (e.g., *alleged* misconduct; *apprehended* criminal; *confirmed* stabbing victim);
- present participles (e.g., *reporting/signalling* possible break-in);
- phraseology and crystallised nominal constructions (e.g., *in pursuit of* a suspect);
- post-modifying locative specifications (e.g., need backup *at/ at the corner of … and …*).

These features demonstrate an in-absence level of interaction between speakers that the dialogic on-screen image display confirms. Such iterative events, indeed, often belong to radio-informative descriptions via a dispatcher-to-RMP code regulated by 'heterogloss' criteria of engagement, where the multiple points of view are also imposed by turn-taking, latching and overlapping enunciations.

The geographical rendition and contextualisation of the dialogues often adhere to the Québécois police linguistic environment. The recurrent mentions of Montreal street names and surrounding areas support plausibility (Table 6.10). Some cultural markers also vividly contribute. For instance, the skyline proposes frequent Montreal views, and the *fleur-de-lis* flag is omnipresent inside public offices (even though, by law, it should be next to the Canadian maple leaf remarkably missing here).

The recognition procedure operates linguistically, too. Field-related acronyms indicate such fictionalisation pertinence and legitimacy, mostly in sequences about the abuse of power or corruption allegations afflicting cops (Table 6.7). Under these circumstances, as praxis demands, some external professionals of the area are involved with resolving the issues to proceed with a formal arrest or the clearance of agents' names. Some peculiar characters from specific departments occasionally arrive for narrative coherence and plot plausibility. Yet, considering the Québécois context, authorities have to respect the Francophone linguistic environment even in the Anglophone adapted version. However, the production dynamics have operated via Francophone terms erasure. Thus, it would have probably sounded quite out of context to name such agencies using their original labels.

Nonetheless, those same divisions could not die *ex abrupto*, supplanted by Anglophone equivalents. That would have produced fake institutional alterations. Subsequently, the best linguistic option consists of acronymic forms for shortening those offices whose name is just not unpacked in English. For example, SQ remains an acronym even if it stands for the French-speaking Sûreté du Québec, the division in charge of enforcing provincial and municipal laws. In the TV serial, the final result was to collocate the original Francophone department with the related English shortening RPC charge, or Regional Police Commander, clarifying and *re-contextualising* the events.

The acronymisation procedure is one most recurrent feature of specialised discourses regularly used for abbreviating long crystallised and standardised

## 274 F. P. Gentile

**Table 6.10** *19-2*, s01e05. RMP chitchat multimodal observation

| Min./ Description | Visual image | Kinesic action | Soundtrack | Phases and metafunctions |
|---|---|---|---|---|
| 00:01:22–24 O/I: car windshield visual salience; Ben's visual salience (facial expression; head nods; gaze) CUT: Nick's visual salience (facial expression; gaze) | NmovA; CP: Shaky, CLS-FV, O/I; VS > Car; P: M; Ph + SP1; SP2 | Movt: Participant #1 head movements; Participant#2 head movements; Tempo: Fast; | AS: Car; Overlapping radio; ST: Piano music (acute tone); | Single narrative phase reporting a dialogue between cops while on patrol supported by three subphases, two of which dedicated to each participant accordingly, and a third side-view inclusive of both EXP: Car + actors INT: Camera position offers an outside-to-inside perspective (except for SP3) keeping the spectator out of the scene, as mere observer TEX: Single thematic phase: 1. overlapping radio communication; 2. participant #1 sense of privacy contrasting participant #2 objecting attitude |
| 00:01:31 O/I: driver's window; CLS-SV: Nick and Ben talking | CP: Shaky, CLS-SV, I VS > Car; P: M; M; SP3; | Movt: participants' head movements; | AS: Car; | |
| 00:01:37–42–43 O/I: car windshield (MS) Nick talking (head movements); Ben listening (stiffly) | CP: Shaky, MS-FV, O/I VS > P: M; Ph; | ≈ | ≈ AS: Car; Overlapping radio; AS: Car; | |

### Dialogue

Radio: ((radio on the background. Unit contacting the dispatcher)) 34-6 we're coming up to De Lorimier ((Disparther's answer)) (..) =OK, copy that

Ben: ((Start talking after a long silence without looking at Nick)) I'm taking a sick day tomorrow

Nick: ((While driving, peeps at Ben twice to check him)) You don't <u>look</u> sick-

Ben: No: I gotta go home to tie up some loose ends around the house

Nick: ((Rises his eyebrows)) =Mm-hmm. (..) °What's°⇒ home <u>again</u>

Radio: //Man asking for (()) station 29*

Nick: =(..) <u>Lachute</u>^

Ben: =Morin-Heights:

noun strings to be communicated promptly. The same motivation typically justifies the coinage of other samples attested within the Corpus. Police need a consistent number of easy-to-use short terminology describing illicit events. Thus, the *19-2* serial includes the Canadian and US police enforcement acronym APB, meaning 'all-points bulletin': a broadcast containing all the crucial information about dangerous persons of interest or missing individuals who are wanted or looked for. Other entries to be mentioned are SPCA (Society for the Prevention of Cruelty to Animals), and the very famous K-9. This last term represents police enforcement units supported by trained dogs, mostly adopted in situations requiring the individuation of explosives or narcotics. On the linguistic ground, it originates from the univerbation of /ˈkeɪ/ and /ˈnaɪn/, spelling out the equivalent of *canine* (/ˈkeɪnaɪn/), hence resulting in a phonological metonymy.

## Specialised Knowledge, Subcodes and Popularisation

The TV crime drama themes necessarily involve a lot of action in terms of cinematic content and yet may also imply other contexts in a tight connection with the police and criminal narrative scopes. The legal and medical areas of expertise are two frequent cases—other than the police— covered by this type of television seriality. Unexpectedly, though, such categories are linguistically irrelevant within the analysed *Corpus*, since the *19-2* TV serial, as police procedural drama, mostly focuses on the protagonists' professional protocols and the workplace repercussions into their civilian lives. Consequentially, the prime linguistic interest remains the *police* legal language rather than the overall legal discourse. Similarly, even when investigating the most violent and harsh cases, the narratee is always closely tied to the narrator's observation slant, concentrating on the patrols. Therefore, when homicides, gunshot wounds or scuffles happen, the camera stays as long as the police-man/woman does and then abandons the scene with them. Sequences save no time to dawdling on nearby lifeless bodies and doctors handling scraps of medical terminology to eavesdrop. Instead, they prefer to indulge in the geared cops (uniforms and vests) moving into the piano sequence.

# 276  F. P. Gentile

Nonetheless, the examined data collection is not merely verbal (and much less written) discourse.

Communication (general as well as professional) takes place multi-modally. Considering sectorial interactions in *19-2*, a qualitative selection of specific sequences omitting significant and substantial verbal interactions would, without doubt, rendition the *medium* visual iconicity and transmit fragments of what still *is* specialised knowledge via non-verbal and para-verbal strategies, which—instead of concentrating on the formal utterings—exalts performativity (Example 6.3 and Table 6.11):

### *Example 6.3  19-2 Corpus, 19-2, s01e01, min. 00:21:02–00:23:50*

| | |
|---|---|
| Ben: | ((Shouts from the store. Spotting the suspect from the car)) Red^⇒ ha:t |
| Nick: | ((While getting off the car)) Get the victim |
| Ben: | ((Preceeds his colleague in the chase)) <u>You</u> get the victim^ (.) Hey↑ |
| Nick: | ((On the radio)) 19-2 (.) Del Camino Bonsecours .h Stabbing victim (.) ((Wheezes and shouts from inside the store)) Partner's in pursuit of suspe:ct need <u>ba</u>ckup and a paramedic right away (.) All right .h |
| Dispatcher: | Copy 19-2. |
| Nick: | I need a clean cloth (..) Give↑⇒ me <u>that</u> |
| Owner: | WHAT WERE YOU DOING .h WHY DON'T YOU <u>THINK</u> |
| Nick: | //Please^ sir* ((to the stabbing victim)) What did you do that for (.) It's okay, okay (.) Listen to me (.) You're gonna be just fine .h <u>all right</u> (.) What's your name^ |
| Julian: | ((Coffing)) J-J-<u>Julian</u>^ |
| Nick: | Julian^ Julian^ (.) ((Victim coffing)) Okay (.) |
| Julian: | ((Crying)) //O::h^⇒ ma:n* |
| Nick: | =Don't look (.) It's okay Hey^ (..) I got you, Julian It's gonna be fine ((Via radio)) I need a paramedic <u>now</u> ((Passage to Ph2, min. 00:21:40–43)) Julian stay with me (.) Stay with me (.) You got a girlfriend (.) Huh^ <u>Yeah</u>^ °What's°⇒ her name^ |
| Julian: | ((with stentoreous voice)) Mau:de |

## 6  The *19-2* Anglified Police Procedural *Noir*    277

**Table 6.11**  *19-2*, s01e01. 'Nick performing CPR' multimodal observation

| Min./Description | | | |
|---|---|---|---|
| 00:21:02 | 00:21:03 | 00:21:05 | 00:21:06 |
| Outdoor: Suspect is spotted | Ben shouts (CLS: face) | O/I: car windshield; | MS: Ben runs in pursuit |
| MovA; | NmovA; | Nick and Ben leave the vehicle | MovA; |
| CP: Tracking, MS-FV, I/O; | CP: Stationary, CLU-SV, O/I; | | CP: Shaky, D-BS; |
| VS > Shop; P: M; M; M; | VS > P: M; M; | MovA; | VS > Streetr; P: M; M; |
| Ph1; | SP1; | CP: Shaky, MS-FV, O/I; | Ph2; |
| AS: Car; shouts; steps; | AS: Car; | VS > Car; P: M; M; | AS: Ambient noise; |
| Tempo: Fast; | Tempo: Fast; | SP1.2; | ST: Piano music; |
| | | AS: Car; car doors; | Tempo: Fast; |
| | | Tempo: Fast; | |
| 00:21:09 | 00:21:16 | 00:21:17 | 00:21:34 |
| Nick approaches the store | O/I: store glass door | Det.: stubbed thigh | Det.: Nick's gloved hand tamponing |
| MovA; | Nick crouches to check the stabbing victim | MovA; | MovA; |
| CP: Shaky, MS-FV; | | CP: Shaky, CU-in > ECS; | CP: Shaky, CU-in > ECS; |
| VS > P: M; | MovA; | VS > P: M; | VS > P: M; M; |
| Ph3; | CP: Shaky, MS-FV; | SP3.1; | SP3.1; |
| AS: Ambient noise; | VS > P: M; | AS: Ambient noise; | AS: Ambient noise; |
| ST: Carillon music; | Ph3; | ST: Agitated music; | ST: Agitated music; |
| Tempo: Fast; | AS: Ambient noise; | Tempo: Fast; | Tempo: Fast; |
| | ST: Agitated music; | | |
| | Tempo: Fast; | | |
| 00:21:38/48 | | 00:22:26–27 | |
| Nick keys-in radio/Checks victim's vitals | | Nick asks owner's help, then performs CPR | |
| MovA; | NmovA; | MovA; | MovA; |
| CP: Shaky, ECS-FV; | CP: Shaky, CU-in > ECS; | CP: Shaky, D-BS; | CP: Shaky, MS-OSS; |
| VS > P: M; | VS > P: M; M; | VS > P: M; M; | VS > P: M; M M; W; |
| SP3.3; | SP3.2; | M; W; | M; |
| AS: Ambient noise; radio switch; | AS: Ambient noise; wheeze; | Ph3; | Ph3; |
| ST: Agitated music; | ST: Agitated music; | AS: Ambient noise; | AS: Ambient noise; |
| Tempo: Fast; | Tempo: Slow; | ST: Agitated music; | ST: Agitated music; |
| | | Tempo: Fast; | Tempo: Fast; |

*(continued)*

# 278    F. P. Gentile

**Table 6.11** (continued)

| Min./Description | | | |
|---|---|---|---|
| 00:22:58–23:38/44 | | | 00:23:50 |
| Paramedics arrive and they take over for Nick | | | Victim is secured |
| MovA; | MovA; | MovA; | MovA; |
| CP: Shaky, D-BS; | CP: Dolly, CLS-SV; | CP: Shaky, CLS-SV; | CP: Shaky, MCS; |
| VS > P: (x4) M; W; | VS > P: M; M; | VS > P: M; M; | VS > P: M; M; M; |
| Ph3; | SP3.3; | W; M; | SP3.2; |
| AS: Ambient noise; | AS: Ambient noise; | Ph3; | AS: Ambient noise; |
| ST: Agitated music; | ST: Piano music; | AS: Ambient noise; | ST: Piano music; |
| Tempo: Slow; | Tempo: Slow; | ST: Piano music; | Tempo: Slow; |
| | | Tempo: Slow; | |

| | |
|---|---|
| Nick: | Mau:de^ (.) You know, you're gonna see her <u>soon</u> (.) I promise (.) You just gotta <u>stay</u> with me stay with me, Jul-Julian^ (.) Julian^ ((Passage to Ph2, min. 00:21:57–22:17)) Hold^⇒ here ((to the cashier while starting CPR; back-ups arrives)) (5.0) .h Stay↑⇒ with me, <u>Julian</u> |
| Bear: | What^ the hell <u>happened</u>^ |
| Nick: | Red hat (.) .h Chartier ran after him (.) Well↑ don't^⇒ stand there GO (..) GO |
| Tyler: | ((Via -radio)) //Chartier (.) where you at^ What's your lo:cation- ((Passage to Ph2, min. 00:22:33–57)) |
| Paramedic#1: | Okay (.) we'll take over^ (.) We'll take it from here sir^ |
| Nick: | You're^⇒ not gonna <u>die</u> Julian ((Nick keeps talking but his voice is silenced. Flashbacks of Harvey's gunfight; piano music. Back to the present, nick is still performing CPR)) °Oh°⇒ don't do this to me (.) Don't do this to me <u>come on</u> ((passage to Ph2, mn. 00:23:27–36)) *Stay°⇒ with me |
| Paramedic#2: | I have a pulse^ |
| Nick: | ((Very fleebly, still CPR-ing)) °Please stay with me° |
| Paramedic#1: | We'll take it from here ((Nick sits on the floor exhausted, sliding backwards to lean his back against the counter. Julian reflates)) |

## 6 The *19-2* Anglified Police Procedural *Noir*

The unavailability of spoken medical language or discourse does not coincide with the lack of medical communication (being this latter an amalgam of oral formulations, prosodic peculiarities, sensory aspects, gestural and mimic communication; see Daniele & Garzone, 2016). In Example 6.3, the related knowledge is not transmitted by whatsoever form of verbal enunciation describing acts through terminology. It is revealed via a direct visual display of procedural and routine performances (described through Table 6.11), hence increasing the informativity and the communicativeness of the scenario (more than any associable dialogic exchange filling silent frames of narration with words).

Table 6.11 integrates Example 6.3 dialogues. It reports three narrative phases (with a total duration of 2′48″), where the first one only lasts a few seconds and is inserted to introduce the following two. There, the main sequence shows a cop *assisting* a victim (of the duration of 1′49″ and almost doubling the latter). The other cop's *chase-phase* (56″) is minor in screen display but more relevant for the plot development. Focusing on the *assistance-phase*, one would notice a dialogic inconsistency (Example 6.3) with sparse iterative events inclusive of high-frequency verbs (Table 6.3; e.g., listen; stay) and collocations (e.g., in pursuit of) compared to the visual salience of the narration (Table 6.11). Besides the first fourteen character lines—the former five of which occur within the initial 7″ and the latter nine within the next 41″—almost two minutes of screen narration exclusively is image flow and music. Even in the absence of any dialogic data (Example 6.3), the perusal of a similar iconicity (in Table 6.11) would let the observers understand the context and trace the outlines of generic first aid procedures shown frame by frame. Indeed, the example presents the cop noticing a *stabbing victim* and running towards him to see the situation. Nick does not need to *check* Julian's *vitals* since the man is *conscious*. However, the policeman immediately wears his latex *gloves*, grabs a *clean cloth* and *applies direct pressure to the wound* to prevent the *exsanguination*. Subsequently, once the situation has *stabilised*, the cop asks for *paramedics* and backups via radio since Ben is solo and chasing the assailant, and then restarts questioning Julian to keep him *alert*. Eventually, as the victim *loses consciousness*, Nick instructs the shop-owner to continue limiting the *bleeding*. At the same time, he moves close to Julian's chest and starts *CPR (cardiopulmonary resuscitation)*.

280 F. P. Gentile

As paramedics arrive, they control the situation and let the rescuer stop the *manoeuvre* as they *feel a pulse* and the victim finally *reanimates*.[4]

Nonetheless, highly involving music also utterly supports the exemplified sequence. Ambient sounds dominating the scene initial seconds cease when some unidentifiable piano music starts, setting a fast tempo indicating the beginning of a salient narrative segment. Rhythm changes from fast to agitated piano music underline the emotional connotation, informing viewers about the severe situation. Music also speeds up frame cuts and emphasises the victim's suffering that paves the way to Nick's CPR performance. The soundtrack's final pressing pace suddenly decelerates to a piece of mild carillon-like playing, suggesting to spectators that Julian is safe thanks to the agent's assistance and paramedics' arrival. To that extent, the unimportance of verbal exchanges compares to other communicative channels' expressive power. When paramedics tell the cop they are there to take care of the victim, the man—mentally disconnected from the context—continues CPR-ing Julian. He shouts at the young man to resist until falling into a flashback of Harvey's accident. His mouth opens wide, and the tension is perceivable through his facial muscles. Yet, his voice goes silent and the crying unheard because of the prominence given to music imports, capable of narrating the events more strongly than words can (min. 00:22:58–00:23:27).

## The Linguistic Characterisation

From a comparative perspective, legal procedures and knowledge render courtroom situations as well as medical ones. They do not endeavour to structure intricate summations nor technical dialogic lawyer-to-client exchanges, but allow the spectators' eyes to assess the atmosphere and enter the place to 'ghostly' witness *unvoiced* trials. Trials and arrest consequences are unimportant to the TV serial storylines since *19-2*, as said, merely cares to rendition its protagonists' laborious professional experiences and private intriguing events.

So far, the chapter examination has discussed a limited range of expressions, mostly about the popularisation of specialised communication, discourse and knowledge-procedural descriptions. A consistent part of the *19-2* TV serial involves dialogues and expressions that equally include

# 6 The *19-2* Anglified Police Procedural *Noir*     281

formal situations and ordinary (extra)linguistic episodes concerning everyday life or informal interactive circumstances. Hence, the user would effortlessly understand that the *product* is rich in vivid language, epithets, colloquialisms and slang. Moreover, such iterative contexts are mainly useful to the linguistic characterisation of stereotypical heroes and villains within the scriptwriter's plot narrative path and grant verisimilitude to the television product. Therefore, the category of professionals structuring the screenplay (despite their expertise) includes socially influenced individuals with their peculiar beliefs and linguistic-expressive qualities. Hence, the writing task must make plenty of different protagonists forged by diverse personal experiences, internal conflicts and relationships. Those subtextual recounts have to stay untold since the screenplay is nothing like literature and has no narrative space for emotional and psychological digressions. Those features must, in most cases, only belong to the actors' expressiveness itself (Trottier, 1998), challenging their performance.

One way of dissimulating the communal authorial linguistic creation shared by two characters is the insertion of connotative expressions. They differ from one hero to the other and contribute to construe the individual's idiolect. In like manner, individuals became easily recognisable by merely hearing their words (even when speakers are off-scene or third parts are reporting their speech; Table 6.12). One recurrent saying that makes users flank one precise speaker with his linguistic formulations, even without evidence of him pronouncing them, belongs to J.M.:

**Example 6.4  *19-2 Corpus, 19-2, s02e08, min. 00:22:05–11***

| | |
|---|---|
| JM: | (To the immobilised protester)) Settle↑⇒ do:wn |
| SWAT agent: | ((While handcuffing another one on the floor)) I got this one |
| JM: | ((Holding the grip, to the resisting arrested protester, while descending the dark narrow and steep staircase)) Hey↑⇒ HEY (.) You↑⇒ wanna go down the stairs face first^ HUH (.) YOU WANNA^ That's↓⇒ it (.) settle down (.) Attaboy^ Relax |

**282**    F. P. Gentile

**Table 6.12** *19-2 Corpus*, "atta-" prefixation word sketch

| ATTA-, AFFIX. [ATTABOY/ATTAGIRL; 6 COUNT] | | | | |
|---|---|---|---|---|
| Rank | Concordance list | | | |
| 1 | STARTING OFF WITH A BANG, MAN! **ATTABOY**! | | | |
| 2 | **ATTABOY**! WELL, I HATE TO DO THIS TO YOU, VINCE. I REALLY DO | | | |
| 3 | WANNA GO DOWN THE STAIRS FACE FIRST? HUH? YOU WANNA? THAT'S IT, SETTLE DOWN. **ATTABOY** | | | |
| 4 | ON THE COUNT OF THREE, YOU'RE GONNA GET UP. DON'T HURT YOURSELF. THREE, ALRIGHT, **ATTAGIRL**. YOU'RE SURE YOU'RE GOOD? | | | |
| 5 | LET'S DRINK IT UP BOTTOMS UP! DRINK IT ALL, DICK, YOU GOT IN YA! **ATTABOY, ATTABOY**! | | | |
| MODIFIERS OF "*A.*" | MODIFIED BY "*A.*" | V. WITH "*A.*" AS O. | "*A.*" AND/OR ... | PREP. PHRASES |
| / | / | / | ATTABOY | / |

Jean Mark Brouillard's name is markedly Francophone (like many other characters in the series). Still, he oxymoronically uses the same connoted Anglophone signal to end a dialogical sequence or produce exclamation points. The gender declined "attaboy" or "attagirl" compliment—labelled as 'attitude-judgement' in terms of the linguistic Appraisal framework—represents J.M.'s trademark. It is a misspelt variation of a 'that's the boy/girl!' encouragement that people habitually address to pets or children (Example 6.4.1). Thus, it also reflects the control procedures linguistically underpinning one speaker's preponderance over the other within a dialogue.

Based on "unequal encounters" (Simpson & Mayr, 2009, p. 12; Thomas, 1988, p. 33), such expression establishes a hierarchical and intimidating dominant-to-subdued relationship between a prominent addresser and the tamed addressee. However, the described leading attitude is not always as peremptory as despotic. On some occasions, J.M. also employs the expression to encourage or compliment his interlocutor by showing off.

Indeed, notwithstanding the common praxis of recurrently pronouncing the iteration to demonstrate his paramount egocentrism, J.M. often

## 6 The *19-2* Anglified Police Procedural *Noir*        283

heartens people and colleagues through the 'attaboy/girl' saying. In this second case, his friendly purpose emphasises some effective lines he hears or behaviours he witnesses:

**Example 6.4.1 *19-2 Corpus, 19-2, s02e08, min. 00:23:14–22:11***

JM:        ((Off scene voice)) You good^
Audrey:   Yeah↑⇒ I'm <u>fine</u> (..)
Radio:     They're trying to get out
Audrey:   Alright^ (.) Sit↓⇒ up
JM:        ((Approaching the cuffed protester laying on the floor)) Get your one leg forward okay^ On the count of three you're gonna get up (.) Don't hurt yourself (.) Three (.) alright <u>attagirl</u> ((While bringing the arrest out, to Audrey)) You^⇒'re sure you're <u>good</u>
Audrey:   °Yeah° .h

Like J.M., other characters have linguistic pattern stereotypes. They often occur in interjectional forms as well. The instance case of Tyler Joseph's idiolect, related to backchannels and cultural backgrounds, confirms that:

**Example 6.5 *19-2 Corpus, 19-2, s03e09, min. 00:06:54–07:28***

Tyler:      You↑⇒ see that^ (..) Boy↑⇒ scout got to be <u>prepared</u> my=ma:n. (.) Chartier's↓⇒ showing you up son (.) Just saying [...] ((Change of scenario. Joseph and Dulac's RMP))
Richard:   Pretty messed up (.) Nick's sister
Tyler:      Mm-hmm
Richard:   It's like the squad is cursed
Tyler:      Hey (.) don't use that wo:rd
Richard:   I can say what I want to
Tyler:      It <u>sounds</u> like you're trying=to=put=a ji:nx on=us
Richard:   The jinx (.) was here <u>before</u> I got here

The man has a tall, massive physicality frequently associated with a resolute deep tone emphasised by the constant manner of expressing both agreement and disapproval—or just signalling phatic connection—through a pursed lips interjective murmur ("Mm-hmm," 90 count; see Example 6.5) at different levels of sound. The over-insertion of similar features within the cop's utterings much intensifies the characterisation procedure, like the "my man" expression abuse (29 collocation count). The individual almost pronounces this saying in all his sentence endings with the same value of a full stop. Besides the linguistic connotation applied to Tyler's language, the man's figure is also peculiar because of his cultural background. Despite his size and the deep voice (sometimes contrasted by acute pitches), the cop shows a naively superstitious attitude emphasised by 'focus-softening' graduation appraisals ("*It sounds like* you're trying=to=put=a ji:nx on=us") in Example 6.5. That verbally attempts to diminish or deflect one's attention to situations that he perceives as uncomfortable and associate his arguable professionalism with puerile angsts. Indeed, Tyler fears the dark and suffers from the severe personal issue of alcoholism, conferring the character a regretful weakness that induces viewers to sympathise.

In terms of idiolect definition and expressive relevance, many characters in *19-2* (mainly cops) are nitwit no-brainers. They lack particularly intense and contentful exchanges. Conversely, their dialogues are trivial, dealing with animal instincts or simplistic links (and interjections), and almost automatically executing their jobs without actually pondering over them.

Many individuals in precinct 19 are stereotypes identifiable via the use of peculiar distinctive traits revealing their ethnicity or place of origin, such as Nick's connoted language:

**Example 6.6 *19-2 Corpus, 19-2, s01e05, min. 00:24:43–52***

Nick: ((Gets off the car and approaches the pub. Before entering his mobile rings and he picks up)) Ce:d^⇒wah gwan^

Landlord: ((Voice from Nick's mobile)) Nick man (.) I got a place for your frie:nd

## 6 The *19-2* Anglified Police Procedural *Noir* 285

While the rest of the African-American protagonists in the TV serial are not associated with any precise homeland, Nick Barron's characterisation (Example 6.6) seems strictly connected with his strong bond towards his birthplace, Jamaica. His ethnicity and nationality are mentioned numerous times throughout the three seasons analysed. It often accompanies the insertion of sporadic Patois vernacular phrases or expressions such as "wah gwan" (Example 6.6), the friendly and informal equivalent of a 'what is going on?' rhetoric question used to greet people. Further speculations involving the answerer also let the users comprehend that the man on the phone clearly understands Nick's colloquialisms. Thus, he has familiarity with the cop (since used to sudden vernacular interjections) or Jamaican-English itself.

Moreover, some interesting linguistic speculations on the grounds of appraisal framework theorisations (see Chap. 2) would infer more police enforcement characterisations. Dialogues hierarchically structure relationships between cops and their superiors, often rendered by commander-to-sergeant 'monoglossia' engagement perspectives. Their role imposes them to articulate their statements and deliver instructions in a univocal, one-sided, and peremptory manner. Here, the message salience also increases employing graduation 'focus-sharpening' and 'force-raise' (Table 6.4). Oppositely, the dialogic context pragmatics involves cops inaction. This second case recurs to 'heterogloss' engagements and graduation 'focus-softening' whenever the speakers chitchat while on patrol, since communication consists of non-essential empty-talks (Examples 6.4.1 and 6.5). 'Judgement' (Table 6.1) and—rarely—'affect' (Example 6.4.1, "You're *sure you're good?*") attitudes occur when emotional concern expresses consideration for the tasks they are assigned, or the vicissitudes they—and their colleagues—live. Once more, what is riveting here, is the impossible observation of apparently missing features. Every shade and branch of the generalised appraisal framework scheme (see Chap. 2, Fig. 2.6) seems to be covered, counting out the 'appreciation' one to various degrees.

As a legal discourse characteristic, the normative tone usually displays a mandatory denotation that justifies unequivocal points of view ('monoglossia') as well as the reference to other possible perspectives ('heteroglossia'). Also, police cases' diverse nature linguistically reflects through

## 286   F. P. Gentile

'force' and 'focus' flattening formulae and attitudes. They demand the agents to esteem both the situation they are involved in ('judgement') and colleagues' wellness supporting them on the scene (admitting 'affect'-oriented linguistic formulations). Nonetheless, even in those episodes, where hints of emotional connotation are required, they only allow an assessing perspective, which has to remain the more objective as possible, in adherence to shared and accepted procedures and codes. To that extent, 'appreciation' attitudes would hardly ever enter the police-talk domain since they work as carriers of aesthetic evaluations, which do not match the legal context.

## Lingo, Slang and Jargon

The criminal, narrative and thematic context seasoning the *19-2* TV serial display more. The fictional stereotyping of the characters and their communicative, dialogic and discoursal schemata and patterns would not involve the protagonists' idiolects' sole differentiation. Therefore, the insertion of vivid, emblematic expressions would not be enough. Likewise, the attribution of interjectional specificity banks allotted to the numerous individuals participating in the onscreen charade would certainly fulfil the diaphasic and diamesic (e.g., formal written constructions versus informal oral expressions such as 'attaboy'), or diatopic (e.g., Nick's patois language) emulative needs. Yet, they would not be exhaustive. Indeed, these heroes have to imitate a recognisable and plausible interaction. Agent Dulac's surname merges with his rookie status, producing the gross syneresis of 'Dickie'; Ben's place of origin is famous for countryside and woods, and that costs him the nickname of 'Bambi', the Walt Disney deer. However, officers cannot limit themselves in the simple colloquialisation of formal constructions or the insertion of colleagues' nicknames in their dialogues to provide structures and epithets. One could find those aspects in the de-technified workplace informality of professional-to-professional communication instead of the most obscure and stiff expert-to-expert one. But, once more, this would not be it.

For the same reason, the language techniques of television crime drama screenplay often require police lingo intrusions. That would be the ad hoc expedient   useful   for   the   credible   rendition—and   thus   the trustworthiness—of the final product to be accessed by the largest audiences. Jargons have an openly exclusive, elitist and connotatively deictic nature. Nonetheless, the law enforcement argot—coined for brevity and conciseness purposes—is proven to be a very eloquent encrypted code with an apical degree of preciseness (Roufa, 2019). Nowadays, it trickles down the ordinary language levels of knowledge and competence thanks to the proliferation of media formats dealing with the genre and creating affiliation.

More specifically, the lingo itself was born for radio transmissibility goals through which patrols achieved the communication of informative content-significant directives. It initially involved the ten-code usage (originated between the 1920s–1930s), where "saying 'ten' before the numeric code helped to ensure the message was delivered", since "older radio systems had to warm up when the microphone was keyed [and] officers were encouraged to pause a second between keying the mic and speaking" (ibid.). In the time being, praxis urges cops to use plain language to outcome the *impasse* of being misinterpreted because of the different code schematisation undertaken by various agencies. Yet, this sort of old-fashioned legacy contributes to the conveyance of an audience-charming destabilising sensation. TV series are still using the ten-code to deliver pieces of information that viewers can interpret correctly, disregarding their proficiency on the matter and acquaintance with the legal discourse because of visual support.

As per the medical knowledge context (Table 6.11), another selected qualitative instance, in Table 6.13, evaluates visual communicativeness supportive (and setting the meaning) of its related verbal expressiveness. Yet, though the utter 10-35 code significance is not sizeable (Table 6.13, dialogue), the multimodal support aid through image sequence displays is fundamental. The lack of visual narration would have involved the possible misinterpretation of the scene, where the lone linguistic (verbal) data could have been unclear. The isolated additional information "partner's been shot" and "need a paramedic right away" would have, without doubt, conveyed the feeling of urgency. Instead, it is only in association with the frames that the viewer can understand the extent of the damage. The scene, therefore, has numerous dialogic pauses, and the moments of silence play a critical role.

## 288    F. P. Gentile

**Table 6.13** *19-2*, s01e01. Gunfight multimodal observation

| Min./Description | | | |
|---|---|---|---|
| 00:02:59<br>WS (Indoor): Nick gets shot<br>MovA;<br>CP: Shaky, MCS-SV;<br>VS > Building inside;<br>P: M; M; M; Ph;<br>AS: Machinery; shot;<br>Tempo: Slow; | 00:03:01<br>Nick falls on the ground (off the scene); Harvey extracts the gun and fires back<br>MovA;<br>CP: Shaky, MS-SV;<br>VS > Building inside; P: M;<br>AS: Machinery; shots;<br>Tempo: Fast; | 00:03:02<br>Harvey gets shot in the head; falls<br>MovA;<br>CP: Shaky, MS-SV;<br>VS > Building inside; P: M;<br>AS: Machinery; splash; lament;<br>Tempo: Fast; | 00:03:03<br>Nick suddenly sits up and fires; Harvey lays prone, motionless<br>MovA;<br>CP: Tracking, MS-SV;<br>VS > Building inside; P: M; AS: Machinery; shots;<br>Tempo: Fast; |
| 00:03:05<br>WS (from the distance): the criminal falls wounded<br>MovA;<br>CP: Shaky, D;<br>VS > Building inside;<br>P: M; SP1;<br>AS: Machinery; shot;<br>Tempo: Fast; | 00:03:08/17<br>Nick checks the vest where the bullet had hit /<br>Nick's CLS (facial mimics + mouthpiece det.)<br>MovA;<br>CP: Shaky, MCS-SV;<br>VS > Building inside; P: M; Ph<br>AS: Machinery; pats;<br>Tempo: Slow; | NmovA;<br>CP: Shaky, ECS-SV;<br>VS > Building inside; P: M; Ph<br>AS: Machinery;<br>Tempo: Fast; | 00:03:33<br>Nick knees to check Harvey; consistent puddle of blood on the ground<br>MovA;<br>CP: Tracking, MS-FV;<br>VS > Building inside; P: M; M; Ph<br>AS: Machinery;<br>ST: Piano music;<br>Tempo: Slow; |

**Dialogue**

Harvey: NICK↑!
Nick: HARVEY↑! (3.0) 19-2^⇒ 10-35. (.) Partner's=been=shot (.) I
  need=a=paramedic right=away
Dispatcher: Copy that 19-2 (.) 10-35.

# 6 The *19-2* Anglified Police Procedural *Noir*          289

Nick calls the code only after checking his partner's vitals, meaning 10-35 *is not* the numerical string for 'dead body'. As a consequence, in the uncertain identification of the sense proffered by such terminology, any spectator observing the event via screens could eventually narrow down the alignment of the exemplified cypher with two ideas: the request for medical support, *or* the (equivalent and formally neutral) advisory of a seriously injured cop. Therefore, it would limit the situation to two different perspectives leading to the same conclusion of summoning paramedics and backups.

Once more, multimodal approaches disallow to consider the diverse layers of communication separately. Despite the primary and intense informativity of the image sequence, the scene utter understanding operates via the synthetic process of merging dialogic passages with visual access and acoustic features. Effects like shot echoes, blood splashes and laments reverberating louder than machinery ambient noises emphasise the mediatic situation high impact. They cooperate with camera techniques (mostly shaky and tracking) to provide credible audience points of view and remarking the emotional charge attributed to flat terminology. Nick's suffering at seeing his friend on the ground in a puddle of blood is not only given by rhythmic and prosodic elements like shouts and pauses surrounding the 10-35 code delivery via radio. It also emerges through the final piano music that narrates his sadness and escorts screen-viewers to the following scene.

Together with similar examples, the *19-2* TV show proposes other codifications. As said, they are easier to understand because they are already part of the everyday language colloquial dimension. Among them, one could find combinations like '10-20' or (in the form of a short question) 'What is your 20?', where the second double-digit stands for 'location', expressing the desire of telling or acknowledging someone's position. Precisely so, argot expressions recur throughout the *19-2* serial (and corpus), being of prompt interpretation since construed based on the meant word-length truncated at its last syllable(s) or deprived of *superfluous* pre-/post-modifiers to benefit from linguistic economy licences. There, one would notice 'perp' for the perpetrator; 'juvie' for the juvenile; 'recert' meaning recertification; 'range' standing for shooting/qualification range; 'rook' for a rookie. Other instances employ rhetoric

Fig.s, metaphorisation or resemantisation. In this second case, one would find 'uniform(-s)' for police officers; 'flagged' for marked out; 'mole' for corrupt (also 'crook') informant. A list of eponyms would include the notorious 'Amber alert' named after the 1996 US Amber Hagerman's abduction and murder case, nowadays known as 'AMBER alert' for America's Missing: Broadcast Emergency Response. Similar shortenings would, instead, originate from anonymisation and condensation, like 'APB', all-points bulletin, "kids casing B&Es" for 'juveniles inspecting houses to performing a *breaking-and-entering* double violation'. More numerical codes may establish an escalating order: "I'll pick up anything code 2 or higher" to signal the willingness to answer any call higher than a code 2 priority, labelled as 'Urgent. Expedite, but obey all traffic laws. No red light or siren'.

Like police jargon, felonies and "the pains of imprisonment" (Sykes, 1958) must properly occur within the *19-2 Corpus*. Thus, in conjunction with the lingo, they maintain a certain level of police language verisimilitude. For this reason, the television serial has to convey some quantity of anti-social communication capable of rendering the same gloomy atmosphere associated with the prison argot and its world. Quoting Michael A.K. Halliday, it is possible to affirm:

> The antilanguages of prison and criminal countercultures are most clearly defined because they have specific reference to alternative social structures, as well as the additional attributes of secret languages and professional jargons; and hence they are full of overt markers of their antilanguage status. (Halliday, 1978, pp. 181–182)

The said subversive context consequently happens to be in a sort of relexicalisation process of mainstream expressions or linguistic patterns (Mayr, 2012) to construe its specific premises and consolidate upside-down social values morality (see Halliday, 1978; Devlin, 1996). From this point of view, the proliferation of swear words, profanity, aggressiveness and grudges towards the conformed systems and the agents granting their existence seems legitimate in a self-devouring mechanism. In light of such conflictual context, the usage of controls linguistically determines the speakers' social and communicative roles. It also establishes

## 6 The *19-2* Anglified Police Procedural *Noir*  291

hierarchical positions within the related dialogic situations. That is once more observable in some primary verbal displays (Table 6.3) conjugated in the imperative mode to set a dominant-to-subdued exchange. The same verb employed by Houle in the sergeant-to-cop interaction and originating the described communicative situation—"Listen!" (Table 6.4)—is now used by the cop, who aims at building up a monitored and paternalistic dialogue with his younger (and socially at risk) interlocutor:

***Example 6.7 19-2 Corpus, 19-2, s01e06, min. 00:26:35–27:23***

Nick:  Listen↓⟹ (..) I'm not here as a police officer (.) okay^ (..) I'm here as a friend of Tarique and your father's ((Moves his head from side to side for emphasis))
Mo:  But↓⟹ you're still a cop (..) and I'm no snitch ((In a tough but childish way))
Nick:  Do you realize that if I didn't show up there were half a dozen Sixers ready to be:at your ass^ (3.5) You're just a runner Mo. (..) You think you really matter to the man in charge^
Mo:  Christo runs the park (.) Everybody knows that [...] He^⟹ ain't scared of <u>you</u>
Nick:  Is that right^
Mo:  He put a <u>biscuit</u> in a cop's face (..) and the cop didn't do shit.

However, the *19-2* TV serial mediatic environment rigidly centres upon the police force experiences. Hence it is hardly interested in the actual display of the prison antilanguage peculiarities. For this reason, on the linguistic ground, criminals always appear while cursing the cops they bump into. However, they seldom use jargon, which sounds incomprehensible to both officers and spectators (Example 6.7). In the instance, the addresser knows he is sending his message towards a non-cooperative addressee. Thus a stiff approach would result ineffectual. Nick's tone-down modulation contrasts the peremptory value of the imperative ("Listen↓⟹"). His 'heterogloss' engagement (appraisal framework) supports that, reassuring the boy he is not there as a cop but as a friend. This verbal behaviour deflects Mo's attention from the hostile label he would

# 292     F. P. Gentile

default attribute to the man and tries to reduce the emotive gap between them (looking for backchannels—"okay?"—and helping himself with gestural implementations like head-nods). Mo's non-cooperation, however, is recognisable via his repulsive 'judgemental' attitude, definitely diverting from the cops' perspective. In turn, the boy articulates his 'heterogloss' answer ("**but** you're **still** a cop **and** *I'm no snitch*"). Again, the escalating empathy arranged by Nick ("Do you realise …"; "you're just…"; "You think you really …") to lead Mo to more profound thoughts contrasts the receiver's obstinacy based on pre-construed knowledge ("He ain't scared of you"; "… the cop didn't do shit"). The receiver does not accept the control triggered by the former speaker; Mo's "reverse discourse" (Foucault, 1980) refuses his interlocutor's authority. He rejects Nick's tone and responds via adopting a distant register contributing to identifying the kid's ideology as reverse discourse "draws on the very vocabulary of categories of dominant discourses in order to make a case for oppressed groups" (Pelissier Kingfisher, 1996, p. 541).

The code recurs to incorrect usages like the ungrammatical negation in "I'm no *snitch*" associated with the slang word for 'spy' (in italics). Other antilanguage terminology examples are 'biscuit' for the gun and verbal usages like 'pull', meaning to extract the weapon. Contrarily to criminals, in the rare occasions when the argot emerges, it is entirely handled by the cops (somehow delegitimating the language purpose itself). In some other cases, it is even delivered *to* (and thus also *by*) unaware children prematurely choosing the wrong side, confident enough that using the code is already a sufficient condition to becoming a gangster.

## The *19-2 Corpus* Results

The analysis of the *19-2 Corpus* (by itself) has led to a series of interesting facts about the linguistics of the Canadian contemporary television crime drama. The preliminary research results will compare to those inferred from the other two corpora—the *Flashpoint Corpus* (Chap. 4) and the *Motive Corpus* (Chap. 5)—at the end of the present study (see Chap. 7). The contrastive analysis will outline the narrative-linguistic peculiarities of the genre in association with the binomial conveyance and use of natural language and specialised communication (here intended to include technical language, discourse structures, terminological *thesauri*, and professional knowledge via verbal, non-verbal, and para-verbal channels). In like manner, the survey will effectively apprehend the amount of multimodal information, whose transmission and alignment with the related linguistic data are responsible for a clearer and facilitated visual supportive, receptive and cognitive process triggered into the audience's mind.

Statistically, the parsing of the *19-2 Corpus* immediately displays some data about the word-count within the textual transcription. It reports ~105,247 tokens (instead of the ~112,387 after the empty-words deletion) and 1547 word-types. Thus, 1.46 per cent ratio in terms of vocabulary variation, meaning the introduction of one new word each 68.03 partial or full repetitions (Table 6.14). Hence, a minimal overturn, especially in correlation with the intense array of scenarios proposed onscreen and the numerous amount of characters involved in the interactive (verbal) situations providing the current data.

When applying the same statistical focus on the isolated seasons, the results seem to vary. The count ranges from ~33,238 (first season) to the ~37,339 (third season) tokens and the ~770-to-825-gap of word types, defining an average of 2.26 per cent of lexical variation corresponding to the conveyance of one new term every 44.25 ones (Table 6.14). Similar data, thus, reveal a more sensible percentage (0.8 times higher than the *19-2 Corpus* total ratio) associated with an ampler vocabulary spectrum whose perception could be doctored otherwise (Table 6.14).

The all-inclusive perspective—on this occasion—would consider the *Corpus* as a unitary and synchronic entity. However, it is worth noting

**Table 6.14** The *19-2 Corpus* results

| 19-2 CORPUS [SEASONS 1 TO 3 > (2008–2010)] | | | |
|---|---|---|---|
| Tokens (T) | Types (t) | 19-2C T/t ratio | |
| ~105,247 | ~1547 | **1/68.03 (1.46%)** | |
| SEASON 1 (2014) T/t | SEASON 2 (2015) T/t | SEASON 3 (2016) T/t | Avg $(T_1 + T_2 + T_3)/$ $(t_1 + t_2 + t_3)$ |
| 1/43.166 (2.31%) | 1/44,325 (2.26%) | 1/45,259 (2.21%) | **1/44.25 (2.26%)** |
| VOCABULARY HETEROGENEITY (Avg T/t vs. *19-2C* T/t) | | | |
| **+0.8%** differentiation | | | |

that it is constituted by a collection of thirty episodes equally distributed within three different and a-synchronic narrative bubbles, whose *trait d'union* is the thematic consequentiality set by the TV serial product. Therefore, if interpreted without paying attention to the seasonal subdivision, the overall data's sole consideration could be misleading. Season intervals represent a separation into three correlated sub-corpora contributing to sketch the general image according to a top-to-bottom slant rather than a bottom-up one.

Besides the overall outlook regarding word repetition or substitution counts, one more differentiation involves the terminological recurrence within the *19-2 Corpus* and its three annual broadcasts. The primary concern regards the misdemeanours mentioned throughout the screenplay transmission over the years. The perspective highlights seventy-eight types of violations divided into six categories: generic felonies (17), violent crimes (16), traffic issues (10), domestic contravention (6), sexual offences (13), and PD.. internal bureaucracy and affairs (16), as schematised in Table 5.1. Nonetheless, the general classification also has to face particularised observations concentrating on the seasonal broadcast conveyance of linguistic data dealing with crimes (Fig. 6.2). Once more, the mathematics applied to the current examination reveals an interesting point, where the best part of the terminological recurrence is inherent in the first two annual transmissions. Season 1 (2014) scores 37 per cent with 200 violations, and season 2 (2015) reaches 38 per cent with 207 ones, while the third follows with 25 per cent (130 crimes).

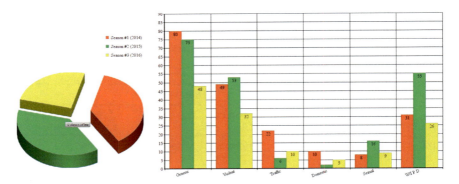

**Fig. 6.2** *19-2 Corpus* law violations chart (Fig. is mine)

The visual differentiation offered by the chart (Fig. 6.2) appears quite emblematic of a decreasing trend in creativity after the peak of 2015, although the acceptance of such a hypothesis merely based on quantitative observations would be untrue. On a qualitative level of analysis, if the second season is the one that reports more crimes, they, in fact, mostly consist of partial or full repetitions of the same deeds. Here, violations roughly correspond to different kinds of 'robberies' (the 'generic' one is distinguished from *armed* robbery, which is 'violent') and hence attested in as many groups according to their eventual premodifier. These reiterated cases have little relevance along with other minor misdemeanours, also contrasted by the neat sorting of violations related to the sphere of sex offences on different impacts.

Contrarily to the 207 repetitive mentions of second-year scripts, the first season is the most creative one. It shows a list of 200 crimes and the lesser reiterative rate, involving the most significant variation percentage in criminal identification terminological conveyance. Entries range from the peculiar 'open fire hydrant' to the 'child in a car' as much unusual report. Similarly, the same vocabulary limitations adopted in 2015 persist in the 2016 broadcast examination. Although, in this case, the repetitive pattern is unpreferred. As per the first season, the third one swarms with uncommon (in the *19-2 Corpus* perspective) advisories like 'serial arsonist' or the procedural 'officer not responding'. The three seasonal terminological rates also allow retrieving a thematic evolution. It starts from a general police procedural milieu (2014) setting, where the focus concentrates on identifying a corrupt agent belonging to precinct 19. Here, the mole permits criminals *of any kind* to get away with their malicious acts (thus the violation of lexical heterogeneity). After that, the serial theme moves onto the thorny subject of sexuality (2015). Eventually, it switches back again towards law enforcement friendly relationships with organised crime associated with the bureaucratic point of view in the third season (2016).

Also, notwithstanding seasons number 1 and 3—the last one proposes interesting aspects of juvenile and social worker profiles—season number 2 is the one which seems to be particularly interesting for its themes. There, Nick becomes (despite his already known borderline sense of duty) a real womaniser having affairs and casual encounters with plenty of old and newly introduced (also random) female characters. J.M.'s violence within the domestic context emerges as strong and unpredictable at the expense of his wife, Justine. Beatrice's lesbian orientation meets other female characters' bisexual occasional behaviours (such as Audrey's). This latter character's storyline involves a brief and perverse sentimental backfire with an ex-sweetheart with whom she has an almost-explicit public oral sex scene, too. The list of sexual narrations would also continue.

Nonetheless, the most significant description—above all—is Julien Houle's profile. Indeed, the first seasonal plot commences insinuating a *mole* within the police department. The doubt proved legit in the second year and proved to be non other than Sergeant himself. Houle is not a mole by chance. The man undergoes organised crime blackmails and briberies to hush him being a paedophile involved in pornography scandals. As anticipated, the narrative approach provides very harsh contextualisations, often associating the characters' private lives with long lists of arguable social conduct. Nick and J.M. are simultaneously cops and baffling heroes, whose sense of decency and morality tends to surrender to a feral (but private) sexual instinct and brutality, accordingly. Houle is corrupt, and the stain marking his professionalism also condemns him to suicide to avoid a public lapidation. The character's substitute, Sergeant Suarez, secretly shares Beatrice's (which happened to be the *ad interim* officer in charge in between Houle and Suarez) declared orientations. This storyline *fil rouge* gives homosexuality a huge mediatic resonance right after paedophilia. The 2015 season thematic narration seems to discuss the central sexual topic under a very provocative-to-morbid approach. Producers could have chosen it for its bombastic magniloquence and socially acknowledged expressiveness which could easily intrigue the voyeuristic television needs of its spectators, according to the "Cancon" (Gittins, 1999, p. 95) commodification praxes (see Chap. 3).

Eventually, many of the features summarised are comprehensible thanks to communication levels, which do not include verbal interaction. Still, contexts result are transparent because of the non-verbal and paraverbal approaches. Renditions deliver information to the audience through prosodic scansions of linguistic enunciations (contrasting the merely written data), visually iconic image displays (supportive of textual annotations), noises and soundtracks (which can only be reported indirectly). All those aspects influence the screen-mediated perception of the broadcast.

Along with visually integrated dialogues, some parts of the *19-2* television product (and the *Flashpoint* and *Motive* ones) occur in the form of iteratively silenced scenes. Only the flow of image sequences and noises narrates them. Off-scene gunshots, for example, are vital to increasing pathos levels and the understandability of severe events. Likewise, the unvoiced pain expressed by a scream conveyed through facial expressions and body language is also fundamental (see Chap. 4, Table 4.8). Multimodally, through the perception of similar filming strategies, the spectators fully understand the significance of the story (i.e., identity maker marks; specialised knowledge iconic conveyance).

The integration of multimodal contents with only-linguistic and extra-linguistic data plays a pivotal role in defining the communicative spirit of the televised narration of crime drama, whose expressiveness is also per se conditioned by the format structure of the product. The already mentioned lexical variation related to occurrences and collocations of violations and felonies depends on the serial-storytelling-modes supposing plots to create *correlated* chains of events that culminate in the seasonal epilogue. According to a similar focus, the array of discourses within the different topical bubbles makes three separate micro-thematic gravitation fields polarising linguistic domains. Consequently, the need for complying with the seasonal recount undoubtedly bribes the terminological differentiation. It produces some specific contextualized glossaries rather than thoroughly ranging from one extremity to the other of the entire lexical appurtenances of the legal language. However, the union of such limited *thesauri* contributes to defining *one* macro-thematic area, inclusive of those particularities shaping the trade-off. Other discoursal patterns are observable in the *19-2* TV series, appearing even more relevant than terminological findings. In conclusion, they allow the examination to portray some generalisable models about the police procedural show interaction. Their situational control displays exert different hierarchical grades in formal and informal environments, plus a limited number of formulaic strategies and emotional permissibility of police talk (as well as the jargon, lingo and argot) through appraisal processes.

298     F. P. Gentile

From a narrative point of view, a similar police-oriented focus strengthens narrations utilising the cinematic techniques that attempt to coherently render the urban scenario of a contemporary Montreal (Table 6.8; Fig. 6.1).

The mediatic transpositions of the city attribute political connotations to the sequences. Building filmings correspond to what Michael O'Toole defines as "functional machines [whose] practical functions are written all over them" (O'Toole, 1994, p. 85), where the *reading* of the city discloses further understandings of the community inhabiting it. The Montreal context is recognisable via a terrific panorama in the very first epised of the series, already ('Partners'. *19-2*. *Bravo!*, Vancouver. Jan. 29, 2014). The sparse skyline includes the CIBC tower, de la Gauchètiere tower, and the Tour McGill. Its thick low edifices glitter in the Québécois night opposite to the characters dominating the hill via a top-down. This extremely wide visual salience represents a singularity that does not correspond to the extensively broadcast product. Contrarily, the most widespread narration of *19-2* Montreal matches a horizontal dimension emphasising the amplitude of the urban milieu surrounding and encasing the related events. A balanced and even visual salience requires cops to move back and forth all over the streets, at ground level, binding them to the pedestrian world or their cars, following the prominent serial title.

Indeed, the skyscraper construction motivations have always adhered to North American political ideologies, economic implicatures, and psychological goals of hierarchical supremacy over competing societies, mostly concerning land prices and spacial availability (Frank, 1985). However, the Québécois architectural conservatism aiming to preserve ancient Victorian Heritage structures has been struggling over the years to limit the proliferation of inhuman towers failing the very "notion of urban planning" (Scott, 2019). This tendency, less familiar to Montreal, has contributed to defining the ideal police procedural environment hosting the *19-2* TV show vicissitudes. Subjects of plot events need to remain the characters alongside their stories. There are plentiful crimes in different parts of the city. Patrols have to reach every corner onboard their RMPs in the briefest time. It is worth noting that Canadian (and the US) streets have peculiar length, stretching from one end of the city to the other. This contingency often needs linguistic specifications like the closest crossing to the crime scene (Example 6.2, 'He is *in the alley between* Brefeuf *and* De la Roche'; see Fig. 6.1, plus Tables 6.7 and 6.8). Thus, the visual power of the cinematic sequences *multimodally* benefits from the widths of spaces rather than in their heights (see also Chap. 4, Fig. 4.5).

Consequently, given the paramount importance of horizontal protractions, any vertical narration acquires different contextualised (and connoted) meanings delivering more multimodal and multilayered pieces of information. The large and bright main streets skirted by maple trees turn into the angst and oppression perceived by spectators witnessing perpetrators' pursuit throughout overwhelmingly narrow alleys. Steep staircases and gloomy interior corridors onscreen are an expedient forming the tension building comprehension of sequences, whose finality underlines certain characters' emotional behaviours that would facilitate the narration. The contrast between outer and internal spaces matches the oxymoronic metaphor opposing bright moments and the individuals' inwardness.

## Notes

1. The project initially was a *CBC* one. After that, at the time, it was subsequently undertaken by *Bravo!* (Wilford, 2014).
2. Also in contrast with the Bill 101 or *Charte de la langue française* (*Loi 101*) introduced in Québec in 1977 and sanctioning French as the official language of the Province "as well as making it the normal and habitual language of the workplace, of instruction, of communications, of commerce and of business" (Behiels & Hudon, 2015) in the ultimate effort to protect the founding Francophonicity of the territory from the devouring dominance of English (Laframboise, 2017).
3. Italics are mine for emphasis.
4. Italics are mine to highlight the terminology that is verbally omitted in the passage in Table 6.11 but corresponding to the performative procedure imaged onscreen. The description emphasises the relevance of specialised 'knowledge' (knowhow) along with specialised 'language', 'discourse' and 'terminology'.

## References

*1-2. Bravo!*, Vancouver. Jan. 29, 2014–Aug. 22, 2016.

Adolphs, S., & Carter, R. (2013). *Spoken Corpus Linguistics: From Monomodal to Multimodal.* Routledge.

Aijmer, K., & Stenström, A.-B. (Eds.). (2004). *Discourse Patterns in Spoken and Written Corpora.* John Benjamins Publishing Company.

Austin, J. L. (1962). *How to Do Things with Words.* Oxford University Press.

Baldry, A., & Thibault, P. J. (2001). Towards Multimodal Corpora. In G. Aston & L. Burnard (Eds.), *Corpora in the Description and Teaching of English-Papers from the 5th ESSE Conference* (pp. 87–102). Cooperativa Libraria Universitaria Editrice Bologna.

Baldry, A., & Thibault, P. J. (2006). *Multimodal Transcription and Text Analysis: A Multimedia Toolkit and Course Book.* Equinox.

Bednarek, M. (2010). *The Language of Fictional Television: Drama and Identity.* Continuum.

Behiels, M. D., & Hudon, R. (08/18/2015 [2013]). Bill 101 (Charte de la lague française). *The Canadian Encyclopedia.* Retrieved August 25, 2019, from https://www.thecanadianencyclopedia.ca/en/article/bill-101

Brendan, K. (2012). English Version of Quebec Cop Show 19-2 Being Made for CBC. *Montreal Gazette.* Retrieved February 18, 2019, from https://montrealgazette.com/entertainment/english-version-of-quebec-cop-show-19-2-being-made-for-cbc

Brundson, C. (2010). *Law and Order.* Palgrave Macmillan.

Burgoon, J. K., Buller, D. B., & Woodall, W. G. (1996). *Nonverbal Communication: The Unspoken Dialogue.* McGraw-Hill.

Calabrese, R. (2019). *Patterns of English Through History, Art and Literature.* Tangram Edizioni Scientifiche.

Carpenter, L. (2016). Montreal Cop Show 19-2 Pulls No Punches. *Cult MTL.* Retrieved January 7, 2019, from https://cultmtl.com/2016/02/montreal-police-tv-show-19-2/

Cavagnoli, S. (2007). *La Comunicazione Specialistica.* Carocci.

Daniele, F., & Garzone, G. (2016). *Communicating Medicine. Popularizing Medicine.* Carocci.

Davis, M. (2021). The TV and Movies Corpora. *International Journal of Corpus Linguistics, 26*(1), 10–37.

Devlin, A. (1996). *Prison Patter: A Dictionary of Prison Words and Slang.* Waterside.

Dorland, M., & Charland, M. R. (2002). *Law, Rhetoric and Irony in the Formation of Canadian Civil Culture.* University of Toronto Press.

Ekman, P., & Friesen, W. V. (1969). The Repertoire of Non-Verbal Behavior: Categories, Origins, Usage and Coding. *Semiotica, 1*(1), 49–98.

Foucault, M. (1980). *Power/Knwledge: Selected Interviews and Other Writings, 1972–1977.* Pantheon.

Frank, R. (1985). The Demand for Unobservable and Other Nonpositional Goods. *American Economic Review, 75*(1), 101–116.

Garside, R. (1987). The CLAWS Word-Tagging System. In R. Garside, G. Leech, & G. Sampson (Eds.), *The Computational Analysis of English: A Corpus-Based Approach.* Longman. Retrieved July 21, 2017, from http://ucrel.lancs.ac.uk/papers/ClawsWordTaggingSystemRG87.pdf

Garside, R., & Smith, N. (1997). A Hybrid Grammatical Tagger: CLAWS4. In R. Garside, G. Leech, & A. McEnery (Eds.), *Corpus Annotation: Linguistic Information from Computer Text Corpora* (pp. 102–121). Longman. Retrieved July 21, 2017, from http://ucrel.lancs.ac.uk/papers/HybridTaggerGS97.pdf

Gentile, F. P. (2020). Rebooting Montreal in English: The *19-2* Case Study. In S. Francesconi & G. Acerenza (Eds.), *Adaptation of Stories and Stories of Adaptation* (*Labirinti*) (Vol. 187, pp. 161–184). Università degli Studi di Trento.

Gittins, S. (1999). *CTV: The Television Wars.* Stoddart.

Grego, K. (2013). *The Physics You Buy in Supermarkets.* Writing Scence for the General Public: The Case of Stephen Hawking. In S. Kermas & T. Christinsen (Eds.), *The Popularization of Specialised Discourse and Knowledge across Communities and Cultures* (pp. 149–172). EDIPUGLIA (Off Print). Retrieved March 9, 2021, from https://core.ac.uk/download/pdf/187907774.pdf

Grice, P. H. (1981). Presupposition and Conversational Implicature. In P. Cole (Ed.), *Radical Pragmatics* (pp. 183–198). Academic Press.

Grice, P. H. (1989). *Studies in the Way of Words.* Harvard University Press.

Hall, J. A., & Knapp, M. L. (Eds.). (2013). *Nonverbal Communication.* De Gruyter Mouton.

Halliday, M. A. K. (1978). *Language as Social Semiotic: The Social Interpretation of Language and Meaning.* Edward Arnold.

Heydon, G. (2005). *The Language of Police Interviewing: A Critical Analysis.* Palgrave Macmillan.

Kendon, A. (1987). On Gesture: Its Complementary Relationship with Speech. In A. W. Siegman & S. Feldstein (Eds.), *Nonverbal Behavior and Communication* (pp. 65–97). Lawrence Erlbaum Associates.

## F. P. Gentile

Knight, D. (2011). *Multimodality and Active Listenership. A Corpus Approach.* Continuum International Publishing Group.

Kress, G. (2010). *Multimodality. A Social Semantic Approach to Contemporary Communication.* Routledge.

Kress, G., & van Leeuwen, T. (2011). *Multimodal Discourse. The Modes and Media of Contemporary Communication.* Bloomsbury Academic.

Laframboise, K. (08/26/2017). How Quebec's Bill 101 Still Shapes Immigrant and Anglo Students 40 Years Later. *CBC.* Retrieved August 25, 2019, from https://www.cbc.ca/news/canada/montreal/quebec-bill-101-40th-anniversary-1.4263253

Leech, G., Garside, R., & Bryant, M. (1994). CLAWS4: The Tagging of the British National Corpus. In *Proceedings of the 15th International Conference of Computational Linguistics (COLING94)* (pp. 622–628). Kyoto, Japan. Retrieved July 21, 2017, from http://ucrel.lancs.ac.uk/papers/coling1994paper.pdf

Lund, K. (2007). The Importance of Gaze and Gesture in Interactive Multimodal Explanation. *Language Resources and Evaluation, 41*(3), 289–303.

Marmor, A. (2014). *The Language of Law.* Oxford University Press.

Martin, J. R., & White, P. R. R. (2005). *The Language of Evaluation. Appraisal in English.* Palgrave Macmillan.

Mayr, A. (2012). Prison Language. *The Encyclopedia of Applied Linguistics.* Retrieved January 15, 2019, from https://onlinelibrary.wiley.com/doi/10.1002/9781405198431.wbeal0054

Mehrabian, A. (1972). *Nonverbal Communication.* Aldeine-Atherton.

Moore, N. (2010). *Nonverbal Communication: Studies and Applications.* Oxford University Press.

Moorti, S., & Cuklaz, J. (2017). *All-American TV Crime Drama: Feminism and Identity Policy in Law&Order – Special Victims Unit.* I.B. Tauris.

Newcomb, H. (Ed.). (2007). *Television. The Critical View.* Oxford University Press.

Norris, S. (2004). Multimodal Discourse Analysis: A Conceptual Framework. In P. LeVine & R. Scollon (Eds.), *Discourse and Technology. Multimodal Discourse Analysis* (pp. 1–6). Georgetown University Press.

O'Halloran, K. L. (Ed.). (2004). *Multimodal Discourse Analysis. Systemic Functional Perspectives.* Continuum.

O'Toole, M. (1994). *The Language of Displayed Art.* Leicester University Press.

Olanrewaju, F. R. (2009). *Forensic Linguistics. An Introduction to the Study of Language and the Laws.* Lincom Europa.

Oswald, B. (2016). Canadian Cop Drama Goes Out with a Bang. *Winnipeg Free Press.* Retrieved February 18, 2019, from https://web.archive.org/web/2017

0917191802/https://www.winnipegfreepress.com/arts-and-life/entertainment/TV/canadian-cop-drama-goes-out-with-a-bang-401917995.html

Pelissier Kingfisher, C. (1996). *Women in the American Welfare Trap*. University of Pennsylvania Press.

Piazza, R., Bednarek, M., & Rossi, F. (Eds.). (2011). *Telecinematic Discourse. Approaches to the Language of Films and Television Series*. John Benjamins Publishing Company.

Pinar-Sanz, M. J. (Ed.). (2015). *Multimodality and Cognitive Linguistics*. John Benjamins Publishing Company.

Pozzo, B. (Ed.). (2005). *Ordinary Language and Legal Language*. Giuffré Editore.

Richardson, K. (2010). *Television Dramatic Dialogue. A Sociolinguistic Study*. Oxford University Press.

Richmond, V. P., McCroskey, J. C., & Payne, S. K. (1991). *Nonverbal Behavior in Interpersonal Relations*. Prentice Hall.

Rimé, B., & Schiaratura, L. (1991). Gesture and Speech. In R. S. Feldman & B. Rimé (Eds.), *Foundamentals of Nonverbal Behavior* (pp. 239–284). Cambridge University Press.

Roufa, T. (2019). Law Enforcement Lingo and Police Codes. *The Balance Careers*. Retrieved January 15, 2019, from https://www.thebalancecareers.com/police-speak-how-to-talk-like-a-cop-974868

Royce, T. D. (2007). Intersemiotic Complementarity: A Framework for Multimodal Discourse Analysis. In T. D. Royce & W. L. Bowcher (Eds.), *New Directions in the Analysis of Multimodal Discourse* (pp. 63–110). Lawrence Erlbaum Associates.

Scollon, R., & LeVine, P. (2004). Multimodal Discourse Analysis as the Confluence of Discourse and Technology. In P. LeVine & R. Scollon (Eds.), *Discourse and Technology. Multimodal Discourse Analysis* (pp. 1–6). Georgetown University Press.

Scott, M. (05/01/2019). Montreal's Heritage at Stake: What Kind of City Do We Want? *Montreal Gazette*. Retrieved May 1, 2019, from https://montreal-gazette.com/news/local-news/city-needs-blueprint-to-guide-development-heritage-montreal

Scott-Phillips, T. (2015). *Speaking Our Minds: Why Human Communication is Different, and How Language Evolved to Make It Special*. Palgrave Macmillan.

Searle, J. (1969). *Speech Acts. An Essay in the Philosophy of Language*. Cambridge University Press.

Searle, J. (1979). *Expression and Meaning. Studies in the Theory of Speech Acts*. Cambridge University Press.

Searle, J., & Vanderveken, D. (1985). *Foundations of Illocutionary Logic*. Cambridge University Press.

Simpson, P., & Mayr, A. (2009). *Language and Power*. Routledge.

Stubbs, M. (1983). *Discourse Analysis. The Sociolinguistic Analysis of Natural Language*. University of Chicago Press.

Swain, E. (Ed.). (2010). *Thresholds and Potentialities of Semantic Functional Linguistics: Multilingual, Multimodal and Other Specialized Discourse*. EUT.

Sykes, G. M. (1958). *The Society of Captives: A Study of a Maximum Security Prison*. Princeton University Press.

Thomas, J. (1988). *Discourse Control in Confrontational Interaction* (Lancaster Paper in Linguistics) (Vol. 50). University of Lancaster.

Trottier, D. (1998). *The Screenwriter's Bible*. Silman-James Press.

Wilford, D. (2014). 19-2 Review: This Is Not Your Average Cop Show. *The Huffington Post*. Retrieved January 7, 2019, from https://www.huffington-post.ca/denette-wilford/192-review-cop-tv-show_b_4681439.html?guccounter=1&guce_referrer_us=aHR0cHM6Ly93d3cuZ29vZ2xlLm NvbS8&guce_referrer_cs=VTJC4-DHj5wQ5MmHYb2-kw

Zipf, G. K. (1949). *Human Behaviour and the Principle of Least Effort. An Introduction to Human Ecology*. Addison Wesley Press. Retrieved January 10, 2019, from https://archive.org/details/in.ernet.dli.2015.90211/page/n11

# 7

# Contrastive Analysis and Results

Throughout the current survey, the analysis has aspired to find and describe the most interesting expressive features and narrative peculiarities of three main televised products—all observed by their respective third seasons—attributable to the Canadian seriality of crime drama/police fiction: *Flashpoint* (*CTV*, 2008–2010; Chap. 4), *Motive* (*CTV*, 2013–2015; Chap. 5), 19–2 (*Bravo!*, 2014–2016; Chap. 6). The said diverse types of broadcast have immediately displayed their different thematic and recounting focus. With that in mind, examining each TV sell-off has proceeded through the transcription of its episode dialogues. Thus the study does not lean on written scripts per se, contrariwise relying on transcribed spoken-*into*-written renditions of verbal actorial performances (Aijmer & Stenström, 2004; Biber, 2012; Adolphs & Carter, 2013). The researcher's next step was to synchronise transcripts with the extra-linguistic data that have provided additional—fundamental—pieces of information about non-verbal and para-verbal aspects (Barthes, 1977; Bavelas, 1994; Beattie & Shovelton, 1999; Baldry & Thibault, 2001, 2006; De Saint-Georges, 2004; Bateman, 2008; Bateman & Schmidt, 2012). Indeed, as explained in the analyses, the study's investigative purpose links to the multimodal observation of onscreen products

© The Author(s), under exclusive license to Springer Nature Switzerland AG 2021
F. P. Gentile, *Corpora, Corpses and Corps*,
https://doi.org/10.1007/978-3-030-78276-4_7

referring to one of the most prolific genres (in TV as in literature) like the police procedural (Sparks, 1992; Pender, 2007; Oswald, 2016; Moorti & Cuklaz, 2017; Yeo, 2018). From this perspective, multimodality is used to comprehend the most significant communication dynamics triggered by mediated onscreen renditions of monitored expressive contexts under two main directions.

On the one hand, it operated to narrow down the number of significant patterns that the medium itself funnelled and used to convey particular pre-elaborated meanings. Under this circumstance, viewers cannot interpret the cinematic contents they are viewing, as they can only follow the charming narrative schemata arranged and offered by plot-bound vicissitudes (Chatman, 1980; Bordwell, 1985; Branigan, 1992; Wolf, 2005; Rühleman, 2013; Eco, 2016a, 2016b, 2016c; Puckett, 2016).

On the other hand, the survey wanted to assess the role of verbal features in communication. Interactive modes and codes undoubtedly have a polyhedral stratification, as demonstrated so far. Verbal communication is only appreciable in its contrastive observation against other informative strategies (Kress & van Leeuwen, 1996; Norris, 2004; O'Halloran, 2004; Lund, 2007; Royce, 2007; Kress, 2010; Swain, 2010; Knight, 2011; Jewitt, 2013; Pinar-Sanz, 2015; Sindroni et al., 2017).

Diverging from the purely wordy dimension, television as a device characterises suggestive expressiveness. Its final quality connects to the visual ground primary perception rather than concentrating on incomplete only linguistic approaches.

Suppose we consider every corpus individually and compare those isolated results only. In that case, the outcomes seem to guide the comprehensive examination of some preliminary data on the statistical level. Different token (T) versus type (t) counts—about the three TV series analysed here (Table 7.1)—shift from the relatively significant values of the *Flashpoint Corpus* (~210,892) to minor ones in the *19–2 Corpus* (~105,247). A similar gap conversely corresponds to some relevant type reaches in the latter (~1547) like in the *Motive* one (~2734). They score a higher percentages of variation rates (1.46 per cent *19–2*, and 1.45 per cent in *Motive*) compared to the older *Flashpoint Corpus* (1.23 per cent). Indeed, the two more recent corpora display a lexical overturn that ranges from 1/69.12 to 1/68.03. It involves a 0.22 per cent rise from the

## 7 Contrastive Analysis and Results

**Table 7.1** *Flashpoint, Motive* and *19–2 Corpora* total statistics

| Corpus | Tokens | Types | Lexical variation score[a] |
|---|---|---|---|
| FLASHPOINT (2008–2010) | ~210,892 | ~2586 | 81.55 relationship [1.23% RATIO] |
| MOTIVE (2013–2015) | ~188,988 | ~2734 | 69.12 relationship [1.45% RATIO] |
| 19–2 (2014–2016) | ~105,247 | ~1547 | 68,03 relationship [1.46% RATIO] |

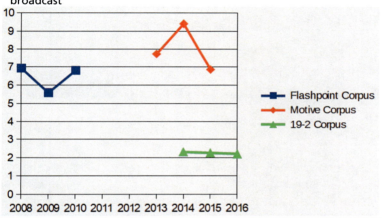

Series differentiation graph per year of broadcast

[a]The scores in Table 7.1's upper part resume Tables 4.10, 5.14, and 6.14 statistics

*Flashpoint Corpus* lower results, alternating one new word or term insertion only after its 81.55 partial or full repetitions. This contingency limits the esteem of that expressive *thesauri*.

Such relationships are observable through a more detailed year-focusing perspective, too (Table 7.1, 'series differentiation chart per year of broadcast'; Table 7.2, 'seasonal differentiation chart per corpora').

The concave curve of the *Flashpoint Corpus* linguistic trend (Table 7.1, squared pins) opposes the almost specular convexity of the *Motive* one (Table 7.1, diamond pins). This divergence signals peaks in diverse moments of their respective broadcasting structures (Table 7.2, bold). The first TV series reaches its highest vocabulary variation in the first season—the one that creates the most affiliation. Instead, the second shows an increasing trend culminating in season 2 and then dropping 0.89 per cent lower than its starting point. A similar situation statistically indicates minor attention levels in terms of linguistic (and thus dialogic,

## 308     F. P. Gentile

**Table 7.2** *Flashpoint, Motive* and *19-2 Corpora* seasonal statistics

thematic and contextual) differentiation. On the contrary, the *19-2 Corpus* (Table 7.1, triangular pins) substantially seems the more constant. Low rate lexical turnovers disregard irrelevant flickers and stabilise on second season average 2.26 per cent (Table 7.2).

The said mismatches are not just linguistic. Their examination shall fall under many co-occurring conditions determining the nature of the three corpora.

Indeed, vivid, expressive tendencies characterise the *Flashpoint* TV series that do not merely rely on the verbal dimension inferable from its linguistic data. Despite the first season communicative boost immediately parading before the public with its heterogeneous codes, the appealing process capturing spectators' attention seems limited to 2008. In 2009, shows demonstrated some breakdown in script-writing, losing vast amounts of lexical variation compared to the previous year's success.

Such creativity drop could allegedly depend on the product programming schedules, assembling seasons 1 and 2 with only a one-week pause, thus intensifying the scriptwriters' tasks. Therefore, as season 2 terminates, the more extended break leading to the third season (in 2010) also coincides with another variation peak about to equal the first season score (just 0.12 per cent lower).

Unlike *Flashpoint*, the *Motive* TV hybrid behaves specularly. The product rates about lexical differentiation maintain high average percentages throughout the three-year broadcasting period analysed. Nonetheless, after an already promising start in 2013 (7.74 per cent), the real apex is reached during 2014, where thesaurus overturn counts glide 1.66 per cent over the previous year record to precipitate a more dainty 6.86 per cent in 2015 (similar to *Flashpoint*'s third year ratio). Nonetheless, if a similar path could be seen as a lack of solidity, it is also true that format strategies demand fluctuations.

The *Flashpoint Corpus* tactics follow a purely "*centripetal complexity*" mode (Jacobs & Peacock, 2013: 52). They bet the series' entire verbal-linguistic and dialogic fortune on the first season. This way, *Flashpoint* conquered a stable plateau of viewers to be maintained during a more relaxed second year and implemented again for the third season. The *Motive* wake is peculiar, as well. This latter corpus expressive concentration appears solid in the first place. One year later, it increases, attempting an escalating success, giving more communicative relevance to the characters' verbal ground interactive exchanges.

Moreover, if the first season served a contextualising target that was useful to producers to present the concept to their spectators, the series's thematic colours blended with those of the *serial* narrative in 2014. The mix originated an evolved idea, where the initial murderous descriptive salience had embedded in a linear subtext expanding the characters' psychological sides and consequentially enlarging their florid expressive palettes. When the show utterly gave up its series modes for newly encountered serial modalities, all plots hinged upon a single storyline: London Montgomery's. That comported the *Motive* TV hybrid to renounce its original diversity and embrace a limited narrative *spectrum* mostly focusing on one main case plus other collateral minor ones. The drop of thematic diversification compromised linguistic variation compositional patterns as well.

The *19-2 Corpus* represents an even more different case study. The serial modality characterising the entire TV product is responsible for the thematic flattening of the Montreal-based show. Hence, the corpus presents a narrow collection of linguistic data integrated with extra-linguistic pieces of information that support its average 2.26 per cent lexical variation. As for the *Flashpoint* TV series, scriptwriters have seemingly concentrated their abilities in the first season (2014), with 2.31 per cent. During the two years 2015–2016, small adjustments changed thesaurus conveyance and alternation counts to 2.26–2.21 per cent. Like *the Motive* third season, the *19-2* serial narrative mode affected plot construction creativity processes, causing a monotonous standardisation of interactive events via mono-thematic scenarios characterising the whole product. Suppose a similar contingency gave birth to a less blossoming verbal-linguistic environment. In that case, it also allowed the creation of a constant register stabilised on a consolidated and limited vocabulary (Tables 7.1 and 7.2: graphs). The lexicon has become highly and easily recognisable by its spectators over the years. In time, it has facilitated mental association schemata and understood reception activities undertaken by those same individuals.

Nonetheless, the mathematical differentiation between the three TV products analysed here—in terms of the aforementioned statistical counts—is, without doubt, symptomatic of particular dissimilar communicative perspectives undertaken in each corpus. The numbers configuring their enclosed linguistic universes contribute to increasing the perceived unbalance among them, respectively.

## Normalisation and Speech Performance Metrics

From the overall perspective (and despite seasonal quibbling examinations), the *Flashpoint Corpus* almost literally doubles the size of the *19-2* one for token scores, although not replicating the trend on the type level. On the same wake, the *Motive Corpus* is 1.80 times bigger than the *19-2 Corpus* and 1.12 times smaller than the *Flashpoint Corpus* by its token counts. A similar trend follows word-type counts, either.

So far, the top-down approach has delivered some relevant and compartmental information about the corpora within their separated realities. Therefore, the bottom-up slant attempts to provide a functional analysis and description of general communicative and expressive patterns about the *genre*. This procedure would "normalise" (McEnery & Hardie, 2012, p. 51) the corpora, allowing users to appreciate the results on an even level. For the ease of the survey, some projections would rearrange the initial results within comparable cyphers displaying new presumed values of tokens and types, considering the average trends shown in Table 7.1. Normalisation procedures usually scale corpora to 1,000,000 tokens. However, since the examination data's width, the study chose a smaller 500,000-token value (in like manner, it still classifies as a 'small-size corpus').

In line with that, the *Flashpoint Corpus* would possibly reach ~6131 types, and the *Motive Corpus* would count ~7233. The *19-2 Corpus* had appeared as a scanter one, less bound to its linguistic salience. However—interestingly enough—it would jump to ~7349 types, unexpectedly outstanding the other two. That would determine a relevant reconsideration of its verbal-linguistic communicative aspects confidently stabilised at higher levels in the same way the other two do on lower ones. Data would imply a tighter connection between the verbal expressiveness and the non-verbal and para-verbal dimension co-occurring in the serial to produce meaning.

Nevertheless, similar data reading needs to consider one more parameter: respective broadcast durations. Projections could drive users to conjectures that would elect the *19-2 Corpus* as the winner in the linguistic salience game, *immediately* followed by the *Motive* one. Such a contingency would determine the Montreal-based serial verbal lexical variation dominance over the similar Vancouver-based one and neatly distant from the Toronto setting. The latter would prefer other extra-linguistic modes in place of minor iterative schemata.

Conversely, the three corpora comprise *transcribed* data. Those collections of spoken words could compare to their respective transmission lengths to establish eventual elocution speed rate pieces of information. Hence, the ~1260 minutes of *19-2* TV serial broadcast compared to its

~105,247 tokens would produce statistics of ~83.53 WPM (words per minute). The *Motive* TV hybrid ~1677 minutes, compared to its ~188,988 tokens, would give ~112.69 WPM, and the *Flashpoint* TV series quotient of ~210,892 tokens divided per its ~1804 minutes would be ~116.90 WPM. Statistically, similar rates all remain underneath the natural conversational pace reaching among 125–150 WPM (Wong, 2014: 348) and remarkably far from the audiobook 150–160 WPM recommended range (Williams, 1998).

On the one hand, the *Flashpoint* (116.90) and the *Motive* (112.69) TV series mostly adhere to a speech speed rate threshold of 100–125 WPM. This level is more similar to lectures and slide presentations (Wong, 2014, ibid.). Moreover, it seems coherent enough with the compound verbal + visual character of onscreen products. This combination presupposes strictly monitored, pre-arranged and autocratic dialogues, as the audience is not actually in the condition to intervene or interrupt the exchanges.

On the other hand, the *19-2* TV serial, considering all the data mentioned above compared to those newly introduced elements (83.53 MWP), determines the utmost victory of visual and acoustic narrations over spoken dialogues. Here, the verbal-linguistic aspect of communication is only confined to a *marginally* supportive role. The *19-2* WPM threshold does not even brush the minimum gap-limit traced by the discipline in terms of (natural) spoken communication elocution rhythm.

Albeit, the features described so far are not as peremptorily conflicting as one could imagine at first glance. The prime details about lexical reiteration opposite to new word insertions only indicate the corpora linguistic heterogeneity. There, the *19-2 Corpus* arrives at higher results of ~7349 tokens on a projective perspective, hypothetically positioning word counts at half-million values (thus confuting previous conjectures about its scant linguistic relevance). *Motive* follows through a 146 token gap, where the *Flashpoint Corpus* only obtains ~6131. Although numbers merely describe the transcripts chromatic spectra, underlining the former and the second series tends to display more accurate choices than the third TV product *univocal* interactive styles.

Moreover, word-per-minute rates seem to present an inversely proportional pattern, where the hugest quantity of words articulated every 60″

belongs to the less lexically florid series (~116.90 WPM). Per contra, the most recent serial (among those investigated in this survey) pays the price of its linguistic diversification via a formulaic slackening stalled at ~83.53 WPM.

A data all-inclusive concluding statement could infer the inclination of both the *19-2* and the *Flashpoint Corpora* to some unpreferred verbal-iterative usages surpassed by other types of communication.

Nonetheless, a similar perspective mirrors two antithetical reflections. A slow articulatory mode renders the lack of attention towards the linguistic expressiveness in *19-2*. That neutralises its kaleidoscopic lexical thesaurus. Oppositely, the same prevalence of extra-linguistic traits in *Flashpoint* opts for a faster *illusionary* locutory pace, frustrated by a poor vocabulary. The remaining one, *Motive*, reveals an overtly linguistic relevance. At 500,000 token normalised counts, it reaches a ~7233 types elevated vocabulary change tally and iterative velocity of 112.69 WPM. To that extent, while the previous examples outline a *weaker focus* on dialogic, conversational and—more generally—spoken events onscreen, the third instance draws significant attention to verbal-interactive dynamics *assimilated* to other non- and para-verbal dimensions.

## The Languages of the *Corpora*

Despite the importance of the said evaluations, however, languages are not aseptic aggregates of independent aspects deemed separate. Indeed, as remarked throughout the study, the multimodal approach presupposes the existence of polyvalent semiotic modes. They co-occur within the same communicative situation to express complex content-enriched meanings stratified at different signifying layers (Birdwhistell, 1952; Thompson & Massaro, 1986; Rimé & Schiaratura, 1991; McNeill, 1992; Bavelas, 1994; Beattie & Shovelton, 1999; Holler & Bettie, 2003, 2004; Wilcox, 2004; Lund, 2007; see also Chap. 2). These multiple expressive possibilities include speech act connotations, gestural and mimic funnels implementing communicative and receptive contexts, prosodic features, and para-verbal collateral bits of information gained via the appraisal of the environment serving as a scenario for the exchange. Despite the linguistic level of interaction, the scene demands its characters to carry out their performative act employing a set of tools that go beyond the *simplistic* use of flat vocal tones scanning words. The shades of actorial voices have specific aspects mostly retrievable in the prosodic traits of one's utterances. The plot scripture wants all the dialogues exploited in the show as composed and aligned through precise criteria arranging the interaction from its very beginning to the end of the exchange. In like manner, the tonal, rhythmic and prosodic peculiarities of the performance rendition communication via construed intentions and impressions precisely emphasising the preset goal that develops the storyline. Thus, staged cinematic situations realise through caricatural reflexes of natural expressive patterns. Emotionality plausibly transposes onscreen for those addressees who immediately recognise the related character's mood. The audience happens to receive similar data via the acoustic metalinguistic reading of the communicative context.

Many features attributable to the prosodic domain are disseminated throughout the three corpora to reproduce natural language articulatory conditions that should not shine through the TV medium as phony or stilted. To that extent, specific patterns are, without a doubt, more frequent than others and appear via an emphatic discourse connotation delivered utilising tonal fluctuations. Because of the nature of those linguistic occurrences (investigations), many character lines include conjectural or deductive formulations to the proposed or affirmed to their interlocutors. Several slight vocal pitch rises (^) para-verbally implement the verbal utterances variations, wherever questions and exclamations occur.[1] In many other cases, vocal pitch mutations directly relate to different communicative situations. When the speakers are willing to focus their performative attention and their receiver's interest on certain words or phrastic elements, exchanges bear connoted or denotative meanings. They play a significant part in the evolution of the plots. Solid tone-ups (↑) may supplant slight vocal pitch rises. There, a loud and clear voice expresses relevant words and tells assent or disagrees. The strength of said replies concerning previous question/exclamation formulae determines the speaker's position (and power) in the conversation. Tone-ups often contrast tone-down drops (↓) or even muffled and whispered speeches (°word°). These signify that addressers want to deflect one's attention from their utterances via belittling or scuffling attitudes. Performers keep some details quiet, accordingly emphasising the informative relevance of those lines. A similar strategy carries the receiver's implicit invitation to concentrate on what is being crucially said on the scene. Those prosodic features also recur with other procedures, like the intense stress attributed to word pronunciations (<u>word</u>) catching the listener's hearing.

However, in adherence to the law enforcement exchanges' military context (Dorland & Charland, 2002; Heydon, 2005; Pozzo, 2005; Olandewarju, 2009; Marmor, 2014; Roufa, 2019), tone variations may also reflect hierarchical (Simpson & Mayr, 2009) organograms to be respected within the workplace milieu. Cops can converse or dialogue loudly *inter pares*. Notwithstanding a similar habit, they must maintain a standard flat tone when dealing with their superiors. These can oppositely involve speeches with vocal pitch tone-ups and subsequent modulations ($\Rightarrow$) that hold the same volume throughout the elocution (or until the pause). Example cases range from formal internal to public discourses and from reprimands to schedules and order delivery through monologic formulations. The rigour and the discipline inferable from those contexts could sometimes result in screaming (WORD) single words or entire discourse passages to reveal even more distant roles and ranks between the participants—e.g., shooting range instructor-to-instructee context; cops commanding perpetrators to surrender during a chaotic arrest.

Prosodic traits always come together with more rhythmic peculiarities providing other significant details on the speakers. One addresser's hierarchical authority over another transmits through clearer and louder vocal tones compared to the lower interactive modes undertaken by inferior-rank agents within the same communicative event. Monologic formulations originate from the linguistic controls that those individuals exert on their interlocutors during the unequal exchange. Their authoritative professional and social dominion pours into the language they use as well. People relating to influential individuals are generally submissive (or just cooperative), letting leaders carry out their locutory or perlocutory acts without cutting them off. This last type of speaker is well aware of its communicative dominance. Thus, they often operate through discourse patterns, which can afford rhythmic slow-downs, expanding their statement duration because of the *formal* impossibility of being

**316**    **F. P. Gentile**

interrupted. Dominant interlocutors, in these contexts, display a certain tendency to ample usages of empty pauses of different length. Clear punctuation marks—signalled by the standard '(.)' multimodally annotative symbol—alternate to other longer breaks—'(..)' or '(number of seconds)'— even within passages where they are not necessary. That silence redundancy determines the linguistic command position of their users. Opposite such cases, when balanced dialogues erase social and professional disparities, they indicate interactions among colleagues or friends. Here, speakers cannot indulge in long performance of their lines, plus they need to be very transparent. In *inter pares* communication, whenever articulatory modes are too lengthy or personal opinions are reckoned as disputable, turn-taking crumbles. The linguistic message delivery pace may give up on interruptions and intrusions of other people's comments or speeches. The whole information chain and its understandability could fade.

Similar aspects are common in natural language contexts. However, the cinematic *controlled* language planning admits simultaneous linguistic superimpositions in cases where utterings are not fundamental or, contrarily, only occur to be hushed. Those events lead to the recognition of the dominant speaker in the dialogue at the silenced weaker one's expense. In colleague-to-colleague situations, linguistically dominant roles are not permanent. Turn-taking breaks can change multiple times, handled by different speakers rebounding and redefining their communicative roles in the exchange systematically. Occurrences of this kind often parade in police procedural interactive occasions, where cops pettifog about the shifts they were assigned, conjecture suspects' pursuit and apprehension, or mutually exchange friendly interpersonal remarks.

When diverging from colleague-to-colleague communications, interruptions happen for authority motivations. For instance, one could notice Sergeant rebuking other patrols or cops shouting at criminals to surrender. On the same trend of the emphatic expedients mentioned above, pauses and rhythmic peculiarities can draw the listener's attention to some precise parts of one's discourse.

To that extent, TV viewers often witness other prosodic phenomena inclusive of syllable lengthening patterns (indicated by ':' for each syllabic lengthening) and latching strategies (see '='). For example, they may express a set of in-context meanings ranging from irony to pure denotation. This latter locutory technique is adopted when the speakers are aware of the risk of being interrupted by their addressees, and they articulate their formulations with no pauses. In this eventuality, the audible in- ('.h') or out-breaths ('h') usually signal the efforts. In some other cases, orators may merely undertake a fast elocution pace deemed to characterise their prosody.

In communication, the primary role of one dimension over the other changes from context to context. Thus, non-verbal aspects supportive of para-verbal features (or vice versa) are also fundamental to the complete communication transfer among the interlocutors, and between the speaker, the receiver and the spectator as well, within the onscreen display. Verbal utterances and para-verbal metalinguistic data about rhythm and prosody require third-party non-verbal dynamics to implement the expressiveness via gesture (-in-talk), facial mimics, head nods and body language characteristics (see Chap. 2). As for the prosodic features, the stereotyped scenic bios of the characters presupposes performative acts to include attitudes and emotions. These aspects televise using universally identifiable behavioural schemes (Ekman, 1971, 1982; Ekman & Friesen, 1969, 2003; Ekman et al. 2013) that the viewer's receptive mind needs to elaborate unconsciously. Indeed, given the immediate comprehensibility associated with body language and emotionally connoted facial expressions, many times, non- and para-verbal communication utterly substitute verbal formulations of any kind.

In *19-2*, certain prosodic peculiarities diversely apply to different speeches in synch with recognisable idiolects. That produces linguistic externalisations univocally ascribable to single characters' expressive patterns and behaviours. To that extent, a cop's utterances are not only linguistically salient compared to the other interpreters' lines, thus defining the set of contexts where an individual is more likely to be present. They also permit the underlining of the communication typology deployed onscreen through its prosodic scansion. The prevalence of monologic lines reveals a massive influx of dominant-to-subdued communication. Here, a relevant construction of plot-related events transmits the said linguistic dichotomy, where hierarchically determined linguistic situations create some rigid separation between the speaker and one (or more) receiver. Such a hypothesis proves right through the exceptional occurrence of commander/sergeant-to-cop and cop-to-criminal interactions. The former case includes unequal exchanges where one speaker delivers instructions or briefs the team about updated mission details. In the latter, dominant subjects verbally assault (through shouts and mandatory orders) their receivers to induce their subjugation and participative surrender finalised at the apprehension. Here, they potentially fire up reverse discourse or "resistance" phemonena (Haworth, 2006: 739-ff). The linguistic articulation coexists with the extra-linguistic additional information. In this binomial relationship, the characters' physicality and movements shift from a docile attitude—of people tamed by workplace contexts and social praxes—to a more aggressive animal instinct—when approaching criminals, noting ethics principle violations, or narrating private-life sexuality. It is worth noting that this second instance also includes events shattering the utopistic portrayal that blindly associates police to absolute righteousness. On that wake, one could think of Nick's bashes physically damaging J.M. Brouillard, once in the know of the man's cruelty towards his wife, Justine.

Similar to *19-2*, the *Flashpoint* TV series also prefers monologic expressions, where utterances are seldom interrupted by other participant's intrusions into one's speech. Nonetheless, the Toronto-based product has demonstrated a complex communicative *texture*. *Flashpoint* lacks a similar feature. The simultaneous inconsistency of character lines clutches overwhelming initial statements. A similar situation depends on comprehension factors aiming at the precise conveyance of a thematic slant concentrating on the harmonious and structured intervention schemata enacted by the entire task force, rather than giving prominence to its singularities. Although leadership roles are neat in the SRU, its members' collaborative and co-dependent attitude supposes everyone can finish (and thus let finish) one's formulation before agreeing or contradicting it with other externalisations. There, turn-taking procedures rigorously apply to grant to all the participants the possibility of expressing their opinion. Everyone shall have the chance to talk without linguistically prevaricating colleagues.

# 7  Contrastive Analysis and Results    319

Still, communication dominances are present within the series. They mostly occur during the instructor-to-instructee patterns (when an expert tells its cadets how to perform their assignments).

Once again, body language is essential to define meaningful communicative contexts. Some clear aggressive, connoted episodes of gesture-in-talk and facial mimics describe cop-to-subject communication. Perpetrators are demanded to surrender, employing powerful and intimidating verbal and corporeal languages. However, other than that, given the psychological perspective of the series, body language actions and reactions to *stimuli* often underline the evaluative goal that SRU members and supervisors adopt. This extra-linguistic behaviour assesses the dangers implied in the stressful situation faced by those trained experts. Also, it evaluates the posthumous consequences that similar events can have in the agents' minds (e.g., cold-blooded sniper killing of escalated subjects in non-negotiable situations).

Conversely, the *Motive* TV series dedicates excellent attention to linguistic expressiveness, which is more prevalent here than in the other two shows. *19-2* has less relevant occurrences and verbally interactive modes. *Flashpoint* prefers body language appraisals prominence. Subsequently, *Motive* juxtaposes those traits to some linguistic usages in terms of prosodic peculiarities. For narrative reasons, the observed product dialogues need to maintain a univocal conjectural nature. That would aim—first—at guessing the reasons behind some murderous deeds and—secondarily—corroborate the hypotheses with further factual deductions supported by pieces of evidence or confessions. Hence, detectives formulate their utterances with a very fluctuating tone alternation of ups and downs. These aspects characterise their purely reconstructive assumptions when confronting each other. Emphatic articulations of crucial terms bearing the entire lucubrations implement expressivity. If hierarchical separations of communicative contexts are missing, the deficiency lurks in the abuse of interruptions telling of dissent. Indeed, in *Motive* (especially in season 1, less relevantly in seasons 2 and 3), apparent rank differences between department captain and detectives are not substantial. The protagonists' scuffing attitude even weaken the said disparity, instead highlighting authority respect issues. The formal turn-taking linguistic chain in the series is always in jeopardy, and thus, as a mechanism of defence, elocution paces rise through rhythmic latching techniques.

Other characters, like the medical examiner, seem to prefer flat expressive tones in private-life scenarios as much as in the workplace. The praxis televises some occupational hazards associating (popularised) medicine discourse (Bhatia & Gotti, 2006; Garzone & Archibald, 2007 [2010]; Gualdo & Telve, 2011; Daniele & Garzone, 2016) neutrality with a lack of emotion in friend-to-friend remarks and exchanges.

These same linguistically contradicting styles also surface in the extra-linguistic features. Body language and gestures are mostly supportive of verbal formulations (and *not* vice versa). Mimics always co-occur with speech or come after such elocutions to emphasise meanings that the listeners have already grasped. In some other cases, like autopsy contexts, the coroner's linguistic formality is also mirrored and enhanced by a postural stiffness that terminates only after the specialised discourse delivery ends. Given the thoughtful nature of the TV product, apprehensions always follow thick interrogatories nailing the culprits as well. In these situations, law enforcement agents' physicality never really emerges through the strength of the arrest.

Despite the differences in terms of the non-verbal and para-verbal usages, it is verbally possible to outline the three series' preliminary communal tendency. From the appraisal framework observation, the 'engagement' level of the language used in the shows tendentially starts from a 'monogloss' perspective. The trend initially establishes a type of narration that concentrates on the protagonists speaking as singularities. Only secondarily (once the audience has acknowledged the speakers' personality), 'monoglossia' becomes 'heteroglossia', including others' perspectival points of view. Cinematically, the strategy deflects original focuses from the primary speakers, as they are presented, towards the other heroes of the series, introduced in the dialogues in turn. Most exchanges in the series have a police procedural nature. Considering that, 'attitude' aims to formulate conjectures or evaluate potentially risky situations.

On the one hand, it involves ample 'judgemental' displays where adverbs and adjectives serve the analytical goal; contextual 'affect' statements declare equal aspects through a more emotional lens.

On the other hand, the 'appreciation' label is rarely attributable in the TV series contexts examined in this study. Its canons, more keen on pure aesthetics, are rare in the crime drama environment.

In line with the police procedural plot's severe and rigorous attitude, attention levels are always relatively high. Consequentially, the 'graduation' marks vary from the 'low force' and 'softened focus' to 'focus sharpening'. In the former case, the sequence protagonists only mind their businesses or take care of interpersonal and friendly relationships. The latter refers to the numerous moments in which climaxes must build some tension (e.g., the suspect's pursuit and arrest). Nonetheless, law enforcement roles frequently link to the crime individuation and the criminal's apprehension. Therefore, many linguistic choices opt for 'lower graduation force' (e.g., possible; alleged; suspect) in place of 'force raises' that spoil unwanted emotional connotations.

## Popularised Knowledge, Natural Language and Characterisation Blend

The linguistic appraisal framework (Martin & White, 2005) analytical application has not always been the most efficient technique for adequately understanding all the expressive contexts rallied in the study. The methodology classifies many emotional and connoted interactions in adherence to stiff unrealistic labels. In turn, the attribution of those flags is always qualitative. It may involve the observer's misjudgement or questionable perception of ambiguously interpretable situations (e.g., use of sarcasm or irony, potentially subverting negative attributions with positive connotations). Moreover, when natural language exchanges blend up with sectorial discourses and specialised knowledge (even though popularised), the matter is even more significant. Those cases rarely adopt positioning too. Aseptic linguistic formulations emulate detechnified specialised discourses mostly entrusted to some terminological employments. They would ban appraisal evaluations to solely lend themselves to other criteria more concerned with syntactic, lexical and textual specificity levels (e.g., formal register; ungrammatical usages due to linguistic economy) lacking emotional supports.

## 322    F. P. Gentile

Among the many kinds of languages involved with *Flashpoint, Motive* and the *19-2 Corpora*, few were linguistically relevant for the frequency and data observation. Besides the *fil rouge* of police procedural focuses (even these having divergent ramifications), the three series' common points seem less than expected. The 2014–2016 seasons of the Montreal-based TV serial report a narrow list of linguistic domains. The primary role of police language and jargon never really contrasts any other verbal expressive contextualisation (as it does on the visual one). The city criminological framing mostly marks the simultaneous delivery of different violation sets at diverse priority levels. Crimes are immediately located across Quebec's main centre, using a detailed map to pinpoint illicit activities from East to West and South to North. Other than such misdemeanours, the language is peculiar because of the precise characterisation of its numerous protagonists. It makes every performer (and performance) recognisable because of some traits stereotypically mirroring their personality and social skills. Flirty tones and vocabulary signal the womaniser. Arrogance, disrespect or scoffing indicate the bullied rookie. Tyler's naivete contrasts with his massive body. The woman displaying a masculine attitude may be a lesbian. Again, most *19-2* cases seriously emphasise sexual-life narrative developments.

The *Motive* TV hybrid between series and serial modes from 2013 to 2015, instead, offers more equilibrium among its multiple language contexts. The topographic narration of the series is irrelevant. Despite sparse identifiable Vancouver areas, the setting likely seems a police drama heterotopy, where the physical environment chosen as the ideal milieu for the recount is just functional as any other place would have been. The series does not mention any salient urban spots, possibly because the product is for the international trade. Nonetheless, the linguistic prominence of a clearly Canadian-English speaking handful of protagonists (apart from the medical examiner interpreted by the US-born Lauren Holly, who—anyhow—became Canadian in 2008)[2] makes the *Motive* series an overtly Canada-oriented format. Linguistic inflexions aside, the limited range of thematic vicissitudes—all dealing with the carrying out of a murder—does not favour the conveyance of long law-breaking events either. Having no city places to wander in or other crimes to solve, the Vancouver homicide department only linguistically concentrates on

# 7 Contrastive Analysis and Results 323

portraying the deadly events. Thus, the police procedural verbal communication essentially shows a reconstructive pattern. The abductive approaches puzzle out the *mens rea* behind the assassinations and, above all, its motivations. Yet, along with procedures, other domains are present in the series. The said reconstructions summon IT language and terminology plus economic discourse passages, wherever the computer researches lead detectives to browse victims' or suspects' financial statuses.

Nonetheless, the most intense specialised communication funnelled in the British Columbia show is medical. The abundant corpses presuppose the coroner's dissecting job. She (it is a female role, here) examines the victims and reports the results. Interesting passages are determinable via linguistic economy assertions implemented by peculiarly sectorial verbal usages and prepositional dependencies. Phraseology and terminological occurrences also increase the verbal dialogue narrative appeal (always supported by their related and intense visual salience).

Different from the other two, *Flashpoint* proposes other situational contexts entrusted to orality. Like in *19-2*, the Toronto setting (2008–2010) brings back toponyms and reassures the urban space its legitimacy, although only focusing downtown. Similar to *Motive*, the list of crimes perpetrated within the SRU jurisdiction is narrow. It does not concentrate on reporting all the possible violations; instead, the detailed identification of a weaponry lexicon mastering all the show's scenarios. In *Flashpoint*, the police slant becomes action-hybrid, and procedures turn into performative protocols for neutralising social threats. In line with a similar contingency, psychology emerges as one major linguistic, disciplinary field. Plots do not bureaucratically follow any aseptic instructions. The linguistic relevance prefers the interpersonal, reflective and emotional developments of character's inner statuses concerning the tasks they must fulfil for the Torontonians' sake (such as killing radical terrorists who refuse dialogue options). Fundamental in- versus out-group dynamics associate with psychological appraisals and negotiation theories. They apply to the interactive contexts escorting the events to their apical ending (in these very cases, the dialogues appraisal framework represents a useful resource again).

In the examination, the different linguistic and thematic areas have revealed a heterogeneous expressive world. Its narrative techniques

## 324   F. P. Gentile

preliminary (and unexpectedly) appear less numerous than its possible points of discontinuity. Highly diversified verbal, communicative and expressive contexts dominate the natural and specialised codes mustered onscreen and emulated before the public.

# Narrating the *Corpora* Visual and Acoustic Dimensions

Users often consider language as the most expressive communication possibility (see Chap. 2). Per contra, receivers should always keep in their mind that diverse channels cooperate to deliver messages. It primarily happens when dealing with the emotional sphere. In that case, the verbal dimension contributes to minimal percentages to such conveyance as non- and para-verbality perform the best part of the work. For instance, the study has already described prosody and body language (among other aspects, aplenty) as determinants to those exchanges.

As a medium, television operates via vast arrays of other techniques playing a significant role in shaping and reshaping contextualised meanings to reach beyond the screen limit. The television modes present—as already said—an *autocratic* personality (see Chaps. 2 and 3). The medium only allows its spectators to witness what its plots have scheduled to happen. No viewers' eye could peep, nor could an ear eavesdrop anything else than that, escaping the device attentive controls. Similar praxes influence the narrative scopes of those products and affect their related thematic diversity.

The *19-2* TV serial has operated via a remarkable Anglophonisation of a Franco-Québécois environment (Brendan, 2012). The *Motive* TV hybrid has given linguistic prominence to a Canadian-English speaking crew. The *Flashpoint* TV series has pushed forward this same goal utilising advertising campaigns (mostly related to interviews to its producers) underlining the cast's (and consequently the series' itself) pure Canadianness. Moreover, the three TV products focus on various thematic units. *19-2* concentrates on patrolling activities and faces bureaucratic issues related to the job. *Motive* prefers the investigative slant familiar with the archaeologist's historiographic goal with fossils: detectives dig in the individuals' past to reconstruct their stories by examining fresh corpses. *Flashpoint* urges people to face globalised society risks via the proposal of terroristic threats, weaponry availability and psychological evaluations.

Nevertheless, the television target provides appealing representations of actual social groups through what Benedict Anderson called "imagined communities" (Anderson, 2006) brought to life after ideologisation processes. The process simplifies complex real-world social dynamics into fictional categorising and functionally representative frameworks. Police TV dramas upholster themselves with a non-porous skin enclosing their storyline articulations within well defined airtight narrative bubbles on both the linguistic and extra-linguistic levels. All the events irrevocably remain within those boundaries. Onscreen situations never really leave the urban fabric of the city they belong to. Naming procedures connecting the recount to precise toponyms work as chains, forcing the stories to stay anchored to those same places reiteratively. Products like *19-2* and *Flashpoint* forge dialogues constricting their characters in Montreal and Toronto cities, respectively, with no ways out. *Motive*'s lack of Vancouver place names could seem a looser context where its protagonists are free to wander wherever they want. On the only occasion that Angie Fynn leaves her comfort zone—the city—to continue her investigation elsewhere—she goes to Toronto—she feels displaced. Toronto's climate is hostile to the heroine, and in a different space (far from 'home'), she finds herself alone and with no jurisdiction. The characters who decide to relinquish their original bubbles of hermetic containment become abandoned outcasts deprived of their human essence as much as of their social roles and powers. Detective Angie Flynn's dexterity and intuit in Vancouver turned into a lone woman's anonymous traits in Toronto. She has to fight against the bureaucracy and non-cooperative agents' stubbornness to regain her legit credentials and solve the case before reacquiring the narrative right to come back home (*Motive*, Canada: *CTV*, s01e06).

Narratively, the three series look for some enfranchisement from the US-dominant styles, as well. The *Flashpoint* goal is to become the consolidated alternative to North America SWAT recounts. It emphasises the dialogic and psychological perspective in place of punches and gunfights.

However, the series' primary visual salience still centres on weapons and geared-up squads in want of some action.

The *Motive* show proposes investigations, which are scantly inclusive of splatter details of the bodies. Some hyper-technological devices unrealistically reveal murderers, as in the *CSI* franchise (Allen, 2007). Despite giving enormous relevance to talk, the stories' narrative development sets a protagonist (a woman), followed by a few secondary characters. She trusts her instinct over paperwork to cut her sergeant's leash, confirming the overused North American cliché of the outsider detective solving cases against all odds.

The *19-2* serial was promising. Remaking an original Francophone product in English could have determined a breakthrough in the Quebec esoteric culture, disclosing its world to the rest of Canada—and other Anglophone end-users. The introspective slower narration connoted to Québécois patois, although, gets lost in the artefact Anglophone reboot of the serial. The remake introduces a faster narrative slant supported by many action expedients and *noir* elements. The first version presented cops as defenceless vigilante preyed on by the relentless vices of a sick society. The new rendition gets closer to the US police procedural style than the more talkative original.

The topics of the three series and the ways producers have chosen to televise them, therefore, distinguish the said products from their US relatives. However, the difference does not emerge in the solid *otherness* they aim at. All those mentioned characteristics—some of which also considered representative affinities—transpose the thematic orientation of the products into their related visual and acoustic displays. Suspense and tension constitute a constant couple of elements essential to police procedural format development and plot evolution. Well-designed music and soundtracks (almost) ubiquitously accompany the verbal dimension. The strategy simmers the uncertain and suspicious climate rendered as the transmitted scenarios' dominant features. The viewer witnesses a dexter alternation of wind and string instruments and percussions played at low tones within the three case studies. Those gloomy notes escort the narrative pathos to its climaxes, mostly adumbrated by other prominent piano notes emphasising the recounts. Fluctuations between lower and more acute tones also permit the association of said instruments with gender-diversified speakers.

The technique implements the verbal dialogic exchanges with more music accompaniments increasing informativity and expressiveness. This consideration is especially valid for *19-2*. Yet, although the theme song is very intriguing, it does not serve any other occasions than the TV serial presentation.

The *Flashpoint* TV series goes beyond that. Instrumental supports do not just underline narrations. The product appears quite attentive to the acoustic dimension on a deeper level. The most intense sequences of the Toronto trade-off emphatically render through the linguistic and extra-linguistic *strata subversion*. Verbal expressiveness becomes secondary to para-verbal contextualisation. Some well-known song stanzas or refrains tell the rhythm of narrations, emotions and sub-textual meanings into the spectator's receptive mind. In addition, when even famous songs are not enough, adapted versions of the series theme song convey intensely emotional passages that are strictly related to the intra-group micro-universe of the SRU team. Its notes play slow rather than fast, through a piano prominence over other instruments and vice versa.

Diametrically opposite, *Motive* lacks its TV series theme song. Moreover, the series linguistically displays sparse dialogic events where sarcasm and irony occur. Such a tendency acoustically corresponds to eccentric music choices underlining facts via fitting serious-to-funny manners. A similar peculiarity already emerges in the pilot episode: the victim first appears while singing a karaoke version of *Hit me with the Best Shot* before being beaten to death.

A considerable part of the show's expressiveness is equally rendered by music and ambient noises on the acoustic level. Pleasant background instruments direct the scenic emotionally driven assessments. The viewer's comprehension of the events also relies on the on-the-scene noises s/ he can hear through the screen. They are not naturally captured throughout the instalment shootings but sampled and synchronised afterwards to meet neat quality needs. On the one hand, the diegetic ambient noises semiotic insertion enhances the narrative coherence of the scene. It drives the spectator's attention to some precise action or detail (e.g., the rustle of paper documents handed over or slammed on a table; footsteps approaching or leaving).

On the other hand, extradiegetic sounds (which characters could not concretely hear on the scene) serve the narration on a purely sensational dimension. They function to frame the viewers as the only individuals entitled to experience them. The cinematic narrative strategy invests the audience with some sensory qualities that the series characters cannot achieve (like hearing the assassin's breath through the crawlspace secretly separating him/her form the agents searching the house on the chase). It creates a tighter bond between the spectators and the onscreen product. Like music and soundtracks, extradiegetic noises belong to the commodification aspects of TV productions, influencing people's reactions and creating affiliation.

Other visual supports flank the acoustic dimension. They align with the actorial body language expressive and performative charge. Shifting to the image comprehension, the reading of cinematic techniques communicates diverse perspectival narrations of a story. The scenic salience frames the sequences via moving or non-moving actions. Accordingly, these two main possibilities focus on specific characters' significant presence and deeds or the primary role of the environmental contextualisation and details emphasis. Suppose some actions are not as essential as the setting. In that case, the filming prefers a non-moving strategy that gives special prominence to the place (e.g., dining room; street; crime scene examination; morgue; headquarter, police station). Oppositely, it gleans on the iconic power of gesture-in-talk or facial mimics to focus on the protagonists' acts disregarding the surrounding dynamism.

Those two main choices involve other narrative expedients, uncovering even more informative tassels in the overall communicative mosaic. All three surveyed TV products have a predisposition to using moving action techniques. They describe evolving plots, where environmental portrayals are undoubtedly essential but, more importantly, contextualise the situations. Moving strategies dynamically contribute to launching subsequent investigative recounts that lead to the resolution of the cases. Camera amplitude also helps such schemes.

Non-moving actions statistically build more sweeping shots and include front views that allow the audience to access the entire compound of the scenic elements. On the contrary, moving sequences tend to undertake narrower camera angles using middle-to-close shot alternations (also inclusive of close-ups and details increasing the narrative salience). Here, front views make room for side, over-the-shoulder, or back views. These angles embed the external spectators into the scene and position them at varying proximities to the interaction participants for a facilitated involvement. In wide shots, the spectators are distant. Middle, close and close-up shots let them gradually approach the speakers.

Similarly, more inclusive side-, back- and over-the-shoulder views substitute fronts to suggest slightly lurking attitudes. Not only does camera amplitude correspond to the observer's eye line and visual field. It coincides with their head movements as well. The tracking techniques emulate the spectator's gaze on the 3D horizontal axis or dolly vertical salience. Thus, visual narrations slide from side to side, back and forth, or reproduce up and down eye movements concerning the context. Tracking expedients recur when the narrations propose, for instance, interrogation rooms. Here, tennis-like interactions summon an intense dialogic alternation of elocution rhythm and the speaker's salience. The camera eye hinges upon a pivot placed inside the room or on the desk, sliding from left to right and vice versa as the interlocutors formulate their questions and answers. Other emblematic tracking sequences involve dynamic passages like classic cops-and-robber pedestrian or car chases. In these other cases, back and forth progressions often fragment their narrative consistency via extreme close-up or cut-in shots detailing inside-to-outside or outside-to-inside car views and aerial sequences. This strategy is preferential in the *19-2* and *Motive* series.

Oppositely, dolly techniques emphasise the hierarchical differentiation of the narrative *strata*. They imply that possible dangers coming from any direction could jeopardise the horizontal progressions connected to police procedural patrolling tasks and interrogatories. The cop drama action slant—as in *Flashpoint*—translates into top/bottom views (and vice versa). On this silver tread, the tactical planning takes off. It moves on the rooftops; snipers up above control the area where a hostage-taker is threatening civilians.

Moreover, besides overtly notable camera movements, framing techniques influence the cinematic rendition as well. Cold and aseptically denotative stationary camera shots portray non-moving actions. They focus on characters or objects disseminated on the scenes for specific reasons and with contingent relevance. Contrariwise, shaky movements connote shot framing patterns mirroring the real-life authenticity of the stage. The trembling strategy facilitates a realistic slant in place of ad hoc constructed and fake (also unemotional) shootings. Such unstable camera shots emulate gait-related movements attributed to the cinematic eye following the sequence. In like manner, they copy the observer's point of view (fidgeting within its assigned spot) or confuse reactions to something happening collaterally in the surrounding area (e.g., a bomb going off).

Similar expedients equally occur in all the three TV products analysed. However, differences in narrative tempos accordingly divert each case towards slightly superior displays of one technique over the others. The *19-2* serial has a slower verbal scansion supported by the same acoustic and visual implementations pace. Camera techniques majorly prefer non-moving action contextualisations to alternate stationary action frames and shaky tracking progressions of medium-to-long duration.

The *Motive* show prefers cinematic strategies that are quite similar to those of *19-2*. Here, the preponderance of fast tempos hurries the sequences to quicker tracking movements. Most cases result in over-fragmentation by speaking/gesturing characters' close shots. Narratively, this process fires up theme-rheme alternations via the introduction of multiple cinematic phases and subphases.

Such a tendency is even more evident in *Flashpoint*. Its narration is the fastest in the whole survey. The TV product counts very brief phases shattered into countless salient frames (since the many characters). For example, shaky camera movement dominates when singularly portraying the team members while carrying out their tasks. Tracking strategies serve precise moments of the plots, such as the small phases narrating the unit's physical transferral from the headquarter to the hotspots and back. Camera movements galore (compared to *Motive* and *19-2*) emphasise the factual vertical rendition. Distant visually iconic focuses locate ant-like sharp-shooters up high, having subjects framed in their gunsights until the negotiating operations succeed or fail (and in these latter situations, they shoot). Nonetheless, the *Flashpoint* particularity also resides in its action and psychological developments thematic turnover. In those second narrative bubbles, the rhythm slows down and brakes the fast pace of the series.

Among the cinematic strategies varying the shows' rhythm, such as the dense framing fragmentation mentioned above, one would note many narrative ellipses. In *19-2*, flashbacks mostly connect to the *psychological* and reflective dimension of one main character—Nick. The strategy frequently associates the events he lives in the present with a past tragedy crippling his former partner due to an almost deadly wound and having repercussions on the man's current efficiency in the workplace.

In *Motive*, episodes always start via immediately identifying the victim and the killer. Then, a sudden flashforward teleports the narrative context after the performance of the murder, when detectives have already arrived on the scene. Subsequent *reconstructive* usages of flashbacks oppose the initial flashforward to emphasise the investigative slant of the series.

Eventually, *Flashpoint* employments of those techniques are for *climax needs*. The instalments kick off *in media res* when events have already escalated. Thus, someway, the beginning of every show could classify as 'flashforwards', per se. The same impulse projecting *Motive* detectives forward in time conversely rewinds the events within a varying range of hours before the situation happens to subsequently—and linearly—lead the spectators through the story.

Indeed, the three TV products' characteristic is a peculiar rendition of non-linear timelines. They leap back and forth in and from the past to recall crucial episodes. The differently arranged narrative goals fascinate the spectators and distinctively identify the diverse formats of cinematic recounting modes.

In conclusion, photography and lighting choices also contribute to enhancing the sequence visual expressiveness. Dark colours in place of brighter filters could determine a character's dominance and relevance over the other or the narrative inclination that the director wants to attribute to the scene. The *noir* narrations of Montreal's imaginary corrupted and stifling society, in *19-2*, correspond to dull colours impairing sunlight vividness and majorly concentrating on the gloominess of nighttime renditions.

## F. P. Gentile

Similar to *19-2*, Vancouver's fictionalisation, in *Motive*, appears as a grey urban context. Its euphemistically whimsical weather originates a sick community inclined to murderous deeds. Continuing the parallelism with the Montreal setting, Canada's enormous external spaces of British Columbia central city dichotomously contrast the oppressive inwardness of in-door boundaries. There, neither lively colours and shades of day-time settings can outstand the neutral and depressive atmosphere of the narrated territory. On the other hand, the *Motive* production emerges for its peculiar use of a photographic filter applying to the 'victim' and 'killer'. These flagging procedures provide characters with the extra-emphatic relevance that captures the viewer's attention.

Unlike the two just described examples, the *Flashpoint* TV series opts for more luminous solutions possibly adopted to contrast SRU uniforms' greyness and the seriousness of the threats presented throughout the show. It renditions a more positive orientation to success transmitted by photography choices in the first place. The vastness of Toronto's urban and sub-urban areas also allows cinematographic directors to face different challenges alternating downtown with other natural environments like parks and woods, taking advantage of the suggestive locations. The enclosed spaces of building interiors do not match *19-2* and *Motive* smallness either. Narrow settings in the former two case studies represent the investigations' dreary effort. Nevertheless, this latter format's amplitude and width narrate the dangers of Toronto's televised equally degenerate social comminations, potentially targeting anybody from whatsoever perspective and for infinite reasons.

On the overall ground, the synchronisation of all the diverse dimensions and dynamics described permits some generalisable hypotheses on the genre communicative and expressive patterns and schemata. However, some more aspects still have to be scrutinised.

## The Canadian Contemporary TV Crime Drama

Several corpus-based data combine with more projective hypotheses to survey the three TV series.

## 7 Contrastive Analysis and Results 333

Despite those statistics, the genre expressive peculiarities observation would not be complete, yet. A contrastive, separate examination of the *19-2, Motive* and *Flashpoint* worlds could fit the constrastive slant. The codes employed would result in concordant as much as opposite communicative features. Similar qualities emerge to mould a generalisable shape of the Canadian TV crime drama (Thompson, 2000; Beaty & Sullivan, 2006; Jewitt, 2013; Bianculli, 2016; Jenner, 2016).

Nonetheless, the cinematic film's negative-like portrayal would work as a cast, whose functional voids must refill to reproduce its solidified and final status. This comparative phase aligns with some more deductions from the observation of an all-inclusive data collection that originates from the three separate corpora assemblage into a single unit. The result is a more comprehensive annotated entity containing the totality of those multilayered stratified (meta- and extra-) linguistic pieces of information. For ease of reference, this product is labelled *Total Corpus*.

Its collection consists of the sum of the three initial corpora token levels (Tables 7.1 and 7.2) lacking empty words to count ~505,127 tokens. However, since the evident and communal employment of similar narrative contexts, the word type count does not reach the ~6867 mathematical sum of those individual linguistic compounds. It settles on a minor ~4824 items. From this perspective, the vocabulary variation determines a tremendous reiterative relationship of one newly inducted word in 104.71 full or partial repetitions and a 0.95 per cent ratio of types/tokens. Also, relating the token number to the broadcasting hours resulting from the addition, the 4741 minutes of televised contents match a ~106.54 WPM rate.

This last percentage is 2.08 per cent higher than the ~104.37 average score. The *Total Corpus* locutory pace seems faster than expected, yet adjacent to hypothetical dividends. Decidedly higher than the *19-2 Corpus* pace ~1.28 times—its 106.54 WPM are still less than *Motive's* 112.69 and *Flashpoint's* 116.90. It translates into a 14.77 per cent brake significantly behind minimum threshold levels for natural conversation rates. Nevertheless, the said value is perfectly coherent with the 100–125 gap typical of oral presentations implemented by visual supports (Wong, 2014, ibid.), extendable to the television modalities. A similar minimal standard and a scant variation percentage (0.95) determine an expressive

**334**  **F. P. Gentile**

**Table 7.3** *Total Corpus* noun frequency list

| RANK | NOUN | | RANK | NOUN | | RANK | NOUN | |
|---|---|---|---|---|---|---|---|---|
| 1 | GUY | [1,379] | 11 | MAN | [504] | 21 | LOOK | [406] |
| 2 | TIME | [1,193] | 12 | **BOSS** [498] | | 22 | PHONE | [404] |
| 3 | RIGHT | [1,127] | 13 | CAR | [491] | 23 | HAND | [401] |
| 4 | **SOMETHING** | **[835]** | 14 | YEAR | [480] | 24 | **SPIKE** | [400] |
| 5 | WAY | [834] | 15 | PEOPLE | [473] | 25 | PLACE | [398] |
| 6 | ANYTHING | [739] | 16 | **GUN** [473] | | 26 | **TEAM** | [394] |
| 7 | THING | [716] | [...] | | | 27 | FRIEND | [392] |
| 8 | DAY | [537] | 18 | NAME | [469] | [...] | | |
| 9 | NIGHT | [535] | 19 | **SOMEONE** [449] | | 43 | MONEY | [315] |
| 10 | KID | [514] | 20 | HOME | [434] | 44 | **POLICE** | [312] |

environment where the flamboyant role of non- and para-verbality adumbrate the verbal communication limit. Formulaic articulation pattern speeds remain unimportant, and a mainly poor vocabulary harnesses the corpus-linguistic and thematic heterogeneity.

Table 7.3 shows common nouns. They differ for characters' growth ('guy', 'kid', 'man'), social relationships (from the distant 'people' to the more connoted 'friend'), temporal contextualisations ('time', 'day', 'night', 'year'), and locative associations ('car', 'home', 'place'). The noun frequency list of the *Total Corpus* highlights some leading recurring entries as corresponding to some generic words. This information would add no connoted or denotative meaningful details to the study, hence seemingly neutralising the scheme usefulness. Generic names do not belong to police procedural slants of cop dramas but an everyday lexicon fund in commonplace texts or descriptions. A few elements provide some hints about the investigative attitude of linguistic data characterisation. For example, 'something' (rank 4, with 834 count) and 'someone' (rank 19, 449 count) emphasise the expressive focus on the happening of certain unidentified events and the involvement of unknown individuals (Table 7.3, in orange: something, someone). However, even in those cases, the attempt to reconnecting the highlighted words with their respective procedural contexts would be unnatural and detrimentally biased.

Notwithstanding the said hurdles, by positions #16 and #44, two emblematic nouns—'gun' (473 count) and 'police' (312 count)—signal

## 7 Contrastive Analysis and Results    335

the crime story narrative perspective preliminarily recounting style summoning the genre. Besides them, other coherent instances are observable further in the list—'shot' (rank 62), 'murder' (rank 70), 'victim' (rank 71), 'cop' (rank 73), 'weapon' (rank 81), 'killer' (rank 100). They are very scant, ranging from 233 to 168 count, thus diminishing the given occurrences linguistic significance.

Some other relevant data reach outstanding frequency scores positioning their related words at prominent ranks, in Table 7.3 (in light grey). However, those words and names immediately suggest their original belonging to the *Flashpoint Corpus* ('boss', rank 12, 498 count; 'Spike', rank 24, 400 count; 'team', rank 26, 394 count) and its thematic topicalisation.

Indeed, suppose the most frequent nouns recurring in the all-inclusive archive of the *Total Corpus* are labellable as generic. In that case, some other terms are entirely indicative of their primary corpus source only. Figure 7.1 reports six examples of some significantly regular nouns. The horizontal width—from 0 to 100 per cent—determines the *Total Corpus* amplitude. Here, the x-axis is separate into three sectors where the left side (0–41.75 per cent) gathers the 210,892 tokens of the *Flashpoint Corpus*. The central area represents the 188,988 tokens of the *Motive Corpus* (41.75–79.16 per cent, through a total of 37.41 per cent). The right part (20.84 per cent) hosts the 105,247 tokens of the *19-2 Corpus* (79.16–100 per cent). Some peculiar noun recurrence patterns demonstrate the actual repartition of tokens in the *Total Corpus*. Examples are qualitatively selected in consideration of the thematic areas of the narrations; however, they also mirror the quantitative perspective. Despite the assemblage of the three initial case studies into a single sample, one could comprehend that the final type number (~4824) comes from an over-fragmented use of the various *thesauri* as the three corpora rallied into one.

Narrative-specific patterns confine terms in binding shallow portions of the scheme belonging to one observable linguistic archive rather than another. Words like 'subject' (rank 69, 220 hist; Fig. 7.1a) and 'team' (rank 26, 394 count; Fig. 7.1b), thus remain the exclusive property of the *Flashpoint* technicality. It expresses through the proficient use of psychologically evaluative labels (e.g., 'subject' in place of the perpetrator,

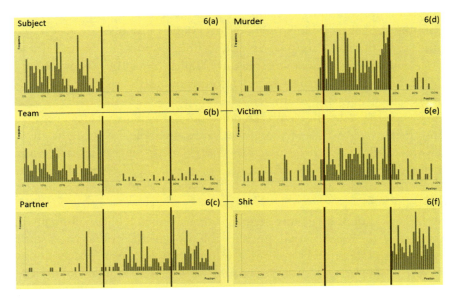

**Fig. 7.1** *Total Corpus* noun topicalisation. (The figure is mine)

criminal, violator) and the socially relevant in-group thematic slant (where 'team' dynamics prevail over the individualistic mentality).

Oppositely, this precision seems marginal in the other two corpora. The monothematic homicidal perspective in *Motive* determines the intensely 'murder'-oriented (rank 70, 219 count; Fig. 7.1d) recounts of the show. Nonetheless, the smaller number of characters participating in the investigative narrations reflects the *19-2* praxis, grouping the many protagonists in duos for patrolling tasks. The Vancouver- and Montreal-based shows achieve quite even scores via a comparative observation of words like 'partner' (rank 85, 189 count; Fig. 7.1c), and some more spread graphic schemata of other terms like 'victim' (rank 71, 213 count; Fig. 7.1e). Despite being strictly related to assassination cases (in *Motive*), the acceptation of these terms is broad enough to comprise wider arrays of crimes. Hence, they find significant matches in both the left and the right sectors as well.

In like manner, the first forty entries of the noun frequency list also report swearwords such as 'shit'. The said iteration is utterly absent in former 79.16 per cent of the *Total Corpus* but monopolising its final right side assigned to the *19-2* TV serial (rank 39, 324 count; Fig. 7.1f). The contingency is useful to determine one more expressive characteristic of this latter case study. The *19-2* serial often concentrated on the conveyance of blue language being indistinctly adopted by cops and perpetrators and emphasising the emotional connotation and the diastratic variation of this TV product's very language.

To that extent, the visual and acoustic meaningful communicative patterns remain dominant. They characterise each series of narrative modes and provide a general overview of the expressive delivery of genre-related content. However, the all-inclusive simultaneous parsing of the outer linguistic data belonging to the investigated products contributes to proffering a deeper understanding of Canadian contemporary TV crime drama dynamics.

Inside the *Total Corpus*, each of the three smaller corpora kept its identity distinguished, and it never really linguistically blended with the others. For this reason, the synchronisation of those narrative bubbles and expressive realities could seem unproductive on a superficial level.

Nonetheless, the limited shared vocabulary emerges per contrast with the unmatching verbal choices that substantiate the dialogic differentiation of the products in adherence to particularised phenomena of topicalisation. The initial and partial conjectures determine the main relevant iterative domains of the observed series. This point is solidly proven within the *Total Corpus*.

The *Flashpoint* TV series, analysed solo, has originally shown certain tendencies to prefer verbal contexts dealing with weaponry lexicon and psycho-social dialectics centred on team-work cooperative structures. The contrastive examination confirmed those features. Its data even accentuated the vocative function usage via the paramount conveyance of characters' names (e.g., Spike, Sam, Jules) and hyponym-to-hypernym scansions (e.g., boss, team, police; Table 7.3). Both those aspects tightly associated language with the visual—and hermeneutic (Ricoeur, 1997)—*thatness* consolidating the denotative expressive slant of the series terminological choices (Figs. 7.1a, and 7.1b). Gestural and proxemic semantics charged words employing non-verbal or il-/per-locutory paraverbal amounts of information.

The investigative perspective in *Motive* answers its specific focus, which concentrates on the killings. However, the prominent linguistic and verbal recurrence of terms like 'murder' and 'victim' is not as characterising as expected (Figs. 7.1d and 7.1e). The television product core is, without a doubt, bound to the occurrence of deadly events launching detectives' fatigues in the eternal struggle against evil intents. The narrative pattern proposes murders and solutions, case after case, without any breaks.

Notwithstanding the Vancouver plots' deterministic certainty, the ordinary acceptation of similar terms in the crime drama context causes them to trickle down other series' domains differently. In *Flashpoint*, since the action and thematic rendition of fictional terroristic threats, 'murder' and (especially) 'victim' communicate the presence of some collateral events and casualties happening during the main narration. Conversely, the extensive array of topics involves the need for those verbal occurrences, in *19-2*. In this latter example, murders are rare (even more than in *Flashpoint*), yet the term 'victim' is overused. A range of criminal contexts resemantise and remodulate it through premodifying additions (e.g., stabbing; gunfight; car accident victim). In *19-2*, this linguistic procedure continually redefines the monoreferential value of the *Motive* terminological vocabulary, where 'victim' equals '*murder* victim' (a label attributed regardless of the kind of murder).

As anticipated throughout the survey, the *Motive* and the *19-2* TV products have more in common than the *Flashpoint* show. The action perspective is crucial to the Toronto product. In like manner, the other two series tend to emphasise the procedural recount—even though all the three shows display both action and procedural slants at different rates—in their verbal dimension and through their visual iconicity. The *19-2* TV serial gives prominence to the police environment, often reproducing onscreen contents concentrating on police precinct in-/out-sides and salient car sequences. A similar relevance attributed to team-work discourses in *Flashpoint* is also present in *19-2*. The former instance treats this theme from the psycho-social perspective aiming at constructing cooperation and trustworthiness among its members (thus, often like team-building operations). Instead, the latter case study discusses police *équipe* gatherings through a paradoxically uncosy scenario, where law enforcement members are unwillingly forced to cooperate and work together. Here, the psycho-social narration becomes the transmission of police procedural and bureaucratic chores of 'partner' *duo* combinations. A similar quality is also widespread in *Motive*, although with no polemical or recalcitrant connotations (Fig. 7.1c).

Along with such examples, the *19-2* serial is the case study drawing more attention to its protagonists' linguistic characterisation in the entire survey. Many heroes display some expressive peculiarities in the Montreal-based programme. For instance, Nick intermittently recurs to the Jamaican patois or the omnipresent Tyler's fearful and attitudinal weaknesses mismatching his massive black-guy status. Nonetheless, vulgar formulations reiterative abuse represents the most intense and relevant aspect of such linguistic characterisations. The Montreal-based rendition proposes heroes and villains indistinctly (e.g., 'shit'; Fig. 7.1f) uttering blue language expressions connoting the serial with a colourful-to-explicit use of verbal branding.

As described, the three cases have many points of both continuity and discontinuity on the multimodal communication perspective. These contribute to assess, define and understand the main expressive traits of the Canadian contemporary crime drama genre proposed by the television medium and reaching end-users behind and beyond the national limit. Thus, this multimodal perusal also participates in the constant reshaping process befalling Canada's linguistic, cultural and imaginary identity simultaneously on- and off-screen.

## Notes

1. Moreover, considering the transcription task originating from the oral dimension, no punctuation marks are present in the corpora. Every sentence and clause uttered onscreen is contextualised through its rhythmic scansion. Thus, it is separate (or not) from the previous and the following ones only through vocal pitch perceivable alterations of length-variable pauses, often presuming the presence of commas or full stops.
2. *The Canadian Press* (2 March 2013). 'Holly has a pretty good motive for moving to Canada'. *The Hamilton Spectator.* https://www.thespec.com/entertainment/2013/03/02/holly-has-a-pretty-good-motive-for-moving-to-canada.html (accessed March 14, 2021).

## References

*19-2. Bravo!* (n.d.). Vancouver. January 29, 2014–August 22, 2016.

Adolphs, S., & Carter, R. (2013). *Spoken Corpus Linguistics: From Monomodal to Multimodal.* Routledge.

Aijmer, K., & Stenström, A.-B. (Eds.). (2004). *Discourse Patterns in Spoken and Written Corpora.* John Benjamins Publishing Company.

Allen, M. (Ed.). (2007). *Reading CSI: Crime TV under the Microscope.* I.B. Tauris.

Anderson, B. (2006 [1983]). *Imagined Communities. Reflections on the Origin and Spread of Nationalism.* Verso. Retrieved June 28, 2019, from https://is.muni.cz/el/1423/jaro2016/SOC757/um/61816961/Benedict_Anderson_Imagined_Communities.pdf

Baldry, A., & Thibault, P. J. (2001). Towards Multimodal Corpora. In G. Aston & L. Burnard (Eds.), *Corpora in the Description and Teaching of English-Papers from the 5th ESSE Conference* (pp. 87–102). Cooperativa Libraria Universitaria Editrice Bologna.

Baldry, A., & Thibault, P. J. (2006). *Multimodal Transcription and Text Analysis: A Multimedia Toolkit and Course Book.* Equinox.

Barthes, R. (1977). *Image, Music, Text.* Fontana.

Bateman, J. A. (2008). *Multimodality and Genre.* Palgrave Macmillan.

Bateman, J. A., & Schmidt, K. H. (2012). *Multimodal Film Analysis. How Films Mean.* Routledge.

Bavelas, J. B. (1994). Gestures as Part of Speech: Methodological Implications. *Research on Language and Social Interaction, 27*(3), 201–221.

Beattie, G., & Shovelton, H. (1999). Mapping the Range of Information Contained in the Iconic Hand Gestures that Accompany Speech. *Journal of Language and Social Psychology, 18*, 438–463.

Beaty, B., & Sullivan, R. (2006). *Canadian Television Today.* University of Calgary Press.

Bhatia, V. K., & Gotti, M. (2006). *Explorations in Specialized Genres'. Linguistics Insights: Studies in Language and Communication* (Vol. 25). Peter Lang.

Bianculli, D. (2016). *The Platinum Age of Television: From 'I Love Lucy' to 'The Walking Dead'. How TV Became Terrific.* Doubleday.

Biber, D. (2012). Corpus-based and Corpus-Driven Analyses of Language Variation and Use. In B. Heine & H. Narrog (Eds.), *The Oxford Handbook of Linguistic Analysis* (pp. 160–191). Oxford University Press.

Birdwhistell, R. L. (1952). *Introduction to Kinesics: An Annotated System for the Analysis of Body Motion and Gesture.* University of Louisville Press.

Bordwell, D. (1985). *Narration in the Fiction Film*. University of Wisconsin Press.

Branigan, E. (1992). *Narrative Comprehension and Film*. Routledge.

Brendan, K. (2012). English Version of Quebec Cop Show 19-2 Being Made for CBC. *Montreal Gazette*. Retrieved February 18, 2019, from https://montrealgazette.com/entertainment/english-version-of-quebec-cop-show-19-2-being-made-for-cbc

Chatman, S. (1980). *Story and Discourse. Narrative Structure in Fiction and Film*. Cornell University Press.

Daniele, F., & Garzone, G. (2016). *Communicating Medicine. Popularizing Medicine*. Carocci.

De Saint-Georges, I. (2004). Materiality in Discourse: The Influence of Space and Layout in Making Meaning. In P. LeVine & R. Scollon (Eds.), *Discourse and Technology. Multimodal Discourse Analysis* (pp. 71–87). Georgetown University Press.

Dorland, M., & Charland, M. R. (2002). *Law, Rhetoric and Irony in the Formation of Canadian Civil Culture*. University of Toronto Press.

Eco, U. (2016a, 1st ed. 1990). *I Limiti* dell'Interpretazione. La Nave di Teseo.

Eco, U. (2016b). *Lector in Fabula*. Bompiani.

Eco, U. (2016c, 1st ed. 1962). Opera Aperta. Forma e Indeterminazione nelle Poetiche Contemporanee. Bompiani.

Ekman, P. (1971). Universal and Cultural Differences in Facial Expression of Emotion. *Nebraska Symposium of Motivation, 19*, 207–283. Retrieved July 29, 2017, from http://www.ekman international.com/ResearchFiles/Universals-And-Cultural-Differences-In-Facial-Expressions-Of.pdf

Ekman, P. (1982). *Emotion in the Human Face*. Cambridge University Press.

Ekman, P., & Friesen, W. V. (1969). The Repertoire of Non-verbal Behavior: Categories, Origins, Usage and Coding. *Semiotica, 1*(1), 49–98.

Ekman, P., & Friesen, W. V. (2003). *Unmasking the Face: A Guide to Recognising Emotion from Facial Clues*. Malor Books.

Ekman, P., Friesen, W. V., & Ellsworth, P. (2013). *Emotion in the Human Face: Guidelines for Research and an Integration of Findings*. Pergamont Press Inc.

*Flashpoint*. (n.d.). CTV. Toronto. July 11, 2008–February 6, 2011.

Garzone, G., & Archibald, J. (Eds.). (2007 [2010]). *Discourse, Identities and Roles in Specialized Communication*. Peter Lang.

Gualdo, R., & Telve, S. (2011). *I Linguaggi Specialistici dell'Italiano*. Carocci.

Haworth, K. (2006). The Dynamics of Power and Resistance in Police Interview Discourse. *Discourse and Society., 17*(6), 739–759.

Heydon, G. (2005). *The Language of Police Interviewing: A Critical Analysis.* Palgrave Macmillan.

Holler, J., & Bettie, G. W. (2003). How Iconic Gesture and Speech Interact in the Representation of Meaning: Are Both Aspects Really Integral to the Process? *Semiotica, 146*(1–4), 81–116.

Holler, J., & Bettie, G. W. (2004). The Interpretation of Iconic Gestures and Speech. *5th International Gesture Workshop.* Genova (Italy). Springer Verlag. pp. 15–17.

Jacobs, J., & Peacock, S. (Eds.). (2013). *Television Aesthetics and Style.* Bloomsbury Academic.

Jenner, M. (2016). *American TV Detective Dramas: Serial Investigation.* Palgrave Macmillan.

Jewitt, C. (Ed.). (2013). *The Routledge Handbook of Multimodal Analysis.* Routledge.

Knight, D. (2011). *Multimodality and Active Listenership. A Corpus Approach.* Continuum Internation Publishing Group.

Kress, G. (2010). *Multimodality. A Social Semantic Approach to Contemporary Communication.* Routledge.

Kress, G., & van Leeuwen, T. (1996). *Reading Images: The Grammar of Visual Design.* Routledge.

Lund, K. (2007). The Importance of Gaze and Gesture in Interactive Multimodal Explanation. *Language Resources and Evaluation, 41*(3), 289–303.

Marmor, A. (2014). *The Language of Law.* Oxford University Press.

Martin, J. R., & White, P. R. R. (2005). *The Language of Evaluation. Appraisal in English.* Palgrave Macmillan.

McEnery, T., & Hardie, A. (2012). *Corpus Linguistics: Method, Theory and Practice.* Cambridge University Press.

McNeill, D. (1992). *Head and Mind: What Gesture Reveal about Thought.* University of Chicago Press.

Moorti, S., & Cuklaz, J. (2017). *All-American TV Crime Drama: Feminism and Identity Policy in Law&Order—Special Victims Unit.* I.B. Tauris.

*Motive.* (n.d.). CTV. Vancouver. February 3, 2013–June 7, 2015.

Norris, S. (2004). Multimodal Discourse Analysis: A Conceptual Framework. In P. LeVine & R. Scollon (Eds.), *Discourse and Technology: Multimodal Discourse Analysis* (pp. 1–6). Georgetown University Press.

O'Halloran, K. L. (Ed.). (2004). *Multimodal Discourse Analysis. Systemic Functional Perspectives.* Continuum.

Olandewarju, F. R. (2009). *Forensic Linguistics. An Introduction to the Study of Language and the Laws*. Lincom Europa.

Oswald, B. (2016). *Canadian Cop Drama Goes Out with a Bang*. Winnipeg Free Press. Retrieved February 18, 2019, from https://web.archive.org/web/20170917191802/https://www.winnipegfreepress.com/arts-and-life/entertainment/TV/canadian-cop-drama-goes-out-with-a-bang-401917995.html

Pender, T. N. (07/20/2007). Cop Action in the Works for CTV. *Playback*. Retrieved May 3, 2019, from http://playbackonline.ca/2007/07/20/critical-20070720/

Pinar-Sanz, M. J. (Ed.). (2015). *Multimodality and Cognitive Linguistics*. John Benjamins Publishing Company.

Pozzo, B. (Ed.). (2005). *Ordinary Language and Legal Language*. Giuffré Editore.

Puckett, K. (2016). *Narrative Theory. A Critical Introduction*. Cambridge University Press.

Ricoeur, P. (1997). *Il conflitto delle interpretazioni*. (R. Balzarotti, F. Botturi, & G. Colombo, Trans.). Milan: Jaca Books. [Original Title: *Le Conflict de Interprétations. Essais d'Herménetique, I*, 1969].

Rimé, B., & Schiaratura, L. (1991). Gesture and Speech. In R. S. Feldman & B. Rimé (Eds.), *Foundamentals of Nonverbal Behavior* (pp. 239–284). Cambridge University Press.

Roufa, T. (2019). Law Enforcement Lingo and Police Codes. *The Balance Careers*. Retrieved January 15, 2019, from https://www.thebalancecareers.com/police-speak-how-to-talk-like-a-cop-974868

Royce, T. D. (2007). Intersemiotic Complementarity: A Framework for Multimodal Discourse Analysis. In T. D. Royce & W. L. Bowcher (Eds.), *New Directions in the Analysis of Multimodal Discourse* (pp. 63–110). Lawrence Erlbaum Associates.

Rühleman, C. (2013). *Narrative in English Conversation: A Corpus Analysis of Storytelling*. Cambridge University Press.

Simpson, P., & Mayr, A. (2009). *Language and Power*. Routledge.

Sindroni, M. G., Wildfeuer, J., & O'Halloran, K. L. (Eds.). (2017). *Mapping Multimodal Performance Studies*. Routledge.

Sparks, R. (1992). *Television and the Drama of Crime: Moral Tales and the Place of Crime in Public Life*. Open University Press.

Swain, E. (Ed.). (2010). *Thresholds and Potentialities of Semantic Functional Linguistics: Multilingual, Multimodal and Other Specialized Discourse*. EUT.

The Canadian Press. (2013, March 2). Holly Has a Pretty Good Motive for Moving to Canada. *The Hamilton Spectator.* Retrieved March 14, 2021, from https://www.thespec.com/entertainment/2013/03/02/holly-has-a-pretty-good-motive-for-moving-to-canada.html

Thompson, R. J. (2000). *The Story of Viewers for Quality Television. From Grassroots to Prime Time.* University of Syracuse.

Thompson, L. A., & Massaro, D. W. (1986). Evaluation of Integration of Speech and Pointing Gestures during Referential Understanding. *Journal of Experimental Child Psychology, 42*(1), 144–168.

Wilcox, S. (2004). Language from Gesture. *Behavioral and Brain Sciences, 27*(4), 524–525.

Williams, J. R. (1998). Guidelines for the Use of Multimedia in Instruction. *Proceedings of the Human Factor and Ergonomics Society Annual Meeting, 2,* 1447–1451.

Wolf, W. (2005). Metalepsis as a Transgeneric and Transmedial Phenomenon: A Case Study of the Possibilities of 'Exploring' Narratological Concepts. In J. C. Meister, T. Kindt, W. Schermus, & M. Stein (Eds.), *Narrative Beyond Literary Criticism* (pp. 83–107). De Gruyter.

Wong, L. (2014). *Essential Study Skills* (8th ed.). Cengage Learning.

Yeo, D. (01/03/2018). Canadian TV Crime Drama. Cardinal Returns to Its Elements. *The Star.* Retrieved June 14, 2018, from https://www.thestar.com/entertainment/television/2018/01/03/canadian-tv-crime-drama-cardinal-returns-to-its-elements.html

# 8

# Concluding Remarks

Once this study has concluded the contrastive analysis, much important data and other considerations emerge from the comparison.

Resuming the title of the survey, three keywords emerge—a recurrent number in the examination. The basic multimodal approach analysed could summarise within the actual and metaphorical concepts of *Corpora*, *Corpses* and *Corps* in the acceptation of three differently conceived 'bodies'.

'Corpora' overtly references the linguistic and textual dimensions granted by the tangibility of the materials collected. As anticipated, the entire study concentrates on some television contexts that, per se, occur on various communicative *strata*, none of which generally contemplates the written mode. Hence, the *readable* 'body' results from intense transcription procedures reporting the series' entire verbal contents onto the morphologic layer. The process has constructed analysable materials following the elocution manners adopted by the performers on the scene. The data that form the three corpus *thesauri* report their articulation qualities. For example, words are truncated, where elision phenomena intervened. They abruptly cut when dialogic interruptions required

---

© The Author(s), under exclusive license to Springer Nature Switzerland AG 2021 **345**
F. P. Gentile, *Corpora, Corpses and Corps*,
https://doi.org/10.1007/978-3-030-78276-4_8

turn-taking alterations. Misspelling is present whenever the actor operated some incorrect iteration.

Moreover, further symbolic insertions implement the denotative characteristics of prosodic, rhythmic and emphatic peculiarities. Other transcriber's comments appear as metalinguistic data supporting the linguistic pieces of information, turning the three standard corpora into their updated multimodal versions. This analysis stage represents the linguistic layer of communication that brings to life some expressive peculiarities of television products. Here, dialogues bolster up main affiliation criteria and recognisability in force with the crime TV series genres and formats. Indeed, the languages funnelled onscreen represent one relevant aspect of television trade-offs. They directly reach their audience's ears to form the product's verbal expressive-model and create a prime linguistic imprint charming those end-users. To that extent, the combination of diverse codes (ranging from words to terms and from natural language to specialised discourse) resolves around the palatability of these prominent dialectic structures, seemingly bestowing the "anchorage" (Barthes, 1977, p. 38) a leading role in the mediatic *mise en scène*.

Nonetheless, the etymological value of labels like 'spectator', from Latin *spectare*—to watch—conversely put the entire discourse back on track of the "relay" (ibid., 41) concept elicited by the *visual* 'body'. The second term evoked in the title, 'Corpses', signals the medium's covenant with sight. This bond grants iconicity a semi-autonomous essence that signifies beyond the textual (here intended as verbal) support. The cop shows have become dominant TV products since the 1970s (Richard Sparks, 1992, p. 27; see also Chap. 3). The atmosphere contributes to the bodies' reification (Jacobs & Peacock, 2013, p. 2010) as fetishes on which inhuman perpetrators unleash their fiendish wrath. Simultaneously, corpses are idols observed with the worshipper's care because serving as means for the defilement actuation and condemning proofs.

The mere verbal mode benefits from constant para-verbal implementations. However, the non-verbality of the cinematic sequences is most impressive. It shows cadavers wherever sensational narrations have to quench the viewers' eagerness for carnage. Corpses turn into ghostly echoes of the deeds accomplished by some murderous hands. The narrations ubiquitously float back and forth in time through flashbacks and

## 8 Concluding Remarks 347

flashforwards that need to efficiently explain the facts and guide those individuals cosily observing the scenes in their couches to the end of the story. Images slide one after another with diverse salience focuses that alternately film positive or evil characters from varying angles. Those multiple techniques transmit preconceived portraits of each (anti-)hero even *before* the cognitive assessment of the linguistic performance of his/her lines. In like manner, these communicative features' visual relevance complements equally valid acoustic aids that recount plot-developments and significant events using emotional background music, ambient noises and soundtrack.

From this multimodal perspective, the weaponry display is, again, one emblematic aspect. Notwithstanding its significant law enforcement focus (and despite its primary thematic interest towards murder), *Motive* almost ignores the cliché association of cops and firearms. Here, the infrequent verbal occurrences mirror the para-verbal ones. Instead, the *Flashpoint* and *19-2* TV products extraordinarily *emphasise* such equipment in two different ways. The former adopts a colossal display of guns, bombs and tools of any sort, seldom being critically involved in a gunfight (given the team's most talkative/negotiating goal). The latter is more parsimonious in showing weapons (compared to *Flashpoint*, not generally speaking). However, the director and the scriptwriters make sure that every time a gun is imaged onscreen, it fires at least once. This practice consequently elects those deadly tools as one of the main distinctive traits of both the Toronto and Montreal products on a visual level.

Thirdly, 'Corps' represent the *ideological* 'body'.

Law enforcement units personify the most inherent aspect of the surveyed series. Nevertheless, they work as an unconscious abstract subtext defining the skeleta of the given representations. In light of that, it is evident that no language or image montage could size its target audience's interest if lacking an appealing topic to be dealt with. Explicit dialogues and hard-boiled splatter displays are only as striking as their ideologically connoted taste for the mass-mediatic exorcism of the sombre social fears afflicting North American countries (Canada included). Assassinations, terrorism and (generally) crime allegorically mirror the illnesses corrupting the rule-of-law of modern world nations, where police agents represent hopes and virtues decimating their counterparts in the televised contexts (see also Miller & Stam, 2004, p. 2).

From there, the making of the commodified product originates a cultural substratum. It blends formerly non-existent social minorities (Jenner, 2016, p. 49) and actual pieces of news (i.e., the *Flashpoint* pilot episode) with fictionalised catchy ideas of imagined communities (Anderson, 2006) that would enchant the public. On this ideological stage, the parallelism—or perhaps the contrast—among the three series is evident.

The Québécois TV show, as said, corresponds to some rebuttal of the Francophone Montreal reshaped into its Anglophone alter ego (Chap.6). The social and political statements it contains are implicitly ascribable to the onscreen rendition (O'Halloran, 2004, p. 55).

Nonetheless, the *Motive* case is peculiar for opposite reasons. *19-2* aimed at English-speaking embezzlement of a historically Francophone 'elseworld'. Conversely, the Vancouver product—per se already Anglophone—most likely hankers for anonymity. *Motive*'s international film industry reputation is in tight cooperation with the US cinematic franchise. Therefore, any openly (and strictly) Canadian narrativity cannot afford to jeopardise the latter's broader contextual setting in terms of both trades and investments. The city of Vancouver serves the location functionally. It is not essential to making the series (any other Canadian centre would have fitted; see Chap. 5).

*Flashpoint*'s perspective is also political. The Toronto-based series does not concentrate on any linguistic or geographic connoted frame. It prefers a purely ideological identification employing the establishment of the most cold-blooded rationality undertaken by Canadian tactical units (as a societal metaphor) utterly opposed to the childish 'fist first' philosophy of its US neighbour (Chap. 4).

The analysis of similar case studies allows the examiner to shift from East to the utmost West of the Canadian territory (excluding the Northern *weltanschauungen*). It slides along the 49th parallel drawing the border between Canada and the United States: a border which neither performers and spectators cross or mention as if it were located far away from the narrated places. The observation also permits distinguishing the narrative characteristics among diverse urban context fictionalisations within the

## 8 Concluding Remarks 349

same confederation. Here, spaces longitudinally detach from each other via three time zones.

Montreal is the first largest city in Quebec and the second most populated centre in Canada, right after Toronto (Ontario). Vancouver—British Columbia—demands its portrayal as well, as it represents one major harbour on the Pacific coast. Moreover, the city is the third Canadian agglomeration (a statistic that also grants the metropolitan area the fourth position in the most densely populated cities list in North America, preceded by New York, San Francisco and Mexico City).[1] The census, then, together with high crime rates[2] majorly contributes to televising Vancouver's relevant fascination concerning its police procedural approach.

Eventually, *Flashpoint* is different from *19-2* Montreal. The latter's goal is *merchandising* the unique reality of Quebec as if it were a deeply rooted Anglophone relocalisation. Instead, the former presents Toronto megacity as an evident Canadian *brand*. It also dichotomously branches from *Motive*'s Vancouver, which opts for a more sombre non-iconic transposition (conversely retrievable on the series verbal dimension).

Similar considerations clarify how TV crime drama content communicates on a general stage. Here, the linguistic domain occurs in a co-dependent but slightly minor relationship with a visually palpable one, where both levels link to an ideological/cultural premise.

Some more pragmatic investigation speculations move deeper.

The three corpora, gathered together, have shown 0.95 per cent of vocabulary variation and 106.54 words-per-minute rates on the linguistic ground. It immediately contrasted the average esteems of 1.38 per cent of tokens versus types and 104.37 WPM. Those numbers involved a mild elocution pace, anyhow ascribable to the oral dimension. This rhythm positioned far from the originally written nature of fundamental scripts that the actors interpreted on the scene. Yet, one should bear in mind that the corpora is based on the sole performed acts, through the transcription procedures disregarding the said written modes. Data also corresponded to low rates in terms of vocabulary heterogeneous choices.

As already explained, the direct consequences of those observations summon certain linguistic (verbal) usages. The shows' spoken language demonstrates a little attention to the interactive oral dimension. Shared

## 350  F. P. Gentile

verbality aspects (language and idiolects) characterise the conversation participants, but they remain minimal and monotonous.

These same expressive pattern generalisations extend to the crime drama genre. Indeed, the all-inclusive scores do not represent a perfect match with the three series of individual results per se. There, slight statistical deflections tend to mould the curve towards one direction or the other, accordingly preferring faster elocution rhythms or higher lexical turnovers.

From the overall point of view, natural language occurrences use plain English. The sentences adhere to an S-V-O standard phrastic order and grammatical constructions of the verbal syntagms. For example, the present/past perfect tenses co-occur with auxiliary verbs in middle positions distancing from the spoken discourse praxis elliptical articulations.

Despite similar elements, other aspects diverge from standard levels. The pronunciation criteria adopted in the series are quite often markedly Canadian-English set of varieties. One may notice frequent open-vowels, starting point alterations typically determined by British Columbia Canadian rising. For instance, it would occur in the emblematic pronunciation of 'about' as /əˈbəʊt / in place of /əˈbaʊt/, and in the backed and rounded /o/ and the accentuated raise of /aɪ/ phonemes. Other phonological peculiarities are the Canadian shift phenomena (e.g., the retraction of /æ/ sounds turning RP /ˈænd/ into the peculiar /eɪnd/ pronunciation of the conjunction 'and') and the consonant merging praxis ('Toronto' becomes /toˈɹɒɾo/ instead of the standard /təˈɹɒntoʊ/) of Ontario regionalisms.

Those traits are even more evident and unexpected in *19-2*, which, set in Montreal, has been defined here as an *Anglo-phony-sation* of its actual Franco-Québécois milieu. The show relinquished every influx from Francophone phonetics and pronunciation to speak an accent-free English meant to reach the TV sets of all Canada's spectators and beyond.

When natural language alternates to specialised communication, the tables turn to a more emotionally neutral and unconnoted stage. Discourses dealing with police jargon and hierarchical organisation tend to blend natural language and low-specialisation terminology to propose detechnified professional usages of specifically designed codes that translate into popularisation. Other professional domains happen to intrude into those speech contexts like legal procedures (in interrogatories), medical discourse and specialised knowledge (when narrations require pivotal autopsies or cop-performed first-aid rescues), IT and finances (checking persons of interest statuses).

The sectorial precision has to strike TV viewers, who should plausibly receive and interpret them as actual 'specialised' language. Those occurrences emulate the formal characteristics of the discourse, simultaneously avoiding the emblematic obscurity of high-technicality levels. That would circumvent useless and intricate meanings and misinterpretations that could fail the accessibility of the said lay end-user contents. On these occasions, natural language juxtaposes to facilitated professional codes (tending to the divulging dimension). This combination mediatically fakes specialised communication via emulative discoursal patterns reproposing wanted ungrammatical formulations. For example, technical utterances under linguistic economy principles would erase superfluous sentence elements conventionally mandatory for correct usages. Still, they would indulge in denotative formal register and tone (with passive voice and deagentivisation preferences in place of active verbs). Some significant terminology supports and semantic densifications would operate through domain-specific alterations of verbal regencies and preposition dependencies. Suppose those expedients successfully manage the goal of resulting credible ESPs. In that case, more work is performed by laconism. It would influence either the syntactic structures (via linguistic economy) and the utterly unemotional communicativeness of those specialised communication passages. Moreover, it would negate any connoted implementations to purely denotative speeches.

On the communication level, the pronunciation-characterising features possibly represent one of the main expedients contributing to the connoted commodification aim. In the national broadcast (see Chap. 3), they apply to increase the percentages of wanted "Cancon" ('Canadian content', Gittins, 1999, p. 95) onscreen.

The crime genre fortune relates to police tasks mostly associated with criminals' apprehension (sometimes fugitives) or real-time city hot-spots interventions. Here, the verbal support sustains the process making the genre nationally identifiable. Language flags the many violations occurring within the shows to let law enforcement officers catch the

**352    F. P. Gentile**

perpetrators. Consequentially, emulating once more actual police discourse conventions, the prime linguistic (verbal) formulations often relate to street names or urban areas. This naming procedure determines the TV product recognisability with a given Canadian territory and the represented community imaginary. Visual toponym displays *non-verbally* mirror those *verbal* 'Cancon' deployments. They contextualise the narrations in the city—thus nation and national ideology—hosting the product. On that level, the *Flashpoint* TV series is quite attentive to its onscreen representability. Even here, however, there are exceptions.

Despite Canada's willingness to *invade* US television companies with its national productions, many Canadian locations run broadcasting business partnerships with other television companies moving their merchandise up North. In light of that, some urban centres in Canada (like Vancouver, in British Columbia) have no interest in being labelled as 100 per cent Canadian, since they are related to an enormous US TV production trade-off setting North American series in the city and marking them up as US places nonetheless.[3] The same Canadianness that *19-2* and *Flashpoint* funnel at different degrees is less consistent in *Motive*. This latter case televises an almost anonymous city that could have located anywhere else. In the show, the only Canadian mark remains its phonological binding inflexion.

The genre expressiveness consists of (mostly) non-verbal and para-verbal features. Extensively described in Chap. 7, those aspects of communication are potent meaning-carries to the television genre. The linguistic relevance of verbal-dimension dialogues seems secondary to the prosodic and rhythmic traits of the para-verbal layer. They serve as meta-linguistic, informative data that describe the medium expressive context. In like manner, interactions can deliver the emotional charge essential for the exchanges' utmost understandability.

The non-verbal acoustic salience supports cinematic phases and dialogic passages with highly explanatory and descriptive ambient noises and music narrating the situations. Sight is one more crucial sense stimulated by TV contents for the appraisal of its plots and themes.

The visual salience of the Canadian crime drama, as observed so far, peremptorily focuses on thematically relevant scenic elements. They could implement the descriptive and narrative aim of the product.

## 8 Concluding Remarks 353

Moreover, they would serve the investigative slant of similar products, allowing the viewer to peruse some details and launch their deductive lucubrations to resolve the stories. Because of the cop-show primary goal of recounting the righteous, officers always have the foreground. Main front or side views and middle-to-close shots turn into close-ups or cut-ins whenever character-related details represent essential storyline elements. In many cases, gears and uniforms are as fundamental as cops, underlining the absolute equipment value in helping the officers with their jobs.

Oppositely, evil is always proposed in the shadow. Darker and gloomier atmospheres emphasise dangerous and corrupted contingencies. Concerning the different slants of the narrations, malicious individuals rendition through the psychological pains, driving their actions or the instinctive inhumanity that passionately caresses their eagerness for death. Nonetheless, their visual salience is always pressing but fleeting. Until their final apprehension, those people frequently appear as lurking or fugitive, or even brazenly coming up against the detectives accusing them. According to the criminal's social statuses, this representation changes from scared adolescents/lower-class labourers to presumptuous upper-class managers. In between heroes and villains are the victims.

Criminal investigations would frequently involve bodies when the plots are not about open clashes among law enforcement agents and serial perpetrators of all sorts. Experts analyse them to comprehend the illegal dynamics leading to someone's demise. On that level, the camera (as much as the spectator's) eyes' voyeuristic attitude would plausibly indulge in the details of the death. The strategy would frame flesh, blood and bones, livid limbs and lifeless orbs until the vulture-like famine of such a saprophagous curiosity would extinguish them. As for the characters, their narrations differ in line with the episodical recount of the stories. Sweeping horizontal sequences preliminarily contextualise the facts. Then, they turn into narrower vertical passages as tension rises to lead to climaxes subverting the events. Frame structures approach the situations more closely, facilitating a pressing pathos that ultimately breaks free at the end of the episodes. This narrative event translates into the filming, returning ampler aerated conclusive sequences re-establishing the peace.

Overall, the characterising traits described in Chap. 7 may summarise the crucial communication structures of the Canadian contemporary TV crime drama.

Low levels of linguistical density and a limited vocabulary select relevant words and terms borrowed from different natural and specialised domains and registers. Linguistics adheres to the police investigative skeleton and actively resolutive conducts disseminated throughout the narrations. The verbal dimension remains a solid third-level aspect. Secondary para-verbal expressiveness surpasses it via vocally performative acts varying the scenes' emotional charges and descriptive emphases. Those acts mostly funnel suspense and tension as the main feelings recounted onscreen.

Nonetheless, both modes come after the primary visual communicativeness of the non-verbal traits. This latter channel constitutes the most complex skeleton of the TV medium per se. One the one hand, it is an inextricable simultaneous combination of body language, gesture-in-talk and facial mimicry. They transmit all the shades of the emotional and performatively expressive *spectra* of natural and sectorial communication. On the other hand, cinematic techniques come along, ranging from camera movement, position and framing salience to montage strategies, plus photography supports. Together, the non-verbal qualities perfectly synchronise with the other two dimensions for a multimodal rendition of targeted exchanges.

The protagonists handle the most relevant visual salience through closer shots than the villains. Many sequences of bodies, evidence and tools (e.g., uniforms, weapons, vehicles) reel in intense static-to-moving frames describing details better than any spoken words. Verbality, here, would be unable to display their actual fascinating circumstances that seize the spectator's attention. Similarly, horizontal and vertical narrative sequences alternate the vastness of Canadian open spaces to shallow indoor passages. Bright or gloomy colours reveal meta-narrative data about the scenes accessed through superficial observations. They tell the dangers and risks that an individual placidly loitering in a tight corridor in the night-time would run compared to other unaware passer-by people exposed in the middle of an uncluttered square at midday.

## 8 Concluding Remarks 355

The different communicative and expressive rates of the various dimensions give the multisemiotic nature of the languages involved (meant as multimodal and multilayered *strata* extending beyond the mere linguistic sides). This expressivity co-occurs harmonically to produce coherent meanings in the TV artificial and emulative context.

Moreover, crime drama expressive slants could originate from many descriptive models. The characteristics retrieved in the examined corpora and contrastively observed to outline the genre's generalisable communicative patterns can only function as *one* of them. In addition to that, the three products analysed are representative of a small slice of the entire narrative panorama focusing on this theme.

Several differences have emerged between the narrative and communicative modes of the *19-2* TV serial (as police procedural), the *Motive* TV hybrid (as *whydunnit* investigative) and the *Flashpoint* TV series (as action cop show). Nonetheless, these do not just derive from the different format structures preferring centripetal (mostly serial-related) or centrifugal (mostly series-related) complexity levels. They correspond to the diverse perspectival focuses, leading plot-determined narrative events. Other subcategories of this massively prolific genre could produce as many expressive deflections, possibly modifying this study's results. A hard-boiled narration would inevitably emphasise splatter details of corpses and killings that would alter the salience of genre-descriptive tendencies (concentrating more on blood and weapons than procedures). A heist drama could adopt harsh linguistic solutions closer to underworld situations than police station settings. Its filming rates could give more prominence to criminals (oxymoronically playing as heroes instead of being villains) than cops, too.

In conclusion, the present examination is a pioneering one, since the literature on the matter has, so far, only targeted the cultural *or* the narrative layers of the TV contents. It has never reached a similar all-inclusive analysis of artistic, cultural, narrative, (extra-)linguistic and communicative co-occurring modes. Besides, the multimodal channels surveyed gather around the pivotal expressive power of the Canadian contemporary crime drama. Still, they are generally valid for the broaderr understanding of the genre. The investigation workings represent part of a more prominent study to be implemented in time, along with the

**356**     F. P. Gentile

evolution of the involved disciplinary methodologies and the analytical goals approaching further case studies, always expanding and reshaping the current state of the art, the genre and media.

## Notes

1. Statistics Canada. 'Population and dwelling count, for census metropolitan areas and census agglomerations, 2006 and 2001 census'. http://www12.statcan.ca/census-recensement/2006/dp-pd/hlt/97-550/Index.cfm?TPL=P1C&Page=RETR&LANG=Eng&T=201&S=3&O=D&RPP=150. See also World Population Review. 'Vancouver population 2019'. http://worldpopulationreview.com/world-cities/vancouver-population/ (accessed May 11, 2019).
2. Vv. Aa. (Nov. 2018) 'West Vancouver ranked one of Canada's 100 most dangerous places'. *Daily Hive*. https://dailyhive.com/vancouver/west-vancouver-dangerous-places-macleans-ranking (accessed May 11, 2019).
3. Vancouver is one of the most preferred places for shooting both Canadian and US television shows, also concerning low production costs (see Chap. 5). One emblematic instance is North Vancouver, often picked up to be the cinematic alter ego of Seattle city because of their relevant urban structure affinities.

## References

*19-2. Bravo!*(n.d.). Vancouver. January 29, 2014–August 22, 2016.

Anderson, B. (2006 [1983]). *Imagined Communities. Reflections on the Origin and Spread of Nationalism*. Verso. Retrieved June, 28, 2019, from https://is.muni.cz/el/1423/jaro2016/SOC757/um/61816961/Benedict_Anderson_Imagined_Communities.pdf

Barthes, R. (1977). *Image, Music, Text*. Fontana.

*Flashpoint*. (n.d.). CTV. Toronto. July 11, 2008–February 6, 2011.

Gittins, S. (1999). *CTV: The Television Wars*. Stoddart.

Jacobs, J., & Peacock, S. (Eds.). (2013). *Television Aesthetics and Style*. Bloomsbury Academic.

Jenner, M. (2016). *American TV Detective Dramas: Serial Investigation*. Palgrave Macmillan.

## 8 Concluding Remarks 357

Miller, T., & Stam, R. (2004). *A Companion to Film Theory*. Blackwell.

*Motive*. (n.d.). CTV. Vancouver. February 3, 2013–June 7, 2015.

Numeris. (n.d.). en.numeris.ca

O'Halloran, K. L. (Ed.). (2004). *Multimodal Discourse Analysis. Systemic Functional Perspectives*. Continuum.

Sparks, R. (1992). *Television and the Drama of Crime. Moral Tales and the Place of Crime in Public Life*. Open University Press.

Statistics Canada. (n.d.). Population and Dwelling Counts for Census Metropolitan Areas and Census Agglomerations, 2006 and 2001 Census. Retrieved May 11, 2019, from http://www12.statcan.ca/census-recensement/2006/dp-pd/hlt/97-550/Index.cfm?TPL=P1C&Page=RETR&LANG=Eng&T=201&S=3&O=D&RPP=150

Vv.Aa. (2018, November). West Vancouver Ranked One of Canada's 100 Most Dangerous Places. *Daily Hive*. Retrieved May 11, 2019, from https://daily-hive.com/vancouver/west-vancouver-dangerous-places-macleans-ranking

# Appendix

## List of the *Flashpoint* Episodes

**Table A.1**  List of the *Flashpoint* episodes, season 1

| *FLASHPOINT*, SEASON 1 (JULY 2008–FEBRUARY 2009) | |
|---|---|
| EP. N°  TITLE—DIRECTOR/WRITERS | AIR DATE |
| 1  *Scorpio*—D. Frazee/S. Morgenstern, M. Ellis | 07/11/2008 |
| 2  *First in line*—D. Frazee/S. Morgenstern, M. Ellis | 07/18/2008 |
| 3  *The element of surprise*—D. Frazee/S. Morgenstern, M. Ellis | 07/24/2008 |
| 4  *Asking for flowers*—C. Johnson/T. Cameron | 07/31/2008 |
| 5  *Who's George?*—H. Dale/A. Barken | 08/07/2008 |
| 6  *Attention shoppers*—H. Dale/T. Forbes | 08/14/2008 |
| 7  *He knows his brother*—S. Surjik/A. Barken | 08/21/2008 |
| 8  *Never kissed a girl*—C. Binamé/E. Spalding | 09/11/2008 |
| 9  *Planets aligned*—K. Makin/T. Forbes | 09/18/2008 |
| 10  *Eagle two*—S. Surjik/T. Cameron | 01/09/2009 |
| 11  *Backwards days*—E. Canuel/E. Spalding | 01/16/2009 |
| 12  *Haunting the barn*—D. Frazee/S. Morgenstern, M. Ellis | 01/23/2009 |
| 13  *Between heartbeats*—Frazee/Morgenstern, Ellis, Cameron | 02/13/2009 |

© The Author(s), under exclusive license to Springer Nature Switzerland AG 2021
F. P. Gentile, *Corpora, Corpses and Corps*,
https://doi.org/10.1007/978-3-030-78276-4

360     Appendix

**Table A.2** List of the *Flashpoint* episodes, season 2

FLASHPOINT, SEASON 2 (FEBRUARY 2009–NOVEMBER 2009[a])

| EP. N° | TITLE—DIRECTOR/WRITERS | AIR DATE |
|---|---|---|
| 1 | *Business as usual*—D. Frazee/S. Morgenstern, M. Ellis | 02/27/2009 |
| 2 | *The fortress*—E. Canuel/I. Weir | 03/06/2009 |
| 3 | *Clean hands*—D. Frazee/A. Barken | 03/13/2009 |
| 4 | *Aisle 13*—S. Surjik/J. Hurst | 04/03/2009 |
| 5 | *The perfect family*—E. Canuel/A. Barken, J. Callaghan | 04/10/2009 |
| 6 | *Remote control*—C. Binamé/R. Cochrane | 04/24/2009 |
| 7 | *Perfetc storm*—H. Dale/T. Cameron | 05/01/2009 |
| 8 | *Last dance*—C. Binamé/S. Morgenstern, M. Ellis | 05/08/2009 |
| 9 | *Exit wounds*—D. Frazee/R. Cochrane | 05/15/2009 |
| 10 | *One wrong move*—D. Frazee/S. Morgenstern, M. Ellis, J. Hurst | 09/25/2009 |
| 11 | *Never let you down*—K. Girotti/J. Hurst, S. Scarrow | 10/02/2009 |
| 12 | *Just a man*—H. Dale/R. Adams | 10/09/2009 |
| 13 | *Custody*—P.A. Kaufman/B. Carney | 10/16/2009 |
| 14 | *Coming to you live*—C. Binamé/I. Weir | 10/23/2009 |
| 15 | *The Farm*—E. Canuel/I. Weir, M.R Byer, T. Hancock | 10/30/2009 |
| 16 | *You think you know someone*—D. Frazee/A. Barken | 11/06/2009 |
| 17 | *The good citizen*—T. Southam/P. Mitchell | 11/13/2009 |
| 18 | *Behind the blue lines*—D. Frazee/S. Morgenstern, M. Ellis | 11/20/2009 |

[a]The second season of *Flashpoint* was aired simultaneously in both Canada and the US. The two countries transmitted the series over the same dates from episodes 1 to 9, while the remaining nine episodes were televised with different broadcasting dates in the US, where the *Flashpoint* TV series finished on 9 July 2010 instead of 20 November 2009

**Table A.3** List of the *Flashpoint* episodes, season 3

FLASHPOINT, SEASON 3 (JULY 2010–FEBRUARY 2011)

| EP. N° | TITLE—DIRECTOR/WRITERS | AIR DATE |
|---|---|---|
| 1 | *Unconditional love*—D. Frazee/S. Morgenstern, M. Ellis | 07/16/2010 |
| 2 | *Severed ties*—H. Dale/T. Hancock, M.R. Byer | 08/06/2010 |
| 3 | *Follow the leader*—D. Frazee/J. Hurst | 08/13/2010 |
| 4 | *Whatever it takes*—H. Dale/G. Manson | 08/20/2010 |
| 5 | *The other Lane*—E. Canuel/B. Theodore | 09/03/2010 |
| 6 | *Jumping at shadows*—K. Makin/S. Morgenstern, M. Ellis | 09/10/2010 |
| 7 | *Acceptable risk*—D. Frazee/P. Davis | 09/17/2010 |
| 8 | *Collateral damage*—K. Makin/A. Brindle | 01/04/2011 |
| 9 | *Thicker than blood*—D. Frazee/A. Stevens | 01/11/2011 |
| 10 | *Terror*—E. Canuel/M.R. Byer, T. Hancock | 01/18/2011 |
| 11 | *No promises*—C. Binamé/R. Cochrane | 11/25/2011 |
| 12 | *I'd do anything*—H. Shaver/P. Davis, B. Theodore | 01/01/2011 |

*(continued)*

**Appendix** **361**

**Table A.3** (continued)

| FLASHPOINT, SEASON 3 (JULY 2010–FEBRUARY 2011) | | |
|---|---|---|
| EP. N° TITLE—DIRECTOR/WRITERS | | AIR DATE |
| 13 *Fault lines (part 1)*[a]—D. Frazee/S. Morgenstern, M. Ellis | | 01/06/2011 |

[a]In the episode finale, Ed—still wearing his uniform but devoid of his weapon—has an altercation with a man at a traffic light: the man eventually gets off the car and pulls his gun against the officer and fires a shot, then the scene is cut also terminating the season. The instalment is proposed by means of a suspended end continuing in season 4, episode 1—*Fault lines (part 2)*—in order to increase the *Flashpoint* TV series spectators' affiliation in light of their irrevocable curiosity to finding out whether the protagonist has died or not (although the fourth season is not included in the current investigation).

Considering the *Flashpoint* TV series three seasons (aired between July 2008 and February 2011) analysed in this survey, one would notice the relevance of the titles as well, finding out that in the forty-four intalments observed, only 15 (34.1 per cent) actually are eligible of a clear police/crime drama slant—highlighted in bold type in the tables—and ranging from the strictly terminological value (*Scorpio; Eagle two; Exit wounds; Custody; Behind the blue lines; Collateral damage*) to the conveyance of a thrilling feeling (e.g., *The element of surprise; The fortress; Jumping at shadows; Terror*) mirroring the aim of the product. Other minor 11.36 per cent (five episodes signalled in light pink boxes) emphasise binding relationships of family or brotherhood; there, *Thicker than blood*—s03e09—is even more relevant in terms of ideology, by resuming the 'blood it thicker than water' idiom and moulding it in an even stronger manner, which alludes to the indistructible connection build by team members of corps units. The remaining 54.54 per cent of *Flashpoint Corpus* instalments adopt a different communicative strategy, where titles are formulated through an appealing—more topically-neutral—procedure (especially in season 1, and secondarily in season 2) mostly ascribable to a mixture of action and romanticised plots (e.g., *Asking for flowers; Never kissed a girl; Planets aligned; Last dance; Unconditional love; Whatever it takes*).

On the rating perspective, the series also demonstrates it has constantly met the favour of its wide public of spectators, always maintaining its level of TV viewers over the years and reaching peaks of more than 1.8 million end-users many times (mostly in season 2), positioning itself on a high-average ratio on the crime drama Canadian TV market, also

**362**    Appendix

outnumbering other similar North American products like *NCIS: Los Angeles* (USA), *Cold Case* (USA), *Law&Order: SVU* (USA), *The Mentalist* (USA), even if remaining underneath major series like *CSI Miami* (USA), *Criminal Minds* (USA), *NCIS* (USA), *CSI* (USA), *Bones* (USA).[1]

## List of the *Motive* episodes

**Table A.4**    List of the *Motive* episodes, season 1

| *MOTIVE*, SEASON 1 (FEBRUARY–MAY 2013) | | |
|---|---|---|
| EP. N° | TITLE—DIRECTOR/WRITERS | AIR DATE |
| 1 | *Creeping Tom*—B. Hughes/D. Cerone | 02/03/2013 |
| 2 | *Crimes of passion*—D. Frazee/D. Heaton | 02/10/2013 |
| 3 | *Pushover*—C.H. Smith/W. Zmak | 02/17/2013 |
| 4 | *Against all odds*—C. Johnson/T. Cameron | 03/03/2013 |
| 5 | *Public enemy*—B. Hughes/J. Thorpe | 03/10/2013 |
| 6 | *Detour*—S. Gunnarsson/K. Collins | 03/14/2013 |
| 7 | *Out of the past*—A. Mikita/D. Heaton | 03/21/2013 |
| 8 | *Undertow*—K. Makin/D. Frykland | 03/28/2013 |
| 9 | *Framed*—S. Gunnarsson/D. Frykland | 04/04/2013 |
| 10 | *Fallen angel*—A. Mikita/W. Zmak | 04/25/2013 |
| 11 | *Brute force*—C.H. Smith/D. Heaton | 05/02/2013 |
| 12 | *Ruthless*—S. Pleszczynski/K. Collins | 05/09/2013 |
| 13 | *The one who got away*—D. Frazee/J. Thorpe | 05/16/2013 |

**Table A.5**    List of the *Motive* episodes, season 2

| *MOTIVE*, SEASON 2 (MARCH–MAY 2014) | | |
|---|---|---|
| EP. N° | TITLE—DIRECTOR/WRITERS | AIR DATE |
| 1 | *Raw deal*—D. Frazee/D. Heaton | 03/06/2014 |
| 2 | *They made me a criminal*—S. Gunnarsson/S. Dodd | 03/13/2014 |
| 3 | *Overboard*—M. Almas/K. Collins | 03/20/2014 |
| 4 | *Deception*—D. Frazee/J. Thorpe | 03/27/2014 |
| 5 | *Dead end*—A. Mikita/D. Schreyer | 04/03/2014 |
| 6 | *Bad blonde*—S. Gunnarsson/D. Heaton | 04/10/2014 |
| 7 | *Pitfall*—F. Gerber/K. Collins | 04/17/2014 |
| 8 | *Angels with dirty faces*—A. Mikita/D. Frykland | 04/24/2014 |
| 9 | *Abandoned*—T.J. Scott/W. Zmak | 05/01/2014 |
| 10 | *Nobody lives forever*—J. Chechik/J.Thorpe | 05/08/2014 |
| 11 | *A bullet for Joey*—A. Mikita/P. Redford | 05/15/2014 |
| 12 | *Kiss of death*—S. Gunnarsson/D. Heaton, T. Pound | 05/22/2014 |
| 13 | *For you I die*—S. Pleszczynski/J. Thorpe | 05/29/2014 |

**Appendix** **363**

**Table A.6** List of the *Motive* episodes, season 3

| *MOTIVE*, SEASON 3 (MARCH–JUNE 2015) | | |
| --- | --- | --- |
| EP. N° | TITLE—DIRECTOR/WRITERS | AIR DATE |
| 1 | *6 months later*—D. Frazee/D. Heaton | 03/08/2015 |
| 2 | *Calling the shots*—S. Gunnarsson/S. Dodd | 03/15/2015 |
| 3 | *Oblivion*—J. Chechik/K. Hill | 03/22/2015 |
| 4 | *The Glass house*—D. Frazee/T. Pound | 03/29/2015 |
| 5 | *The suicide tree*—S. Gunnarsson/M. MacLennan | 04/05/2015 |
| 6 | *Fallen*—B. Hughes/J. Puckrin | 04/12/2015 |
| 7 | *Pilot error*—S. Pleszczynski/S. Dodd | 04/19/2015 |
| 8 | *Reversal of fortune*—S. Gunnarsson/D. Vignale | 04/26/2015 |
| 9 | *Best enemies*—A. Mikita/K. Hill | 05/03/2015 |
| 10 | *Purgatory*—A. Kroekoer/M. MacLellan | 05/10/2015 |
| 11 | *The amateurs*—S. Pleszczynski/D. Heaton | 05/24/2015 |
| 12 | *Frampton comes alive*—M. Herndl/D. Vignale | 05/31/2015 |
| 13 | *A problem like Maria*—A. Mikita/S. Dodd, D. Heaton | 06/07/2015 |

On the linguistic level, an evaluation of the *Motive* TV hybrid instalment titles would highlight some semantic peculiarities in line with the *Flashpoint* ones. Here, the total number of thirty-nine episodes could be read through a separation into three groups: 35.9 per cent (fourteen episodes) related to evident criminal cases and thriller stories (e.g., *Crimes of passion; Public enemy; Brute force; They made me a criminal; A bullet for Joey; The suicide tree;* in light blue boxes), 17.9 per cent (seven episodes) recounting plot developments from the personal-emotional state of mind of the characters involved in the series (*Against all odds; Out of the past; Ruthless; Abandoned; Oblivion; Fallen; Reversal of fortune;* in light pink boxes), thus, putting under the spotlight the passionate dimension relating broken people and homicides, 46.2 per cent (eighteen episodes) of less specific (yet charming) titles.

Moreover, it is worth noting a stronger syntheticism in the ideation of these summing up captions serving as titles of the *Motive* TV series episodes than in *Flashpoint*. While the first product opted for some more elaborate options, this other case study evidences a lot of 'essential' choices limited to the use of just one precise and evocative term providing its users with all the preliminary bits of information they need before the actual observation of the related instalment, mirroring in the selection of

**364** Appendix

the *Motive*'s titles the same accuracy demonstrated in the construction of the dialogic sequences structuring the *Corpus*.

A symptomatic difference between the *Flashpoint* and the *Motive* products is also appraisable through this latter TV trade-off viewership. If the former series premiered with a relatively high rating that physiologically flattened in the second episode of the first season to subsequently readjust its scores upwards throughout the duration of the show, this second case study represented a less appreciated showcase, where fluctuations in terms of share remained wide and constant all over the broadcasting period and often declined under the 1 million spectator threshold, although brushing against the 1.45–46 million roof a couple of times between seasons 2 and 3.[2]

## List of the *19-2* Episodes

**Table A.7**   List of the *19-2* episodes, season 1

| 19-2, SEASON 1 (JANUARY–APRIL 2014) | | |
|---|---|---|
| EP. N° | TITLE—DIRECTOR/WRITERS | AIR DATE |
| 1 | *Partners*—L. Choquette/B.M. Smith | 01/29/2014 |
| 2 | *Deer*—L. Choquette/B.M. Smith | 02/05/2014 |
| 3 | *Welfare day*—L. Choquette/B.M. Smith | 02/12/2014 |
| 4 | *The party*—L. Choquette/B.M. Smith | 02/19/2014 |
| 5 | *Home*—E. Canuel/J. McKeown | 02/26/2014 |
| 6 | *Turf*—E. Canuel/D. Vignale | 03/05/2014 |
| 7 | *Lovers*—E. Canuel/J. McKeown | 03/12/2014 |
| 8 | *Medals*—L. Choquette/J. McKeown | 03/19/2014 |
| 9 | *Islands*—L. Choquette/E. Spalding | 03/26/2014 |
| 10 | *Winter*—L. Choquette/B.M. Smith | 04/02/2014 |

**Table A.8**   List of the *19-2* episodes, season 2

| 19-2, SEASON 2 (JANUARY–MARCH 2015) | | |
|---|---|---|
| EP. N° | TITLE—DIRECTOR/WRITERS | AIR DATE |
| 1 | *School*—D. Grou (aka Podz)/B.M. Smith | 01/19/2015 |
| 2 | *Disorder*—L. Choquette/J. McKeown | 01/26/2015 |
| 3 | *Borders*—L. Choquette/B.M. Smith, N. Troubetzkoy | 02/02/2015 |
| 4 | *Tribes*—L. Choquette/J. McKeown | 02/09/2015 |
| 5 | *Rock garden*—E. Canuel/D. Vignale | 02/16/2015 |
| 6 | *Tables*—E. Canuel/B.M. Smith | 02/23/2015 |

*(continued)*

**Table A.8** (continued)

| 19-2, SEASON 2 (JANUARY–MARCH 2015) | | |
|---|---|---|
| EP. N° | TITLE—DIRECTOR/WRITERS | AIR DATE |
| 7 | *Property line*—E. Canuel/N. Troubetzkoy | 03/02/2015 |
| 8 | *Babylon*—L. Choquette/D. Vignale | 03/09/2015 |
| 9 | *Orphans*—L. Choquette/J. McKeown | 03/16/2015 |
| 10 | *Bridges*—L. Choquette/B. M. Smith | 03/23/2015 |

**Table A.9** List of the *19-2* episodes, season 3

| 19-2, SEASON 3 (JUNE–AUGUST 2016) | | |
|---|---|---|
| EP. N° | TITLE—DIRECTOR/WRITERS | AIR DATE |
| 1 | *Burn pie*—S. Gunnarsson/B.M. Smith | 06/20/2016 |
| 2 | *Rescue*—S. Gunnarsson/J. McKeown | 06/27/2016 |
| 3 | *Chicken*—S. Gunnarsson/N. Troubetzkoy | 07/04/2016 |
| 4 | *Bitch*—S. Pleszczynski/B.M. Smith, L. Kamm | 07/11/2016 |
| 5 | *Protest pants*—S. Pleszczynski/J. McKeown | 07/18/2016 |
| 6 | *City*—S. Pleszczynski/A.L. Bingeman | 07/25/2016 |
| 7 | *Honeymoon*—S. Pleszczynski/B.M. Smith | 08/01/2016 |
| 8 | *Fall*—L. Choquette/N. Troubetzkoy | 08/08/2016 |
| 9 | *Gone*—L. Choquette/A.L. Bingeman | 08/15/2016 |
| 10 | *Water*—L. Choquette/B. M. Smith | 08/22/2016 |

Observing the *19-2* serial in comparison with the other two cases investigated in this study, one would without doubt indulge on the evaluation of its episode titles. Where the *Flashpoint* and *Motive* TV series adopted a mixture of different topics in their titles as well as in the contents of their related plots (associating law enforcement perspectives with familiar relationships, emotions, everyday situations and catchy idioms), the laconism of the *19-2 Corpus* utterly corresponds to its serial hermetic procedure naming the instalments. Here, indeed, only four in thirty episodes are presented via two-word titles (*The Party*, s01e04, is not included in the count since the first word merely is a definite article, hence it does not even represent a polyrhematic phrase), and yet none of the entire collection can be recognised in accordance with relevant salient implicatures. As a consequence, the Montreal-based television product appears as a definitely aseptic environment, in which police procedural operations are set. The only episode title somehow recalling the crime theme possibly is *Rescue*—s03e02—although such a word does not bindingly imply the intervention of public service agents, thus leaving the title's merits in a dull limbo. Contrariwise, about one third of the instalments (eight in total) examined shows a sort of proclivity that, rather than criminological, seems to aim at declaring a political-like statement (*Welfare Day*; *Disorder*; *Borders*; *Tribes*; *Property lines*; *Bridges*; *Protestant pants*; *City*; in light grey boxes) on some major Canadian—fictionalised—social issues. A similar 'monotony', however, could conceivably derive from the solid coherence carried out in the serial on the ground of its director/writers restricted group selected to working on the elaboration of the subjects, in lieu of the very ampler heterogeneity displayed in *Fashpoint* and *Motive*.

## Notes

1. Data retrieved from BBM Canada, 'Top Programs—Total Canada (English)' of 21–27 September 2009. https://web.archive.org/web/20110706165224/http://www.bbm.ca/_documents/top_30_tv_programs_english/nat09212009.pdf (accessed 08/28/2019).
2. See 'Top Programs—Total Canada (English)' files of 10–16 March 2014, and 24–30 March 2014 issued by BBM Canada www.bbm.ca, and of 23–29 March 2015 issued by Numeris en.numeris.ca

# Further Reading

Balirano, G. (2014). *Masculinity and Representation: A Multimodal Critical Approach to Male Identity Construcitons*. Paolo Loffredo, Iniziative Editoriali.

Baumann, K.-D. (2007). Communicative-Cognitive Approach to Emotion in LSP Communication. In K. Ahmad & M. Rogers (Eds.), *Evidence-Based LSP. Translation, Text and terminology* (pp. 323–344). Bern: Peter Lang.

BBM Canada—Bureau of Broadcasting Measurment. www.bbm.ca

Bhatia, V. K. (1993). *Analyzing Genre: Language Use in Professional Settings*. Longman.

Byrnes Media. (03/07/2011). CRTC Approves BCE's Purchase of CTV Globemedia. Retrieved June 12, 2018, from https://byrnesmedia. com/2011/03/07/crtc-approves-bces-purchase-of-ctvglobemedia/

Cadlin, C. N., & Gotti, M. (Eds.). (2004). *Intercultural Aspects of Specialized Communication*. Peter Lang.

Cortese, G. (1996). *Tradurre I Linguaggi Settoriali*. Edizioni Libreria Cortina.

De Silva-Joyce, H., & Thomson, E. A. (Eds.). (2015). *Language in Uniform: Language analysis and Training for Defence and Policing Purposes*. Cambridge Scholars Publishing.

Derrida, J., & E. Prenowitz. (Summer 1995). Archive Fever: A Freudian Impression. *Diacritics, 25*(2). The Johns Hopkins University Press, pp. 9–63. Retrieved April 28, 2018, from http://www.jstor.org/stable/465144?orig in=JSTOR-pdf

**368**    **Further Reading**

Douglas, D. (2000). *Assessing Languages for Specific Purposes*. Cambridge University Press.

Faini, P. (2018). *Terminologia, linguaggi specialistici, traduzione*. Tangram Edizioni Scientifiche.

Frank, R. (1985). The Demand for Unobservable and Other Nonpositional Goods. *American Economic Review, 75*(1), 101–116.

Gálová, D. (Ed.). (2007). *Language for Specific Purposes—Searching for Common Solutions*. Cambridge Scholars Publishing.

Gawlinski, M. (2003). *Interactive Television Production*. Focal Press.

Gläser, R. (1995). *Linguistic Features and Genre Profiles of Specific English*. Peter Lang.

Goodman, N. (1976). *Languages of Arts*. Hackett.

Gunter, B., & McLaughlin, C. (1992). *Television: The Public's View*. John Libbey.

Hofstede, G. (1983). The Cultural Relativity of Organizational Practices and Theories. *Journal of International Business Studies, 14*, 75–90.

Holden, S. (1977). *English for Special Purposes*. Modern English Publication Ltd.

Jacoby, S., & McNamara, T. (1999). Locating Competence. *English for Specific Purposes, 18*(3), 213–241.

Johns, A. M., & Dudley-Evans, T. (1991). English for Specific Purposes: International in Scope, Sspecific in Purpose. *TESOL Quarterly, 25*(2), 297–314.

Latour, B., & Woolgar, S. (1979). *Laboratory life: The Construction of Scientific Facts*. Sage.

Laurén, C., & Nordman, M. (1989). *Special Language*. Multilingual Matters.

Lorend, R. (2002). *Television: Aesthetic Reflections*. Peter Lang.

Manghani, S. (2013). *Image Studies. Theory and Practice*. Routledge.

McNary, D. (11/06/2007). WGS strike could go into 2008. *Variety*. Retrieved May 3, 2019, from https://variety.com/2007/scene/markets-festivals/wga-strike-could-go-into-2008-1117975495/

Palusci, O. (Ed.). (2016). *Green Canada*. Peter Lang.

Palusci, O., & Rizzardi, B. (Eds.). (2014). *Crossing Borders: Variations on a Theme in Canadian Studies*. ETS Editions.

Raboy, M. (1990). *Missed Opportunities: The Story of Canada's Broadcasting Policy*. McGill-Queen's University Press.

Robinson, P. C. (1989). An Overview of English for Specific Purposes. In H. Coleman (Ed.), *Working with Language: A Multidisciplinary Consideration of Language Use in Work Contexts* (pp. 395–427). Mouton de Gruyter.

Sager, J., Dungworth, D., & McDonad, P. (1980). *English Special Languages: Principles and Practice in Science and Technology*. Brandstetter.

Scarpa, F. (2008). *La Traduzione Specializzata*. Hoepli.

Scott, M. (05/01/2019). Montreal's Heritage at Stake: What Kind of City Do We Want? *Montreal Gazette*. Retrieved May 1, 2019, from https://montreal-gazette.com/news/local-news/city-needs-blueprint-to-guide-development-heritage-montreal

Selinker, L. (1979). On the Use of Informants in Discourse Analysis and Language for Specific Purposes. *International Review of Applied Linguistics., 17*, 189–215.

Selinker, L., & Trimble, L. (1976). Scientific and Technical Writing: The Choice of Tense. *English Teaching Forum, 14*(4), 22–26.

Selinker, L., Trimble, M. T., & Trimble, L. (1976). Presuppositional Rhetorical Information in EST Discourse. *TESOL Quarterly, 10*(3), 281–290.

Slade, A. F., Narro, A. J., & Givens-Carroll, D. (Eds.). (2015). *Television, Social Media and Fan Culture*. Lexington Books.

Trompenaars, F. (1993). *Riding the Waves of Culture: Understanding Cultural Diversity in Business*. Nicholas Brealey Publication.

Van Dijk, T. (2014). *Discourse and Knowledge. Asociocognitive Approach*. Cambridge University Press.

Wheatley, H. (2016). *Spectacular Television. Exploring Television Pleasure*. I.B. Tauris.

Wood, A. S. (1982). An Examination of the Rhetorical Structures of Authentic Chemistry Texts. *Applied Linguistics, 3*(2), 121–143. Retrieved September 1, 2017, from https://academic.oup.com/applij/article-abstract/III/2/121/222092/An-Examination-of-the-Rhetorical-Structures-of?redirectedFrom=PDF

Yngve, V. H. (1970). On Getting a Word in Edgewise. *Papers from the 6th Regional Meeting of the Chicago Linguistic Society*, pp. 567–577.

# Index[1]

## A

Abercrombie, D., 16
Adolphs, S., 110, 118, 182, 184, 247, 305
Aijmer, K., 118, 182, 183, 247, 305
Alias, S., 147, 241
Allen, M., 92, 326
Althusser, L., 91
Altman, R., 46
Anderson, B., 325, 348
Arango, T., 84
Archibald, J., 320
Arp, R., 169
Austin, J. L., 29, 260
Ayaß, R., 79

## B

Baldry, A., viii–ix, 2, 21, 36, 94, 118, 182, 247, 305
Bammer, G., 129
Barber, C. L., 49
Bargainnier, E. F., 99
Barr, M., 111
Barr, R., 90
Barthes, R., 28, 92, 305, 346
Bartlett, F., 38
Bartol, C. R., 164, 171
Base, R. E., 85
Bateman, J. A., 2, 4, 24, 25, 30, 37, 39–41, 94, 182, 305
Bavelas, J. B., 30, 305, 313
Beattie, G., 30, 305, 313

---

[1] Note: Page numbers followed by 'n' refer to notes.

© The Author(s), under exclusive license to Springer Nature Switzerland AG 2021
F. P. Gentile, *Corpora, Corpses and Corps*,
https://doi.org/10.1007/978-3-030-78276-4

## 372 Index

Beaty, B., 82, 84, 85, 98, 180, 333
Bednarek, M., 10, 36, 38, 94, 113, 182, 254
Beers-Fägersten, K., 79
Behiels, M. D., 299n2
Bellugi, U., 33
Berry-Flint, S., 45, 46
Bettie, G. W., 21, 22, 313
Bhatia, V. K., 320
Bianculli, D., 333
Biber, D., 15, 16, 195, 305
Bird, S., 34
Birdwhistell, R. L., 30, 31, 313
Black, D. W., 30
Bluem, A. W., 90
Bock, K., 30
Bolinger, D., 32
Bonsignori, V., 58n14
Booth, W. C., 44, 49
Bordwell, D., 36, 38, 39, 42, 306
Branigan, E., 36, 306
Bredin, M., 82, 83, 180
Brendan, K., 243
Brookes, S. A., 113
Brooks, P., 6
Brooks, V., 42
Brown, R., 30
Buckland, W., 195
Burgoon, J. K., 33, 261
Burnard, L., 17
Burton, T., 48
Bush, G. W., 84
Butler, J., 29

### C

Cabrè, M. T., 52
Calabrese, R., 16, 195, 247
Callaghan, J., 125, 136, 157–159, 163, 165

Cameron, D., 33
Campbell, D., 159, 171
Carpenter, L., 242
Carroll, J.B., 18, 75
Carter, R., 110, 118, 182, 184, 247, 305
Carveth, R., 169
Cavagnoli, S., 254
Cawelty, J. G., 193
Centini, M., 207
Cerrato, L., 19, 30
Chandler, R., 97
Charland, M. R., 83, 109, 180, 243, 315
Chatman, S., 38, 306
Chirck-Gibson, P., 80
Chomsky, N., 30
Clark, H. H., 22
Colantoni, E., 124
Cole, A. W., 33
Coletti, V., 49
Collins, R., 84, 109, 180
Conrad, S., 15
Cooley, C., 156
Crane, G., 17
Creeber, G., 109
Crosthwaite, P., 17
Cuklaz, J., 9, 243, 306
Currie, G., 39, 47

### D

Dance, F. E. X., 77
Daniele, F., 226, 279, 320
De Beaugrande, R. A., 20, 94, 123, 126
De Bruyn, B., 44
De Saint-Georges, I., 10, 305
Deschênes, J., 242
Devlin, A., 254, 290

Dillon, H., 124
Disney, W., 286
Donaldson, L. F., 94
Dorland, M., 83, 109, 180, 243, 315
Doyle, J., 98
Dressler, W. U., 20, 94, 123, 126
Dudley-Evans, T., 49, 50
Durbridge, F., 90
Durovicova, N., 38, 182

E

Eco, U., 34, 37, 39, 43, 44, 47, 182,
    202, 306
Efron, D., 32
Eisenstein, S., 40
Ekman, P., 30, 32, 33, 49, 261, 317
Ellis, M., 111, 112
Engwall, L., 17
Ewer, J., 51

F

Faini, P., 49
Fairclough, N., 49
Fill, A., 3
Firth, J., 19
Foster, M. E., 19
Foucault, M., 292
Frank, R., 298
Freeze, C., 113
Fremeth, H., 85, 86
Friesen, W. V., 32, 49, 261, 317

G

Garside, R., 20, 247
Garzone, G., 129, 192, 226,
    279, 320

Gentile, F. P., 189, 193, 242, 243
Gerhardt, C., 79
Giannoni, D.S., 50
Gibbons, J., 101
Gittins, S., 86, 98, 109, 180, 181,
    296, 351
Goldman, E., 172n4
Gotti, M., 50–52, 320
Gramley, S., 49
Granata, P., 3, 76
Grant, B. K., 45
Grego, K., 129, 192, 244, 254
Gregory, M., 28
Grice, P. H., 29, 263
Griffin, Z. M., 30
Gualdo, R., 52, 227, 320
Gunnarsson, B. L., 49

H

Haiman, J., 32
Hajič, J., 57n6
Hale, M., 180
Hall, E. T., 188
Hall, J. A., 188, 254, 261
Halliday, M. A. K., 3, 27, 28,
    32, 94, 290
Hardie, A., 311
Hardwick, C., 1
Harper, S. J., 98
Hasan, R., 32
Haworth, K., 318
Hazelwood, R., 164, 171
Heydon, G., viii, 36, 101, 184, 234,
    243, 315
Hill, J., 80
Hobbs, R., 42
Hochberg, J., 42
Hoffman, L., 51

**374**   **Index**

Holler, J., 21, 22, 313
Hoskins, C., 83
Hoslanova, J., 17
Houser, N., 1
Howatt, A. P. R., 50
Hudon, R., 299n2
Hughes, B., 99
Hulob, R. C., 44
Hutchinson, T., 50, 51
Hyland, K., 54, 56, 200

**I**

Ingarden, R., 44
Iser, W., 44

**J**

Jacobs, J., 79, 94, 95, 168, 178, 309, 346
Jenkins, H., 41
Jenner, M., 9, 92–94, 207, 333, 348
Jensen, K. B., 41
Jernyn, D., 92
Jerome, J. K., 90
Jewit, C., 10, 306, 333
Johnson, A. J., 125, 172n4
Jones, T., 172n5

**K**

Kellner, D., 91
Kendon, A., 30, 32, 261
Kennedy, G. D., 18
Kilgarriff, A., 20
Kipp, M., 19
Klein, J. T., 129
Knapp, M. L., 188, 254, 261
Knight, D., 32, 254, 261, 306

Kocsis, R. M., 164, 171
Kozloff, S., 79
Kracauer, S., 6
Kress, G., 2, 3, 10, 22, 23, 47, 94, 110, 113, 251, 254, 306
Kristine, D., 23, 126
Krych, M.A., 22
Kübler, S., 195
Kuhn, R., 80

**L**

Labov, W., 34
Laframboise, K., 299n2
Lamberti, E., 3, 74
Lapsley, R., 36
Larson, C. E., 77
Latorre, G., 51
LeChevallier, M., 189
Lederman, M., 98
Leech, G., 20, 247
LeVine, P., 24, 26, 53, 251
Levinson, J., 24, 25
Levinson, P., 77
Levote, D., 164, 171
Lewin, K., 160, 171
Lewins, A., 35
Liberman, M., 34
Longworth, J.L., 9
Lowry, B., 180
Lund, K., 23, 251, 254, 306, 313

**M**

Manwell, R., 90
Marcus, M., 57n6
Marmor, A., 109, 243, 315
Marr, D., 47

Martin, J. R., 54, 123, 153, 172n3, 208, 257, 321
Massaro, D. W., 30, 313
Matthiessen, C. M. I. M., 94
Maynard, S. K., 30
Mayr, A., 123, 172n3, 186, 254, 256, 282, 290, 315
McClausand, T., 82
McCormick, P. J., 44
McEnery, A., 18, 311
McFayden, S., 83
McLuhan, M., 3, 74–76
McNeill, D., 16, 30, 32, 313
McPhail, B., 81
McQuail, D., 71, 72
Mehrabian, A., 2, 16, 128, 252
Messaris, P., 4, 47
Metz, C., 4, 40, 41
Miller, T., 4, 42, 348
Mitchell, W., 25
Mittal, S., 164, 171
Monaco, J., 4, 40
Moore, N., 33, 254, 261
Moorti, S., 9, 243, 306
Mühlhäusler, M. P., 3
Myerson, B. R., 186

**N**

Nelson, R., 9, 79, 207
Newcomb, H., 79, 95, 254
Newman, K., 38, 182
Norris, S., 26, 31, 251, 306

**O**

O'Halloran, K. L., viii–ix, 10, 17, 22, 28, 33, 36, 113, 115, 241, 306, 348

O'Toole, M., 10, 298
Oberlander, J., 19
Ogden, C. K., 74
Olandewarju, F. R., 109, 315
Ong, W. J., 77
Oswald, B., 243, 306

**P**

Paetkau, D., 125
Palermo, G. B., 164, 171
Pätzold, K. M., 49
Peacock, S., 79, 94, 95, 168, 178, 309, 346
Peirce, C.S., 1, 2
Pelissier Kingfisher, C., 292
Pender, T. N., 111, 306
Piazza, R., 4, 36, 94, 182, 254
Pinar-Sanz, M. J., 251, 306
Plummer, K., 87
Postman, N., 3, 76
Potts, C., 29
Pozzo, B., 243, 315
Puckett, K., 45, 306
Pudovkin, V. I., 40
Pylyshyn, Z., 47

**R**

Richards, I. A., 74
Richardson, K., 9, 36, 79, 113, 182, 254
Richmond, V. P., 31, 32, 261
Ricoeur, P., 77, 337
Rimé, B., 30, 261, 313
Roelcke, T., 129, 202
Roufa, T., 243, 254, 287, 315
Royce, T. D., 94, 251, 306

# 376 Index

Rühleman, C., 118, 306
Russo, K. E., 56

**S**

Saferstein, B., 17, 18
Santorini, B., 261
Schegloff, E. A., 32
Schiaratura, L., 30, 261, 313
Schier, F., 47
Schlesinger, J., 84
Schmidt, K. H., 2, 4, 24, 25, 37, 39–41, 182, 305
Scollon, R., 24, 26, 53, 251
Scott, M., 298
Scott-Phillips, T., 1, 254
Searle, J., 29, 131, 256, 260
Segre, C., 44
Selinker, L., 50
Shannon, C. E., 24
Shengelaia, N., 57n5
Shovelton, H., 30, 305, 313
Sikov, E., 4
Silver, C., 35
Simpson, P., 123, 186, 256, 282, 315
Sinclair, J., 19, 33
Sindroni, M. G., 29, 306
Singh, T., 164, 171
Skhiri, M., 19, 30
Smith, L., 42
Smith, N., 247
Smith, R., 42
Sokorin, P. A., 156, 171
Sparks, Richard, 90, 346
Sparks, Robert, 86, 87, 306
St. John, M. J., 49, 50
Stam, R., 42, 348
Stelter, B., 83

Stenström, A. B., 118, 182, 183, 247, 305
Stewart, C., 58n14
Strassel, L., 33
Straw, W., 83
Stubbs, M., 15, 54, 129, 254
Sullivan, R., 82, 84, 85, 98, 180, 333
Swain, E., 251, 306
Swales, J. M., 49
Sykes, G. M., 254, 290

**T**

Taylor, A., 21
Taylor, M., 125
Telve, S., 52, 227, 320
Thibault, P. J., 2, 21, 94, 118, 182, 247, 305
Thomas, J., 282
Thompson, J., 72
Thompson, K., 36
Thompson, L. A., 30, 313
Thompson, R. J., 333
Thomson, D., 77–79
Todorov, T., 6
Tognini-Bonelli, E., 16
Treble, P., 112, 113
Trimble, L., 50, 51
Trottier, D., 281
Trudgill, P., 45, 54, 182
Tulloch, J., 79, 91
Turvey, B. E., 164, 171

**V**

Van Leeuwen, T., 2, 3, 10, 22, 26, 94, 110, 113, 254, 306
Vanderveken, D., 131, 256

## W

Wallace, D., 48
Walzlawick, P., 31
Waters, A., 50, 51
Weaver, W., 24
Wees, W. C., 40
Weinrich, H., 44
Westlake, M., 36
White, P. R. R., 54,
        123, 153, 208,
        257, 321
Widdowson, H. G., 51
Wilcox, S., 18, 32, 313
Wild, D., 111
Wildfeuer, J., 4, 37, 182
Wilford, D., 299n1
Williams, J. R., 312

Wilson, A., 18
Wolf, W., 41, 306
Wong, L., 312, 333
Wong, T., 89, 98
Wonner, B., 17
Wood, A. S., 50
Wynne, M., 33

## Y

Yacoob, Y., 30
Yeo, D., 98, 306

## Z

Zinsmeiter, K., 195
Zipf, G. K., 262